THE REVELS PLAYS

Founder editor
Clifford Leech, 1958–71

General Editors
F. David Hoeniger, E. A. J. Honigmann and J. R. Mulryne

TWO TUDOR INTERLUDES

THE INTERLUDE OF YOUTH
HICK SCORNER

The title page of the sixteenth-century first quarto, reproduced by courtesy of His Grace the Archbishop of Canterbury and the Trustees of Lambeth Palace Library.

THE REVELS PLAYS

TWO TUDOR INTERLUDES

THE INTERLUDE OF YOUTH
HICK SCORNER

Edited by

Ian Lancashire

MANCHESTER
UNIVERSITY PRESS

THE JOHNS HOPKINS
UNIVERSITY PRESS

© Ian Lancashire 1980

First published 1980
by Manchester University Press
Oxford Road, Manchester M13 9PL
ISBN 0 7190 1523 5

Published in the United States of America, 1980, by
The Johns Hopkins University Press
Baltimore, Maryland 21218
ISBN 0–8018–2338–2

Library of Congress Catalog Card Number 79–3123

British Library Cataloguing in Publication Data

Two Tudor interludes.—(The revels plays).
 1. English drama—Early modern and
 Elizabethan, 1500–1600
 I. Lancashire, Ian   II. Worde, Wynkyn de.
 Interlude of youth   III. Waley, John
 IV. Copland, William   V. Worde, Wynkyn de.
 Hick Scorner   VI. Series
 822'.2'08   PR1262

 UK ISBN 0–7190–1523–5
 US ISBN 0–8018–2338–2

Printed in Great Britain
by W & J Mackay Limited, Chatham

Contents

Illustrations

To the Memory of
ELIZABETH AND ERNEST LANCASHIRE

General Editors' Preface

The series known as the Revels Plays was conceived by Clifford Leech. The idea for the series emerged in his mind, as he explained in his preface to the first of the Revels Plays in 1958, from the success of the New Arden Shakespeare. The aim of the new group of texts was 'to apply to Shakespeare's predecessors, contemporaries and successors the methods that are now used in Shakespeare editing'. The plays chosen were to include well known works from the early Tudor period to about 1700, as well as others less familiar but of literary and theatrical merit: 'the plays included,' Leech wrote, 'should be such as to deserve and indeed demand performance.' We owe it to Clifford Leech that the idea became reality. He set the high standards of the series, ensuring that editors of individual volumes produced work of lasting merit, equally useful for teachers and students, theatre directors and actors. Clifford Leech remained General Editor until 1971, supervising the first seventeen volumes to be published.

The Revels Plays are now under the direction of three General Editors, F. David Hoeniger, E. A. J. Honigmann and J. R. Mulryne. The publishers, originally Methuen, are now Manchester University Press, with Johns Hopkins University Press as co-publisher. Yet, despite these changes, the format and essential character of the series will continue, and it is hoped that its editorial standards will be maintained. Except for some work in progress, the General Editors intend, in expanding the series, to concentrate for the immediate future on plays from the period 1558–1642, and may include a small number of non-dramatic works of interest to students of drama. Some slight changes have been forced by considerations of cost. For example, in editions from 1978, notes to the Introduction are placed together at the end, not at the foot of the page. Collation and commentary notes will continue, however, to appear on the relevant pages.

The text of each Revels play, in accordance with established practice in the series, is edited afresh from the original text of best authority (in a few instances, texts), but spelling and punctuation are modernised and speech headings are silently made consistent. Elisions in the original are also silently regularised, except where metre would be affected by the change; since 1968 the '-ed' form is used for non-syllabic terminations in past tenses and past participles ('-'d' earlier), and '-èd' for syllabic ('-ed' earlier). The editor emends, as distinct from modernises, his original only in instances where error is patent, or at least very probable, and correction persuasive. Act divisions are given only if they appear in the original or if the structure of the play clearly points to them. Those act and scene divisions not found in the original are provided unobtrusively in small type and in square brackets. Square brackets are also used for any other additions to or changes in the stage directions of the original.

Revels Plays do not provide a variorum collation, but only those variants which require the critical attention of serious textual students. All departures of substance from 'copy-text' are listed, including any relineation and those changes in punctuation which involve to any degree a decision between alternative interpretations; but not such accidentals as turned letters, nor necessarily additions to stage directions whose editorial nature is already made clear by the use of brackets. Press corrections in the 'copy-texts' are likewise included. Of later emendations of the text, only those are given which as alternative readings still deserve attention.

One of the hallmarks of the Revels Plays is the thoroughness of their annotations. Besides explaining the meaning of difficult words and passages, the editor provides comments on customs or usage, text or stage-business—indeed, on anything he judges pertinent and helpful. Each volume contains a Glossarial Index to the Commentary, in which particular attention is drawn to meanings for words not listed in *O.E.D.*

The Introduction to a Revels play assesses the authority of the 'copy-text' on which it is based, and discusses the editorial methods employed in dealing with it; the editor also considers his play's date and (where relevant) sources, together with its place in the work of the author and in the theatre of its time. Stage-history is offered, and in the case of a play by an author not previously represented in the series a brief biography is given.

It is our hope that plays edited in this fashion will promote further scholarly and theatrical investigation of one of the richest periods in theatrical history.

F. DAVID HOENIGER

E. A. J. HONIGMANN

J. R. MULRYNE

Preface

This edition of *The Interlude of Youth* is based on the three early quartos by Wynkyn de Worde, John Waley and William Copland, and that of *Hick Scorner* on de Worde's quarto *c.* 1515–16. Modernised texts are provided, together with appropriate textual notes and commentary, an introduction and appendices. Besides explicating the interludes for literary and theatre students, this apparatus shows how *Youth* and *Hick Scorner* reflect, and to judge by their probable auspices evidently participated in, early Henrician political history. I have stressed its contribution to the plays in the hope that historians and readers of social history in general will look to the Tudor interlude, not only as a vivid statement of English character, but as a source of information about the period itself.

This research developed from my University of Toronto doctoral thesis, 'A Critical Edition of *Hycke Scorner*', which had the encouragement, criticism and support of John Leyerle, David Bevington, Brian Parker and those who gave it the A. S. P. Woodhouse Prize in 1968–69. In the ensuing years my debts to both institutions and individuals have been many. For the use of books and facilities, and for the provision of microfilm or photocopies and information, I am grateful to the staff of all the libraries I visited in preparing this edition, especially the Bodleian Library, the British Library, Harvard University Library (and Katharine F. Pantzer), the Henry E. Huntington Library, the Institute for Historical Research, Lambeth Palace Library, the National Library of Ireland, the Carl H. Pforzheimer Library, the University of Toronto Library, Trinity College Library, Dublin, and Yale University Library (the Elizabethan Club). For financial support I am thankful to the University of Toronto and to the Canada Council, which gave me a Research

Grant in 1971 and a Leave Fellowship in 1973–74, during which this edition was largely written. My specific debts to individuals who answered my questions and saved me from mistakes are indicated throughout this book, but special thanks for help over some years are due to R. W. Van Fossen, Jean Christie and Erindale College, which has also provided a generous grant towards the publication of this edition. John Bradley of the University of Toronto Computer Center helped me to concord both plays with his program COGS, and Geoffrey Matthews of the Cartography Office found time to be a genial mapmaker. My special guides through a decade of research have been three editors: my wife, Anne Lancashire, who asked me once if Henry VIII had any enemies called Richard; Clifford Leech, the former General Editor, a regular Malvern Festival visitor who shared its interest in these old plays; and David Hoeniger, a present General Editor, who has been a most patient, exacting and kind master of these revels.

IAN LANCASHIRE

Toronto
December 1976

Abbreviations

As well as abbreviations of previous editions of *The Interlude of Youth* and *Hick Scorner* (see Intro., pp. 15–16), the following are used.

Abbott	E. A. Abbott, *A Shakespearian Grammar*. 1870; rpt. 1966.
A.G.	*The assemble of goddes*, ed. Francis Jenkinson. 1906. Line references are to *The Assembly of Gods*, ed. Oscar L. Triggs. E.E.T.S. E.S. 69. 1896.
Ane Satyre	*The Works of Sir David Lindsay of the Mount: 1490–1555*, ed. Douglas Hamer. Vol. II. *Ane Satyre of the Thrie Estaitis.* Scottish Text Society, 3rd ser., 2. 1931.
Ashby	'Notes and extracts relating to old English and French plays . . . by the Rev. George Ashby, B.D., Rector of Barrow, co. Suffolk', British Library Additional MS 29, 793.
Bevington	David M. Bevington, *From 'Mankind' to Marlowe*. 1962.
Brook	G. L. Brook, *English Dialects*. 1963.
Chambers, *E.F.-P.*	Sir Edmund Chambers, *The English Folk-Play*. 1933; rpt. 1969.
Chambers, *E.S.*	E. K. Chambers, *The Elizabethan Stage*. 4 vols. 1923; rpt. 1967.
Chambers, *M.S.*	E. K. Chambers, *The Mediaeval Stage*. 2 vols. 1903; rpt. 1963.
Chronicles	*Chronicles of London*, ed. Charles L. Kingsford. 1905.
Cocke Lorelles bote	*Cocke Lorelles bote*. Wynkyn de Worde, n.d. *S.T.C.* 5456.

Collier	J. Payne Collier, *The History of English Dramatic Poetry to the Time of Shakespeare*. 2 vols. 1831.
C.P.	G. E. C[okayne]., *The Complete Peerage*, new edition, ed. Vicary Gibbs *et al.* 13 vols. 1910–59.
Craik	T. W. Craik, *The Tudor Interlude*. 1958; rpt. 1967.
Cruickshank	C. G. Cruickshank, *Army Royal: Henry VIII's Invasion of France, 1513*. 1969.
Digby Plays	*The Digby Plays*, ed. F. J. Furnivall. E.E.T.S. E.S. 70. 1896; rpt. 1967.
D.N.B.	*The Dictionary of National Biography*, ed. Sir Leslie Stephen and Sir Sidney Lee. 22 vols. 1921–22.
Dobson	E. J. Dobson, *English Pronunciation, 1500–1700*. 2nd ed. 2 vols. 1968.
Eclogues	*The Eclogues of Alexander Barclay*, ed. Beatrice White. E.E.T.S. O.S. 175. 1928.
E.E.T.S. E.S., O.S., S.S.	Early English Text Society Extra Series, Original Series, Supplementary Series.
Everyman	*Everyman*, ed. A. C. Cawley. 1961.
Flügel	Ewald Flügel, ed., 'Kleinere Mitteilungen Aus Handschriften. 3. Die Proverbs von Lekenfield und Wresil (Yorks).', *Anglia*, 14 (1892), 471–97.
Four Elements	*The Nature of the Four Elements*, ed. John S. Farmer. T.F.T. 1908.
Four Years	*Four Years at the Court of Henry VIII*, trans. Rawdon Brown. 2 vols. 1854.
Fulgens & Lucres	Henry Medwall, *Fulgens & Lucres*, ed. F. S. Boas and A. W. Reed. 1926.
Greg	W. W. Greg, *A Bibliography of the English Printed Drama to the Restoration*. Bibl. Soc. Illustrated Monographs, no. XXIV. 4 vols. 1939–59.

Halle	Edward Halle, *The Union of the Two Noble Families of Lancaster and York: 1550*. Scolar Press Facsimile. 1970.
Hawes	'The Example of Vertu', in *Stephen Hawes: The Minor Poems*, ed. Florence W. Gluck and Alice B. Morgan. E.E.T.S. O.S. 271. 1974.
Heath	Peter Heath, *The English Parish Clergy on the Eve of the Reformation*. 1969.
Hodnett	Edward Hodnett, *English Woodcuts: 1480–1535*. 2nd ed. 1973.
H.S.	This edition of *Hick Scorner*.
Johan the Evangelist	*The Interlude of Johan the Evangelist*, ed. W. W. Greg. M.S.R. 1970.
Laing	David Laing, ed., *Early Popular Poetry of Scotland and the Northern Border*, rev. W. Carew Hazlitt. 2 vols. 1895.
Libr.	*The Library.*
L.P.	*Letters and Papers, Foreign and Domestic, of the Reign of Henry VIII*, ed. J. S. Brewer, J. Gairdner and R. H. Brodie. 21 vols. 1862–1918. Vol. I, rev. R. H. Brodie. 1920. *Addenda.* 2 vols. 1929–32.
Lupton	J. H. Lupton, *A Life of John Colet, D.D.* 2nd ed. 1909.
Macro Plays	*The Macro Plays*, ed. Mark Eccles. E.E.T.S. O.S. 262. 1969.
Magnyfycence	John Skelton, *Magnyfycence*, ed. Robert Lee Ramsay. E.E.T.S. E.S. 98. 1908; rpt. 1958.
Manners and Meals	*Manners and Meals in Olden Time*, ed. Frederick J. Furnivall. E.E.T.S. O.S. 32. 1868.
M.E.D.	*Middle English Dictionary*, ed. Hans Kurath and Sherman M. Kuhn. 1954–. Published up to Part M2. 1975.
M.S.R.	Malone Society Reprints.

Nature	Henry Medwall, 'Nature', in *Quellen des Weltlichen Dramas in England vor Shakespeare*, ed. Alois Brandl. Quellen und Forschungen, 80. 1898.
Non-Cycle Plays	*Non-Cycle Plays and Fragments*, ed. Norman Davis. E.E.T.S. S.S. 1. 1970.
O.E.D.	*The Oxford English Dictionary.*
Percy 1	*The Regulations and Establishment of the Household of Henry Algernon Percy*, ed. T[homas]. P[ercy]. 1770.
Percy 2	'The booke of All maner of Orders Concernynge an Erles hous', Bodleian MS Eng. hist. b. 208.
Potter	Robert Potter, *The English Morality Play.* 1975.
Pugh	Ralph B. Pugh, *Imprisonment in Medieval England.* 1968.
Relation	*A Relation, or rather a true account, of the Island of England . . . about the year 1500*, trans. Charlotte A. Sneyd. Camden Society, 37. 1847.
Remains	*Remains of the Early Popular Poetry of England*, ed. W. Carew Hazlitt. 4 vols. 1864–66.
Rendle	William Rendle, *Old Southwark and its People.* 1878.
R.E.S.	*The Review of English Studies.*
Scarisbrick	J. J. Scarisbrick, *Henry VIII.* 1968.
Schell	E. T. Schell, '*Youth* and *Hyckescorner*: Which Came First?' *Philological Quarterly*, 45 (1966), 468–74.
Select Cases	*Select Cases in the Council of Henry VII*, ed. C. G. Bayne and William H. Dunham, Jr. Selden Society, 75. 1958.
Sermons	*Middle English Sermons edited from British Museum MS. Royal 18 B. xxiii*, ed. Woodburn O. Ross. E.E.T.S. O.S. 209. 1940.

Ship of Fools	Alexander Barclay, *The Ship of Fools*, ed. T. H. Jamieson. 2 vols. 1874.
Songs	*Songs, Carols, and other Miscellaneous Poems*, ed. Roman Dyboski. E.E.T.S. E.S. 101. 1907.
Southern	Richard Southern, *The Staging of Plays before Shakespeare*. 1973.
Spont	Alfred Spont, ed., *Letters and Papers Relating to the War with France, 1512–1513*. Navy Record Society, 10. 1897.
S.R.	*The Statutes of the Realm*, ed. A. Luders, J. Raithby *et al*. Great Britain Record Commission, Publication no. 8. 11 vols. 1810–28.
S.T.C.	*A Short-Title Catalogue of Books Printed in England, Scotland, & Ireland . . . 1475–1640*, ed. A. W. Pollard and G. R. Redgrave. 1926. 2nd edition, begun by W. A. Jackson and F. S. Ferguson, completed by Katharine F. Pantzer. Vol. 2, I–Z. 1976. *S.T.C.* numbers for A–H with asterisks are from work in progress at the Houghton Library, Harvard University.
Stevens	John Stevens, *Music & Poetry in the Early Tudor Court*. 1961.
Stow	John Stow, *A Survey of London*, ed. Charles L. Kingsford. 2 vols. 1908.
Sugden	Edward H. Sugden, *A Topographical Dictionary to the Works of Shakespeare and his Fellow Dramatists*. 1925.
T.F.T.	Tudor Facsimile Texts.
Tilley	Morris P. Tilley, *A Dictionary of the Proverbs in England in the Sixteenth and Seventeenth Centuries*. 1950.
Towneley Plays	*The Towneley Plays*, ed. George England and Alfred W. Pollard. E.E.T.S. E.S. 71. 1897; rpt. 1952.

T.R.P.	*Tudor Royal Proclamations. Volume I: The Early Tudors (1485–1553)*. 1964. *Volume II: The Later Tudors (1553–1587)*. 1969. Ed. Paul L. Hughes and James F. Larkin.
Utopia	*The Complete Works of St. Thomas More*, IV, ed. Edward Surtz, S.J., and J. H. Hexter. 1965.
Venice	*Calendar of State Papers . . . Relating to English Affairs, Existing in . . . Venice*, ed. Rawdon Brown. Vols. I–II. 1864, 1867.
Winchester MS	'Lucidus and Dubius' and 'Occupation and Idleness', Winchester College MS 33, fols. 54v–73v. I am grateful to Professor Norman Davis for permission to quote from his transcript of these plays.
World	*The World and the Child*, ed. John S. Farmer. T.F.T. 1908.
Wyld	Henry C. Wyld, *Studies in English Rhymes*. 1923.
Y.	This edition of *The Interlude of Youth*.

Quotations from the Bible are, where exact wording is unnecessary, taken from the King James Version, and the Vulgate Latin from *Biblia Sacra*, 4th ed. (Bibliotheca de Autores Cristianos, 1965). With the exception of *The Pardoner's Tale*, which is quoted from the *Caunterbury tales* Wynkyn de Worde printed at Westminster in 1498 (*S.T.C.* 5085), references to Geoffrey Chaucer's poems are to his *Works*, ed. F. N. Robinson, 2nd ed. (1957). All quotations from John Skelton's poems are from *The Poetical Works*, ed. Alexander Dyce, 2 vols. (1843). The titles of Shakespeare's plays are abbreviated as in C. T. Onions's *A Shakespeare Glossary*, 2nd ed. (1919), and line references are to, and quotations from, the one-volume Pelican edition (1969) by Alfred Harbage.

Introduction

a. The Interlude of Youth

Youth exists in three undated sixteenth-century black-letter editions: Q1, a fragmentary first sheet in Lambeth Palace Library; Q2, published by John Waley; and Q3, printed by William Copland.[1] As Q1 lacks colophon or printer's device, and the careers of Waley and Copland overlap, the order of the three editions must be decided by bibliographical evidence, principally an analysis of type founts and woodcut states.

Q1, Lambeth Palace Library **Z240.1.25, entitled *Thenterlude of youth.*, was discovered as an end-paper in a library bookbinding.[2] The sheet was cut down for that purpose because the pages were incorrectly imposed in the formes during the printing.[3] The positions of what should be sigs. A2v and A4v in the outer forme, and of sigs. A2r and A4r in the inner forme, were reversed when the eight pages were locked into the two chases, so that the printed sheet, when folded, had its signatures in the order, A1, A4, A3 and A2. The signatures, and four or five lines of type at the bottom of all eight pages,[4] are clipped off, and one side has also been substantially cut away so that the speech prefixes and line-beginnings on sigs. A3v and A4v are missing.[5] Otherwise uncut, and without the stitching holes that would exist if the sheet had once been bound with the other two sheets, Q1 evidently survives only because of a pressman's blunder.

R. B. McKerrow, in editing a facsimile of Q1 in 1905, used the title-page factotums,[6] woodcut figures with blank name-scrolls that were filled in as needed, to identify the printer and date the edition. McKerrow compared its right-hand and left-hand factotums with other impressions of the same woodcuts in the undated, imperfect Bodleian *Kalender of Shepherds* (*S.T.C.* 22411; Bodl. Douce K.97), which he incorrectly took[7] to be another copy of the Wynkyn de Worde edition of 24 January 1528 now in the Huntington Library. Both Q1 factotums occur in the Bodleian edition in two states, one full-size, and one cut down (as in Q1). The Q1 right-hand woodcut, required late in the Bodleian book for a space smaller than its size (sig. L6v), loses there the bottom row of leaves and part of the figure's gown, both of which print at the start (sigs. A6v, C3v, E4v); and the left-hand one is also noticeably clipped between its first (sig. R3r) and second (sig. R6r) appearances. McKerrow argues rightly that, since Q1 shows these cut-down states (even further worn), as well as other features of de Worde's presswork,[8] Q1 must come from the same (de Worde) shop as the Bodleian edition, and must date after it, though before de Worde's death in 1535. McKerrow's argument in dating Q1 after 1528 is technically wrong, because the Huntington edition too contains both factotums *only* in cut-down states, and de Worde uses a cut-down Q1 right-hand factotum as early as 30 May 1526 (*S.T.C.* 6897, sig. A3v), but recent methods for dating by type fount in fact prove his conclusion right. The main typeface in Q1 is de Worde's distinctive post-1521 95 Textura with $s^3v^3w^2w^3y^2$ (in Frank Isaac's keyplate), and the title is printed in de Worde's large Textura 220, which he first used in 1532.[9] In addition, some Q1 peculiarities, a seldom (by then) employed small w^2 and a damaged large w^2 (where its top horizontal strokes are often missing and leave the uprights open above) regularly found as a capital at the start of lines, appear throughout de Worde's late productions, but seem dominant in 1532–33, until de Worde by 1534 evidently begins replacing the large w^2 with w^3 in capital position.[10] De Worde must consequently have printed Q1 in 1532–33.

Between 19 July 1557 and 9 July 1558 an entry, licensing the printing of the following books, was made in the Stationers' Register of London:

To master John wally these bokes Called *Welth and helthe / the treatise of the ffrere and the boye / stans puer ad mensam* another of *youghte charyte and humylyte* an *a b c for cheldren* in englesshe *with syllabes* also a boke called *an hundreth mery tayles* . . . . .ij[s] [11]

The fourth book here must be Q2, *Thēterlude of youth.*, which was, according to the colophon, 'Imprinted at London, by John waley dwellyng in Foster lane' (sig. C4v). The following six copies[12] are extant:

BL   British Library, C.34.b.24 (slightly cropped; donated by David Garrick in 1779; his book by about 1756).[13]

Bodl. 1 Bodleian, Oxford, Malone 231 (slightly cropped; donated by Edmond Malone in 1821; cf. Bodl. Malone 132, opp. pp. 534, 556; and Malone 156, p. 169).

Bodl. 2 Bodleian, Oxford, Douce I.224 (sig. A2 cropped; donated by Francis Douce in 1834; his book before 1803; not in Bodl. TS. R.6.91, his purchases 1803–34).[14]

Yale   Yale University Elizabethan Club Library 246 (Sotheby 1906 'Irish Find', Bernard Quaritch's copy to 1908, donated by A. S. Cochrane in 1911).

Hunt.   Henry E. Huntington Library (San Marino, California) 129016 (cropped and defective; Thomas Pearson's copy to 1788, John Philip Kemble's to 1821, from then to 1914 owned by the duke of Devonshire).[15]

Pforz.   Carl H. Pforzheimer Library, N.Y., 526 (Lord Mostyn's copy to 1919, J. L. Clawson's to 1926).

Typographical evidence shows Q2 to be this licensed play. On unstated grounds, W. W. Greg correctly identifies the Q2 printer (John Waley published from 1546 to 1586, but had no press) as John King,[16] whose press worked from before 1554 to 1561, and who did several books for Waley *c.* 1555 (*S.T.C.* 4728, 16067). Greg's attribution must be based on Q2's striking resemblances to King's 1560 editions of *Impatient Poverty* and *Nice Wanton* (*S.T.C.* 14114, 25016): all use the same type, a 94 Textura with $s^3v^3w^{5d}w^{12}w^{13a}y^2y^8$ (and possibly w^{5b}), and share various details of format, such as identical leaf ornaments preceding the colophon (both Q2 and *Impatient Poverty* also print the same ornamental woodblock upside-down on the last page).[17] Within King's known career Greg dates Q2 1555–58, that is, before 17 November 1558, the day of Queen Mary's death, because Q2 includes certain Roman terms, 'mass' (36) and 'beads' (770), replaced in Q3. These limits, however, probably should be advanced to late 1557–59. Q2's use of w^{5d} and w^{12}, and of y^8 instead of y^5, dates it after King's 1557 work (*S.T.C.* 21287), and with his 1560 output.[18] Yet the play must have been printed before Elizabeth's 'Injunctions for Religion', issued before 19 July 1559, which prohibited 'praying upon beads, or suchlike superstition', and proscribed the printing and sale of 'pamphlets, plays, and ballads' unless licensed by her royal commissioners.[19]

The colophon of Q3, entitled *The Enterlude of Youth*, states that it was 'Imprented at London in Lothbury ouer against Sainct Margarytes church by me Wyllyam Copland'. Two copies [20] are extant:

BL   British Library, C.34.e.15 (donated by David Garrick in 1779; his book by about 1756).

Hunt. Henry E. Huntington Library (San Marino, California) 61802 (Lord Mostyn's copy until 1919).

The colophon address indicates that Q3 was not printed before the end of 1562 (previously Copland's press was at the Three-Crane Wharf in the Vintry), and probably not before 1565, after which time he worked at Lothbury until his death in poverty by 1569.[21] Few of the thirty-odd extant Lothbury books are dated, but a comparison of types suggests that Q3, with an old and mixed 94 Textura with $s^2 s^3 v^3 w^3 w^{5b} w^{12} w^{13a} w^{8\ (1.c.)}\ y^2 y^8$ and an odd italic capital Y, is from the last years of Copland's press, when his financial situation must have been poor. Many Lothbury editions employ a simple 94 Textura with $s^3 v^2 w^{5b} w^{12} y^2$, a type found in the Three-Crane-Wharf period, and some of these Lothbury works contain the three Q3 title-page factotums in apparently earlier states: *S.T.C.* 3385 the right-hand (sig. G1v) and centre (sig. G3r) ones, and *S.T.C.* 24829 the right-hand one (sig. B1v).[22] Q3 should, then, be a late Lothbury edition, probably with limits 1566–68/69.

There may be later editions of *Youth*, but henceforth it and *Hick Scorner* (whose latest extant quarto may also be printed by Copland) are mentioned together as old pieces. In 1575 among the popular books of Coventry's famous Captain Cox are listed 'hiz auncient playz. Yooth & charitee, Hikskorner, Nugize, Impacient pouerty'.[23] The two also appear in a Stationers' Register entry on 15 January 1582, when Sampson Awdeley's (John Sampson's) printing rights to forty-three books, among them six 'Plaiebookes', John Heywood's *'The weather'*, *'iiij P'*, and *'Love'*, as well as *'youthe'*, *'ympacient pouertie'* and *'Hicke Skorner'*, were transferred to John Charlewood, though this registration must be a blocking entry, because Awdeley died in 1575 and virtually no editions from it are extant from either his or Charlewood's presses.[24] Perhaps Awdeley obtained *Youth* and *Hick Scorner* from Copland. From Charlewood, at any rate, the rights passed to his widow's second husband, James Roberts, on 31 May 1594, and possibly from him to William Jaggard in 1615, and to Thomas and Richard Cotes in 1627.[25] Because the 'Enterlude of youth' listed for sale in Edward Archer's 1656 play-catalogue reproduces the title spelling of Copland's edition, however, it may have been a copy of Q3, and Q3 may have been the last early edition.[26]

R. B. McKerrow, though unable to date accurately Q2 and Q3, stated the basic relationships of these three quartos.[27] Q3 can hardly be derived from the earlier Q2 in view of a number of correct Q3 readings that, occasionally shared with Q1, appear so distorted in Q2 as to make their restoration in Q3 highly improbable (20, 136, 345, 411); and any conflation of texts for cheap, popular editions, while not impossible, is unlikely. In addition, neither Q2 nor Q3 can be based on Q1 because there are nearly fifty significant readings where Q2 and Q3, independently, agree against Q1. McKerrow concludes that Q2 and Q3, then, must be separately based on an unknown edition,[28] either one directly descended from Q1, or a parallel edition from a text ultimately identical with that underlying Q1. Several variants, such as Q2–Q3 retention (against Q1) of some northern forms (227, and cf. 134), lend some slight support to this second possibility, as *Youth* is evidently from the north. If so, Q2 and Q3, though late and corrupt, might possess some pre-Q1 textual readings, and Q1's early date should not itself decide where authority lies. Only a look at each variant in the 218 lines up to line 247 in which all three quartos are extant can show to what extent the late quartos are trustworthy.

Joint Q2–Q3 readings are obviously better than Q1 only twice, when it transposes three successive speech prefixes (90, 97, 105), and once when it misprints (199), but any printer might easily rectify these self-evident errors. About half the other joint Q2–Q3 variants from Q1 are either clearly wrong or very doubtful. Common Q2–Q3 readings damage good Latin (15, 110), hide one rhyme (223), weaken grammar (211, perhaps 94), and depart from the play's customary idiom (135, 177). Eight relatively archaic or uncommon words or expressions in Q1 are modernised or altered, three of which are northern forms, notably the term 'new' (232), for which Q2–Q3 has 'newegate', a homograph that seriously distorts meaning.[29] Two other common Q2–Q3 variants also tend to damage the sense (129, 242), and several more (66, 72) are likely corrupt. In all but two of the about fifteen important variants where either Q2 or Q3, though not both, agrees with Q1, it is certainly right.[30] The dissenting quarto, often by apparent misprint, alters lines in ways inconsistent with their dramatic context (20, 48, 111, 162), disturbs grammar (5, 123, 184), introduces religious censorship (36), destroys rhyme (221, 233) and erodes *Youth*'s usual idiom (176, 225), all which quasi-editorial changes typify the early Tudor printer's work.[31] There are, then, reasonable grounds to reject Q2, Q3 or both in favour of Q1 in the remaining cases where a variant's own character or context does not itself indicate where textual authority lies, and so these Q1 readings have been retained in this edition. Q1, however, must itself conceal misreadings, as they are endemic to de Worde's press, and only a few have been traced.[32]

The 577 lines where only Q2 and Q3 exist give a much less satisfactory text. Least problematic are the approximately forty-five Q2 and Q3 substantive variants where Q1 is not extant. Though on their account alone Bang and McKerrow chose to edit all three quartos together instead of one critical text, all but a few can be settled on the individual variant's merits. While committing almost twice the misprints of Q3, Q2 often gives the better text, as where it preserves three northern forms lost in Q3 (11, 665, 687), and another word sacrificed in Q3 to religious censorship (770). Otherwise each quarto corrects the other's misprints and bad Latin (389.1), Q3 supplies a rhyme lost in Q2 (698), and Q3 gives two Q2 lacunae of a line and a half (182, 793). Syntax decides five, and dramatic context thirteen, more variants.[33] Three difficult ones may be judged by *Youth*'s customary usage (325, 471, 772), and two others (324, 684) by Q2's tendency to accidental omission,[34] though in these instances neither quarto is decisively better. *Youth*'s most serious textual problem, rather, is that, if proportions remain the same, in these 577 lines Q2 and Q3 should *jointly* depart from Q1 (and so a consistently better text) over a hundred more times, of which scarcely a quarter should be discernible.[35] Fewer still, only fifteen, have in fact been confidently emended: six rhymes are retrieved from varied corruptions, and eight misreadings arising largely from mechanical printing errors are corrected.[36] Nine further emendations, relineating run-together verses,[37] are made, but these treat a problem that probably developed long before Q2–Q3, in the original manuscript text. There are a somewhat larger number of places where some corruption, from whatever source, occurs, but these invite no certain explanation or reconstruction,[38] and because the text of *Youth* evidently has some problems for which its use of sources is responsible (364, 516, and perhaps 435) this edition preserves rather than emends some questionable readings.

b. Hick Scorner

This also survives in three undated sixteenth-century black-letter editions: Q1, published by Wynkyn de Worde; Q2, a

two-leaf fragment in the British Library; and Q3, published by
John Waley.[39] Though Q1 must precede Q3 (Waley's career
began in 1546, eleven years after de Worde's death), only type
and woodcut tests can identify their specific limits and Q2's
printer and date, and so indicate which one has textual priority.

Q1, the de Worde edition, exists in a unique copy, British
Library C.21.c.4. Its known history begins on 18 October 1762,
when Thomas Percy mentions having on loan from a fellow
antiquarian, Thomas Astle, an old, small volume of six black-
letter editions, *Robert the Devil*, *Secretary and Jealousy*, *Cock
Lorel's Boat*, *The Parliament of Birds*, *Hick Scorner* and *Everyman*.[40] By 12 May 1763 David Garrick had been given the
volume by Astle, who addressed it from his native Staffordshire,
where the copy of Q1 could evidently have been found as early as
1529/30.[41] By 1779, when *Hick Scorner* and *Everyman* were
bequeathed to the British Museum with the rest of Garrick's
play-collection, they had been individually bound.[42]

Entitled *Hycke scorner*, Q1 was, the colophon says, 'En-
prynted by me Wynkyn de Worde' (sig. C6v), and sold, from
the device,[43] at the sign of the sun in Fleet Street. Q1's ordinary
95 Textura with $s^2v^3w^{2\,(\text{large and small})}w^3y^2$ and about a dozen
instances of a recut type, s^3, gives limits of 1514–21, since s^3 is
not found in de Worde's work before 1514, and s^2 disappears
after 1521.[44] Comparison of the variant states of two of Q1's ten
woodcuts moves the upper limit back to 10 March 1518. The
Free Will and Hick Scorner factotums (sig. A1) appear, considerably damaged, in de Worde's *Nychodemus gospell* (*S.T.C.*
18568), published that day, where they have lost (sigs. A5v,
C4r) all but the bottom lines and suspended curls of the complete scrolls they had in Q1.[45] Finally, the state of de Worde's
Q1 device, employed up to 1519 when it was recut, makes, as
W. W. Greg says, '1515 or the beginning of 1516 the most likely
date of printing'.[46] Comparison of this device's states in de
Worde's dated 1511–18 editions reveals a complex pattern of
growing damage that places Q1 after 8 June 1515, the date of his
Expositio sequētiarū (*S.T.C.* 16126), and before 5 September
1516, the date of his *Promptuarium paruulorū* (*S.T.C.* 20438).[47]

Q2 exists only in two adjacent leaves, with neither title-page nor colophon, now British Library C.18.e.2[4], which first appeared at the sale of B. H. Bright's library in 1845, and was only at last identified by W. C. Hazlitt in 1876 on the advice of F. J. Furnivall.[48] Greg has shown that Q2 must comprise the second and third last leaves of a quarto with a collation like $A^6B^4C^6$, and is 'probably out of a binding'.[49] Referring without explanation to Frank Isaac's type-studies, Greg identifies its printer as Peter Treveris, who published in Southwark from 1522 to 1532, and its date as about 1526–27. The Q2 type, a 93 Textura with $s^3w^{5b}w^{12}v^3y^2$ and a peculiar, over-large sh ligature, can indeed only have belonged to Treveris, but since it appears in his dated editions uniformly from 1525 to 1529, and since no dated books before, and only three dated books after (two in a non-Textura fount), are extant, Greg's should probably be taken just as a convenience date.[50] Q2, however, definitely follows Q1 and precedes Q3.

Q3 is also extant in a unique copy, Bodleian Library Malone 330, bequeathed in 1821 by Edmond Malone, whose copy, perhaps with a *Youth* Q2 transcript, came from the library of the actor John Henderson.[51] Entitled *Hycke scorner* on sig. A1r and *the enterlude of Hycke scorner* on sig. E4r, Q3 was, the colophon says, 'Imprinted at London in Foster laene by Johñ Waley'. Its limits are 1546, when Waley's career began, and 6 July 1553, when Edward VI died, since the colophon is preceded by the prayer 'God saue the Kynge'. The printer to whom Waley contracted Q3 out, as *Youth* to John King, may have been either William Copland or Robert Wyer, or both.

Greg attributed Q3 to Copland's press *c.* 1550, presumably because he printed plays for himself and other works for Waley (e.g., *S.T.C.* 2861, 3007, 19495.3*),[52] and because four Q3 woodcuts occur in similar or later states in Copland editions that, though undated, were printed at the Rose Garland, his 1548–57 London address. For instance, his edition of Andrew Borde's *Introduction of knowledge* (*S.T.C.* 3383; *c.* 1555?) has the large Q3 woodcut of the two gallants and the Q3 centre factotum both in later states, his sumptuous *Valentine and Orson*

(*S.T.C.* 24572a, *c.* 1555) has all four Q3 cuts in such late states (on sigs. I4v, Cc1v, Nn4v and M1v), and other editions share one or more of them.[53] However, as these Q3 woodcuts exist in earlier states only in other printers' editions, Copland may not have had them when Q3 was published.[54] Its type, a 95 Textura with $s^2v^3w^3w^{5b}w^{14}y^2$ and a distinctive capital *Y* not in Isaac's keyplate, was not, moreover, employed by Copland in his extant editions, but belonged to Robert Wyer (who printed from 1526 to 1560) about 1540–42 and survives in three works (*S.T.C.* 12206a.7*, 18844 and 22880.2*).[55] John Waley's undated edition of John Heywood's *Play of Love*, again attributed by Greg to Copland's press, also shares the Q3 type and certain features of its format (such as centred speech headings preceded by a leaf), as does a third Copland attribution, Waley's *Johan the Evangelist*, which uses Q3's distinctive triangle of three large leaves in the colophon.[56] There are several plausible explanations of this problem; one is a three-way business deal. Knowing de Worde's will bequeathed to Robert Copland (William's father) ten marks' worth of books, Waley might have approached Copland to release his copy of de Worde's early *Hick Scorner* (and perhaps *Johan the Evangelist*) along with the four woodcuts to Robert Wyer for the mechanical printing, since the Coplands probably had not got a press for themselves before about 1547.[57] Alternatively, Wyer might simply have sold his old type to them at that time.

Other and later editions are possible. The title-character was proverbial in the Tudor period, *Hick Scorner* (after *Youth*) occurs in Captain Cox's old play collection in 1575, and both plays were transferred from Sampson Awdeley to John Charlewood in the Stationers' Register on 15 January 1582, and from him to James Roberts in 1594.[58] By the 1656 play-catalogue of R. Rogers and W. Ley, however, the play was known only as *Dick Scorner*, in 1675 Edward Phillips in misreading an earlier list by Francis Kirkman included it in the work of Robert Baron (a late seventeenth-century author), and by 1691 Gerard Langbaine said he 'never saw' the play and did not 'know what species of *Dramatick Poetry*' it was.[59]

The relationship of the three extant quartos is uncertain, but Q2 and Q3, as with *Youth*, must descend indirectly from Q1 through one or more unknown de Worde editions.[60] Shared Q1–Q3 corruptions, such as 'Jeltron' (51), 'and' (392), 'wyfe' (569) and the speech heading at 142, suggest that Q3 is indeed printed from a de Worde edition inherited by Copland. Common Q2–Q3 variants from Q1, like 'Thomas' (941) and several word-omissions (838, 925), show Q2 also belongs in this line, though Q2 variance from Q1–Q3 where Q3 cannot well independently restore the Q1 reading (844, 846, 938) indicates that Q3 cannot be based on Q2. Both must derive ultimately from the same post-Q1 de Worde edition (hence the common Q2–Q3 variants), which Peter Treveris may have pirated.[61] Conflation of underlying texts for either Q2 or Q3 is again improbable where such cheap, popular reprints are concerned.

On many grounds almost all the nearly five hundred Q2 and Q3 substantive variants appear to be printing-house accretions without textual authority. Q2 variants obscure rhymes (862, 870, 898) and twice give corrupt homographs, 'mely' or 'mellay' for 'mele' (938) and 'Thomas' for 'Tyburn' (941), while the four times Q2 corrects Q1 (839, 904, 926, 949) the older reading is self-evidently wrong or misleading. Though rife with misreadings, Q3 is a cleaner, better proof-read text than Q1, which has numerous accidentals, and the later edition improves on Q1 by restoring rhymes (22, 340) and a dropped word (79), righting reversed speech headings (298–99) and even correcting a printer's apparent misreadings of the original underlying MS (628, 756), notably where abbreviations may have occurred (643, 711).[62] These errors are also self-evident, however, and Q3 editorial care extends to updating and clarifying the text. An inability to interpret words like 'lode' (84), 'gyved' (198), 'threwe' (483), 'guyded' (527), 'fared' (528), 'fewte' (536), 'sin' (583), 'brachis' (828) and 'a le' (836) produces several dozen homographs.[63] Inappropriate alterations also stem from the printer's inability to understand the play's rhyme scheme,[64] and he is very insensitive to staging matters. Q3 confuses a piece of stage business (611), mixes up those whom speakers address or refer to (435, 771, 903, 989, 1025, 1028), and freely changes speech headings. Probably because Q1 never indicates that Pity exits about line 152, Q3 assigns one of Free Will's lines to him later (250–51; cf. 444); and a possible Q1 confusion in headings (101–02) may produce the Q3 headings at 71–74. Less clearly non-authorial are stylistic changes. Nevertheless, archaic or rare terms and forms like 'brast' (35), 'let' (175), 'lineages' (265), 'Constantine' (319), 'yede' (680), the verb 'thou' (705), 'miss' (848) and 'halp' (961) are given modernised equivalents,[65] and occasionally synonyms destroy rhyme (272, 281) and conceal the influence of *Youth* (845, 970). Grammar is simplified, often unnecessarily or incorrectly,[66] and scores of minor alterations in word-choice, verb tense, number and word-order are made. Most defy classification, but certain pervading changes suggest overall revision by someone other than the original writer.[67] Finally, as in Q3 of *Youth*, post-Reformation censorship takes its toll of oaths in *Hick Scorner*, as by God (243, 249; cf. 846) and the mass (784), and eliminates one curse (922) and various allusions, as to Northumberland poverty (321), royal preachers (343), the supremacy of Christ in the Trinity (869; cf. 76), current political strife (380) and the monks (345), whose monasteries were dissolved in 1538. Other alterations (31, 46, 93, 634 and 786) seem inspired by compositorial piety.

On the other hand, Q1 was printed within months of the play's composition in 1514, and may well be the first edition. The many printing errors suggest rapid presswork, and there is likewise little attempt to hide difficulties that an unclear MS may have presented (e.g., 370–71). As already noted, Q1 seems susceptible to misconstruing abbreviations (392, etc.), and the not uncommon MS practice of running short lines into longer ones without break also occurs in Q1 (550–51, 691–92, and cf. 484, 644). Three kinds of corruption, however, are perhaps the printer's responsibility here. De Worde thought of *Hick Scorner* less as a play than as a verse satire,[68] since nowhere is it called an interlude and no stage directions appear. One consequence may be his reassignment of some speeches: the tidings at 101–22 may have been transferred from Perseverance (?) to Pity because they tell how 'men complain piteously' (103); and Pity's exit speech at 142 is assigned to Contemplation evidently because de Worde thought Pity stayed in sight until the binding.[69] Secondly, in mechanically standardising the orthography of his MS base-text, de Worde destroys rhyme (22, 179, 517, 521, 649; and perhaps 480, 573, 960), and normalises one and possibly more inversions in sentence structure (944; cf. 203, 306, 491, 866), if lacunae in the rhyme scheme are significant. Finally, line-justification (only twice are there run-on verses, at 297 and 1028) may occasion the omission of some end-words (513, 801) and so other rhyme lacunae, though a few of them may be deliberate.[70] If these corruptions are all, the play is lucky, as in other, admittedly more important, texts de Worde's alterations were massive and approached translation.[71]

c. Principles of this edition

The texts of this edition are based directly on those copies of all extant sixteenth-century quartos in the British, Bodleian and Lambeth Palace Libraries.[72] Modern spelling, whether in English, French or Latin, is used for both texts, without collation, and the minimal pointing of the early quartos is silently amplified by light modern punctuation. Contractions are expanded, roman numerals written out, archaic letters transliterated into modern equivalents, and English words capitalised, joined or split up, and spelled according to O.E.D. usage. Normally obsolete terms included in the O.E.D. as a main entry have been retained, but obsolete forms varying from modern orthography and pronunciation, yet without separate O.E.D. entries, have been modernised,[73] except (so as to avoid the danger of translation) for the following kinds: obsolete plurals or comparatives (e.g., Y. 368, H.S. 293, 797), strong forms of verbs that have since become weak (e.g., H.S. 354, 952, 961), old forms of proper and place names where modernisation would seriously distort their character, and any word with a high individuation (like terms not in the O.E.D. in any spelling). A few still familiar archaic forms are kept, and no modernisation occurs where substantive meaning might be altered or hidden, as in phonetic spelling of uncertain value (e.g., *H.S.* 182), possibly intended miswriting (e.g., *H.S.* 319), and forms whose recasting would conceal deliberate ambiguity or that bear a sense not held by their modern equivalents. Finally, archaic forms are also kept when their absence would obscure unmistakable metre or rhyme, though where quarto spelling itself consistently modernises a rhyme or where either the rhyme scheme or the original pronunciation is conjectural and in doubt, modernisation is preferred.[74] Here the Commentary will draw attention to any possibly to-be-overlooked rhymes or metrical effects, and some general principles governing the plays' versification are discussed below (see pp. 26, 32). Rhyme schemes could not be clarified by stanzaic line-indentation within the texts themselves because they employ, irregularly and often uncertainly, couplets, triplets, quatrains, tail-rhyme and blank lines.

The collations give, for speech headings, stage directions and the texts themselves, all quarto variants that are, or might reasonably be held to be, substantive. Besides differences that affect meaning, whether through punctuation, capitalisation, word-spacing, term substitution or morphology (e.g., case forms of nouns, or tense and mood verb endings), some variants that affect neither function nor signification are listed: inversions in word order, alternate inflectional verb forms (e.g., third-person singular verbs in *-th*), the two indefinite articles, alternate plurals in *-en*, and the like. Any variant representing an alternate main *O.E.D.* entry has been noted. Quarto spelling variants, where recognised as such by the *O.E.D.* or *M.E.D.*, have been omitted from the collation, as well as quite unambiguous misprints unless they bear on a textual or linguistic point. Just as the black-letter types are particularly susceptible to foul case, turned letters and bad (smeared or incomplete) inking, so word-spacing in these quartos, whether by loose type or sloppy compositors, is erratic, unstandardised and often impossible to judge, and consequently misspacings are collated only when they may affect meaning. Similarly, mislineation of the speech headings is ignored when the line's indentation shows the heading's proper position. In addition, selected variant spellings appear in the collation, as where justifiable modernisation involves choosing between two meanings, where metre or rhyme is in question, where spelling bears on the development of substantive variants, and where terms have no standard spelling. Finally, the collations record the source for possibly controversial editorial (bracketed) stage directions, all editorial emendations, and other or variant emendations and conjectures (abbreviated 'conj.') by this and previous editors where such readings offer plausible alternatives.

The following modern editions have been collated:

The Interlude of Youth

Henderson	John Henderson, transcriber, 'Thēterlude of youth'. British Library MS Kings 297 (before 1786); Q2 slightly emended.
Maitland	S. R. Maitland, ed., 'Thenterlude of Youth', *A List of Some of the Early Printed Books in the Archiepiscopal Library at Lambeth* (London, 1843), pp. 309–16; Q1.
Halliwell	James Orchard Halliwell, ed., *The Enterlude of Youth*, in his *Contributions to Early English Literature* (London, 1849); Henderson, modified by Q1 and Q3.
Hazlitt	W. Carew Hazlitt, ed., 'The Interlude of Youth', *A Select Collection of Old English Plays*, 4th ed., II (London, 1874), pp. [i]–iv, 5–40; eclectic (based on Halliwell).
Bang-McKerrow	W. Bang and R. B. McKerrow, ed., *The Enterlude of Youth*, Materialien zur Kunde des älteren Englischen Dramas, XII (Louvain, 1905); a Q1 facsimile, Q2 and Q3 old spelling reprints, and full introduction, notes and apparatus.
Farmer	John S. Farmer, ed., 'Interlude of Youth', *Six Anonymous Plays (Second Series)* (London, 1906), pp. 91–116; eclectic.

Birmingham   *The Interlude of Youth: A Morality. As Edited and given in the month of October, 1907, in Birmingham* (Birmingham Printers, 1907); Hazlitt, edited and censored for acting by Barry Jackson for the Pilgrim Players.

Gowans   A. L. G[owans]., ed., *The Interlude of Youth*, intro. John Drinkwater (London, 1922); modernised, eclectic (based on Hazlitt, favouring Q3).

Hampden   John Hampden, ed., *Everyman: The Interlude of Youth: The World and the Child* (London, [1931]); Hazlitt-Gowans, censored for acting.

Schell-Shuchter Edgar T. Schell and J. D. Shuchter, ed., 'The Interlude of Youth', *English Morality Plays and Moral Interludes* (New York, 1969), pp. 140–65; eclectic.

Happé   Peter Happé, ed., 'Youth', *Tudor Interludes* (Penguin Books, 1972), pp. 113–38, 391–94; eclectic.

Hick Scorner[75]

Hawkins   Thomas Hawkins, ed., 'Hycke-scorner. A Morality', *The Origin of the English Drama* (Oxford: Clarendon Press, 1773), I, 69–111; Q1.

Hazlitt   W. Carew Hazlitt, ed., 'Hickscorner', *A Select Collection of Old English Plays*, 4th ed., I (London, 1874), 143–95; Hawkins.

Manly   John Matthews Manly, ed., 'Hyckescorner', *Specimens of the Pre-Shaksperean Drama*, I (Boston, Mass., 1897), 386–420; Hawkins and Q1. G. L. Kittredge, one of the General Editors, suggested certain readings here.

Farmer   John S. Farmer, ed., 'Hickscorner', *Six Anonymous Plays: First Series* (c. 1510–1537) (London, 1905), pp. 123–60; Hazlitt.

Emendations unique to this edition are noted 'This ed.'. Only the first modern edition to adopt a collated reading is listed. Where this edition's punctuation and use of apostrophes agree with previous editions, no attribution is made, but when disagreement results in a substantive variant interpretation, that fact is recorded. In that case, however, the omission of Q readings in the collation always signifies that no punctuation or apostrophe whatsoever exists in the quartos, and the citation of another edition as the source of this edition's practice indicates only agreement about meaning, not identical pointing. Likewise, the lemma is always taken from the modernised text, and the reading's source or sources, which follow the bracket, will sometimes differ from it in minor ways that do not affect the particular variation in question. Where the lemma consists of a complete stage direction, the abbreviation 'S.D.' is often used. Variant readings in the collation after the lemma agree exactly with their source (contractions, for instance, have not been expanded), except in two cases: where accidental differences occur between two sources in substantive agreement on the matter in question, and 'subst.' follows the differing source; and where doubt occurs as to a text's reading because of worn type, smudged ink or the like, in which case the probable reading is assumed and the alternative possible reading follows. Finally, because the slash appears in these quartos as pointing, line-breaks in the collation and elsewhere are indicated by a vertical bar.

Textual points from the collation are discussed in the Commentary (and above, pp. 5–7, 11–13). Meanings are glossed, normally, only once. All quotations, whether in the Commentary, the appendices or elsewhere, appear in their original spelling. Titles are also unmodernised, except where no specific edition is cited and the early printings offer different spellings.

2. DATE

a. The Interlude of Youth

Youth must have been written after its sources, *Everyman*,

Medwall's *Nature* (both *c.* 1495) and Hawes's *Example of Vertu* (1503–04), and before September 1516, the latest date for *Hick Scorner* Q1, which in turn adapts *Youth*.[76] Four topical allusions in *Youth* narrow these limits to August 1513 – May 1514, and various dramatic features of the interlude suggest a date about Christmas 1513 or Shrovetide 1514.

One allusion is Youth's quip (a sarcastic reply to Charity's claim at 696 that God 'bought' his soul), 'Iwis, he bought not my cap, | Nor yet my jolly hat' (703–04). To have any point—Youth could scarcely be sporting both at once—this remark must refer to their current expensiveness (at least as dear as his soul) after the spring and summer of 1512. The parliament of 4 February 1512 enacted that from 1 May no foreign caps or hats, whose previous cheapness apparently resulted in 'the great Idelnesse enpov'ysshyng and utter undoing' of English craftsmen, could be bought, except by lords and knights.[77] Besides creating this artificially protected market for local goods, the statute prescribed price ceilings for both hats (2s) and the four qualities of caps (3s 4d for the finest) that exceeded ceilings legislated in 1489 (by 4d and 8d respectively) to correct what were then termed 'outrageous' prices.[78]

The second allusion is Youth's taunt that 'holy caitiffs' guilty of stealing 'would be hanged as high | As a man may see with his eye. | In faith, this same is true' (140–44). Youth emphasises that this punishment is in fact meted out because up to 1512 all clerics, whether in minor or holy orders, were able to escape a secular court's sentence of death or imprisonment for a felony like theft by claiming 'benefit of clergy', whereby convicted clerics who proved themselves by reading a Latin verse or two were delivered to the more lenient bishops' courts.[79] This exemption, already weakened by a statute in 1488/89, was half destroyed on 4 November 1512, when parliament enacted a further statute limiting benefit of clergy only to those in holy orders where cases of robbery or murder were concerned.[80] Those in minor orders were evidently subject to hanging for a simple felony. Because this law was only made until the next parliament, which met 2 February 1515 and was dissolved before it could re-enact the legislation,[81] Youth's remark can have been true only for the intervening period of just over two years.

A third satirical comment, when Youth notes how common the Tudor knight's gold collar has become and compares it to a felon's hanging rope, advances the play's *terminus a quo* to about August 1513. Youth tells Riot that he deserves for his crimes to be 'dubbed' a 'knight of the collar' (270–72) and to get a rope about his neck as that order's mock-ensign 'because gold collars be so good cheap' (278), too plentiful to bear distinction. This jest could not have developed until Henry VII added a chain-like gold collar (with a pendant St George image) to the ensigns of the Garter—probably before the 14 November 1501 marriage of Prince Arthur and Catherine of Aragon, at which 'massy' gold chains were much in evidence and Henry installed fifty-eight Knights of the Bath and twenty-six Knights Bachelors[82]— and must, as McKerrow thought, reflect a time when many, probably newly created knights wore gold chains. While Henry VII's last years were niggardly and his court was rather drab, the early years of his son's reign were extravagant and spendthrift.[83] At Henry VIII's coronation in June 1509 Halle reported gold-smiths' work 'in more plentie and abundaunce, then hath been seen, or redde of at any tyme before, and thereto many and a greate nombre of chaines of Golde, and Bauderikes, bothe massy and great', so that even the sixty horsemen preceding the entrance of Pallas' knights for the celebratory jousts afterwards wore such gold collars on chains.[84] Youth must refer to the climax of this showiness, Henry's victories in August–September 1513 (at Thérouanne and Tournai over the French, and at Flodden Field over the Scots, when no fewer than two hundred new English knights were dubbed) and their after-math.[85] By late 1513, when success was intoxicating the Tudor court, not only had the golden collar become knighthood's general trademark, but a variant of Youth's own witticism was in vogue. When Leonardo Spinelli, the Pope's emissary, gave Henry the papal sword and cap of maintenance on 21 May 1514, the Venetian diplomat Nicolo di Favri thus described the London court: 'All bore such massive gold chains that some might have served for fetters on a felon's ankles, and sufficed for his safe custody, so heavy were they, and of such immense value.'[86] Parliament's revised act of apparel in February 1515 reacted to this glut of collars by adding a regulation not in the act of 1510, 'that noman under the degre of a Knight were any cheyne of gold or gilte or colour [collar] of Gold or any gold aboute his neke'.[87]

A fourth political allusion supports this evidence for a date of composition after the summer of 1513 and suggests a final limit of May 1514. Pride's last bribe for Youth's loyalty, 'Ye may be Emperor or ye die' (674), was an ambition within Henry VIII's reach in late 1513 and early 1514. The king had indeed just begun to think of himself as ruler of an empire in 1513. That year Polydore Vergil's *Anglica Historia*, especially commissioned by Henry VII, was completed in manuscript form. It argued that centuries earlier Rome had invested English kings with its imperial rank; and Henry VIII must have agreed, because in 1513 he named two new royal ships the *Henry Imperial* and the *Mary Imperial*.[88] With this sudden promotion in rank, Henry was in many minds (not least his own) a candidate for the very title that Pride mentions: Holy Roman Emperor, then held by Maximilian I. The Emperor himself in fact encouraged Henry in this thought. As early as 23 July 1513, when imperial diplomats told Henry's ambassador Sir Robert Wingfield that Maximilian would join Henry in the French campaign (they first met at Rincq, between Thérouanne and Aire, on 10 August) and would 'trust him as his own son', Henry must have pondered being created heir to the Empire.[89] This 'father–son' relationship was noted in August by others, including Henry himself and Maximilian's daughter, Margaret of Savoy; and by September the Emperor was said to love Henry 'more than a son', and as 'his king' and 'his brother'.[90] About Christmas the wily Maximilian did formally offer Henry 'the Imperial crown, and other offices', but apparently demanded in return certain impossible concessions by the English. On 12 June 1514, by which time the gesture had been retracted (though it was to be repeated three more times in 1516–18), Henry wrote to Margaret of Savoy that the offer was made just before he took ill—Henry had smallpox in late January 1514—when he needed time and his Council's advice before replying.[91] Evidently the Emperor's proposal still hung fire on 20 May, when Wingfield looked to answer Maximilian 'upon the subject of the Roman crown and the vicariate of the Empire', but the English cannot have entertained the idea seriously after news reached them of Maximilian's truce with France and Scotland on 13 March 1514 (a total betrayal of Henry's enterprise and previous agreements).[92] The expectations that Pride arouses in Youth for the Holy Roman Empire, then, were probably only shared realistically by Henry in the six to eight months from late summer 1513 to late March 1514.

From other internal evidence *Youth* appears to have been written for a major feast occurring in this period. Both Christmas and Shrovetide are possible. Interludes, *Youth*'s drinking and 'cheer' (205, 235), and Riot's instruction in cards, dice and like sports (679–89) traditionally belonged to the twelve holidays from Christmas to Epiphany (6 January) and to Shrovetide, which lasted from the Saturday before Shrove Tuesday (28 February in 1514) sometimes to the day after Ash Wednesday, when the religious said goodbye to rich food, plays and gaming until Easter had passed.[93] *Mankind* is probably a Shrovetide play, and *The World and the Child* a Christmas one.[94] Chapel gentlemen, by whom *Youth* gives some signs of having been acted, generally performed plays for their noble patrons at both principal feasts in pre-Reformation England.[95] *Youth*'s riddle about mustard and salt fish (120) makes sense as a joke about lenten prohibition of meat, but the Advent that preceded Christmas as well as the Lent that followed Shrovetide both enjoined abstinence.[96] The confession of sins that Youth finally recites on his knees (733–34, 738–41) was required preparation for a medieval Lent, and the choice of Charity's main theme, Christ's passion (1–2, 165–69, 724–25), would also befit that season, so that Shrovetide may be preferable. On the other hand, composition of the play in late February in Yorkshire

would not leave much time for its printing, which would seem to
have been done before June, when another playwright apparently used *Youth* as a main source to write *Hick Scorner* for a
noble household several hundred miles south at London.[97]

b. Hick Scorner

The strict limits of this interlude are August 1513–September
1516, but it was probably written between March and September 1514, and some evidence exists for a date shortly after
Whitsun week (4–10 June that year), a popular season for
plays.[98]

The *terminus a quo* can be well defined. As Alois Brandl
argued long ago, *Hick Scorner* must have been composed after
10 August 1512, when the principal warship of Henry VIII's
navy, the *Regent*, one of thirteen ships that the play's title-
character describes as having sunk in the Irish Sea (332, 362),
foundered near Brest as it grappled, afire, with the French
carrack *Cordelière* in the first major naval battle of the 1512–14
war between England and France.[99] Charles M. Gayley and
Willy Bang disputed the historicity of Hick Scorner's story, and
dated the interlude while the *Regent* was still active, but the
playwright clearly would not have dared, for both superstitious
and political reasons, to report this king's ship as lost unless it
truly were.[100] Scorn stating a known fact inaccurately is one
thing; rumour spreading false news that (even in a play)
weakens the nation's morale and touches the king's honour is
quite something else. Government records also identify nine of
the dozen other ships that Hick Scorner says are wrecked, and
information about two of these further advances the interlude's
date. Because a second royal ship, Henry VIII's purchased
merchantman the *Anne of Foy* (333), otherwise called the *Anne
Gallant*, sank in Plymouth haven just before 7 May 1513, where
she remained for refloating and repairs through 26 March 1514
and up to her return to full service by late April,[101] *Hick Scorner*
could not have been written before May 1513. In addition,
various other unidentified English ships, some of them perhaps
mentioned in the play's list, went to the bottom in the summer

1513 war, and of the English merchantmen that foundered in the subsequent bad winter weather one may have been Hick Scorner's *Mary Bellouse of Bristow* (336). She disappears from customs records after sailing for Ireland on 12 September 1513,[102] and an Irish Sea disaster of the sort the play refers to may have overtaken her. At any rate, because the interlude's principal source is *Youth*, and as its earliest possible date of composition is August 1513, *Hick Scorner* must have been written after that month. The play must be later still, if *Youth* was written for Christmas 1513 or Shrovetide (late February) 1514.[103]

The play's terminal limit is of course the last possible date for the printing of Q1, September 1516,[104] but *Hick Scorner* is undoubtedly much earlier. R. B. McKerrow argued that it must have been composed before 30 September 1514 because Hick Scorner's ship-catalogue fails to mention Henry VIII's *Lubeck* or *Great Elizabeth*, which sank then in a storm with several hundred men just west of Calais at Sangatte.[105] Given the magnitude of this catastrophe (the just-purchased *Lubeck* preceded Henry's sister Mary to France for her marriage with Louis XII, and Mary herself nearly did not reach Boulogne a few days later because of similar bad weather), the ship's omission is puzzling unless the interlude had already been written. *Hick Scorner* includes many other current allusions, as to the (Scots') devastation of Northumberland, to the threat of legislated emigration by Englishmen to Ireland, to the benefit-of-clergy and sanctuary controversies, to the great cannon named the 'twelve apostles' that Henry VIII had made for his 1513 invasion of France (761), and probably even (in Imagination's character) to a notorious Genoa merchant whom Empson and Dudley under Henry VII had employed as a promoter, John Baptist de Grimaldi, but these references cannot be exactly dated and used to confirm McKerrow's suggestion. One which can, however, is Hick Scorner's parody of the Yorkist pretender to the throne, Richard de la Pole, whom London understood by at least late May 1514 to be in Normandy with a large army waiting to board ship for an invasion of England.[106] Hick Scorner's arrival from

France in a ship of five thousand warlike vices clearly draws on the pretender's scheme, but such dramatic satire is unlikely to have been written after the 7 August Anglo–French treaty, for it obliged Louis XII to cut off Richard's financial support, disband his army, cancel the invasion and force him into exile at Metz in Lorraine. Free Will and Imagination could hardly have expected the pretender's arrival after this date.

These March–August 1514 limits can probably be further narrowed, because the play apparently satirises, in the brawl scene where Hick Scorner's 'poule' (450) is broken, a humiliation that overtook the pretender in late June or July, when his German mercenaries rioted in Normandy and had to be transported, in disgrace and in a hurry, to Saint-Malo. A Paris report of 15 June locates de la Pole's army still in Normandy, but by August there is evidence of French warships at Saint-Malo, so that the riot should have occurred in June or July and *Hick Scorner* accordingly written during that six-week period. Documentation of this riot is slender, but Free Will's confusion of Easter Day and Whitsunday, 4 June in 1514, as well as his mockery of the traditional Easter–Whitsun ales (745–53), lend some support to a date in this month. Perhaps the interlude was designed as part of the entertainment of the French ambassadors who were then in London to work out a peace treaty with the English. At his last entrance Free Will, interestingly, commands the audience's attention in both English and French (646–47).

3. STAGING, AUSPICES AND AUTHORSHIP

a. The Interlude of Youth

Youth was written, like most interludes,[107] for indoor performance at a hall banquet, 'among all this cheer' (205), as Youth says, where a riddle about mustard and salt fish (120) would be topical. Humility's entrance from evensong (570) suits a banqueting hour, and what stage conditions can be inferred from a text with only one stage direction (389.1) are consistent with a hall play. The staging 'place' (640), a term meaning 'manor-house' as well as 'acting area',[108] offered the interluders a space that, visible to the audience 'beforn' (547), must have been at ground level, since Youth enters brushing through the spectators (40–41, 589), and since Riot, as he comes in talking to them, overlooks and discovers Youth in a way that suggests he blends with the crowd (215–19).[109] The playwright's dialogue reflects some care in working out actors' movements (e.g., 541n), and these sometimes also need the 'space' (201) of a hall floor, as when Riot flirts with Lechery and she in turn quarrels with him while Youth and Pride, seemingly oblivious to them, talk together (411–25), or later when Humility, trying to get at Youth, has to speak first to an evidently intervening Pride and Riot (654–64).[110] That Charity in entering stops Youth as he goes to the tavern (476; cf. 292–93) suggests that the players used a single entrance-exit, like the Tudor hall's screened double doors. Finally, *Youth*'s flexible costuming, as well as such easily portable properties as Youth's dagger and purse, Riot's two chains for Charity's hands and feet, Humility's beads, and possibly a book for Charity (cf. 14, 25, 109),[111] all point to interluders at work in an area made ready for them only minutes before performance time. One item alone need have been there before the play began, a seat for Charity during the fettering so that he would be visible for his complaint, but at a banquet, as Youth implies (151–52), stools would have been readily at hand.[112]

Youth was acted by an economical, mobile Tudor troupe of familiar make-up, 'Foure men and a boy'.[113] Restricted to these few actors, the playwright needed to alter his source material structurally. Because one actor had to double as Lady Lechery and Humility, her part had to be suppressed when that virtue was needed.[114] A monologue such as Charity's complaint was introduced to allow time for role-changing, and both characterisation and action were compressed, sometimes awkwardly; hence Lechery's solitary departure for the tavern. However, Youth, Riot and Pride behave in their two three-part songs, for the first of which Pride becomes 'rector chory' (473–75, 546), less like itinerant interluders than like chapel gentlemen, perhaps tenor, bass and counter-tenor, respectively; and the parts of 'little' Lechery (411) and meek Humility suit a child or adolescent, possibly from a choir. These four players, with a man whose relative seniority shows up in Charity's noted age, schoolmaster manner and Latin, might well be permanent servants in a noble household for the deference they show their 'masters' (196, 547, 761) throughout. Youth jokes about heaven's ladder with the spectators, not with Charity (97), and alludes rather self-consciously to that actor's part (163); in turn, Charity assures the audience, not Youth, of his intention to return (196–98); and the players' final benedictions and plea for approval compliment the onlookers no less than four times.

Youth's original auspices, as Willy Bang thought, must have been northern. Besides various widespread northern word-forms, such as 'dead' (2) and 'yate' (QI 16),[115] certain fairly localised words appear, in particular 'agate' (475) and the noun 'new' (QI 232), a term only found elsewhere in the York Corpus Christi cycle. Rhymes also support this provenance, once a few misrhymes are discounted, the many cases of assonance before nasals and *p*, *t* and *k* are understood as typical of early moral interludes (such as *Lucidus and Dubius* and *Occupation and Idleness*), and certain apparent irregularities are explained.[116] Here important northern forms include 'fand' (267), and 'world' (760) rhyming as 'ward' with 'hard'.[117] Northern *s* (from Old English *sc*) in final position where *sh* is usual elsewhere may account for several couplets (119–20, 679–80), and the loss of [g] from [ŋg] in rhymes like 'rings'/'shins' (507–08) is a sign of an eastern dialect.[118] Other dialectical evidence has disappeared with the original spelling, levelled to East Midland English by decades of printing and reprinting in London, but one external document tends to confirm the north-east as the play's provenance. *Youth*'s text partly survives in a Lincolnshire variant of the northern sword dances and plough plays, the so-called 'Revesby Play', an artful, hybrid mummers' entertainment copied down for a 1779 performance at Revesby Abbey.[119] *Youth* was written, it seems, in the area extending from southern Yorkshire, about York and Beverley, down to Lincoln, parts of

England that produced (and still were acting into the mid-sixteenth century) much of the extant medieval English drama.

The northern household that probably sponsored the interlude, during the winter of 1513–14, is that of Henry Algernon Percy, fifth earl of Northumberland, whose seats were at Leconfield and Wressle, near Beverley. His players were paid by Henry VII on 7 January 1493, presumably for acting the previous (Twelfth) night, and they also performed at Thornbury, in Gloucestershire, the seat of Edward Stafford, duke of Buckingham, the earl's brother-in-law, on 25 December 1507.[120] No other northern magnate at this time is known to have patronised players as much as Percy did, and few could have afforded the luxury. The Percy household books show that during the winter he kept both a four-person troupe, which was employed on Twelfth Night and generally from Christmas to Candlemas for 'Playing of Playe[s] and Interludes', and also his chapel gentlemen and children, who normally performed a Nativity play on Christmas day, a Resurrection play on Easter morning, and (with 'other his Lordshipis Servaunts') an unnamed play, which might have been *Youth* in 1514, on Shrove Tuesday night.[121] The earl's house also sheltered two playwrights: one was his almoner, whom one household book describes in late 1514 as a 'maker of Interludys'; the other was the family poet-historian William Peeris (or Pyers), whom the Beverley governors paid in 1519–20 to do the 'transposing' or 'alteration' of their Corpus Christi play.[122] The north, of course, had other noblemen's acting troupes.[123] Henry, lord Clifford (at Skipton, Yorkshire), Thomas, lord Dacre of Gilsland (near Carlyle, in Cumberland), Thomas, lord Darcy (at Temple Hirst, Yorkshire), and George Talbot, earl of Shrewsbury (at Sheffield, Yorkshire) all were monied enough to sponsor players, but three of these men, Darcy, Dacre and Talbot, held high office under young Henry VIII and would not have tolerated *Youth*'s criticism of the king and his policy in the north.[124] Only Clifford, who was Dacre's enemy and Percy's ally in 1514, was in Henry's reign an outsider: Clifford would marry his son to the earl's daughter Margaret, and about 1517 scathingly denounce his own son (who from at least 1506 had been brought up at court with the future king) to the Privy Council in words strikingly recalling *Youth*.[125] Young Clifford, who was jailed in the Fleet in October 1517, had extorted money from rural churches, threatened and spoiled his father's property, struck his servant Henry Popeley, and 'for maynteinyng his inordinate pride and ryot, as more speciallie dyd apere when he dep'tyd out of ye corte and com into ye contrie, aparellyd himself and hys horse in cloth of golde and goldsmyths wark, more lyk a duke then a pore baron's sonne as hee ys'.[126] If Clifford was as poor as he said, he certainly would not have kept interluders. However, as a satellite of the Percies, and a proponent of their (and the play's) out-of-favour political orthodoxy, he might well have seen *Youth* at home in Leconfield or Wressle, or on the road at Skipton.

A great deal is known about the earl's household and his domestic and political affairs, and *Youth* reflects them in detail. Percy's court had a school, a children's choir and a full chapel, one that, besides offering daily evensong, had rules for the selection of weekly 'rectors chory' from its gentlemen members (473n). Though the administration of the earl's widespread estates occupied his chief counsellors, the household business centred on worship and the education of Percy's heirs, especially his eldest son Henry (born *c.* 1502, and so about twelve years old in 1514). His upbringing was a dogmatically moral one. On his Leconfield chamber ceiling was inscribed a verse dialogue between pleasure-loving, irresponsible youth and moralising adulthood; and in the garret over the bath there was a similar anti-youth dialogue between the parts 'sensatyue' and 'intellectyue', where the first boasted, 'I am yonge lusty and of high corage. | Desscendyd of ryall blode & noble parentage', and exulted in song, wealth, rich clothes, servants and 'assuride councell', and the second preached against worldly vanity and warned that 'Amonge councell myche dissymylynge is'.[127] *Youth* is mainly a dialogue between two such voices, and the two sides of its debate are exactly represented in a stanza belonging to the Sensative Part and in a Leconfield library ceiling proverb:

I floure in youthe delyght and pleasure
To fede all my fantasys I want no treasure.
I synge and daunce I reuell and play.
I am so louede of ladyes I nede not to pray.

How goode so eu^{er} thy werke be
Grownde thyn entente vpon charite
Vayneglory allway fle
Inclyne thy selfe to humylite.[128]

These verses indicate how strongly Percy would have approved of Charity's criticism of Youth's opening boast. One incident late in the earl's life, well after 1514, also proves that he thought his young son ungovernable and might have had the interlude acted for his particular benefit. When Wolsey called Percy from the north to break off his son's marriage pre-contract with Anne Boleyn (he was then serving in Wolsey's household), the earl accused the youth of 'prodigality', of having 'always been a proud, presumptuous, disdainful, and a very unthrift waster', and of intending, of his 'natural inclination', his family's destruction.[129] The conflicting values of father and son were really only a reflection, however, of the reigns of their royal counterparts. Though Henry VII had extorted a huge fine from the fifth earl and had denied him the Percies' traditional control of the north, the two men agreed in principle, whereas Henry VIII, whose cult of youth and new style always had the sixth earl's intense loyalty, irked his father both personally and morally by excluding him from influence and dignity, by abandoning the north to a disastrous period of non-government, by squandering money on court pleasures and foreign adventures, and even, perhaps, by becoming scandalously involved with the sister of the earl's brother-in-law, to the queen's public vexation (one of whose ladies-in-waiting was the earl's sister Anne).[130] There are many reasons to believe, then, that *Youth*'s political and moral criticisms of Henry VIII, as well as its didactic allegory, may have been written for the fifth earl's eldest son. He needed some hard words to prepare him for service at Wolsey's house, where a cardinal (whom Charity may partly represent)[131] held sway, not the king.

The playwright's identity is unknown. If the Percy household provided auspices for *Youth*, however, he must have been the fifth earl's almoner, the 'maker of Interludys'.[132] Some internal evidence supports this possibility. Charity's first Latin quotations were widely adopted in a form of dinner grace (25–26n), and its recitation in a noble household was the job of the almoner.[133] If he had to choose a principal virtue, also, it would obviously have been his own duty, Charity.

Once published, *Youth* entered the repertory of the sixteenth-century common interluders, and from the impact it had on other, later plays the work seems to have been acted up to Elizabeth's reign.[134] The first of its many modern revivals took place on 12 December 1905 by Nugent Monck's English Drama Society at Bloomsbury Hall, London. Barry Jackson's Pilgrim Players, later the Birmingham Repertory, first staged *Youth* publicly themselves on 2 October 1907 at St Jude's Mission Hall, Birmingham, and frequently afterwards, notably with Marlowe's *Doctor Faustus* on the opening night's programme of the 1934 Malvern Festival (24 July, and 1, 6 and 13 August).[135] Only three later revivals, two during the 1951 Festival of Britain celebrations, have come to my notice.[136]

b. Hick Scorner

This also is an interlude[137] designed for indoor performance, perhaps in a hall towards the end of a banquet, for Free Will, entering as a 'gest' (158), calls for the drinking cup to be filled[138] and plays the feast's traditional jester (652n). Perseverance's benediction is also said to conclude '*all* our mirths here' (1027), as if more than a play is involved. The audience hierarchy, from noble 'sovereigns' or 'lords' (2, 546, 767) down to their entourage of 'young men' (297, 568) and the 'fellows' at the doors (156), probably household servants, suits this auspices; and what evidence we have of staging does as well. For instance, differentiating audience from acting areas in 'this place' (93, 545; cf. *Y.* 640) is difficult: Free Will twice warns spectators to stand back (156, 646), Hick Scorner is mooted to enter from the 'bosoms' (297) of the young men, Free Will's assault on Perse-

verance would endanger the audience (718), and when Imagination returns he asks it no fewer than four questions (891–908),
the last of which implies he has overlooked Free Will in the
crowded room. In addition, Hick Scorner could best have 'hid
in some corner' (300), as Imagination suspects, if the audience–actor area was a hall lit by torches that left the room's far
reaches in relative obscurity.[139] There must be at least two
different doors, if Pity's second exit, almost simultaneous with
Free Will's final entrance (645–46), is not to be awkwardly
managed, and any manor hall has several accesses.[140] Otherwise, all the play demands, like any hall interlude with a brawl
(443–48), is space. Properties such as Free Will's rope and
fetters, Hick Scorner's horn, and the virtues' new coats for the
converted rogues, could be readily carried on and off with the
actors, and the one thing the room must supply, a seat for Pity
twice (30, 539), would be available, as in *Youth*, among the
banquet stools.

Though authorial stage directions might confirm this staging,
they may never have been written out at all, even in a prompt
copy, because the playwright consistently, almost on principle,
indicates his stage-business in the text itself. The entrances of
Pity's two fellows are, as Southern says, explicitly 'anticipated'
(31–32n, 72n). Free Will's companions are called in after their
entrances have already been anticipated (186–92, 232–33,
296–303), and their return minus Hick Scorner is predicted
(616–17). Exits too are self-evident, and even permit some
emendation of speech headings (142n). In general the dialogue
makes a helpful guide to the play's original production, and, for
instance, theatrically defines character through implied details
of costuming.[141] Free Will's sordid life is realised concretely
when he talks about or plays with his purse (167–71), hat-
feather (190), codpiece (761) and shoes (790–807), Imagination's new prosperity and rank show up when he returns
daggerless (928; cf. 435), and a clothes-change marks their
conversions. An image possibly on Pity's garment (17n) may
express his allegorical meaning, and his treatment as a thief begins
when he gets new 'stockings' (515). Action, likewise, is at times

implicitly choreographed for us: the brawl is no chaotic scramble, but a play within a play named and perhaps patterned after the newly imported French *farce* (446); and dialogue shows that when Imagination strikes with his dagger it is not just randomly stabbed but falls right on the rogues' heads (437, 450). Free Will's gradual entrapment by Perseverance and Contemplation is another example of how the playwright thinks his blocking into the text.

Hick Scorner shows signs of having been written for a four-man troupe, the doubling assignments for which help explain why Pity and Hick Scorner are absent after line 645; as will be seen, their absence is also accounted for by characterisation.[142] The roles seem to have been split as follows: (1) Free Will, with 286 lines (on stage 156–483, 510–45, 646–1028); (2) Pity (1–152, 456–645) and Imagination (891–1028), with 235 lines; (3) Contemplation (33–155, 602–1028) and Hick Scorner (301–545), with 221 lines; (4) Perseverance (75–155, 602–1028) and Imagination (192–545), with 286 lines. Either of the last two actors could have played the first half of Imagination's split role, but the fourth actor's forceful leadership in playing Perseverance, who heads the conversion attempt and gives the final benediction, would better suit Imagination the brawler, whose first part is longer and more physically demanding than Hick Scorner's.[143] All roles, however, call for mature actors, even Free Will's (693n), which seems youngest in agility and experience.

The interlude's auspices were certainly near London. Wynkyn de Worde's press would have levelled spelling to East Midland usage whatever the original copy had, but linguistic evidence based on rhymes[144] also localises the playwright's dialect there. The loss of [g] from stressed syllables ending in [ŋg], a regular feature in rhymes here, is limited to eastern England, the presence of *o* (from early Old English *a*) before *nd* points to East Midland, and several southern or Kentish word-forms crop up.[145] The interlude's ample, specific reference to its dramatic setting, the London area,[146] corroborates this evidence: Though the city's western suburbs, legal London, figure prominently there, Imagination's attacks on lawyers and judges do not suit an Inns of Court performance, and the play's satirical or flippant comments on mayors, London and otherwise (444–45, 578–79), even suggest freedom from fear of civic displeasure. Hick Scorner's arrival by a ship *from* London (384) may point to auspices somewhere outside the city on the Thames, and while Westminster is mentioned twice (217, 842) the characters' activities centre on Southwark. Free Will's first monologue tells how he slept 'at the stews' side' (184), that is, in a Bankside brothel, Imagination plots to spend the next night there by the Thames (405, 418), and at the end he enters as comptroller of the stews, in particular of the Southwark *Bell* and *Hart's Horn* (898–901). Both rogues plan to rob at Shooters Hill (543, 822) and Free Will fears the gallows at St Thomas-a-Watering (838), both of which places are on the Old Kent Road, which runs south from Southwark's Borough High Street.[147] The best indication of the play's auspices, however, is Free Will's return, after being away off-stage for only twenty-six lines, with the fetters and the rope from (of all London district prisons) the King's Bench (512) in Borough High Street. The play's source here, *Youth*, does not say where Riot got the chains. The King's Bench visit, which appears to be a time-saving device (at 508 Hick Scorner suggests leading Pity away to Newgate), is the playwright's own addition, and may well be a neighbourhood allusion, there to accommodate the interlude to its intended place of performance. Long before the building of the Swan, Rose and Globe theatres, Southwark had put on plays, sometimes just outside the King's Bench, and because the suburbs were outside city jurisdiction actors could there avoid civic prohibitions.[148]

In 1514 two men rich enough to sponsor banquet interludes, and secure enough to countenance an attack on the Church (127–38), had Southwark manors. To Richard Fox, bishop of Winchester and Lord Privy Seal, belonged Winchester Palace, which stood on the Thames bank next to the stews. Charles Brandon, duke of Suffolk, Henry VIII's favourite and close advisor, held Manor Place, also called Suffolk Place after 1514, which was in Borough High Street opposite St George's Church, the King's Bench and the Marshalsea (another prison), and which had a separate Banqueting House located in the garden.[149] Because Fox's diocese controlled the stews that *Hick Scorner* so often satirises, he would probably not have stomached the play, but Brandon's sponsorship of it is very plausible. His 'Place' (to which the actors may have referred at 93 and 545) was opposite the prison Free Will visited during his brief absence, and after February 1510 Brandon was actually the Marshall of the King's Bench.[150] The binding of Pity, a justice figure such as the duke might employ, with chains from his own jail would have been a witty jest (one that Brandon's own disguising as a prisoner in the 1511 tournament at Westminster shows that he would have relished); and other features of the interlude are consistent with Brandon's patronage: the concern for criminals, Pity's mission as a secular justice of the peace, his praise for royal preachers (343), and the allusions to (courtly) farce and songs.[151] Finally, no one would have had a better reason than Brandon for sponsoring an attack on Richard de la Pole (in the title-character): on 1 February 1514, just months before the play's composition, Brandon had been created duke of Suffolk (Edmund de la Pole's title until 1504; maintained by Richard until his death in 1525), and was even then lobbying to get the brothers' estates as well, which were largely granted to him a year later. Any attack on a de la Pole would have been 'mirths' at Suffolk Place that year.

The playwright's name is not known, but if the interlude's auspices were at Suffolk Place he probably belonged to the duke's household, which then had at least one servant with revels experience, Lewis Wynwod.[152] The author of *Hick Scorner* may also be the anonymous poet responsible for *Cocke Lorelles bote*, written *c.* 1506–10 in or about London, since the poem, besides possibly influencing the play, shares with it techniques of composition, themes and formulaic language.[153] The prosody of both works is alike: they have a rough accentual metre where lines often differ in length by half a dozen syllables, they use the same kinds of assonance (before *p* and *t*, *k* and *t*, and p and k), and they mix couplets randomly with a few basic stanzaic forms like *aabccb* and *abba*, though the play also includes variants like *aaabcccb* and *abab*.[154] Each author is fond of name-catalogues and ship jargon, has the knack of inventing proverbial title-figures, and discusses comparable satiric topics: oddities like land-travelling ships of rogues (302, 389, 820–44) and the shoe-making craft, as well as commonplaces like incontinent clerics and the stews. The evidence that both works appear to have two common sources, Chaucer's *Pardoner's Tale* and *The Assembly of Gods*, and to draw different material from each, seems to rule out coincidental imitation.[155] The fact that both *Hick Scorner* Q1 and the poem survive only in unique de Worde editions from the same David Garrick volume (see above, p. 8) is also worth noting. Our knowledge of the entire early Tudor literary world, however, is sketchy.

By the Reformation *Hick Scorner* had evidently entered the repertory of common players, whose productions of it perhaps contributed to the proverbial usage of the eponym's name.[156] By 1656 the interlude had been forgotten, and was not revived until Sir Barry Jackson's 'Five Centuries of English Drama' (his third festival held at Malvern, Worcestershire) presented the play in a programme with Udall's *Ralph Roister Doister* on 3, 10 and 17 August 1931. The forty-minute production, directed by H. K. Ayliff and designed by Paul Shelving, was acted before a set that depicted 'the exterior of a church adjoining an ale-house', and showed the influence of Jackson's *Youth* revivals.[157] G. B. Shaw thought the play

> magical. Not only were the naïve rhythms of medieval stage poetry much more musical than the euphuistic blank verse of the Elizabethans and post-Elizabethans, but the world in which the persons of the drama spoke was our own modern war-wrecked world. The long speech with the refrain 'Worse was it never' might have been written on the very day of the performance.[158]

A shortened radio version of the play's conversion scene (646–1011) was prepared by John Barton and Raymond Raikes for a series in the BBC Third Programme in 1956–57, and was later recorded.[159] This editor also directed the play on 19–21

November 1969 at University College, Toronto, for the Poculi Ludique Societas.[160]

4. SOURCES

a. The Interlude of Youth

Though *Youth* reflects contemporary Tudor politics and includes numerous biblical quotations or allusions,[161] the play's moral allegory, homiletic themes and much dialogue are conflated from three printed sources: Henry Medwall's two-part *Nature* (c. 1495), *Everyman* (translated from the Dutch *Elckerlijc c.* 1495), and Stephen Hawes's *Example of Vertu* (1503–04). Their use, which incidentally shows the priority of *Youth* to *Hick Scorner*,[162] has not been argued before, but is revealed by parallel characterisation and allegorical logic, regular verbal paraphrase, and unresolved dramatic inconsistencies that crop up where the sources conflict. Other as yet unknown sources may exist.

The moral struggle that occurs in Medwall's Man between two sets of opposed counsellors, Reason, Shamefastness, Humility, Charity and other virtues, and Worldly Affection, Sensuality, Pride and other vices, is the basic model for a similar conflict in *Youth*.[163] Charity resembles Reason in *I Nature* in coming from heaven (5) as God's grace to Youth, and in being rejected by him as a 'hangman' (307) oppressor of the senses,[164] but Charity's name and moral dependence on his brother Humility, the one virtue that is a necessary pre-condition of love and good works, are from *II Nature*, where Man is converted, not by Reason, but first by Meekness or Humility, and only then by Charity. Riot's allegorical meaning may have no specific source,[165] but in tempting Youth to commit deadly sin he is influenced by Worldly Affection and Sensuality in *I Nature*. Riot resembles Worldly Affection in having the 'discretion' (245) that Man and Youth admire in one who chooses servants,[166] and Sensuality in picking out Pride for Youth's household service. Sensuality also influences Riot when he advises Youth to reject marriage for fornication (364–73), suggests the rendezvous with Youth's 'leman' in a tavern 'At the wine' (376), and instigates the attack on Charity when he tries to prevent the tavern visit. Youth, the centre of this conflict, takes features from Medwall's Man and Pride. Characterised as the World's governor (I, 207) and as a fellow 'karued out of tre' (I, 194), Man seems to influence Youth when he talks of eternal kingship (592) and of flourishing as the 'vine tree' (45, 75). On the other hand, as a recent heir to his father's lands and as a gallant sporting luxuriant hair and a dagger (48, 84), Youth is modelled on Pride, who also enters praising himself and claiming a noble descent and inheritance (I, 731–39).[167] No Medwall character in fact affects *Youth* more than Pride. The difficulties posed by Pride's first appearance in *Youth*, when Riot sights him off-stage (316), and by Youth's oddly unanswered question about where Pride comes from (328), may well have been caused by the playwright's careless use of the parallel scene of Pride's entrance in *I Nature*, for verbal echoes occur at lines 331–34. Just as Medwall's Pride insists that Man dress like a gallant (I, 1059–61), so Pride in *Youth* advises Youth to wear 'gay' clothes;[168] and this counsel appears in Pride's only long speech, one that paraphrases *Nature* in several other respects (342–46, 348–53). Both Prides also are pandars. Medwall's Pride leads Man to one of the vice's 'kynnesmen', Bodily Lust, who is associated with the prostitutes Kate and Margery whom Man meets at the tavern, and with Lechery, who Sensuality says changes her name to Lust to deceive Man.[169] Similarly, Pride introduces Youth to the vice's sister (372), Lady Lechery. Like Bodily Lust, Kate and Margery, she meets her lover at a tavern; and Lady Lechery takes her name, as well as the wish to fool her lover about it (408–09), from the other Medwall character. The climax in *I Nature*, when Man strikes Reason on the head with a sword in the tavern, is only partly realised in *Youth*: of course Youth does threaten a blow at Charity to make his 'head ache' (131–32; cf. 300) and later does assault him after he too objects to the tavern visit, but the actual binding scene evidently derives from *Everyman*. The next episode, the complaint of Charity as he sits in chains, parallels Reason's complaint after his beating in *I Nature*, even in detail (553–61). Finally, the logic in the concluding moral allegory of both plays is the same: to convert Man and Youth, Charity must first seek the help of and be 'unchained' by Humility or Meekness (as in *I Nature* Reason can only stand by helplessly until Shamefastness brings Man to his senses); and the longest moral speech of the conversion episode in *Youth*, by Charity (717–26), is paraphrased from Meekness's climactic account of Christ's redemption of fallen Adam.[170]

This redaction of Medwall's plot lacks much of his humanist emphasis, apparently because the author of *Youth* still accepted a medieval view of human nature and supplemented *Nature* with other sources. His decision to conflate Medwall's Reason and Charity under the latter's name, for instance, is authorised by Paul's equation of Christ and Charity (15, 26), but seems to have been prompted by *Everyman*, where Good Deeds (identified with 'charity' at 699–700) is shown to be the only virtue that can redeem mankind. The one action in *Youth* not obviously based on *Nature*, the binding of Charity by Youth's sins, Riot and Pride (541)—in *I Nature* Man, not just his companions, strikes Reason at the tavern, and the episode is narrated rather than actually staged—is modelled on Good Deeds' plight: Everyman discovers her lying on the floor, where she has been 'sore bounde' by his sins.[171] In this scene, Charity's otherwise peculiar identification of his death with Youth's own (515–16; cf. 628) must also show the influence of *Everyman*, in which Good Deeds goes with man into the grave. This play is also probably responsible for circumstances that the playwright of *Youth* introduces to lead up to the binding scene: Charity's aggressive entrance (476–77) verbally echoes Death's sudden seizing of Everyman, and the virtue's quickly reassumed submissiveness afterwards (496–504) is an example of an interface of the play's sources. The character of Death may also influence *Youth* in Charity's opening claim to enforce God's laws (6) and in the emphasis on Youth's death (71–72; cf. 648–51, 675) and probable fate thereafter (80, 87, 92–96, 136, 177).

Everyman seems to have a part in shaping still other episodes. Charity's opening remarks on priests who celebrate mass without him (33–39) resemble Knowledge's attack on priests who sell the sacraments. Several aspects of Youth's conversion ritual recall Everyman's: the kneeling before Humility (733–34), Youth's betaking of himself to God (739), and his being simultaneously reclothed (unlike Man in *Nature*) and rechristened Good Contrition (765), a redundant variant of the name of Everyman's new garment, Contrition. Finally, the quickly broken promises of Everyman's false friends may appear in the frail oaths of Riot and Pride, who forsake Youth immediately after they have sworn constancy (744–55).[172] Riot's earlier resemblances to Fellowship, and Kindred and Cousin, in answering Youth's wish for company and help (206–09), in vowing revenge against his enemy and in standing for good cheer and debauchery, confirm such an influence, as do verbal parallels on the themes of need and betrayal (669, 749–50, 757–8).[173]

The playwright's use of the third source, Stephen Hawes's *Example of Vertu*, reveals both a remarkable contempt for its theme, sexual love and *fines amours*, and a close reliance on its courtly dialogue. Presented to Henry VII when Hawes was a groom of the chamber,[174] the poem is a conventional allegorical dream-vision about the moral education of Youth by Dames Discretion, Sapience and Hardiness, and about his marriage to the King of Love's daughter, Dame Cleanness, after the young man has won the name of Virtue by slaying a three-headed dragon (the World, the Flesh and the Devil). Here the playwright finds Youth's name and the strategy of reasoned argument or 'sapience' (rather than love or fear of God *per se*) in converting him. Like Hawes's young man, who begins 'Of vyces full' (68) and only becomes Virtue after undergoing instruction, Youth does not know what 'may avail | Virtue for to make' (554–55) until Charity's two-step argument has showed him. Unlike Hawes, however, the playwright quite rejects sexual love as a means to virtue, though he not only models his *Lady* Lechery (who has no such title in *Nature*)[175] on the poem's Dame Cleanness, 'a lady of meruelous beaute | Spronge out of hyghe and noble lynage' (1058–59), but also simply transfers dialogue from the poem's wooing scene to the episode when Youth and Lechery meet (381–86, 388, 419, 467). If Hawes looks ahead to Spenser's *Fairy Queen*, *Youth* belongs with Henryson's *Testament of Cresseid*. Other miscellaneous debts to the poem occur, the most important of which are passages where Pride echoes Dame Hardiness, Lady Richess, who is also called Pride, and Dame Sapience (337–38, 342–46, 362–63).[176]

Nature, with 2,860 lines to be acted by no fewer than seven persons over several days, *Everyman*, with 921 lines to be acted by no fewer than ten persons, and Hawes's poem of 2,129 lines have among them about fifty-five speaking parts, two plots of man corrupted and four of man restored to virtue. Reducing even some of this material for *Youth*, a five-actor, six-character interlude of under 800 lines, was an exacting business and meant fusing many characters into one, dovetailing unrelated actions, and adjusting inconsistent themes.[177] A few times the playwright fails to solve these problems. With Charity he is successful. Reason, Medwall's Charity, Good Deeds and Death all contribute something here; and what reconciles their incongruities (such as Reason's divine origin and Good Deeds' mortality, or her passivity and Death's arresting manner) is the playwright's decision to model Charity after Christ in words and acts. Youth is in one respect conceived inconsistently. Thinking of Man's erratic moral behaviour in *Nature*, the playwright terms Youth changeable (551–52), but the play shows him hostile to Charity from the beginning to his conversion. Conflating Man's attack on Reason in *Nature* with the scene of bound Good Deeds in *Everyman* makes sense, but retaining Medwall's use of a tavern visit is awkward and perhaps unnecessary once Charity's binding and Lechery's temptation are actually staged. After Riot first suggests a visit to the tavern (283), roughly at the same point in the plot as in *Nature*, three hundred lines and many other references to the proposed trip (375–76, 399, 431, 453, 539) go by. Further, because the actor doubling Lechery and Humility must miss the binding scene in order to dress for Humility's entrance, and Youth must accordingly send Lechery off alone to meet him shortly at the tavern, while he and his fellows sing a song together, Hawes's courtly lady is treated like one of Medwall's tavern prostitutes. Yet these are small points; and despite a wordy double benediction that closes the work because the playwright, in complimenting his audience, copies from both his source plays at once (783–85, 786–91, 795), *Youth* ends showing remarkably few seams for all its varied cloth.

b. Hick Scorner

The author of *Hick Scorner* also draws on many sources. *Youth* gives him neither its moral allegory (the character names are all changed) nor its court satire. He takes from *Youth*, rather, its skeletal action and its miscellaneous stock of dramatic talk, full of ideas, images, rogues' quips, formulaic phrases, questions, maxims and the ordinary, functional language that just verbalises action. For moral theme and allegory he turns to Geoffrey Chaucer and John Lydgate. A late fifteenth-century verse dream-allegory, *The assemble of goddes*, then erroneously attributed to Lydgate,[178] provides or suggests all the character-names in *Hick Scorner* but one (the name of the title-character himself), and hence almost all the allegorical argument as well. For satire on the criminal underworld, the playwright goes to various sources,[179] mainly *The Pardoner's Tale*, where he finds a pattern for many of Imagination's exploits and for details in the fettering scene. Finally, Pity's two monologues (the interlude's principal set moral speeches), by incorporating parts of the anonymous 'Long Charter of Christ' and the 'now-a-days' ballad, are brought into the tradition of the popular verse complaint, a form of religious meditation and social criticism quite absent from Charity's parallel speeches in *Youth*.[180]

Because the extant complete quartos of *Youth* imply that it has a Marian date of composition, the play's many verbal similarities with *Hick Scorner* were first interpreted as evidence that *Hick Scorner* was the source of *Youth*.[181] When in 1905 R. B. McKerrow showed that at least one edition preceded de Worde's *Youth* fragment, however, W. Bang (followed by E. T. Schell in 1966) offered useful, yet inconclusive, arguments for the priority of *Youth*, mainly its alleged artistic superiority (notably its uncomplicated, 'sequential' moral thesis) and the fact that what in *Youth* is simple becomes in *Hick Scorner* elaborated and repetitive.[182] Though both interludes may have been written in one twelve-month period in 1513–14, new internal evidence suggests that *Youth* was first,[183] and what is now known about the two plays' other sources makes a *Hick Scorner–Youth* order impossible. To be the later play, *Youth* would have had to conflate the actions and allegory of *Nature*, *Everyman* and *The Example of Vertu* more accurately than its source *Hick Scorner* did, and to avoid adapting from it any feature derived from *The assemble of goddes*, *The Pardoner's Tale* or the play's other sources.

Its corruption-to-conversion plot basically follows that of *Youth*, somewhat reorganised, with much dialogue transferred fairly intact. The first scene of *Hick Scorner*, Pity's meeting with the virtues, is new, except for his first speech (1–9, 14, 25–29) and exit (145–52), which derive from Charity's, and for Contemplation's opening theme (33), which is moved up from Humility's late entrance in *Youth*.[184] The initial confrontation between Youth and Charity is omitted because the allegory that *Hick Scorner* takes from *The assemble of goddes* delays Free Will's attack on virtue until after he has been subjected to bad counsel, and denies the principal virtue (here Pity) any part in the final conversion. The corruption scene in *Hick Scorner*, however, is clearly structured on that in *Youth*. As Youth summons Riot, who in turn summons Pride, so Free Will, whose first lines are based on Youth's (156–59, 163–67, 170; cf. 685), summons Imagination, who in turn calls in Hick Scorner. The opening words of these two characters (192, 303–06) are adapted from Riot's first speech. While Imagination's jailbird lechery (204), however, resembles Riot's, Hick Scorner's role as pimp, rather, develops from Pride's as pandar. Pity's sudden reappearance, virtuous counselling of the rogues (462–63), enchainment in fetters, and complaint to the audience (546–601) are also patterned on Charity's second scene in *Youth*, though here a complication arises. Lacking an initial conflict between Pity and

Free Will, *Hick Scorner* has occasion for neither Pity's sudden intrusion nor the rogues' ill-treatment of him, and must invent a pretext. This occasion, the brawl, is suggested partly by the Youth–Riot banter about Youth's fighting coin-servants (441–57). His first quarrel with Charity then supplies Imagination's false charge of theft (475–76), and also, with Riot's later abuse of Charity, gives *Hick Scorner* the rogues' threats and mockery of Pity (479, 497–502, 510–11, 515, 525). Their helter-skelter exit (542, 544–45)[185] and the virtues' freeing of Pity (602–20) are adapted, physically and verbally, from the parallel actions in *Youth*. In the conversion scenes, however, *Hick Scorner* departs radically from *Youth* and follows *The assemble of goddes*. Free Will is like Youth in repenting and being reclothed (867–70, 876, 912–13), but Imagination is, in the end, unlike Riot. Though the dialogue that follows Riot's first entrance (891–93, 895–97, 903–05, 908–10) and his talent at getting out of Newgate by 'policy' (683–84) are used by Imagination, he does not, unlike Riot, forsake his master, but is converted and gets, like Youth, a new name (1007; cf. 872). Further, neither Pity nor Hick Scorner, unlike their counterparts in *Youth*, Charity and Riot, takes part in the final scene. Yet little of the conversion argument in *Youth* goes to waste. Youth's mockery of Charity when they first meet contributes, in the conversion scene of *Hick Scorner*, material for Imagination (948–49, 953–57, 972–73, 977–79) and Free Will (700–02, 729, 731, 734–37, 745); and the latter also draws on what Riot says then (793, 807, 844–45). The proselytising of Contemplation and Perseverance is adapted from Charity's first rebukes of prodigal Youth (728, 772–88, 848–49, 942–47, 968–70, 1020–21) and from the parts of both virtues (858, 1015) and vices (855–56, 885–90) in the conversion scene of *Youth*. The benedictions in *Hick Scorner*, finally, are condensed from those in *Youth* (1023–24, 1027–28).[186]

The corruption and conversion episodes in *Hick Scorner* depart allegorically from those in *Youth* mainly where the influence of *The assemble of goddes* is at work. This poem is a moral psychomachia in which the armies of Vice and Virtue fight on the field of Macrocosm.[187] Its lord, Free Will, stays neutral until one of Vice's ambassadors, Sensuality, seeds the battlefield with rank, entangling weeds that put Virtue's army on the defensive, at which point Vice wins the support of the lord of Macrocosm and Virtue is routed. Free Will in *Hick Scorner* is clearly based on this lord in name, in definition (161) and in the circumstances leading up to his corruption. Youth is an enemy to virtue from the beginning, but Free Will has no initial quarrel with Pity, hears his fellows' confessions of vice with scepticism or silence, and provokes, by insulting Imagination, the brawl that cracks Hick Scorner's skull. Free Will agrees to be one of 'three knaves in a lease' (419) for the same two reasons that the lord of Macrocosm turns to Vice: the persuasions of a sensuality figure, and a sudden misfortune for a host of virtues. Like Sensuality's 'seed', Imagination's vice is partly sexual, and he interests Free Will in a night of pimping at the stews after a rallying cry, 'Now virtue shall draw arrear, arrear' (403), that clearly echoes the poem. Secondly, when Hick Scorner brags how a navy of virtues, in sight of his fleet of vices, foundered in the Irish Sea, he impresses Free Will with two catalogues of names largely extracted from the poem's enumeration of those fighting in the armies of Virtue and Vice.[188] The conversion of Free Will and Imagination in *Hick Scorner* follows just as closely that of the lord of Macrocosm and Sensuality. They are forcibly redeemed when Good Perseverance, seizing the initiative from retreating Virtue, enters the field and defeats Vice in a personal encounter. Likewise, in the play Free Will is not converted by Pity, the master of the virtues; instead Good Perseverance (59, 80), a character not in *Youth*, leads the unusually aggressive conversion attempt.[189] Imagination, if he were modelled in this respect on Riot, would not be converted at all. The playwright departs from *Youth* in favour of the poem even to the extent of making Imagination repent, like Sensuality, because of his fear of death.[190]

The assemble of goddes is not only the allegorical model for *Hick Scorner*, but also a convenient repository of moral personifications. Though functioning like Sensuality, Imagination, for example, owes his first name (but not its pejorative meaning) to that of Virtue's messenger in the poem, and takes the name newly given to him after his conversion, Good Remembrance (1007), from one of Virtue's three ambassadors to Free Will. Several other characters in the play owe their names, directly or indirectly, to the poem. Perfect Contemplation (42), one of Virtue's many petty captains, was selected as a passive virtue to balance Perseverance, the active virtuous life. Pity (5), a minor captain mentioned twice at important moments in the poem, perhaps suggested to the playwright, because of the name's association with a portrait of Christ called 'the Image of Pity', an alternative name for Charity, who in *Youth* of course identifies himself with God. The poem may have had an oblique influence on the choice of Hick Scorner's occupation as a sailor. After Barclay's and Watson's translations of Brant's *Narrenschiff* appeared in 1509, the name of Vice's second ambassador to Free Will, Folly, came to be associated closely with a sea-rover on a ship of fools. (Vice's third ambassador, Sensuality, is of course an influence on Hick Scorner's fellow, Imagination.) Brant's work, however, was not a direct source for the play: Hick Scorner is modelled on a historical figure, and the ship anecdotes that he and Free Will tell, in so far as they are literary motifs, appear to be indebted to *Cocke Lorelles bote*, an English satire that exploited the popularity of the German poem.[191]

Our playwright uses Chaucer's *Pardoner's Tale*, the Flanders story of three violent 'yonge folke that hauntedyn folye | As ryot hazarde stewys and tauernys' (463–65), as a sourcebook of criminal exploits. The tale's main influence is seen in the rogues' assault on Pity, where Chaucer supplies the play with some of the rough abuse so lacking in the parallel but sardonically polite binding scene in *Youth*. After swearing his two fellows to a brotherhood where 'thre ben all onys' (696), the Pardoner's first rioter sets out with them to murder Death, whom they drunkenly suppose vulnerable. Instead, they meet an old man, 'a restles caytyf' (728) whom they insult as 'olde churle' (750), arrest, and charge with spying for 'that traytour deth' (753) and with intending their murder: 'thou art one of his assent | To sle vs yonge folke thou fals theef' (758–59). Similarly, Imagination proposes that he, Free Will and Hick Scorner 'keep company all together' that night in robbing and, if necessary, in murdering a 'true man' (410–18), to which brotherhood Free Will readily agrees. The three then also meet an 'old churl' (457; cf. 473), 'thief' (475), 'caitiff' (497) and 'traitor' (505) whom they arrest on the suspicion that he plots their death: 'He would destroy us all and all our kin' (498). Like their Chaucerian counterparts, they associate this 'churl' Pity with Death, whom they too brag they can overcome:

> What, Death! And he were here, he should sit by thee.
> Trowest thou that he be able to strive with us three?
> Nay, nay, nay.
>
> (539–41)

Just as the Flanders rogues leave the old man and walk 'vp this crokyd wey' to a grove, under an oak tree of which a mass of gold (the cause of their deaths) lies (760–65), so Imagination's crew then leaves Pity to go to Shooters Hill (543, 822), a high wood on the London–Dover road where robbers victimised passers-by and risked hanging at nearby St Thomas-a-Watering (838). Another of the play's low-life episodes that the tale may have influenced is Imagination's dagger attack on Free Will and Hick Scorner: this may reflect, besides Youth's 'quarrel' of coins, the dishonour among thieves that the two older Flanders rogues show in stabbing to death their young fellow. In any event, the plot this youth hatches to poison his two elders evidently inspires another exploit by Imagination. His theft of the Ludgate apothecary's money-bag for Free Will's ransom (a trick that involves buying a 'mouthful' of noxious drugs) and his night-walk 'round' London wall to a near-by Newgate inn with the loot (670–81) are adapted from the night visit of Chaucer's youngest Flanders rogue to an apothecary's shop for a box of poison to kill his partners, and from his two walks afterwards, one 'In to the nexte strete' for wine, and another (only planned) to his own house later with the gold (851–75). In fact, the dependence of *Hick Scorner* on Chaucer's writing can be detected in most of the rogues' scenes, and even in some speeches by the virtues.[192]

So plentiful is evidence about the interlude's sources that we can, as with *Youth*, follow the playwright closely as he assembles from them, at times expertly, at times not, his own text. He probably ignored in *Youth* the satire on Henry VIII and its moral theme, the upbringing of a young noble heir, because they were politically sensitive, not to say repugnant,[193] and instead turned to *The assemble of goddes* for a non-controversial allegory, and to Chaucer and current political figures in the king's disfavour for satire. The conflation left some inconsistencies. In combining Charity's Christ-like suffering with Virtue's aggressiveness and inability to convert Free Will, Pity sometimes fails to fit well into the action derived from *Youth*. His motive for exiting separately from Contemplation and Perseverance after their first meeting (Pity must next enter alone) is only implied,[194] his role as justice of the peace in breaking up the brawl and in pursuing Hick Scorner so as to prevent him from gaining sanctuary may seem out of character, and of course Pity's last exit, however sound in allegory, is awkward. The playwright uses Riot's first words, 'who calleth after me?' no fewer than three times; the last occasion, at Imagination's final entrance, is one too many, for no one in fact does call for the rogue this time.[195] Our author nods when Free Will, whom the audience last saw leaving for Shooters Hill, enters from Newgate, where he was jailed for attempted theft at a *tavern*. Here episodes drawn from Chaucer's tale and *Youth* have not been well adjusted. Elsewhere, however, dovetailing of disparate materials testifies to the playwright's good craftsmanship. Imagination hardly betrays that he is based on half a dozen figures. The allegorical point, in *Youth*, of having Riot and Pride enter in succession, to show how one sin leads to another, is partly wasted because Youth enters as a prodigal. By substituting for him the less corrupt Free Will and yet retaining the device of successive entrances from *Youth*, the author of *Hick Scorner* improves on both sources. Impressive also is the careful knitting of the Virtue–Vice psychomachia and current English politics, of the

Flanders rogues' attack on Death and Sensuality's dread of it, and of materials from at least four sources with allusions to contemporary social conditions in Pity's complaint. These examples illustrate not only our playwright's own cast of mind, but the techniques of early Tudor play-making itself.

5. THE PLAYS

Youth and *Hick Scorner* cannot simply be called 'moral plays' like *Everyman* (which is translated from the Dutch *Elckerlijc*) or Tudor imitations of the French *moralité*, a word that has been applied in a misleading, anachronistic way to many early English plays.[196] De Worde, Waley and Copland printed 'interludes'—in general, indoor winter entertainments, from a minstrel's skits to full-length plays performed during breaks at a hall banquet—a term that developed this sense only in England.[197] Perhaps the closest continental relation to this distinctively English dramatic form is the topical, often scatological French *farce*, to which the very early *Interludium de Clerico et Puella* (*c*. 1290–1335), *Hick Scorner* itself—with its miniature internal 'farce' (446)—and later John Heywood's plays are linked. Farces were in fact popular at the early sixteenth-century Scottish court, and by the time of Sir David Lindsay's *Satyre of the Thrie Estaitis* (*c*. 1540–54) one of them was called an 'Interlude'.[198] In England, however, the interlude is unlike both French and Scottish *farces* in the way it mixes, as Elizabethan comedy and tragedy were often to do, quite different kinds of theatre, the moral abstraction of the *moralité* and the topical comedy of the *farce*.[199] *Youth* is not just moral allegory, and *Hick Scorner* is not just humorous social satire: each uses religious matter in allegoric form to frame witty, sometimes slapstick political commentary, a combination well suited to the entertainment of a banquet-hall elite. As in the early Tudor carols that make conventional literary or devotional themes serve topical political allegory,[200] in both plays the topical element is stressed. De Worde's decision to print them, at a time when scarcely any drama was published,[201] shows that they were of broad national interest. In fact the political issues over which these interludes clash are inherited from the Wars of the Roses. *Youth* indirectly attacks Henry VIII, and voices the bitterness of an out-of-favour northern nobility that had supported the last Yorkist kings, Edward IV and Richard III. *Hick Scorner*, a product of Henry's capital city and court, counter-attacks by recasting substantial chunks of *Youth* into a travesty of the king's great enemy, the Yorkist pretender to the throne, Richard de la Pole. Thus these plays are a moral as well as a political diptych of early Tudor England. On one level, they are allegories embodying in universal figures an abstract moral lesson for young men; on another level, the plays' contemporary allusions and social comedy, as well as the compelling individuation that actual performance gives to all allegorical characters, moralise England's sharply divided body politic, the depressed, conservative north, and prospering, innovative London. Like the Wakefield Master and later Tudor dramatists, these playwrights weave together moral paradigm and social history. *Youth* and *Hick Scorner* are reductive plays, but the tension between their solemn general truths and their comic personal attacks generates, in performance, both resonance and piquancy. They have proved repeatedly to be good theatre.

a. The Interlude of Youth

This play interprets its subject, the nature of man's sin and redemption, partly through moral allegory, which sets personified abstractions and a type of mankind into ordinary social relationships or activities that are themselves to be understood as homiletic generalisations.[202] The meaning of the personifications is transparent. The figure of Youth, traditionally twenty-five to thirty-five years old, belongs to the Ages of Man *topos*, which was widely analysed in scholastic encyclopaedic works, described in poems like *The Parlement of the Thre Ages* (*c*. 1352–90) and plays like *The World and the Child* (printed 1522), and depicted in medieval manuscript illustrations, woodcuts and tapestries.[203] Youth is here surrounded by two of the seven major virtues, Humility and Charity, and two of the seven deadly sins, Pride and Lechery. Riot, the main vice, personifies general lawlessness (as in robbing, gaming and playing the bawd) as well as a specific Tudor felony, public assembly to disturb the peace (207n). What the play's action means is perhaps less clear: Youth's rake's progress from initial corruption to redemption is a rough-hewn 'psychomachia', an allegory of internal struggles between good and evil in his soul.[204] Entrances, exits, friendships, quarrels and mischief-making (the liaison with Lady Lechery, the binding of Charity, and the tavern visit) stand for spiritual or psychological changes in Youth himself. Charity's entrance to him from God as 'grace' (111, 147) signifies God's initial gift, to all men, of his son the redeemer, with whom Charity identifies himself (26). In rejecting Charity, Youth shows allegorically his ignorance of the meaning of the atonement (170) and of course his inability to love either God or anyone else. To save Youth from otherwise certain damnation, Charity seeks out help from his brother Humility, another of Christ's virtues and, more important, the root and pre-condition of all virtues.[205] Youth's next steps, the summoning of Riot, Pride and Lechery, follow from the rejection of Charity (Riot's violence and robbery are the opposite of charity, and Pride's self-love defies humility) and sink Youth further in vice. Adding lawlessness to vanity, Youth inclines to lechery and chooses a courtly love and fornication that parody what Charity represents.[206] The virtue was 'planted' (31) in Christ's heart; in Youth this union is perverted as he identifies Lechery's 'heart' with his own (394–96). The 'change of heart' leads Youth to attack Charity (and through him God), not just dismiss the virtue from his mind. Here the action and the allegoric meaning are plainly one: Youth supervises as his Pride holds Charity down and his Riot chains the virtue (536–39). At this point, only a second gift of 'grace' from God (515, 625) can save Youth; and Humility's entrance to free Charity, allegorically the quelling of a personal vanity that inhibits Christian love, is that miracle. Humility does not convert Youth, but the virtue makes conversion possible for the first time. Eventually Youth kneels before Humility to beg for God's mercy (733), that is, for Charity, to whom the sinner is handed; and Youth then renounces Pride and Riot in the reverse of the order in which he first received them (Humility countering the first, and Charity the second). As visible signs of received spiritual grace, Youth gets Humility's beads and Charity's garments.

This moral allegory explains how Youth's mind is changed, but not why. His conversion seems sudden and unmotivated,[207] but it results, not from Humility's entrance or from Charity's unchaining, but many lines later from the completion of a homiletic argument begun at Charity's first entrance. Like most moral plays,[208] *Youth* resembles sermon literature, and when Charity first speaks he asks for 'audience' in the way any preacher would. As speakers rather than actors, the play's personifications are to be taken literally, not allegorically; consequently, *Youth* is as much a debate play as a moral allegory. The 'childe in ʒowthe' Idleness in *Occupation*, a late fifteenth-century moral interlude, ignores all argument until Doctrine uses physical 'maistry' to spank him with a rod into repentance, but Youth's problem is an intellectual one: he 'wotteth not what may avail | Virtue for to make' (554–55).[209] To be virtuous, should one seek to 'inherit' bliss in heaven through moral righteousness (92, 781), or should one work to get 'high degree' (338, 591, 622) on earth? At first Youth thinks of virtue in terms of his body's powers, and when Charity argues that anyone trusting solely in his body will be damned unless he strives for and accepts the mercy earned for man by Christ on the cross, Youth is too vain and impatient to listen to an explanation of why the passion is relevant to him. He says instead, 'God's fast! what is that to me?' (170). Only after Humility has cooled off Youth's brains (599–600) can Charity at last explain what the doctrine of atonement means (716–26). This debate converts Youth; what saves him, the two gifts of divine grace, is of course explained in the moral allegory.

Youth, however, does not break down into two plays, one of conversion, the other of salvation. The debate and the moral allegory run parallel throughout, but they also meet in Charity: the doctrine he uses to convert Youth, Christ's love (as shown in the passion), is also the role Charity plays in the allegory. When he tells Youth that Christ's passion saved his soul, which was 'bond' to the devil (710), Charity refers to the harrowing of hell, but also to his own actions in the play. In his opening monologue the virtue said his origin was in Christ, his essence was Christ's love, and his name was God's name, for *Deus charitas est* (26). Like the Son, Charity comes as a 'king' to represent on earth God's laws and make man an 'heritor of bliss' (23, 28, 92), and the virtue's references to the crucified Christ's spread arms (1, 166) look forward to Charity's fettered arms and legs. Christ, the hanged man, was executed as a thief, and the Corpus Christi plays traditionally included stocking and binding as part of the passion; just so, Charity, the 'hangman' (307), is falsely accused of theft by Youth, who imagines him hanged for it (138–43), but settles for enchainment.[210] Just before the shackles go on, Charity quotes one of Christ's sayings (529); and afterwards Humility, speaking Christ's name (562), and referring to the passion, enters to Charity from evensong (570), which commemorates the passion's aftermath. He can certainly say, with Christ, that he suffered to redeem Youth from hell, for Youth meets Riot 'in the devil way' (220), serves him by invoking the devil's name and refusing marriage (200, 368), and feels his heart 'burn' (388) under Lechery's influence. Youth can at the play's end no longer deny in argument the relevance of the passion to him; the moral allegory has shown him figuratively a participant in it. Like all sinners, Youth in sinning is one of Christ's torturers.[211]

Yet the playwright was not just interested in moral allegory and debate. No one explicitly draws our attention to their existence (as characters or commentators do in the Macro plays or in *Everyman*), and the allegoric logic has many loose ends. Pride, not Riot (an anomalous vice), is the root of all evil and should have entered first to Youth. Charity's second entrance (without Humility, whom he went to get) and Lechery's absence from the binding scene do not work allegorically. The Charity–Christ parallels are never extended into a scriptural allegory, and Youth seems unaware of the binding's figural meaning. More important, abstract characterisation often breaks down as both virtues and vices behave like the man-type Youth is supposed to be. He and Charity, for instance, begin like foils, like antithetical Kings of Life (rather than quaiitatively different man-type and moral trait).[212] Youth's opening monologue, a detailed inversion of Charity's, boasts the sinner to be 'peerless', 'royal', and flourishing 'as the vine tree' with 'bushed' hair, a hazel-stick frame and a cask-like chest (43–49), some of which qualities are traditionally shared between Christ and his folk counterpart, the 'green' man or woodwose.[213] Rather than Youth's vice, Riot is his 'brother' and 'compeer' (207, 216); most of their features are joint ones (particularly 'jollity', nimble legs and recklessness) and Youth even carries the vice's trademark, a dagger. Despite their names, Charity, Youth and Riot seem to be comparable social types at times, all engaged in realistic activities.

They are largely secular household ones. *Youth* can be understood as prudent advice to a landed heir of noble blood and class (343, 487, 489) about how to choose reliable counsellors for his estates. One, Charity, is the Tudor lord's typical 'clerkish' administrator (113): he behaves like an almoner (a fixture in the large manor household) and has a priest's name, 'Sir John' (25–26n, 491). The second, Riot, is hail-fellow-well-met, a tavern-haunting felon from Newgate and Tyburn. In selecting 'one man more | To wait' on him (312–13), Youth mistakes by choosing Riot's 'Master Pride' (317), a gallant and worldly chapel gentleman (cf. 473), rather than Charity's brother, Humility, who says divine service devoutly. Flattery, not frankness, wins the young heir. His feudal principles, which demand that his inferiors be subdued to him 'by right, | As servants to their masters should be' (595–96), are the object of Riot's hypocritical lip-service, as when he mock-chides Youth, 'Let not thy servants fight within thee' (449). Yet Riot's company inverts this feudal hierarchy by making their master the servant. Riot offers to pay for Youth's tavern fun, but Youth actually foots the bill (285, 455–57). Lechery deceitfully keeps her name secret and in leading him from marriage to prodigality this Lady deprives him of heirs as well as economic advantage.

On the other hand, Charity's 'Sir, if it please you to do thus' (632) combines advice with marked deference. How the virtues counsel Youth, to avoid pride in noble kin or stock (487–89) and lawlessness, as in 'unthrifty' wasting of income (64), is exactly how the clergy advised the Tudor nobility, whose right business was thought to be charity and service to the Church.

The play's commitment to depict Tudor individuals (rather than abstractions) in a contemporary setting, however, goes further than this type-cast domestic exemplum. The figure of Youth was often characterised as a king in the middle ages,[214] and in *Youth* there is considerable evidence that he would have satirised Henry VIII, crowned in 1509. After Youth asks the audience, 'Who may be likened unto me | In my youth and jollity?' (46–47), and points out his 'peerless' rank and 'royal' hair, Charity describes him as 'flourishing with royalty' (76), and Riot enters to make 'royal cheer' (225), 'as merry as a king' (238), with his 'compeer' Youth (216). Later, Riot implies Youth's political identity cleverly by characterising his coins, pieces termed a 'noble' (441), as his fighting 'servants' (449; cf. 596); and Youth himself boasts at his second entrance that he is 'king eternal' (592) over all dukes, lords, barons and knights. Only months before the play's composition, in mid-1513, Henry deployed the nobility to defeat the French at Thérouanne, the Battle of the Spurs and Tournai, and the Scots at Flodden Field, and also was judged a king of 'immortal' glory.[215] Youth's promise to make Riot a 'knight of the collar' is another allusion to Henry, in this instance to his creation of so many knights after these campaigns; and Pride's offer of the Holy Roman Empire to Youth refers to Maximilian's identical proposition to Henry that winter.[216] The interlude's title, however, is the best indicator of the play's political satire, for the king in fact called himself 'Youth'. Henry VIII's own songs, of which some thirty-five have survived, do so. 'Yowth woll have nedes dalyaunce', 'The tyme of youthe is to be spent', and 'sum saith that yough rulyth me' are representative of these lyrics, which generally defend his chivalric code of knighthood and courtly love against sceptics.[217]

These allusions, attacking the king's self-conceit and prodigality, do not appear to be unfounded. By 1513, when Henry in his twenty-second year was invading France to claim still more of his 'right and inheritance',[218] his father's tight-fisted and somewhat dingy old court had been thoroughly renovated. Westminster, Greenwich, Richmond and Eltham celebrated the new king's extraordinary physique in tournaments, game sports, hunting and riding, his handsome features in court revels, disguisings and rich dress, and his pride and loves in music and song-making.[219] One song juxtaposes 'Lusti yough' and his 'dysdaynares' and recalls Youth's general objection to Charity's advice, 'wilt thou rede me | In my youth to leese my jollity?' (172):

> Lusti yough shuld us ensue,
> Hys mery hart shall sure all rew;
> For whatsoever they do hym tell,
> It ys not for hym we know yt well.
> For they wold have hym hys libertye refrayne
> And all mery company for to dysdayne;
> But I wyll not so whatsoever thay say,
> But follow hys mynd in all that we may.
> How shuld yough hymselfe best use
> But all dysdaynares for to refuse?
> Yough has as chef assurans
> Honest myrth with vertus pastance.[220]

Despite Henry's vigorous profession of 'Honest myrth', his disdaining critics had plenty of evidence that he shared Youth's 'unthrifty' nature and bodily vanity. By 1514 the king had spent much of his inheritance (as the play's new heir promises to do), partly on revels, attire and general display of wealth, but mostly on war, one week of which, 5–12 June 1513, absorbed half his reign's up-to-then total expenditure of a million pounds (a financial crisis helped stop the war).[221] A single incident amusingly testifies how the king, like Youth (66–70), loved having his body praised: in May 1515, after interrogating Pietro Pasqualigo about Francis I's build, and learning him to be less stout, and possessed of a spare leg, Henry opened his own doublet, put his hand on his thigh, and exhibited his muscular calf to the amazed Venetian diplomat.[222]

The vices that Youth embraces after his opening monologue also link him with Henry VIII generally. He consorted with gamblers who leeched him, as Riot would Youth, of much money: early in 1511 some tennis, card and dice-playing Frenchmen and Italians, having won large sums from the king, were expelled from court, and later he gambled huge amounts with the French hostages taken in 1513.[223] That July, Henry practised another of Riot's sports in shooting 'at the blank' (688) with his own archers at Calais.[224] Like Pride, Henry wore 'the richest and most superb' clothes imaginable,[225] and probably set much credit, by early 1514, in the Emperor's overtures. Youth's affair with Lady Lechery might recall Henry's courtly love cult (he jousted as *Coeur Loyal* in 1511, and wrote at least one song in praise of Venus) and rumoured private liaisons, though on the one occasion we know Henry visited a tavern he went for other reasons.[226] In May 1510 he was implicated in scandal when his favourite, William Compton, some said on behalf of Henry, was caught wooing one of the duke of Buckingham's married sisters, Lady Anne, by the enraged duke himself.[227] The king's reaction, to bar from court those who had (other than the duke) spied on Anne, especially her older sister, one of the queen's ladies-in-waiting, angered Catherine and corroborated the talk. Henry also enjoyed the company of a Belgian lady in the 1513 campaign, was wooing his mistress-to-be, Elizabeth Blount, by early 1514, and contemplated later that year taking Riot's advice about marriage: divorce proceedings were begun at Rome.[228] In brief, the play's satire of the young king in those areas where specific allusions are lacking is entirely apt. *Youth* agrees both with an English opinion of 1510 that Henry 'is young, and does not care to occupy himself with anything but the pleasures of his age', and with a French papal diplomat six years later who said he was only a 'youngling, cares for nothing but girls and hunting, and wastes his father's patrimony'.[229]

Up to this point the attack on the king is a political caricature, but in Youth's fellowship with Riot, a figure not found in the interlude's known sources, there is evidence of political allegory. A very strong criticism of the king's reign, rather than of his personality, was that he badly damaged the law's ability to bring 'riot' or civil disorder to justice, particularly in the north, where the play may have been written. After the fourth earl of Northumberland was murdered at Topcliffe in Yorkshire in 1489 by rebels as he tried to enforce Tudor taxation, Henry VII appointed, as Lieutenants or High Commissioners in the north, at first Thomas Howard, earl of Surrey (1489–99), and lastly Henry's own mother, Margaret, countess of Richmond (1507–09).[230] Because the problem was not limited to the north, and because even there the Lieutenant was often helpless, Henry's parliament in 1495–96 enacted statutes that empowered local justices to try and to convict accused rioters on simple information, in their absence and without jury.[231] Under Henry VIII, however, both these measures were abandoned, to the special dismay of *Youth*'s probable sponsor, the fifth earl of Northumberland. The countess of Richmond died on 29 June 1509, and in August the earl's servants were arguing that he should rule all from the Trent north, and were predicting that 'if ther lord hade nott rowmes in the northe as his fader hade, it shold not long be well'.[232] This lobbying was to no avail: by August 1511 not only had Henry allowed the Lieutenancy to lapse, but he had also appointed the weak Thomas, lord Dacre, as warden of all the northern marches, under whom border law would fall apart by 1522.[233] The worst blow to Henry VII's policy came in 1510, when those who had Empson and Dudley arrested moved to prevent royal agents or justices trying cases on information alone, forced the repeal of the 1496 statute, and left much of England, especially in the north, vulnerable to the old disorders.[234] In cheerfully tolerating Riot, the highway robber of a 'courtier's lad', Youth is allegorically young Henry VIII in his policy of weakening all justice not strictly tied to the court. The snapping of Riot's Tyburn rope is, in this light, the most serious political allusion in the play.

In Youth's conversion by Charity, finally, one other element of political allegory may exist. A single royal advisor, a protégé of Richard Fox, Henry VII's Privy Seal (still in office when the play was written, but increasingly displaced by Henry VIII's favourites), and a man who had entered government well before 1509, had in 1513–14 enough power to sway the young king: Thomas Wolsey, whose management of the 1513 war won him Henry's confidence.[235] If anyone might play Charity to the king's Youth, and turn him against Riot, Wolsey could. As his livings were mainly in the north, at Lincoln and York, and as the fifth earl clearly had some faith in Wolsey (to whose household he sent his oldest son), the priest would presumably have been sensitive to problems in the northern shires.[236] In these circumstances, Charity may have been intended to stand for Wolsey. As Henry's royal almoner from November 1509 to early 1514, Wolsey conventionally represented the king's charity (as that virtue did Youth's) and so came to have a special reputation for aiding the poor.[237] Further, Riot's threat to put Charity in the stocks (304n), a point not in *Youth*'s known sources, could have been recognised as an allusion to Sir Amias Paulet's stocking of Wolsey in 1500–01, a humiliation for which Paulet later paid.[238] Whether or not a compliment to Wolsey was intended or would have been understood is unsure—Riot and his friends have no known political identities[239]—but if one existed it had no effect. The political lesson of *Youth* was partly learned at court, because after 1513 Henry increasingly entrusted government to his Charity, Wolsey, and earned the Pope's thanks with the new title *Fides Defensor*, but neither the fifth earl nor the north gained new powers against 'riot' or greater favour at Westminster.[240]

b. Hick Scorner

Since Thomas Percy said that the author of *Hick Scorner* is 'so little attentive to the allegory, that we need only substitute other names to his personages, and we have real characters and living manners', even readers who have found some allegory have said that it fails to work properly and is irrelevant to the play's realistic depiction of London criminal life.[241] Imagination's account of Tyburn hangings and Free Will's underworld anecdotes are memorable, but the play has seemed puzzling and incomplete. It has been called a degenerate or hybrid 'morality', in that by excluding from the last scene both Pity, who begins the play and leads the virtuous in it, and Hick Scorner, the most corrupt (as well as the title) character, the action does not readily conform to the psychomachia plot, where virtue and vice struggle for man's soul. T. W. Craik leaves the problem characters aside and concludes that *Hick Scorner* is simply a 'conflict between good men and sinners whom they finally convert'.[242] Pity and the eponym, nevertheless, do present a problem. Why is the play named after a figure who is on stage less than a quarter of the time and has fewer lines than anyone but Contemplation? If Hick Scorner had Imagination's zest or Free Will's lines the question might not arise, but the sea-rover speaks little apart from four catalogues of countries, ships, virtues and vices. The vice-tempter also seems peripheral and ineffectual in the play's action: after getting beaten up as a meddling peace-maker by Imagination, Hick Scorner falls in meekly with his schemes for robbery. David Bevington's analysis of the play's doubling requirements gives sensible technical reasons for the early exits, but for the title no brief has been made.[243]

If one can be made, it is that, as in *Youth*, the play's characterisation and action must be understood in terms of not only moral allegory but also the politics of England in 1514. Rather than a simple moral type obedient to the definition of its name, each character behaves partly as individual historical figure or social type, partly as universal religious or moral abstraction. In *Youth* and *Hick Scorner*, as in Marlowe's plays, moral conflict is allegorically conceived and at the same time peopled by the English body politic.[244] Of the play's six figures who represent the Tudor establishment, foreign invaders, corrupt politicians and petty criminals, no one is more historical than Hick Scorner himself. He lends the play its title because he was, in 1514, the land's greatest gangster, Richard de la Pole, the current Yorkist pretender to the throne.

Hick Scorner's landing in England with an army of over five thousand (366), evidently from France (309) but 'over' the Irish

Sea (362–64), represents a much bruited invasion in 1514 from France by Henry VIII's feared enemy,[245] the Yorkist pretender, whose title as Richard IV had been recognised by Louis XII of France in 1512 and theoretically was as good as or better than Henry's. The first name of Richard de la Pole, who styled himself duke of Suffolk and 'White Rose' after the titles of his brother Edmund, executed on Tower Hill in May 1513, is made a diminutive in Hick Scorner's first name (232n). The pretender's second name,'de la Pole'—meaning 'of or at the pool'—is the basis for puns when Free Will remarks that in brawling with Imagination Hick Scorner should be plunged 'in a mill pool above the arse' (447), and when Hick Scorner cries out from Imagination's beating, 'He hath made a great hole in my poll, | That all my wit is set to the ground' (450–51).[246] Like the play's sea-rover (383–84), Richard de la Pole was an exiled Englishman with a history of wandering. After an alleged abortive uprising (with his brother Edmund) against Henry VII in 1501, de la Pole spent over twenty years soliciting European rulers to help overthrow the Tudors. Like Hick Scorner he had been in Germany (310), France and Spain (309): in 1512–13 he led German mercenaries from Gascony (313) with the French into Navarre against the Spanish–English alliance, and he was joint commander of the huge French army that skirmished with Henry's force outside Tournehem after the king had invaded France in person in 1513. Richard's invasion army of 1514, which was first based in Normandy, behaved much like Hick Scorner's five thousand brawlers, murderers and rogues, but still more like skull-busting Imagination, for Richard's mercenaries 'made suche a Riot that many of them were slayn' and he was forced to convey them into Brittany (313) to take ship there. The play's anomalous brawl, and the odd peace-making role that leaves Hick Scorner with a broken 'pole', now make sense as political parodies of Richard's military setback with his lansquenets in Normandy. Their humiliating behaviour 'broke' de la Pole's invasion plans as much as did French diplomacy. *Hick Scorner* was evidently written at the time when news of the riot was recent and London was preparing for the francophile usurper's return with 'Overthwart Guile' (373), 'False Law with Horrible Vengeance' (375) and 'Mischievous Governance' (376); that is, before England's treaty with Louis cancelled the venture and made Hick Scorner's boast, 'they shall nevermore us withstand' (361), an empty threat. That Richard's fleet would have taken a western (Irish Sea) route from France (as he did in a second attempt in 1523) explains the circuitous route that Hick Scorner's navy takes before making for land. And his political identity accounts for Hick Scorner's early disappearance from the play. As his absence from the conversion scene means that he cannot be saved, so Richard's excommunication and his exemption from Henry VIII's general pardon in 1509 excluded him from church and life in the England of 1514. What Hick Scorner says of Pity the justice, 'He would destroy us all and all our kin' (498), was quite true of Henry VIII: after executing Edmund in 1513, the king plotted to have Richard extradited from his sanctuary on the continent and to assassinate him.

Rather than developing his characters into a broad political allegory,[247] the playwright offers caricatures, quick and bright cartoon sketches of famous Tudor rogues. One character, for instance, satirises a Tudor Londoner who had nothing to do with de la Pole. Imagination's exploits are based, loosely, on those of the infamous promoter John Baptist de Grimaldi, who was branded the 'worst' man in England about 1509 and who, like Imagination (the word in this sense figured prominently in accounts of Grimaldi's many unscrupulous money-making schemes), could 'imagine things subtle | For to get money plenty' (215–16).[248] While himself no lawyer, Grimaldi could boast, with Imagination, 'And I were dead the lawyers' thrift were lost' (220), since the notorious merchant-broker had served Henry VII's lawyers Empson and Dudley in providing false or doubtful information against individuals, on the basis of which heavy fines could be levied for violation of royal statutes. Imagination too says that he is 'kin' to great gentlemen, can get 'into lords' favours' and be 'of their privy counsel' (218, 229–30). As such, he functions like a promoter: by trickery he causes some to lose 'both house and land', wrongfully taints others of treason, and bribes judges (222–28, 267–68). What would have especially identified Imagination with the crafty broker is his astonishing combination of a prestigious West-minster Hall career with common vice and mean criminality. The rogue's 'pyrdewy' seduction, pimping proposal and comp-trollership of stews are typical of Grimaldi's behaviour; and Imagination's odd anecdote about the one occasion on which he was found 'reprovable' (269–70), in stealing a reddish-brown (bay) horse, would surely have recalled a notorious Grimaldi device, also the only occasion on which he was found guilty of a hanging theft. To avoid the consequences of certain lawsuits, Grimaldi had himself charged with stealing a reddish-brown horse, an offence that, though normally punished by hanging, could be (and was) settled quite easily with a bought pardon. There are other ways in which Imagination may have been modelled on Grimaldi—his escape to Westminster sanctuary in 1509 following the arrest of Empson, Dudley and many of their promoters may explain Pity's worry (640) and Free Will's conso-lation (842–45); and Grimaldi too apparently underwent a quick conversion—but Imagination did not need to mirror Grimaldi exactly for the caricature to be recognisable.[249]

The entire play can be taken, indeed, as a satirical reflection of the times. In this perspective, *Hick Scorner* begins when a visitor (Pity) meets two men in holy orders, Contemplation, a patron (49) who grants priests their livings, and his subordinate, Perse-verance, whose vocation is helping the poor (85). The news the three discuss is England's double moral crisis. Perseverance says that the rich gentry and nobility oppress the poor, and the visitor reports how the clerics 'use so great sin' (137) and lead astray laymen who are advised by them. Pity is obviously Christ's representative, but as a 'king' leading the 'double reign' (24–25) who visits 'this country' (98) to hear 'many men com-plain piteously' (103) he may well also recall Henry VIII, who during a summer progress in 1510 heard (and later had parlia-ment act upon) 'euery daye more and more complaintes of Empson and Dudley'.[250] Pity's own charges against the clergy too characterise the young king, who sanctioned John Colet's attack in 1511 on the unreformed Church by employing him as a regular royal preacher and by calling him (in 1513) his 'own doctor'.[251] In any case, all three men discuss worldly abuses like public ombudsmen, and the next scene exemplifies the truth of their social commentary when they meet Free Will and Imagination. The latter's confession about how lords use him to usurp other men's lands, and his portrayal of Grimaldi, prove Perseverance's charge. Pity's criticism is justified by Imagination, who explains how he and his kin enter minor orders as 'clerks' (265–66) to get benefit of clergy, by which they can safely commit felonies. Though legislation punishes him for fornication, so that he enters from the stocks (180n), and though he was imprisoned at Newgate once for ten years (236, 949), his clerical 'neck verse' now protects him from the Tyburn gallows. Worse, Imagination, in patronising young 'Will' in crime—in being 'His priest' (432), as Imagination says later in another context—is corrupting a layman, albeit a roguish one.

Hick Scorner's entrance raises external political threats to the state and so worsens its internal crisis. Not only does his landing represent Richard de la Pole's threatened invasion, but Hick Scorner's news ridicules some recent, harsh English losses in the naval war with France—particularly of Henry's own ships the *Regent* and the *Anne of Foy* (332–33)[252]—and plays on fears that the new Irish policy then being discussed in the king's council would have an ill effect on England. One proposal advised Henry to subdue the rebellious Irish by populating the Pale and beyond with one person from every parish in England. Henry took this situation seriously enough to promise (to John Kite, who was sent as bishop of Armagh across the Irish Sea in the spring of 1514) that he himself, as his father Henry VII had planned in 1506, would sail shortly to Ireland in personal command of an army.[253] Thus Hick Scorner's report that his ship witnessed the sinking, on sand bars in the Irish Sea, of thirteen ships 'Full of people that would into Ireland, | And they came out of this country' (327–28), strikes indirectly at a royal enterprise. The news of this catastrophe also of course bears on the social criticism of the opening scene, as the ships foundered with

Perseverance's 'alms-deed doers' (346) and Pity's 'All true religious' (339).

Hick Scorner's arrival and bad news cheer up the two English rogues, who have entered out of cash and somewhat downcast. Their untapped potential for theft is realised shortly. Free Will uses Imagination's tricks to steal a tavern wine-cup (651–2), gets caught, and discovers at first hand the stocks and the Newgate prison conditions that Imagination before described from personal experience. In turn he succeeds in purchasing status as a gentleman and in bribing the law to free a thief from jail when Imagination commits the theft at the apothecary's shop, lodges at the Swan, where 'every man took him for a gentleman' (682), and, on the next morning, pays for Free Will's freedom. Further, Hick Scorner's example urges the two to greater crime. His role as shipboard pimp and pirate (the ship's owner is brother to a Shooters Hill highway robber, Jack Poller) makes Imagination propose a night's adventure of pimping and Thames-side or Shooters Hill highway robbery (404–18, 543). These crimes are technically much more serious than his previous fornication, stews-haunting (immoral but legal) and theft (which did not involve assault). Though the outcome of the rogues' ambush plans is not mentioned, and Free Will tells how Imagination in vain stalked Holborn for a victim, Imagination next enters having been granted, presumably by the bishop of Winchester or his agent, the comptrollership of such Southwark stew-houses as the Bell and the Hart's Horn (901). While still only a frequenter of stews (736–39), Free Will has equally ambitious plans as a 'merchant of the bank' (820), a Shooters Hill highwayman whose trade he describes metaphorically as sea piracy, after Hick Scorner. Most serious is the 'Hatred' (379–80) and stage violence that he precipitates. Free Will insults Imagination's parentage in a sudden fit of scorn (420–26), Imagination responds with a dagger, and Hick Scorner in turn threatens him with a sailor's horn. Forgetting all about the cowardly flight from the catchpoll (211) and the humiliation before the bailie (273), Imagination breaks the sailor's skull and then turns on Pity when he enters, not as a helpless visitor any more, but as a local English justice charged with keeping the peace (460–61). Here Imagination makes good his previous boast to slander men of treason (225) when he lays false witness (522) on the 'traitor' Pity (505), and both rogues flout the law that had up to then kept them in fear or in jail. Fetching chains from the King's Bench prison, Free Will turns the law itself to crime, much as the promoters had done. Pity's binding is, consequently, Perseverance's original fear that 'All is not God's law that is used in land' (115) come true.

The conversion scene presents the law's remedying of this disorder in a similar 'realistic' perspective. After Pity, in summarising how Hick Scorner's gang generally subverts English law, recites a satirical litany of other public abuses (including extortion, heresy and overspending on clothes), Perseverance and Contemplation enter, release Pity and send him, an English justice charged under the Statute of Winchester (633n), to pursue, set watch for, arrest and imprison the escaped criminals lest they reach a sanctuary area outside crown jurisdiction, as Grimaldi did in 1509. In so far as Perseverance and Contemplation 'arrest' (715) Free Will to prevent his 'escape' (717), they also are justices, Pity's 'brethren', but their main role is priestly, as before. Free Will calls Perseverance a 'priest, a doctor or else a frere' (696). The rogue begs the two men to set him penance, a function only priests could perform (864), and is even reclothed in a way that may suggest entrance into minor orders under the 'patron' Contemplation. The play ends with a confessional setting, but the nature of the confession, Free Will's powerful meditation on the outlaw's miserable life and death on the Tyburn or St Thomas of Watering gibbets, could not be less abstract; and even Imagination's change of heart results from personal loyalty, not argument. The interlude never forgets its social theme, the redemption of living London thieves and crooks.

One need not for that reason, however, deny *Hick Scorner* an allegory, as Percy and others have.[254] Interpreting the play as a psychomachia is problematical, but Craik's reading, a struggle between sinners and their converters, seems sound.[255] In five episodes *Hick Scorner* traces how one man-type, saved by God's mercy, converts a second, corrupt man-type who, prompted by a devil's envy, has rejected that mercy. Each figure for mankind has two aspects, there being two kinds of both virtue and vice: Contemplation and Perseverance, representing complementary sides of the universal perfected Christian, are the converter; and Free Will and Imagination, each an aspect of the universal corrupt man, are the to-be-converted.[256] Pity and Hick Scorner superficially allegorise a virtue (mercy) and a vice (scoffing, an aspect of the envy that is antithetical to mercy): as such, they are incapable of fluctuating between good and evil, stand as moral constants between which the man-types move, and leave the play before the conversion scene, which belongs to those who are, as yet, neither redeemed nor damned. A strong case can also be made for seeing the two as semi-religious figures, Pity as Christ's gift to men and Hick Scorner as the devil's opposed offering, where each takes on some features and actions of a supernatural patron. The play's first four scenes (up till Pity's exit), then, allegorise what is meant by a state of grace (man's loving relation with Christ) and what by spiritual peril (man's contempt for Christ); and the last episode shifts from religious to social allegory to represent, ideally, the meaning of the act of conversion.

The allegory begins as Pity, telling of his genesis in Christ's heart (7–8) and paraphrasing his very gospel words (28), associates himself less with abstract virtue than with the Son. Pity's name also makes this identification. Contemporary devotional literature as well as the liturgy called the icon of Christ displaying his wounds (the five 'wells of pity') the 'Image of Pity' (5n, 19). Pity's meditation on the passion, accordingly, is adapted from a popular poem on Christ's testament. The entrances of Contemplation and Perseverance (both invoking Christ's name), then, signify the typical Christian's admission by God's 'grace' (31, 76) to his Pity, the porter of heaven's gate by whom 'all that will to heaven needs must come' (28–29). Perfect Contemplation and Good Perseverance, their full names, are the model Christian life in its two complementary aspects, the passive, contemplative way of retirement from secular business into a life of worship, and the active, militant way of the Christian knight serving God in the world. Contemplation, 'brother to Holy Church' (43), represents desert dwellers and ascetics like John the Baptist, Antony and Jerome, and indeed all high churchmen (43–44, 49). Perseverance typifies the Church at work in society in never turning his face from the 'poor man' (85). Though the active life is beneath the passive—note that Contemplation comes *from* Perseverance (59), and he in turn, 'Still going upward the ladder of grace' (83), seeks out Contemplation (94)—here the two are at one. In the past they met when Contemplation meditated on 'thoughts that is full heavenly' (68–69); here they meet with Pity together (though in an order showing their rank), and each professes roles appropriate to the other, Contemplation as the Satan-fighting knight (50–54) and Perseverance as the solitary worshipper (86–89). After their exchange of bad news, Pity sets out on a 'great errand' that points ahead to the 'passion' scene (146 and n.), a mission to aid those men who, he learns, 'complain piteously' (103).

The next scene, the meeting of Free Will, Imagination and Hick Scorner, parodies Pity's conference with the just man-type. In the first place, Free Will and his 'fellow Imagination' (177) are, respectively, active and contemplative aspects of the typical fallen man: the corrupt will that initiates action and the criminal thinking that feeds it with schemes, plots and lies.[257] Whereas thriving, constant Perseverance is a much wished-for companion for all men, especially the poor (79–85), Free Will, who will 'never i-thee' (185), is quickly wearied of by men, particularly the poor mendicant he steals from (163–69). If Perseverance sleeps, he does so with Contemplation (70), but Free Will sleeps, like Imagination, with whores (172, 187–88, 206). Similarly, Imagination's opening complaint of a stocks' punishment recalls Contemplation's complaint of Christ's suffering, 'to a pillar bound' (35);[258] and just as Contemplation is Christ's kin (40) and Holy Church's brother, so Imagination is a cleric who boasts kinship to 'many a great gentleman' (218) and the advantage of 'lords' favours' (229). The two sides of each man-type are mutually dependent in like ways. Perseverance learns from Contemplation; Free Will is taught by Imagination, and both contemplatives must give way in worldly matters. Perseverance begins the conversion, and Free Will, with the controlling choice (159–60), summons Imagination as a mental tool (189–91), orders him to steal and bribe (660–88), calls him his 'knave' servant (735) and commands his final conversion (984–85). This ranking, incidentally, explains one of the play's cleverest allegorical points, Imagination's generous apology to Free Will (whom he blames for the brawl), 'all mine ill will I forgive thee' (471). Secondly, Hick Scorner, who represents five thousand 'devil's officers' (378) and has been in 'the land of rumbelow, | Three mile out of hell' (317–18), is just as clearly the foil to Pity and Christ, and by personifying scorning (and envy, the name of his ship) directly opposes their divine charity.[259] Born in Christ's 'bosom' (7) and crucified with him (19), Pity comes from New Jerusalem, the heavenly city, to offer men help from the 'maiden [who] so laid his life to wed' (23). By contrast, Hick Scorner, first imagined emerging from the 'bosoms' (297) of the audience's young men, and thought to have been hanged (306), comes from cities like 'Babyland' (319), of whose destruction John speaks in Revelation, to offer the help, not of a virgin, but of three whores on whose performance he will 'dare lay to wed' his life (400). Pity, with Charity, 'of true love leads the double reign' (25), but Hick Scorner is a lecherous pimp. The three rogues are thus inversions of the three virtues. Free Will and Imagination become the devil's disciples, not Christ's, and when they receive the same bad news as was told before—the drowning of 'Right Conscience and Faith with Devotion' (344), for example, corroborates Pity's report when he tells of the many with 'small devotion' (124)—the rogues celebrate.

The moral differences between the virtuous and corrupt man-types show up in their contrary treatments of Pity in the next two scenes. The brawl is the occasion for Pity's entrance, and provides a further example of how he and Hick Scorner are foils, since both interfere with the fight in order to save Free

Will, perhaps allegorically, from his own Imagination. A peace-keeping justice in warning Imagination about the law (436), and a scapegoat in suffering a 'passion' (449), Hick Scorner parodically foreshadows Pity, who also, like a 'peace' officer (460–61), warns Imagination of 'God's law' (463), and like Christ endures a passion in chains. As the expression 'Piteous people that be of sin destroyers' (347) shows, the 'Image of Pity' also stood for stern justice.[260] Free Will and Imagination, however, adopt Hick Scorner's hatred and injustice. Their brutalisation of Pity resembles, as in *Youth*, the torturers' abuse of Christ in medieval representations of the passion.[261] At this point Pity refers to himself obliquely as Christ, Truth (520–21); and his complaint implies that the three are Judas figures (546) and paraphrases Christ's words on the cross (548). Imagination's false witness and Free Will's fetching of the chains allegorically commit them both against Christ in person; and Free Will's later confession of having spent Easter at the *Petty Judas* alehouse (748) is quite in character. When in the next scene Contemplation and Perseverance free Pity, they literally and figuratively undo what the corrupt man-type has done, and take the first step in converting him. Pity then leaves because his function as Christ's gift is not to convert, a task he left to the disciples, but to reward the penitent with mercy and to judge the faithless.[262] This rationale appears later in pleas that Free Will repent for God's 'love' (744, 848): 'Then on thee he will have pity | And bring thee to heaven' (727–28). Hick Scorner's non-return, which is implied here (616–17), places him also outside conversion. He is one who has already gone 'to hell by his will voluntary' (778). As Contemplation says, 'Fiends flee away where they see me come' (54). Scorn by definition rejects offers of help. More than doubling, therefore, lies behind Pity's and Hick Scorner's early exits.

The two man-types have pursued parallel but separate courses so far during the play, but at last face one another in the final scene, which presents a subtle analysis of the different roles played by their active and passive selves. Perseverance leads the conversion, and so the active man-type here confronts his corrupt counterpart (695). Flippantly, Free Will dismisses warnings against fortune (756) and hell (772), as he thinks himself free to avoid them by invoking Imagination (758–59) and caution (776–80). Contemplation's quotation from the Office of the Dead, however, breaks this self-confidence; Free Will comes to recognise that death ignores the individual will. Convincing himself, he voluntarily repents and obtains God's mercy (871). At this point the conversion proper is over; as Perseverance says, only by 'free will' is any penitence possible. What follows is, allegorically, Free Will's ascent to a better life. He first must emulate Perseverance's constancy in 'good will' (883–90; cf. 82). Imagination, Free Will's complementary self, is by definition corrupt, and when he enters, nothing Contemplation and Perseverance say to him has any effect; yet Imagination is converted, instantly and without question (984–85), by Free Will, for he is literally Imagination's will (989). In renaming him 'Good Remembrance' and delivering him into Perseverance's care (1006–07), Free Will allegorically rejects criminal cunning for conscience, and proceeds to the passive life by going to 'dwell with Contemplation' (1008).[263] The play's perfected man-type not only has converted his counterpart, but has instructed him 'upward the ladder of grace' so that their two higher and lower selves are companions. In a costuming effect that confirms this allegory, Free Will is clothed by Contemplation (876) and Imagination by Perseverance (1002).

When our playwright depicts his two universal man-types as London crooks and lawmen, he fuses two techniques, allegory and 'realism', with quite exceptional skill. In doing so he is perhaps most impressive in choosing petty criminals as the play's regenerated man-type. This concern for felons is of course implicit in Pity's allegorical relation to Christ. Just as his passion, in effect a thief's imprisonment, trial, torture and hanging, saved two actual thieves, Barabbas and the man crucified on Christ's right hand (Luke xxiii.39–43), so Pity's fettering as a thief, done by thieves whose own just punishment he assumes on himself, ultimately saves Free Will and Imagination from a thief's hanging.[264] Contemplation and Perseverance in part make this point in telling Imagination that Christ, by dying on the cross, delivered him 'out of prison' (952, 958, 967). The playwright's enlightened attitude to the men whom Shakespeare will call Autolycus, Falstaff and even Pompey makes *Hick Scorner* a moral statement well ahead of its time. Helping debtors out of prison was a traditional act of charity (cf. 350), but thieves were another matter, and the proposals for the rehabilitation of criminals in Sir Thomas More's *Utopia* (1516), which appeared when he was under-sheriff of London, are a remarkable social development.[265] More, and the More circle, would have liked this interlude. It wastes no moral righteousness on 'Saint Tyburn of Kent' (941)—hanging is a 'knavish sight', as Free Will says—and there may be some grounds for calling the playwright a humanist, if only at heart.

NOTES TO INTRODUCTION

1 Greg, I (1939), 94–95, nos. 20*a*–*c*. William Herbert and Edmond Malone each owned an MS copy of Q2: see B.L. C.60.0.5 (Herbert's annotated Ames's 1749 *Typographical Antiquities*), p. 258; and Bodl. Malone 156 (Malone's interleaved 1782 *Biographia Dramatica*, II), p. 169. Herbert's copy was owned by Thomas F. Dibdin in 1819 (his *Typographical Antiquities*, IV [1819], pp. 274–75). Malone probably picked up his MS (with the Q3 *Hick Scorner*) 23 February 1786 for £1 1s at the sale of John Henderson's books (*A Catalogue of the Library of John Henderson* [1786], p. 27, lot 661; annotated B.L. copy 272.k.28[2]). The putative Lambeth Palace Library MS (Carl J. Stratman, *Bibliography of Medieval Drama*, 1st ed. only [1954], p. 240) and the 'fragment in the British Museum' mentioned by Claude Jenkins, a former Lambeth Librarian, in an MS note preceding the Lambeth Q1 are ghosts.

2 Maitland, p. 310. Two earlier shelfmarks (?) appear on Q1: J. M. 45 and 1. E. 12. For a facsimile, see J. S. Farmer, ed., *Youth*, T.F.T. (1909).

3 The MS note preceding Q1 says the edition was scrapped because the characters' names are omitted from the scrolls above the title-page factotums, but such omissions occur in Q2 and *H.S.* Q3. The note was evidently written when the fragment was displayed for a private performance of *Youth* in 1911 in Lambeth Palace Crypt.

4 That is, thirty-four lines: 10–14, 43–47, 78–81, 112–15, 146–49, 180–83, 214–17, 248–[?51].

5 That is, for sixty lines: 150–79, 218–47.

6 They imitate those made for Antoine Vérard's *Therence en Francois*, printed at Paris *c*. 1500, and copied in Pynson's 1506 *Kalender of shepherdes* (*S.T.C.* 22408) after Vérard reused the originals in his 1503 English *Kalendayr* (*S.T.C.* 22407). See Bang-McKerrow, pp. xvi–xix; Hodnett, pp. vii–viii

(where factotums are unlisted); and Alfred W. Pollard, 'Some Notes on English Illustrated Books', *Trans. of the Bibl. Soc.*, 6 (1900–02), 36–40.

7 Following H. O. Sommer, ed., *The Kalender of Shepherdes* (1892), pp. 46–47.

8 McKerrow also noted the Q1 right-hand factotum in de Worde's *Hick Scorner* (sig. A1v), and the title-page capital initial *I* in the Bodleian *Kalender* (sigs. Q1v, R1v, X8v). This initial also occurs in a 5 November 1528 de Worde edition (*S.T.C.* 17974, sig. X2v), and Bang notes it in *S.T.C.* 6833, de Worde's 1520 *Dyetary of ghostly helthe* (sig. A3), printed by Henry Pepwell, a book in Louvain Library in 1914 when it burned down (H. de Vocht, *Professor W. Bang and His Work in English Philology*, Materials for the Study of the Old English Drama, N.S. 25 [1958], p. 45). Q1's middle factotum also is in a de Worde edition (*S.T.C.* 14109, sig. A1r; c. 1528).

9 Frank Isaac, *English & Scottish Printing Types: 1501–35, 1508–41*, Bibl. Soc. Facsimiles and Illustrations, no. II (1930), s.v. Wynkyn de Worde.

10 For the damaged large w^2, see *S.T.C.* 10002 (1528), 25422 (1530), 17975, 14559 (1532), 656, 7500, 14045 and 25423 (1533). It is missing from *S.T.C.* 23152 (16 May 1534) and in *The lyfe of Hyldebrāde* (21 March 1534), though it occurs a few times in its separately collated prologue (*S.T.C.* 23552), where w^3 appears in capital positions.

11 *A Transcript of the Registers of the Company of Stationers of London: 1554–1640 A.D.*, ed. Edward Arber, I (1875), fol. 22.

12 Press variants are limited to loosened (174, 183, 250) or dirty (399) type and uneven inking (664, 710). Putative copies in the Victoria and Albert Museum Dyce Library and the Los Angeles Public Library (Stratman, *Bibliography*, 1st ed. only, p. 240) are ghosts, but other copies may have existed (see nn. 14–15). For a Q2 facsimile, see J. S. Farmer, ed., *Youth*, T.F.T. (1909).

13 Edward Capell's MS inventory-index of Garrick's play-books (B.L. 643 l.30) includes both it and the Copland edition, and was finished by about 1756. The price on sig. C4v of Garrick's Waley copy may be in Gerard Langbaine's hand (for his copy, see his *Account of the English Dramatick Poets* [1691], p. 535), and this book may have come to Garrick from the Harley Library, where Joseph Ames, the first to record a Waley edition (*Typographical Antiquities* [1749], p. 257), could have seen it. For most of this information I am grateful to George M. Kahrl, who is preparing a study of the Garrick collection.

14 George Ashby, between 1773 and 1787, handled a copy that, like the Malone-Douce ones, was missing the bottom of the signature on A2, and belonged to a volume of eleven old plays owned by John Wenyeve, of Brettenham, Suffolk (fol. 27r).

15 *Bibliotheca Pearsoniana* (1788), p. 144, lot no. 3506, sold 30 April (to Kemble, according to B.L. copy 822.d.15); also evidently identified by *The Carl H. Pforzheimer Library: English Literature, 1475–1700* (1940), II, 536, with the Q2 copy in *A Catalogue of the Library of Richard Wright, M.D.* (1787), p. 55, lot no. 1637, sold 1 May. Since the Pearson sale also included a 1568 *Jacob and Esau* (p. 140, lot no. 3401), a copy of which was paired with a Waley *Youth* in the sale of William Fletewode's library (see *Bib-*

liotheca Monastica-Fletewodiana [1774], p. 80, lot no. 1426, sold 12
December), these two Q2 copies may be the same. *The Carl H. Pforzheimer
Library* incorrectly queries the Fletewode to be the Garrick copy (p. 536).

16 Greg, I, 94.

17 Another 1560 King edition (*S.T.C.* 12105) has this inverted ornament (sig.
D4v), and the odd capital initial *I* on Q2's title-page regularly appears in his
1560 editions (*S.T.C.* 16933, 19971). For the type keyplate, see Frank
Isaac, *English & Scottish Printing Types: 1535–58, 1552–58*, Bibl. Soc.
Facsimiles and Illustrations, no. III (1932), fig. 1.

18 Q2 use of w^{13a} instead of w^{8cap} shows it is not before 1555 (*S.T.C.* 9971,
sigs. O$^{1-8}$, P$^{1-8}$). The only other dated book between 1557 and 1560, a 1559
Breviat Chronicle (*S.T.C.* 9973), has the pre-Q2 y^5 and omits the Q2 w^{5d}
and w^{12}, but as it only recounts events to August 1557 the bulk of the
edition was probably printed not long after that date.

19 *T.R.P.*, II, no. 460, injunctions 3 (pp. 118–19) and 51 (pp. 128–29). In
May 1559 a statute was promulgated forbidding the performance of
unlicensed interludes and plays (no. 458, pp. 115–16).

20 Press variants involve inking (the apparent turned letters in one copy at
191, 320, 518, 766) and the periods after the speech headings at 149 and
273. For a facsimile, see J. S. Farmer, ed., *Youth*, T.F.T. (1908).

21 *Jack Juggler*, ed. W. W. Greg and Eunice L. Smart, M.S.R. (1933), pp.
v–vi; E. G. Duff, *A Century of the English Book Trade* (1905), pp. 32–33.

22 *S.T.C.* 24572, a Lothbury book with type similar to a Three-Crane-Wharf
fount, has both Q3 centre (sigs. R8v, Z6v, Cc4v) and left-hand (sig. Hh3r)
factotums in somewhat earlier states. *S.T.C.* 7572, another Lothbury
edition with type like Q3, has its central factotum in the same state (sig.
R3v); this woodcut appears in earlier states in de Worde's *S.T.C.* 24242
(sig. A1r) and Copland's Three-Crane-Wharf *S.T.C.* 14837 (sig. A1r), and
in almost the same state in the Lothbury *S.T.C.* 14837^a (sig. A1r).

23 *Robert Laneham: A Letter* [1575] (Scolar Press Facsimile, 1968), sig. C3r.

24 *Transcript*, II (1875), 186. Awdeley printed *The Play of the Weather* (Greg
15*d*), and Charlewood 'The olde Algorisme' in 1581 (*S.T.C.* 14121).

25 *Transcript*, II, 308–308b; III (1876), 265; IV (1877), 146. Over one-half the
1582 books, including the playbooks, are not mentioned in 1594 or afterwards, but an undated MS, once owned by Thomas Coxeter (1689–1747),
lists them in their 1582 order in a catalogue of Roberts's books (William
Herbert, [Ames's] *Typographical Antiquities*, II [1786], 1031–32). With
Richard Cotes's death in 1653 his wife Ellen carried on the business for a
short time (Henry R. Plomer, *A Dictionary of the Booksellers and Printers
. . . from 1641 to 1667* [1907], p. 53). For some of these transactions, see
Edwin E. Willoughby, *A Printer of Shakespeare* (1934), pp. 24, 74–75,
107–10.

26 Greg, III (1957), 1332.

27 Bang-McKerrow, pp. xxi–xxiii.

28 Two items noted by McKerrow, the quartos' page-by-page correspondence, and especially Q2's provision of 'an extra line on A2, besides altering
the position of a speaker's name on A1v' (p. xxi, n. 1 and 2), to offset a large
woodcut on sig. A1r, strongly imply that Q2 and Q3 were based on an
edition (where the text would already be divided off), not an MS.

29 The others are at 5, 16, 116, 130, 162, 172 and 220.

30 Each variant's readings at 136 and 200 are equally possible.

31 For Robert Wyer's practice (1526–60), see H. C. Schulz, 'A Middle English Manuscript Used as Printer's Copy', *Huntington Library Quarterly*, 29 (1966), 325–36. For de Worde's, see Gavin Bone, 'Extant Manuscripts Printed from by W. de Worde with Notes on the Owner, Roger Thorney', *Libr.*, 4th ser., 12 (1931–32), 289–93; and Robert W. Mitchner, 'Wynkyn de Worde's Use of the Plimpton Manuscript of *De Proprietatibus Rerum*', *Libr.*, 5th ser., 6 (1951), 7–18.

32 Dramatic context permits emendation at 232, and rhyme at 59, but we can only conjecture about problems at 17, 22, 190 and 218.

33 I.e., at 46, 345, 408, 479, 679; 252, 262, 346, 400, 458, 496, 498, 507, 551, 557, 593, 627, 638.

34 For instance, while Q3 omits four words (252, 325, 471, 479), Q2 omits ten (5, 182, 324, 551, 679, 698) and an entire line (793).

35 The ratio of Q1 to non-Q1 text being 218 : 577 or 1 : 2·65, for fifteen Q2 variants from Q3 in the extant Q1 text there should be about forty such variants in the rest. There are in fact about forty-five, and if extrapolation from this ratio is safe, there should be, with about forty known joint Q2–Q3 variants from Q1, about 105 unknown ones.

36 I.e., at 14, 291, 365, 411, 699, 790 (emendation where an uncertain degree of modernisation by the printer obscures rhyme, as at 179–80, 192/195, and 760, is of course undesirable, and various seeming irregularities in rhyme stem from later changes in standard English pronunciation; see p. 26); 154, 232, 325, 350, 434, 461, 507, 684.

37 I.e., at 12–13, 275–76, 395–96, 413–14, 428–29, 433–34, 474–75, 585–86, 728–29.

38 Cf. 114, 397, 398, 410, 435, 469, 491, 493, 683, 685, 687, 705, 708, 716, 723, 772 (mainly rhyme or lineation problems).

39 Greg, I, 81–82, no. *3a–c*. J. S. Farmer says fragments other than Q2 are known (his Q1 facsimile, *Hick Scorner*, T.F.T. [1908], p. v), perhaps because W. W. Greg's *List of English Plays* (1900) does not identify Q2 with the B. H. Bright fragment (p. 139) noted by W. C. Hazlitt in his *Hand-Book* (1867), p. 464, and his *Collections and Notes* (1876), p. 214. James O. Halliwell's note of a Sampson Awdeley edition (*A Dictionary of Old English Plays* [1860], p. 119) is just speculation (see p. 5).

40 Percy's letter to Richard Farmer only names *Cock Lorel's Boat* and *The Parliament of Birds*, but on 25 January 1763 Percy identifies the volume's six pieces (including *Hick Scorner*), explains that, as the book was 'in a very shattered condition', he has renewed its leaves and binding, and offers to buy it if Astle will negotiate with the owner. See S. H. Harlowe, 'Letters from Dr. Percy to T. Astle', *Notes and Queries*, 4th ser., 3 (1869), 53–54; corrected in *The Correspondence of Thomas Percy & Richard Farmer*, ed. Cleanth Brooks (1946), pp. 20–21, and n. 25; and cf. Potter, p. 204.

41 Harlowe, 'Letters', p. 54. Astle's name and birthplace (Yoxal, Staffs., his residence as late as July 1761) are partly legible on the title-page of the volume's first tract (*Robert the deuyll*, now B.L. C.21.c.11), addressed to Garrick. Sixteenth-century scribbles on Q1 mention a bill drawn up in 21 Henry VIII, 1529/30 (sig. A5r), and certain names, Thomas Lotte of

Uttoxeter (Staffs.; sig. B4v), John Less (sig. B4v) and John Stork (sig. C3v).

42 Edward Capell's small booklet want-list of plays for Garrick *c.* 1756 lists 'Dick Scorner' (p. 3, bound in the 'Catalogue of Garrick's Plays', B.L. 643.l.30; see n. 13), but Capell neither catalogued the acquired play (in B.L. MS Kings 309) nor bound it in a Garrick volume (his flyleaves are collected in the 'Index to Garrick Plays', also B.L. 643.l.30). On 20 January 1774 George Steevens asked Garrick to see 'an old quarto volume, which is not in your catalogue', and 'which contains *Cock Lorel's Bote*, is in a parchment cover, has *Hyck Scorner* with it, &c'. See *The Private Correspondence of David Garrick*, I (1831), pp. 607–08.

43 Ronald B. McKerrow, *Printers' & Publishers' Devices in England & Scotland, 1485–1640*, Bibl. Soc. Illustrated Monographs, no. 16 (1913), no. 19.

44 Frank Isaac, *English & Scottish Printing Types: 1501–35, 1508–41* (1930), keyplate and s.v. Wynkyn de Worde. His suggestion that w^3 was introduced in 1519 is misleading, as the letter appears, albeit in small quantities, earlier: see *S.T.C.* 18567 (1511), 3290 (1513), 9985 (1515), 3264 (1517), etc. The odd stray capital *I* in Q1 (sigs. A4r, A8v, B2r, C5r) belongs to a de Worde Westminster Textura fount.

45 *S.T.C.* 18568 has two more Q1 factotums, Pity (sig. A5v) and Imagination (further deteriorated on sig. C4r; note a break in the scroll's roof). All four factotums (see p. 1 and n. 6) occur previously in the 1509 and 1511 editions (*S.T.C.* 18566–67), three in their Q1 states, Free Will in a better state, and are regular elsewhere in de Worde books: *S.T.C.* 12948 (sig. R6r), 13686 (sig. D4v), 14518 (sig. D7r), 17027 (sig. A1r), 20108 (sig. G7v). The Perseverance factotum is in *S.T.C.* 14518 (sig. F3r), but I have not seen the Contemplation figure, though like ones exist, as on the Q3 title-page. Q1 woodcuts on sig. A1r are common to de Worde books: the four workmen (Hodnett 882), the gowned man with sword (*S.T.C.* 24879, sig. F6v), the crowned king (Hodnett 877); the elephant and castle may copy Antwerp craftsmanship, according to Alfred W. Pollard's 'The Transference of Woodcuts in the Fifteenth and Sixteenth Centuries', *Bibliographica*, 2 (1896), 347, n. 1.

46 McKerrow, *Devices*, pp. 7–8; Greg, I, 81. Earlier Frank Isaac told him that the state of the device 'points to 1516–17'; see Greg's 'Notes on Some Early Plays', *Libr.*, 4th ser., 11 (1930–31), 44.

47 Despite inking and clamping variations, and the device's appearance, in early states, in editions bearing a later date but evidently printed before, certain faults are datable: a sharp 1 mm cut in the top border's lower line (about 31 mm from the left) occurs in Q1 and after, but not in *S.T.C.* 16126 or before; and a sharp 1 mm cut in the bottom border's lower line (about 37 mm from the left) occurs in *S.T.C.* 20438 and after, but not in Q1 or before.

48 *Catalogue of the Valuable Library of the Late Benjamin Heywood Bright, Esq.* (1845), p. 359, lot no. 5737*, sold 10 April. Hazlitt, *Collections and Notes*, p. 214. The B.L. annotated copy (S.-C.S. 259[1]) lists [Thomas] Rodd, the bookseller, as paying 5s for it, and a pencil price of 12s is on the verso of the fragment's first leaf, presumably what the B.L. paid when it obtained Q2 with two other non-dramatic fragments, C.18.e.2[2–3], on 30 June 1845 (noted on C.18.e.2[2], sig. D1r; Greg says about 28 June [I, 82]). Q2 was

catalogued under '*Hyckescorner*' on 11 May 1878 according to B.L. records.

49 Greg, 'Notes on Some Early Plays', pp. 45–46; Greg, I, 82. Q1 is collated $A^8B^4C^6$, and Q3 A–E^4.

50 Isaac, *Types: 1501–35, 1508–41*, s.v. Peter Treveris.

51 *Catalogue* (1786), p. 27, lot no. 658, sold 23 February for £1 12s, as annotated in the B.L. copy (272.k.28[2]). Malone identifies his Q3 as Henderson's in Malone's annotated Langbaine, Bodl. Malone 132, opp. p. 534. Q3 was probably sold twice earlier: (1) on 7 April 1773, in the library of James West, President of the Royal Society; see *Bibliotheca Westiana* (1773), p. 104, lot no. 1689 (to John Ratcliffe for 11s according to the B.L. annotated copy, 270.k.7); and (2) on 4 April 1776 at the sale of Ratcliffe's library; see *Bibliotheca Ratcliffiana* [1776], p. 66, lot no. 1287 (sold to a Mr Money for £1 1s, according to B.L. 822.d.6).

52 Greg, I, 82; for Copland's acknowledged play-editions, see nos. 20c, 32, 35a–b, 41b.

53 Greg reproduces the Q3 title-page (I, plate VII). In *S.T.C.* 3383 the gallants' cut (Hodnett 1092) on sig. A1r has several wormholes in the lower right floor (one in Q3), and the centre factotum on sig. G3v is missing the scroll's uprights and top (present in Q3). Otherwise, for Hodnett 1092 see *S.T.C.* 3385, by Copland *c.* 1562–63 (sig. A1r), 24572, by Copland *c.* 1565 (sig. E8v), and 11362, by A. Veale *c.* 1560 (sig. A2v); for the centre factotum, *S.T.C.* 7572, by Copland *c.* 1565? (sig. G1r) and 24572 (sig. N3v); for the right factotum, *S.T.C.* 11362 (sig. A4r).

54 Right and left Q3 factotums appear in *S.T.C.* 10605 by John Scott *c.* 1530–35 (sig. A1v), and the centre factotum in several de Worde editions, *S.T.C.* 9985 in 1515 (sig. b5r), 10002 in 1528 (sig. B5r) and 14518 *c.* 1509–16 (sig. D7r).

55 Frank Isaac, *English & Scottish Printing Types: 1535–58, 1552–58* (1932), s.v. Robert Wyer and William Copland. Copland's 1549–55 95 Textura used w^8 and y^4, and w^{14} only occurs in his 1555–58 72 Textura. For information about Wyer's type I am indebted to Katharine F. Pantzer, reviser of the *S.T.C.*

56 Greg, I, nos. 16b, 26. Cf. my 'Robert Wyer's Alleged Edition of Heywood's *Play of the Weather*: The Source of the Error', *Libr.*, 5th ser., 29 (1974), 441–46.

57 E. G. Duff, *A Century of the English Book Trade* (1905), p. 32; Henry R. Plomer, *Wynkyn de Worde & His Contemporaries from the Death of Caxton to 1535* (1925), pp. 192–93. Circa 1543 H. Dab and R. Banks commissioned Wyer to print a Robert Copland translation (*S.T.C.* 12468).

58 See p. 5.

59 Greg, III (1957), 1323, 1342 (Greg argues on p. 1321 that such errors arose from careless dictation); E. Phillips, 'Eminent Poets Among the Moderns', *Theatrum Poetarum* (1675), p. 160; Gerard Langbaine, *An Account of the English Dramatick Poets* (1691), pp. 529–30.

60 Greg says they are unrelated (I, 82).

61 N. F. Blake, 'Wynkyn de Worde: The Later Years', *Gutenberg-Jahrbuch 1972*, ed. Hans Widmann, pp. 135–36.

62 Q3 also corrects possibly substantive foul-case (130, 239, 282, 322, 365, 544, 607, 801), misspacing (310, 479) and repeated type (320, 358, 737, 813).

63 Also 240, 287, 371, 419, 446–47, 528, 552, 653, 669 (and a factual correction at 842 misses the point).

64 See 182, 202 (?), 249, 332, 370, 372, 478, 491, 509, 626, 739, 784, 1027–28.

65 Also 23, 32, 146, 314, 362, 672, 734, 785, 797, 948, 985, 988.

66 See 25, 125, 364, 426, 462, 547, 870, 882, 956, 965, 1016.

67 E.g., 'to' (with an infinitive), 'I' (with 'beshrew'), the auxiliary 'will', and 'or'/'nor' are added; the adjective 'all', the relative pronoun 'that', and the verb-ending '-th' are excised; aphetic verbs are given in full; and substitutions of 'an' ('if') for 'and', 'in'/'on' for the preposition 'a', and 'ye' for 'you' (or 'you' for 'ye' when the subject and verb are inverted) occur.

68 N. F. Blake makes this point ('Wynkyn de Worde: The Later Years', p. 135).

69 These could be visual slips, but later the compositor seems not to have understood what a 'farce' (446) was, and other problems at 297 and 483 may have involved uncertainty about staging.

70 Hick Scorner may follow Youth in not rhyming the last lines of some speeches (32, 620, 645, 753, 960; see n. 116), rhymeless lines can be found in The assemble of goddes (a source), and see p. 14.

71 The H.S. text may also be defective at 180, 301 and 813; and see n. 31.

72 The Tudor Facsimile Texts include all Youth quartos (1908–09) and the Hick Scorner Q1 (1908), and provide satisfactory reproduction for all but a few readings.

73 Archaic forms so altered include 'euerychone' (Y. 196), 'aumsase' (Y. 685), 'perfyte' (H.S. 42), 'sentwary' (H.S. 640), 'vyages' (H.S. 822), and superseded verb forms like 'stall' (H.S. 270), 'lad' (H.S. 279), 'dronke' (H.S. 650), 'kest' (H.S. 677), 'renne' (H.S. 741), 'shytte' (H.S. 784), 'tred' (H.S. 797) and 'ware' (H.S. 803). Such spellings may well misrepresent both the playwrights' accidentals and their then current pronunciation, however, for printers used a standardised orthography that distorted rhyme, at least in these plays (see n. 36).

74 As the apparent lack of regular metre within the line gives no grounds for choosing between syllabic and non-syllabic verb endings, however, these (-st, -est, -ed, etc.) have been kept in the original form.

75 This editor's Ph.D. dissertation, 'Hycke Scorner: A Critical Edition' (University of Toronto, 1969), is the basis for the present edition. Extracts of the play are to be found in Anecdotes of Literature and Scarce Books, ed. William Beloe, I (London, 1807), 387–88 (ll. 814–45); in English Plays, ed. Henry Morley, Cassell's Library of English Literature (London, n.d.), 12–18 (summary with many quotations); and in Geoffrey Bullough's Narrative and Dramatic Sources of Shakespeare, IV (London, 1962), 292–99 (ll. 296–308, 363–443, 531–45, 865–1028). W. Bang evidently intended to follow his edition of Youth with one of Hick Scorner (p. vii, n. 1), but it never appeared.

76 See pp. 8, 36–41. Bang dated Youth in the late fifteenth or early sixteenth century (pp. xiii–xiv) after McKerrow proved Q1 to be about 1530 (see above, pp. 1–2). Previously Collier's Marian date, just before Q2 (II, 313), was generally accepted. By assuming the priority of Hick Scorner, the Harbage-Schoenbaum Annals of English Drama (1964) dated Youth 1520 with 1513–29 limits, but E. T. Schell in 1966 and this editor in 1971 argued Youth to be prior (see pp. 41–42).

77 *S.R.*, III (1817), 3 Hen. VIII. c. 15, pp. 33–34.

78 *S.R.*, II (1816), 4 Hen. VII. c. 9, p. 534.

79 C. B. Firth, 'Benefit of Clergy in the time of Edward IV', *English Historical Review*, 32 (1917), 175–91; and cf. *H.S.* 266.

80 *S.R.*, II (1816), 4 Hen. VII. c. 13, p. 538 (any convicted cleric was to be branded on the hand 'T' or 'M' as 'thief' or 'murderer'); III (1817), 4 Hen. VIII. c. 2, p. 49.

81 The Church and the House of Lords together suppressed the Commons bill to renew (though benefit of clergy eventually fell when Henry broke from Rome). J. S. Roskell, *The Commons and their Speakers in English Parliaments, 1376–1523* (1965), pp. 319–20, discusses the controversy.

82 Any tenant with £40 yearly could be a Knight Bachelor (though honour attached to the title when the king personally dubbed a man), and two high orders existed, the Bath and the twenty-six member Garter. The Collar of the King's Livery was seldom of gold, could be held without regard to class or sex, and in Edward IV's household in 1478 was shared with relatively minor officials. See William A. Shaw, *The Knights of England* (1906), I, xliii, xlv, 19–20, 145–47; Sir Nicholas H. Nicolas, *History of the Orders of Knighthood* (1841–42), I, xliv–xlv, 120; II, 349–50, lix; A. R. Myers, ed., *The Household of Edward IV* (1959), p. 217. For the wedding collars, see Halle, 'Henry VII', fol. 53r; and *Chronicles*, pp. 249–50, and 254 (where a poem of December 1501 noted on London's streets 'many a semely knyght | In veluet gownes and cheynes of gold').

83 On 27 May 1509 William, lord Mountjoy, wrote to Erasmus: 'Avarice is expelled the country. Liberality scatters wealth with bounteous hand. Our king does not desire gold or gems or precious metals, but virtue, glory, immortality' (*The Epistles of Erasmus*, trans. Francis M. Nichols, I [1901], 457).

84 Halle, 'Henry VIII', fols. 3r, 5r. At the tournament of February 1511, sixty-four persons are depicted with such chains (*The Great Tournament Roll of Westminster*, intro. Sydney Anglo [1968]). At various times Henry distributed these as gifts (*L.P.* II, p. 1450; Nicholas H. Nicolas, *Testamenta Vetusta* [1826], II, 549).

85 Shaw, *Knights of England*, II, 36–42; *L.P.* I.2246.4.ii, and App. 26 (and cf. I.2301).

86 *Venice*, II, no. 445; di Favri repeated this observation when on 13 August 1514 the marriage contract of Henry's sister Mary with Louis XII was celebrated by proxy at Greenwich (no. 505). After this period, the remark became proverbial: cf. Alexander Barclay, *Mirrour of Good Maners* (1885), p. 34 ('The great thieues are laded with great chaynes of golde, | The small thiefe with yron chayned from all refuge'); and Tilley C214 ('CHAINS of gold are stronger than chains of iron').

87 *S.R.*, III (1817), 6 Hen. VIII. c. 1, p. 122; cf. 1 Hen. VIII. c. 14, pp. 8–9.

88 Richard Koebner, '"The Imperial Crown of This Realm": Henry VIII, Constantine the Great, and Polydore Vergil', *Bulletin of the Institute of Historical Research*, 26 (1953), 29–52. The first important royal document to state that England is an empire is the preamble to the act in restraint of appeals of April 1533.

89 *L.P.* I.2114. Scarisbrick discusses these negotiations and suggests the first

offer occurred about August 1513 (p. 97). For the Rincq meeting, see Cruickshank, pp. 90–91. Only once, in 1257, had there been an English King of the Romans, Henry III's brother Richard, earl of Cornwall, and he was never elected Emperor (Neville Williams, *Henry VIII and his Court* [1971], p. 70).

90 *L.P.* I.2166, 2170, 2180, 2265, 2391 (p. 1061).

91 *Lettres du Roy Louis XII* [ed. Jean Godefroy] (1712), IV, 323; *L.P.* I.2992; and Scarisbrick, pp. 97–98. For Henry's sickness, see *L.P.* I.2610 (and for the date, I.2658).

92 *L.P.* I.2725, 2925.

93 Chambers, *M.S.*, I, 390–419, describes secular Christmas entertainments, and A. R. Wright, *British Calendar Customs: England*, ed. T. E. Lones, I (1936), 1–32, Shrovetide ones. Servants and apprentices could only play at cards and dice, *temp.* Henry VII–VIII, during Christmas (see *Y.* 679n), but note the account of Shrovetide from 1553 by the anti-Catholic Thomas Naogeorgus, whose work was translated in 1570 by Barnabe Googe in *The Popish Kingdome or reigne of Antichrist*, ed. Robert C. Hope (1880):

> the Dice are shakte and tost, and Cardes apace they teare:
> In euery house are showtes and cryes, and mirth, and reuell route,
> And daintie tables spred, and all be set with ghestes aboute:
> With sundrie playes and Christmasse games, & feare and shame away,
> The tongue is set at libertie, and hath no kinde of stay.
> All thinges are lawfull then and done, no pleasure passed by . . .
>
> (fols. 47v–48r)

A Shrovetide game not unlike Charity's treatment by Riot and Pride is also mentioned: friends or strangers have their hands bound behind their backs by revellers who, 'Basons ringing great, | Before them do . . . daunce with ioy, and sport in euery streat' (fol. 48v). Chambers also discusses the German *Fastnachtspiele* (*M.S.*, I, 382).

94 *Macro Plays*, p. xlii; and my 'The Auspices of *The World and the Child*', *Renaissance and Reformation*, 12 (1976), 96–105.

95 See pp. 25–26. The earl of Northumberland employed actors throughout the Christmas season, and about 1512 his chapel gentlemen were said to perform customarily on Christmas day and on Shrove Tuesday night (on the latter, a play of possibly non-biblical subject). Henry VIII's chapel gentlemen played on Shrove Sunday 1512, and Cornish produced a play before the court on Shrove Tuesday 1517 (*L.P.* II, pp. 1454–55, 1474).

96 The laity did not always observe fasting in Advent, the four weeks before Christmas (from 27 November in 1513), according to James Ryman's 'Farewele, Advent; Cristemas is cum' (*A Selection of English Carols*, ed. Richard L. Greene [1962], pp. 53–55).

97 See pp. 22–24.

98 See Chambers, *M.S.*, II, 66, 94, 138 and 396; and notes to *H.S.* 745–53, 748 and 876.

99 Alois Brandl, *Quellen des Weltlichen Dramas in England vor Shakespeare*, Quellen und Forschungen, 80 (1898), p. xxviii. For the *Regent*'s history, see Appendix I.D., pp. 245–46. Collier (II, 309) first used this ship to date the play *temp.* Henry VII. Earlier Thomas Percy, *Reliques of Ancient*

English Poetry (1765), I, 124, cited the play's 'new found island' allusion (315) to the same purpose.

100 Believing the *Regent* 'would not probably have been referred to as existing after 1512', Gayley proposed 1497–1512 limits (*Representative English Comedies*, I [1903], lx), and apparently followed the conclusions reached previously by Wilhelm Swoboda (*John Heywood als Dramatiker*, Wiener Beiträge zur Deutschen und Englischen Philologie, 3 [1888], pp. 5–6, n. 2), who, however, misdated the limiting events 1498 and 1513, and thought Hick Scorner's ship imitated Barclay's *Ship of Fools* (published 1509). Arguing a more specific indebtedness to Barclay at 119–20, Bang dated the play between 1509 and (June) 1511, when English warships fought and captured Andrew Barton's (Scottish) ship, the *Lyon* (*L.P.* I.855n). Bang supposed that this ship (which did not sink) would have been included in Hick Scorner's list if the play had been written by then, and argued that the catalogue was fictitious because the historical facts of the *Regent*'s actual foundering were not used (Bang-McKerrow, pp. viii–xii). McKerrow held, on the contrary, that the nature of the reference showed, from superstitious considerations alone, that the ship had already been lost (pp. xii–xiii). Subsequent opinion has followed Brandl-McKerrow: W. W. Greg says 'not earlier than 1513' (I, 81), and the Harbage-Schoenbaum *Annals of English Drama* (1964) 1513 with limits to 1516.

101 For the *Anne*'s complex history, see Appendix I.D., pp. 246–48.

102 Appendix I.D., p. 249.

103 See pp. 17–22, 41–42.

104 See p. 8.

105 Halle, 'Henry VIII', fol. 48r; *L.P.* I.3513, II.68; a slightly different version appears in *The Chronicle of Calais*, ed. John G. Nichols, Camden Soc., 35 (1846), p. 16; and Bang-McKerrow, pp. xii–xiii.

106 The history of Richard de la Pole, in so far as it relates to his early quest for the English crown, is summarised in Appendix I.A. For a discussion of the parody, see pp. 59–61.

107 The John Rastell–George Mayler action in the Court of Requests *c*. 1526–30 (concerning events perhaps *c*. 1520) distinguishes between 'stage playes in the sommer and interludes in the winter' (H. R. Plomer, 'New Documents on English Printers and Booksellers of the Sixteenth Century', *Transactions of the Bibliographical Society*, 4 [1896–98], 175), and so supports Craik's view that the interlude typically had indoor hall auspices (pp. 9–26). In *Occupation and Idleness* the two title-characters meet 'in this halle' (Winchester MS, fol. 68r); and cf. my 'The Auspices of *The World and the Child*', *Renaissance and Reformation*, 12 (1976), 96–105; and p. 48.

108 The term 'place' is discussed by Richard Southern, *The Medieval Theatre in the Round* (1957), pp. 219–36, and Bevington, p. 51. Southern's *Staging* analyses theatrical use of the Tudor great hall (pp. 45–55).

109 Riot's exit to get Pride, which leaves Youth silent on stage for a moment (316–19n), may occur because the source was carelessly condensed, or because the hall access was anticipated as being too crowded for Pride to enter effectively unless someone made room for him.

110 Also noted by Southern, pp. 217–18.

111 The garment with which Charity covered the gallant's outfit (589–90,

703–04) that Pride gave to Youth to replace his 'thin' and less 'gay' clothes (348, 486; see p. 271) was worn by one of the virtues, perhaps as a chasuble (767); it might have had an image of Christ on it (cf. *H.S.* 17n). Riot might show his stolen purse (266), and his cards and dice (679–86), and Pride possibly carried a staff of office (473n).

112 In *Sir Thomas More*, ed. C. F. Tucker Brooke in *The Shakespeare Apocrypha* (1908; rpt. 1967), More prepares for his play-banquet by ordering, 'Place me heere stooles, to set the ladyes on' (IV.i.4; cf. 103).

113 *Sir Thomas More*, IV.i.54. In 1509 Henry VIII had five players (*L.P.* I.20, p. 16). Both Bevington (pp. 114–16) and Happé (p. 9) stress that *Youth* was written for an itinerant troupe.

114 Bevington categorises these structural changes in the course of showing how *World* (c. 1508) miniaturises its source, *The Mirror of the Periods of Man's Life* (pp. 116–24); and he briefly discusses *Youth* (pp. 139–40). See pp. 40–41. He argues that Lechery exited with Youth at 546, and that her later non-appearance is an 'imperfect expedient' of the doubling scheme. If she was sent to the tavern before Youth, however, her return would not be expected. One is tempted to wonder whether Charity's question to Humility, 'Where have ye be so long?' (568), draws attention to this doubling.

115 The second may bear a specifically northern sense. See also 'thought' (Q2 11), the interjection 'A' (90, perhaps 411; but cf. *H.S.* 446), 'ony' (Q1 116; but cf. *H.S.* 444), 'henged' (Q2–Q3 227), the preposition 'be' (Q2–Q3 134, 262; Q2 665), and 'shyll' (687; but cf. *H.S.* 437). Less certain are 'heritor' (92), 'Aback' (40), 'avow' (364, 612) and 'afeard' (498), despite Richard O. Heslop's *Northumberland Words*, I (1892), 5, 7.

116 Ending speeches with a non-rhyming line is a regular practice here (e.g., 39, 89, 96, 104, 125, 132, 144, etc.) and in *Everyman*, but for possibly corrupt rhymes (or passages), see 227–28, 683–84. Typical cases of assonance are at 99–100, 188–89, 258–59, 435–36. See Norman Davis, 'Two Unprinted Dialogues in Late Middle English, and their Language', *Revue des Langues Vivantes*, 35 (1969), 469. Note the loss of *t* after *s* (192), of *r* before *n* (255) and of *d* after *n* (786) – features in the main also true of *H.S.* (see n. 144).

117 As northern dialects generally have *a* for the reflex of OE. *ā* and *ā(w)* (cf. Brook, p. 64), the triplet (?) 'shame'/'name'/'known' (407–09) may be relevant here; and the rhyme at 192/195 apparently depends on a northern form.

118 Brook, pp. 65–66 (but see Dobson, §373, for another explanation); Dobson, §399; Joseph Wright, *The English Dialect Grammar* (1905), §274. Other rhymes that may show loss of [g] (in connection with the commoner loss of *d*) are at 105–06 and 568–70.

119 See Appendix III. Charles R. Baskervill, in his 'Mummers' Wooing Plays in England', *Modern Philology*, 21 (1923–24), first noted this indebtedness to *Youth* (pp. 232–34).

120 Chambers, *M.S.*, II, 184–85, n. 2, and 257; John Gage, '. . . extracts from the Household Book of Edward Stafford, Duke of Buckingham', *Archaeologia*, 25 (1834), 318–19, 324–25. The fourth earl's troupe was at Selby Abbey, in the West Riding, in 1479–80, and his son's players were

there twice *c*. 1500 (Glynne Wickham, *Early English Stages*, I [1966], 332–37).

121 Percy 1, pp. 343–45, 351. This book contains budgets, payment schedules, checker-rolls, model warrants and other administrative articles, some from 1511 (though transcribed, apparently, in September–October 1514), with accretions dated up to 1524. These revels personnel are listed in a customary rewards schedule written after 1524, but they clearly existed as well in 1511–14. The earl also employed (1) a Christmas Abbot of Misrule (Percy 1, p. 344) and Master of Revels to arrange 'his Lordships Playes Interludes and Dresinge that is plaid befor his Lordship in his Hous in the xijth Dayes of Cristenmas' (Percy 1, p. 346); (2) three minstrels (tabor, lute and rebec), and (3) as many as eleven chapel gentlemen (three basses, four countertenors and four tenors), one of whom was master of the chapel's six children (Percy 1, pp. 42, 324–25; cf. 40–41, 44, 198, 254, 257). On Twelfth Night the second household book, containing ceremonialia, directs that 'their be aithir play as an entirlude A comody or trigidy to be plaied afoir the lord and the laidy afoir the disguising', and similar revels were part of a family wedding feast (Percy 2, fols. 40r, 30r; these items date from ? *c*. 1510–15). For a description of this unpublished MS, see D. M. Barratt, 'A Second Northumberland Household Book', *The Bodleian Library Record*, 8 (1968), 93–98. My edition, 'Orders for Twelfth Day and Night *c*. 1515 in the Second Northumberland Household Book', is forthcoming in *English Literary Renaissance*. Entries for 18 (?) and 23 December in P.R.O. MS E 36.226, p. 16, give (disguising) expenses for the earl's 1514 Christmas.

122 Among the earl's household chaplains is 'The Almonar and if he be a maker of Interludys than he to have a Servaunt to the intent for Writynge of the Parts' (Percy 1, pp. 44, 254). The almoner's servant is noted in the household meal schedule in spring 1511 (pp. 87, 95). Historical Manuscripts Commission, *Report on the Manuscripts of the Corporation of Beverley* (1900), p. 171. Play-writing seems to have been one of an almoner's traditional duties. At Westminster Abbey *c*. 1526 the sub-almoner's notebook records a payment of 16*d* for 'wryttyng of a play for the children' (H. F. Westlake, *Westminster Abbey: The Last Days of the Monastery* [1921], p. 35; I am grateful to Alan H. Nelson for this reference).

123 Percy evidently budgeted to pay for twenty players in perhaps four visiting companies over Christmas 1511–12, and had a going rate for earls' and lords' troupes (Percy 1, pp. 22, 340–41; cf. 158). The earl of Shrewsbury's players were in Shrewsbury in 1496 and 1510 (Chambers, *M.S.*, II, 251). The Selby Abbey records note various companies 1431–*c*. 1500 and 1527–32.

124 *C.P.*, III (1913), 294–95; IV (1916), 20–22, 73–76; XI (1949), 707–10; and for *Youth*'s politics, see pp. 56–58. The minor northern nobility also held two Dacre supporters, William, lord Conyers, of Hornby Castle, Yorkshire, and Henry, lord Scrope, of Bolton, Yorkshire, and Richard Nevill, lord Latimer, of Snape Castle, Yorkshire (III, 404–05; XI, 546–47; VII [1929], 481–82). Ralph Neville, fourth earl of Westmorland (at Brancepeth and Raby, Durham), was in 1510 Buckingham's ward (XII, part 2 [1959], 553).

125 A. G. Dickens, ed., *Clifford Letters of the Sixteenth Century*, Surtees Soc.,

172 (1962), pp. 21, 23, 96–97, 130 and n. 11; M. E. James, 'The First Earl of Cumberland (1493–1542) and the Decline of Northern Feudalism', *Northern History*, I (1966), 52; G. R. Batho, *A Calendar of the Shrewsbury and Talbot Papers*, II (1971), 325.

126 *Clifford Letters*, pp. 21–22; the full letter, from which my quotation is taken, is in Thomas D. Whitaker's *History and Antiquities of the Deanery of Craven* (1805), p. 228, where it is dated 1512–13 (p. 229).

127 These poems, extant in a former Percy MS, B.L. Royal 18.D.2, fols. 195v–end, are printed by Flügel, pp. 471–97 (for the cited extracts, see pp. 473–76, 375). Verse proverbs appeared in four other Leconfield rooms, and three Wressle rooms, in several cases (as in poems about Aristotle's advice to Alexander) discussing youth.

128 Flügel, pp. 476, 487 (cf. *Y.* 44–45, 54). For other thematic similarities, see notes to *Y.* 247–48, 348–53, 585, 645–46.

129 George Cavendish, 'The Life and Death of Cardinal Wolsey', ed. Richard S. Sylvester and Davis P. Harding, *Two Early Tudor Lives* (1962; rpt. 1964), pp. 35–36. Family histories include Edward B. De Fonblanque's *Annals of The House of Percy* (1887), I, 310–479, and M. E. James's *A Tudor Magnate and the Tudor State* (1966).

130 The fine is discussed by C. J. Harrison, 'The petition of Edmund Dudley', *English Historical Review*, 87 (1972), 87, 91. Percy was the only attendant earl denied an important role in Henry VIII's coronation (B.L. Add. MS 6113, fol. 72r; Cotton MS Tiberius E.VIII, fols. 92–93). For Henry VIII's other acts and policies, see pp. 54–57.

131 See pp. 57–58.

132 William Peeris's extant writings bear no resemblance to *Youth* whatsoever: see his metrical 'Chronicle of the family of Percy' (*c.* 1516), [ed. J. Besly] (1845) in *Reprints of Rare Tracts* (1847); and *Musicall Prouerbis in the Garet at the New Lodge in the Parke of Lekingfelde*, ed. Philip Wilson (1924). Anthony a Wood, in *Athenæ Oxonienses*, I (1691), noted: 'I have seen also an interlude of youth; Printed at *Lond.* in an old English. Char. *temp. Hen.* 8. but whether *Jo. Heywood* was the Author of it, I know not' (col. 116).

133 'The Boke of Curtasye', *Manners and Meals*, p. 323, ll. 729–30.

134 E.g., R. Wever's *Lusty Juventus* (*c.* 1550), and *Histrio-mastix* (*c.* 1599), ed. John S. Farmer, T.F.T. (1912), where Post-Hast's script for 'the new plot of the prodigall childe' has two lines possibly based on *Youth*: 'Huffa, huffa, who callis for mee? | I play the Prodigall child in iollytie' (sig. C1r; cf. *Y.* 210–11, but also *H.S.* 891–92). Such influence, of course, could derive from the early editions. The Edward VI revels 'playe of yeowthe at crystmas' is probably the dialogue *Riches and Youth*, acted at court 6 January 1551/52 (Albert Feuillerat, *Documents Relating to the Revels at Court in the Time of King Edward VI and Queen Mary*, Materialien zur Kunde des älteren Englischen Dramas, Series I, 44 [1914; rpt. 1963], pp. xiii, 268–69, 278, 299).

135 See Appendix IV. A different Pilgrim Players, comprised of students (including Mavis Walker) from the (London) Central School of Speech and Acting, toured and played in summer 1933 both *Youth* and *Like Will to Like* for various societies and churches, outdoors and indoors (as at Oxford in the Holywell Music Room). The Melbourne Mermaid Play Society, later

the Melbourne Repertory Theatre, also revived *Youth* (Agnes M. Mackenzie, *The Playgoer's Handbook to the English Renaissance Drama* [1927], p. 178n).

136 *Christian Drama*, 2 (October 1951), 10–15 (for the Trade Guild Play Festival, Market Place, Derby, on 24 May, directed by Elizabeth Heward), and 34 (at the Guild Chapel, Stratford-upon-Avon, directed by Henry Clark). *Youth* was directed at Wabash College, Crawfordsville, Indiana, by Professor Thomas P. Campbell on 23 March 1978.

137 Cf. the Q3 colophon for 'the enterlude of Hycke scorner' (sig. E4r), and Appendix II, p. 255.

138 Often termed the 'voidee', passed about at a feast's end (Chambers, *M.S.*, II, 183 and n. 1). London innyard performance (Free Will at 650 says he has just been 'at the tavern') is not documented before 1557 (Chambers, *E.S.*, II, 356), and current scholarship regards such staging for early Tudor plays sceptically (e.g., David Bevington, 'Popular and Courtly Traditions on the Early Tudor Stage', *Medieval Drama*, ed. Neville Denny, Stratford-upon-Avon Studies 16 [1973], 91–98). How interluders at this period would finance a play, at least initially, without a guaranteed sponsor and his house is also unclear.

139 Southern says that Imagination's first entrance is 'concealed among the bystanders so that Frewyll could not see him in the shadows from the torches, and has to call out for him and summon him to "come nere"' (p. 175). Southern makes the same general point about Hick Scorner's entrance and Imagination's apparent failure to see the two men with the converted Free Will (pp. 175, 179), and discusses the problems of lighting a hall (pp. 53–55), which he assumes to be the play's place of performance (pp. 168–80).

140 The separate exits of Pity, and then of Contemplation and Perseverance, followed by Free Will's entrance (152–56), may demand three doors, though here and at 645–46 Southern argues just in terms of the hall's screened double exit (pp. 174, 178). Three entrances were normally available in the Tudor hall (pp. 49–52).

141 The often-reproduced Q1 factotum woodcuts, which antedate the play, do not depict its original costuming: see n. 45, and Alfred W. Pollard, 'Some Notes on English Illustrated Books', *Trans. of the Bibl. Soc.*, 6 (1901), 38.

142 *Magnyfycence*, p. cxxxiii; Bevington, pp. 138–39.

143 The costume change, for which Free Will's thirty-six-line opening monologue exists, may have been speeded up if, as evidently is the case, both Perseverance (cf. 85) and the recently stocked Imagination were poorly dressed.

144 Some rhymes are imperfect: there is pervasive assonance before nasals (93–94, 150–51), before the voiceless stops p, t and k (68/70, 214–15, 635–36), and before g and d (476–77); stressed and unstressed syllables are rhymed; and some couplets apparently depend on plural endings (478–79, 586–88) and syllabic [ŋ] (604–05, 966–67). Other seemingly irregular rhymes are, however, true: in early Tudor pronunciation *th* often becomes *f* (258–59), and *r* is lost before *n* (663, 829), *s* (261, 266, 660) and *t* (183), while the dropping of *d* after *n*, for which see Wyld, p. 115, and Dobson, §410 (i), explains rhymes at 280–81, 515/517, 866/868/870 and 1027–28.

145 Unstressed syllables generally lose [g] in -ing endings (e.g., 137–38, 997/999), but rhymes such as 'strong'/'England' (379–80), 'England'/'long' (565/569; cf. 87–89) and 'him'/'bring' (779–80; cf. 851–52) also appear. See Wyld, pp. 112–13; Dobson, §377 (iii), 399. For -ond as an East Midland characteristic, see Brook, p. 67, Dobson, §71, and H.S. 222–24, 620/624. Rhyme at 525–27 does not usually characterise northern or south-western dialects (see O.E.D., 'iron', sb.¹), and cf. verbal forms at 78 and 362.

146 The play mentions, besides the place-names discussed above, Newgate, Tyburn, Holborn, St Giles-in-the-Field, Ludgate and the Swan at Newgate. Among early plays whose local allusions have been used to identify the place of performance are the Wakefield pageants and Mankind.

147 For another possible Southwark allusion, see 447n.

148 Chambers lists mid-fifteenth-century performances at St Margaret's Church, and a play acted in defiance of obsequies for Henry VIII (M.S., II, 381–82, 222).

149 Survey of London, XXII (1950), ed. Ida Darlington, 46–47; XXV (1955), ed. I. Darlington, 22–3; and C. L. Kingsford, 'London Topographical Gleanings', London Topographical Record, 13 (1923), 47–8.

150 C.P., XII, part I (1953), 454 (and for other biographical information, pp. 454–60); and David J. Johnson, Southwark and the City (1969), pp. 100, 429.

151 Brandon as King's Bench Marshall in the February 1511 tournament at Westminster entered 'Into the ffeeld enclosid In a Towyr and led by a Jaylour holdyng a grete keye In his hand', and wore 'a long & course prisoners wede' over the jousting armour until the queen freed him from both prison and prison clothes (The Great Chronicle of London, ed. A. H. Thomas and I. D. Thornley [1938], p. 372). The play's song-references are at 182, 207, 360 and 692–93, and Brandon's part in Henry VIII's revels can be found described in L.P. II, pp. 1496–98, 1500–01. Imagination's fear that Free Will may be beguiled 'searching on a hill' (906) may allude to Manor Place's site on St Margaret's Hill. A Southwark map c. 1542 that locates these place-names can be seen in Rendle, front.

152 Lewis Wynwod, Brandon's servant in 1514, supplied costumes for Henry VIII's Christmas revels that year, when Brandon took part (L.P. II, p. 1501), and so functioned like Richard Gybson, one of the king's players and his revels' supervisor. The four players who came out of Suffolk to play before the Lord Steward (George Talbot, the earl of Shrewsbury) in Henry's hall in January 1512 (L.P. II, p. 1454) may have been connected with the Suffolk-based Brandon family. By 1525 Brandon was sponsor of a troupe of four interluders (Chambers, M.S., II, 252), and the absence of evidence of his patronage earlier suggests he indeed had no company of players after 1515, when the duke disgraced himself and incurred heavy financial penalties because of his secret marriage to the widowed French queen, Henry's sister Mary.

153 Paul R. Baumgartner, 'The Date of Cocke Lorelles Bote', Studies in Bibliography, 19 (1966), pp. 175–81; and see p. 45. For verbal similarities, see H.S. 183, 622–24, 750, 821 and perhaps 179, 232, 317, 388, 440, 663, 820 and 834.

154 John M. Berdan's Early Tudor Poetry, 1485–1547 (1920) sees 'normal

Medieval Latin measures' in the poem, but notes no other early vernacular use of them (pp. 222, 224); cf. Baumgartner, 'Cocke Lorelles Bote: A Critical Edition', unpublished Ph.D. thesis (Chapel Hill, N.C., 1961), pp. 5–9. For H.S. rhymes, see n. 144. Prosody alone rules out attribution to verse satirists like Skelton, Barclay and Robert Copland.

155 Cocke Lorelles Bote has a pardoner who wearies Cock (cf. Chaucer's Host) with his religious spiel, and interrupts it to drink, as his Chaucerian counterpart did before telling his tale (sigs. B3v–4r, B5v). At the end of a long list of craftsmen (sigs. B6v–C1r) the poet introduces various rogues; and over fifteen of these, including the unique 'Tyburne collopes' ('Tyburn flesh', not elsewhere in M.E.D. or O.E.D.) and the rare 'facers' and 'chylderne quellers' (both also not elsewhere found, though the first recurs c. 1550), appear previously in the A.G. list of Vice's commoners (697, 674, 709), which H.S. adapts differently. Neither source has been argued before.

156 See pp. 9–10, and Appendix II.

157 J. C. Trewin, The Birmingham Repertory Theatre: 1913–1963 (1963), p. 244; Malvern Festival 1931 (programme; the B.L. copy W. P. 5113); 'Malvern Dramatic Festival', The Malvern Gazette, 7 August 1931, p. 5; and Appendix IV. The cast was Eric Stanley (Pity), Grosvenor North (Contemplation), Richard Riddle (Perseverance), Jack Carlton (Free Will), Robert Donat (Imagination) and Gilbert Davis (Hick Scorner).

158 'Dramatic Antiquities at Malvern', Shaw on Theatre, ed. E. J. West (1958), p. 227; cf. The Times, 4 August 1931, p. 8.

159 The record is The First Stage (SW A–12, Part 2; SW–221, side I). Cf. Potter, p. 232.

160 The cast was Joseph Pastor (Pity), William Dean (Contemplation), Stephen Klein (Perseverance), Bruce Salvatore (Free Will), Paul Baker (Imagination) and John Cartwright (Hick Scorner).

161 Ruth H. Blackburn says Youth 'contains so many overtones from Luke 15 [11–32] that it almost, if not quite, qualifies as a native attempt at a Prodigal Son Play' (Biblical Drama Under the Tudors [1971], p. 22). Though Youth, like the Prodigal Son, spends his heritage in part on 'riotous living' ('vivendo luxuriose') and fast women, and is eventually reclothed (Luke xv.13, 22, 30), the play is not based on the parable: Youth has no living father or brother, gets land instead of goods, does not journey from home, is not bankrupted, never becomes a servant, and repents without a family reunion. If Youth is indebted to biblical matter, it is in the allegory of Christ's passion in Charity's binding; and see Appendix III.5.

162 Until recently, Hick Scorner was thought by many to be Youth's source (see p. 41).

163 For the use of some uncommon expressions from Nature, see notes to Y. 130, 210 and 365 (also perhaps 376 and 413); Riot's hybrid oath, 'for God avow' (364, 612), is apparently a Medwall invention.

164 Charity and Pride, like Reason and Sensuality, also quarrel about using 'fellow' in personal address (480).

165 The character may be influenced by Hawes's Example, where Discretion tells Youth, 'And ryotous company do thou not haunt | For that wyll payre and yll thy name' (502–03), but 'Riot' was traditionally held to be a young

man's vice (*Y.* 207n), probably from the Prodigal Son parable, and the abstraction is not uncommon in early Tudor verse. Barclay's *Ship of Fools* yokes all three *Youth* vices in stating that 'many all waste aboute Ryot and pryde' (I, 158) and that hospitality is what 'pryde ryot and Uenus suffreth nat to be' (I, 159), and has Virtue tell Voluptuosity: 'In the is pryde: and all thy wanton wyll | Is set on ryot and wretchyd lechery' (II, 303). Riot appears in 'Old Christmas' (printed in 1533), ed. W. W. Greg, *Collections: Volume IV*, Malone Soc. (1956), pp. 35–37; in Thomas Churchyard's 'Discourse of the Queenes Majestie's Entertainment in Suffolk and Norfolk' (1578), *The Progresses and Public Processions of Queen Elizabeth*, ed. John Nichols, 2nd ed. (1823), II, 194–96; and in Skelton's early 'Bowge of Courte' (*Works*, I, ll. 344–417), where some parallels between its and the play's Riot occur (see notes to *Y.* 255, 679, 681), though Skelton's figure is no felon, and political events have much to do with our playwright's choice of this term (see p. 57).

166 Worldly Affection's offer to take Margery off Man's hands, and his jealous response (II, 239–56), may have suggested Riot's flirtation with Lechery.

167 For other possible uses, by Youth, of Man's social rank, behaviour and dress, see 312, 435 and 486; of Pride's words, 701–05; and of Sensuality's words, 40–41.

168 Other instances of how Pride's clothes-obsession in *Nature* affects *Youth* may be found at 589–90 and 703–04. *Youth*'s Pride alludes at 317 to his namesake's alias, and at 603–04 to his snobbish objection to Reason's birth.

169 Though Medwall does not explicitly equate these figures, none appears in person, and Sensuality implies their identity in saying Man, after seeing Kate and Margery, is 'famylyer | Wyth bodely lust' (I, 1185–86). For *Everyman* figures like these, see n. 173.

170 See also 600, and, for the rogues' debt to *Nature* in counter-attack, 645–46.

171 J. T. Grein first argued there was 'ample evidence to show that the author of the Interlude was deeply influenced by "Everyman"' ('The English Drama Society', *Sunday Times* [London, 17 December 1905], p. 4).

172 Man's seven sins, except Covetous, also desert him in age, but they do not swear such oaths (though *Nature* may be an influence at 755).

173 Riot's wish 'to make good cheer' (235) and to provide Youth with 'a wench to kiss' (287) may reflect Fellowship's proposal to 'ete & drynke & make good chere, | Or haunt to women the lusty company' (272–73), and Cousin's offer of his 'mayde', who 'loueth to go to feestes, these to be nyse' (360–61; cf. *Y.* 412). For other parallels, see *Y.* 4, 47, 245, 393.

174 Hawes's concluding comment that the union of the White and Red Roses is 'In all clennes and vertuous courage' (2091) suggests that he regarded Cleanness and Virtue as types of Elizabeth and Henry, but Hawes also compliments the young prince of Wales as 'Surmontynge in vertue' (2096), and the poem may refer allegorically to his projected, on-again-off-again match with his brother's widow Catherine of Aragon. Later prince Henry was the centre of a cult of Youth and himself took on the allegorical name (see p. 54).

175 Medwall's Kate and Margery, however, are ironically termed 'full curteys' at the tavern (I, 1128; *Y.* 425).

176 Hawes's poem may have influenced *Y*. 92–96, 110 and 245 as well, and see n. 165.

177 Cf. p. 25. The opening scenes with Nature, the World and Innocency in Medwall's first part, and *II Nature*, which deals with Man's middle and old age, are mined for thematic material (362–73, 553–61, 717–26), but are ignored where action is concerned, except for the Humility–Charity relationship.

178 Certain variants in the poem's early texts (see Appendix III.3, ll. 646, 696, 897) show the playwright to have used *S.T.C.* 17006, an edition by Wynkyn de Worde at Westminster *c.* 1500, reproduced in facsimile by Francis Jenkinson (1906), or a later edition derived from it. For the poem's extant MSS and printings, see Triggs's edition, pp. vii–x; Gavin Bone, 'Extant Manuscripts Printed from by W. de Worde', *Libr.*, 4th ser., 12 (1931–32), 303; William Ringler, 'The Fragment "Virtue" and "The Assemble of Goddes": STC 24844a and 17005–17007a', *Papers of the Bibliographical Society of America*, 47 (1953), 378–80; Bradford Y. Fletcher, 'The Textual Tradition of *The Assembly of Gods*', *ibid.*, 71 (1977), 191–94. Henry N. MacCracken, ed., *The Minor Poems of John Lydgate*, E.E.T.S. E.S. 107, part I (1911), discredits the Lydgate attribution (pp. xxxv–xxxvi).

179 There are many resemblances to the anonymous *Cocke Lorelles bote* (see n. 153). John Skelton's 'Bowge of Courte' (see notes to *H.S.* 211–12, 214, 368, 393–99, 652), and the mummers' play (see notes to *H.S.* 308–24, 452, 745–53).

180 See Appendix III.2 and 4, pp. 260–61, 266, and notes to *H.S.* 10–20, 34–38 and 546–601. John Peter, in his *Complaint and Satire in Early English Literature* (1956), follows Hazlitt (I, 174) in noting the similarity of Pity's complaint to the ballad, but sees no echo of it in the play (p. 190). My article, 'The Sources of *Hyckescorner*', *R.E.S.*, new series, 22 (1971), 257–73, discusses the play's debts to all but the 'Long Charter of Christ'.

181 See Alfred W. Pollard, ed., *English Miracle Plays, Moralities and Interludes* (1890), p. liv; Katharine L. Bates, *The English Religious Drama* (1893), pp. 222–24; Charles M. Gayley, ed., *Representative English Comedies*, I (1903), lxxiv; W. Creizenach, *Geschichte des Neueren Dramas*, III (1903), 503.

182 Bang-McKerrow, pp. vii–viii; Schell, pp. 468–74.

183 For instance, *Y*. 441–57 (Youth's fighting coin-servants) parallels *H.S.* 170 (a coin-personification) and at least in part 428–52 (the brawl of Free Will's fellow rogues), and *Youth*'s conflation of these two quite unrelated passages is improbable. The priority problem is discussed at more length in my 'Sources of *Hyckescorner*', pp. 257–60.

184 In *Hick Scorner* the juxtaposition of the three virtues' first monologues with those of their three rogue opposites seems to reflect the balanced opening Charity–Youth monologues.

185 The projected stews visit (405) and Free Will's subsequently revealed tavern wine-drinking (650) are presumably based on Youth's exit to a tavern with Riot and Pride to drink wine with Lechery.

186 For other debts, see notes to *H.S.* 179, 194, 245, 444, 468, 537, 705–10, 768.

187 For a summary, see Appendix III.3. Ramsay perceptively argues that *Hick Scorner* is, of all moralities, closest to Prudentius' *Psychomachia* (*Magnyfycence*, p. clv).

188 *H.S.* 339–52, 368–79. The playwright's catalogue form (phrases linked by 'and' or 'with') and unusual mixture of abstractions and human social types also point to this source. For other possible debts to these lists, see *H.S.* 47, 385, 546–601.

189 The poem's influence can also be detected in Free Will's being brought to 'virtue' (488, 619; personified at 880) and 'Sadness' (881), Free Will's disguised appearance to Imagination (908–10) and the emphasis on 'virtuous living' (618; personified at 1025).

190 Cf. also *H.S.* 987n.

191 See pp. 34–35; and notes to *H.S.* 302, 389, 820–45. Citing a doubtful parallel at *H.S.* 119–20, Bang argues that Barclay's translation is a source, and assumes the general influence (p. ix) that Wilhelm Swoboda earlier saw (*John Heywood als Dramatiker* [1888], pp. 5–6, n. 2). For a useful survey, see Paul R. Baumgartner, 'From Medieval Fool to Renaissance Rogue: *Cocke Lorelles Bote* and the Literary Tradition', *Annuale Mediaevale*, 4 (1963), 57–91.

192 See notes to *H.S.* 116–18, 274–94, 378, 546–601, 751–53.

193 See pp. 53–58. *Youth*'s satire of two preoccupations of the rich and well-born, Pride's clothes-snobbery and Riot's skill at cards, dice and other games are virtually ignored in *Hick Scorner*.

194 Bevington, p. 139.

195 Schell, pp. 470–71.

196 The term 'morality' was first used for early English plays in 1742, only a year after it entered the language in an English translation of Luigi Riccoboni's *Réflections historiques et critiques sur les différents théâtres de l'Europe* (Potter, pp. 197–98, 247; he rightly explains, as 'a non-recurrent borrowing', the use of the term to describe a play by English interluders in 1503 at Scottish court revels for the marriage of Margaret Tudor and James IV).

197 The meaning of 'interlude' is defined or discussed in the *M.E.D.* ('enterlude, -ludi', n.), F. P. Wilson's *The English Drama, 1485–1585*, ed. G. K. Hunter (1969), pp. 10–11, and *Early Middle English Verse and Prose*, ed. J. A. W. Bennett and G. V. Smithers (1966), p. 196. Further examples from medieval records are given in Stanley J. Kahrl's *Traditions of Medieval English Drama* (1974), pp. 101–02. See also n. 107.

198 *Sir David Lyndesay's Works*, ed. J. Small and F. Hall, E.E.T.S. O.S. 11, 19, 35, 37 (1865–69; rpt. 1969), p. 447; and *H.S.* 446n.

199 Despite similarities, the *moralité* and the *farce* are discrete forms. Grace Frank says the first is characterised by 'a didactic intention expressed in symbol and story', and the second by 'an expression of the colourful, everyday life and language of their time' (*The Medieval French Drama* [1954; rpt. 1967], pp. 246–47).

200 See Richard L. Greene, 'The Meaning of the Corpus Christi Carol', *Medium Ævum*, 29 (1960), 10–21, and his 'A Carol of Anne Boleyn by Wyatt', *R.E.S.*, N.S., 25 (1974), 437–39. Both discuss allegorical treatments of Henry VIII's desertion of Catherine of Aragon for Anne Boleyn.

201 As far as is known, no cycle pageant was ever published in this period. Up to 1530 the content of scriptural plays may have seemed, for printers like de Worde, too apolitical and commonplace to appeal to the book-buying public. The script of the Manchester fragment of the Chester 'Resurrec-

tion' play, however, partly imitates black-letter type (R. M. Lumiansky and David Mills, ed., *The Chester Mystery Cycle*, E.E.T.S. S.S. 3 [1974], p. x) and may have been copied from an edition.

202 Robert W. Frank, Jr., 'The Art of Reading Medieval Personification-Allegory', *Journal of English Literary History*, 20 (1953), 237–50, is a helpful discussion.

203 Bartholomaeus Anglicus, *De Proprietatibus Rerum* (1495), fols. m2v–m3r (*S.T.C.* 1536); *The Parlement of the Thre Ages*, ed. M. Y. Offord, E.E.T.S. E.S. 246 (1959); *Ratis Raving, and Other Moral and Religious Pieces*, ed. J. Rawson Lumby, E.E.T.S. O.S. 43 (1870); R. H. Bowers, 'A Medieval Analogue to *As You Like It* II.vii.137–66', *Shakespeare Quarterly*, 3 (1952), 109–12 (B.L. Add. MS 37049, fols. 28v–29r; a dialogue with illustrations); 'The Mirror of the Periods of Man's Life', *Hymns to the Virgin and Christ*, ed. F. J. Furnivall, E.E.T.S. O.S. 24 (1867), pp. 58–78; Campbell Dodgson, *Catalogue of Early German and Flemish Woodcuts preserved in the Department of Prints and Drawings in the British Museum* (1903), I, 116–17, 225; (1911), II, 38; R. Wever, *An Enterlude called lusty Iuuentus, Lyuely discribing the frailtye of youth: of nature, prone to vice: by grace and good counsayll, trayne=able to vertue* (*c.* 1565; *S.T.C.* 25149). Samuel C. Chew, in 'This Strange Eventful History', *Joseph Quincy Adams Memorial Studies*, ed. James G. McManaway, Giles E. Dawson and Edwin E. Willoughby (1948), pp. 157–82, is a general critical overview of the subject. For Youth's traditional age limits, see *The Customs of London, otherwise called Arnold's Chronicle* [ed. F. Douce] (1811), p. 157 (written before 1503?); and cf. Samuel A. Small, 'The *Iuventus* Stage of Life', *Philologica: The Malone Anniversary Studies*, ed. Thomas A. Kirby and Henry Bosley Woolf [1949], p. 236.

204 W. Roy MacKenzie, *The English Moralities from the Point of View of Allegory* (1914), says that 'All the characters, both virtuous and vicious, are to be interpreted solely as forces struggling for supremacy in the heart of the hero' (p. 105). For the controversial term 'psychomachia', see *Magnyfycence*, pp. cxlix–cli, and Potter, pp. 37–38.

205 Walter Hilton's *Scala perfeccōnis* (Wynkyn de Worde, 1494; *S.T.C.* 14042), for example, says that, though both meekness (or humility) and charity are Christ's 'specyall lyuerey', meekness is the 'firste & the last of all vertues . . . [the] kepyng & sauyng of all other vertues', and that Charity, 'a free yefte of god', can be held only by those who are 'perfytly and sothfastly meke' (sigs. e6r, cιv, f8r; chapters 51, 18, 68). *Humilitas* leads the virtues in *The Castle of Perseverance* (*Macro Plays*, p. 62), as Meekness does in *Nature* (see p. 38). See also Adolf Katzenellenbogen, *Allegories of the Virtues and Vices in Mediaeval Art* (1939; rpt. 1964), p. 63.

206 In the middle ages courtly love was widely viewed as cupidity, the antithesis of charity: see D. W. Robertson, Jr., *A Preface to Chaucer* (1962; rpt. 1969), pp. 24–30, 391–503. At Henry VII's court *c.* 1500 interest in courtly love was, to one spectator, non-existent: 'And although their dispositions are somewhat licentious, I never have noticed any one, either at court or amongst the lower orders, to be in love; whence one must necessarily conclude, either that the English are the most discreet lovers in the world, or that they are incapable of love' (*Relation*, p. 24).

207 Happé, for instance, thinks the conversion is 'Dramatically . . . very sudden, and without motivation' (p. 394), as does Joyce E. Peterson, 'The Paradox of Disintegrating Form in *Mundus et Infans*', *English Literary Renaissance*, 7 (1977), 5–6.

208 G. R. Owst, *Literature and Pulpit in Medieval England* (1961), pp. 471–547.

209 Winchester MS, fols. 70r, 73r. Note how Youth thinks Riot 'steadfast of mind' (247–48; cf. 212–13), and accuses Charity of what Riot has done (138; cf. 227–32).

210 In one cycle Caiaphas pledges that he will fast until Christ 'be stald | In the stokys' (*Towneley Plays*, XXI, 202–03), Christ in the buffeting scene is set on a 'stole' (XXIX, 359), and the Second Torturer even describes crucifixion as a punishment where Christ 'syttys in yond sett' (XXIII, 100). While Charity says a 'knight with a spear' (167) stabbed Christ to death, Youth, like Caiaphas (XXI, 443–44), repeatedly threatens the virtue with a dagger, and Riot, 'knight of the collar' (270), fetches chains to bind him.

211 Paul said that backsliders recrucified Christ (Hebrews vi.6); and swearing by his body was compared to the tormentors' 'dismembrynge of Crist' (Chaucer's *Parson's Tale*, l. 590; cf. *Pardoner's Tale*, ll. 708–09). V. A. Kolve, in *The Play Called Corpus Christi* (1966), argues that the cycles' '*tortores* mirror a common human nature' (p. 221).

212 In *The Pride of Life*, the King of Life evidently stresses his youth (*Non-Cycle Plays*, ll. 420, 431).

213 Larry D. Benson, *Art and Tradition in Sir Gawain and the Green Knight* (1965), pp. 65–67, 75. Note how Youth, a recent heir to his late father's lands (57), contrasts with Charity, who would make all men heirs to God the Father (23, 92); and how Youth profanes the mass (55) for the celebration of which Charity is essential (35–39).

214 John W. Jones, 'Observations on the Origin of the Division of Man's Life into Stages', *Archaeologia*, 35 (1853), 174, 176–77. Sometimes the wheel of fortune, with a king at its top, was the model for the wheel of life, with Youth at its top.

215 *L.P.* I.2277 (Cardinal Bainbridge from Rome to Wolsey). An Italian wrote then that 'to everyone the King seems a being descended from Heaven' (*L.P.* I.2265).

216 See pp. 19–21.

217 Stevens, pp. 344, 392, 411. Henry's songs are occasionally echoed in *Youth*: 'Who shall me lett?' (Stevens, p. 344; *Y.* 70), 'Who love dysdaynyth ys all of the village' (Stevens, p. 407; *Y.* 603–04), 'I pray you all that aged be, | How well dyd ye your yough carry?' (Stevens, p. 411; *Y.* 642–46); and note *Y.* 45n. The hero of Hawes's *Example of Vertu* (written c. 1503–04) was Youth, whose adventures may have been intended to instruct the (then) thirteen-year-old prince of Wales. When catalogued *temp.* Mary, the arras hangings of Greenwich Palace included 'The story of youth' and 'The Seven Ages' ([Edward] *Hasted's History of Kent*, ed. Henry H. Drake [1886], I, 60, n. 4).

218 *L.P.* I.2157 (and cf. *Y.* 163n).

219 Excellent contemporary Venetian descriptions of Henry appear in *Four Years*, I, 76, 86–87, and II, 312–13. Cf. Scarisbrick, pp. 3–20, and Frank A. Mumby, *The Youth of Henry VIII* (1913).

220 Stevens, p. 416.

221 Scarisbrick, p. 54; cf. *Four Years*, II, 313; Edward, Lord Herbert of Cherbury, *The Life and Raigne of King Henry the Eighth* (1649), p. 9.

222 *Four Years*, I, 90–91.

223 Halle, 'Henry VIII', fol. 11v; Skelton's 'Why Come Ye Nat to Courte?' mentions a Domyngo Lomelyn winning much from Henry at 'the cardys and haserdynge' (II, 63, ll. 1187–90); *Four Years*, II. 312.

224 Scarisbrick, p. 14; *L.P.* I.2391, p. 1058.

225 *Four Years*, II, 313; also Scarisbrick, p. 16.

226 Stevens, p. 407; Halle, 'Henry VIII', fol. 9r. Henry, disguised as one of his yeomen of the guard, visited the King's Head Tavern in Cheapside to see the watch on midsummer's night, 1510 (*Songs*, p. 156).

227 *L.P.* I.474.

228 *L.P.* I.3163; Scarisbrick, p. 147; Betty Behrens, 'A Note on Henry VIII's Divorce Project of 1514', *Bulletin of the Institute of Historical Research*, 11 (1933–34), 163–64, and *L.P.* I.3206. According to French sources, before Henry left the continent in autumn 1513 he, 'for love of a lady, had clad himself and his court in mourning' (*Venice*, II, no. 355).

229 Mumby, *Youth of Henry VIII*, pp. 349–50; *Calendar of Letters . . . Relating to the Negotiations Between England and Spain*, II, ed. G. A. Bergenroth (1866), no. 44.

230 R. R. Reid, *The King's Council in the North* (1921), pp. 77–91, 487. The other known Lieutenants or High Commissioners were William Sever, abbot of St Mary's of York, and Thomas Savage, archbishop of York (Wolsey's later bishopric).

231 *S.R.*, II (1816), 11 Hen. VII. c. 3, 7; 12 Hen. VII. c. 2; 19 Hen. VII. c. 13 (confirming the two previous statutes, as well as 13 Hen. IV. c. 7). Reid, *King's Council*, p. 83.

232 *Letters of Richard Fox, 1486–1527*, ed. P. S. and H. M. Allen (1929), pp. 43–44. The servants also suggested Buckingham as protector of all England.

233 Reid, *King's Council*, pp. 90–93; *L.P.* I.132.5, 857.19 and 1003.17.

234 *S.R.*, III (1817), 1 Hen. VIII. c. 6 (this repealed 11 Hen. VII. c. 3, on which the riot statutes depended); cf. Appendix I.B, p. 243. From 1509 to 1514 Northumberland was on the Commissions of the Peace for Northumberland, Yorkshire and Sussex (*L.P.* I. App.1).

235 A. F. Pollard, *Wolsey*, 2nd ed. (1953), pp. 13–14. A letter of 2 August 1513 notes 'there are two obstinate men, who govern everything, the grand esquire [Brandon] and the almoner' (*L.P.* I.2141).

236 *D.N.B.*, XXI, 797–98 (Wolsey was made dean of Lincoln in February 1509, dean of York in February 1513, and bishop elect of Lincoln by February 1514); Pollard, *Wolsey*, p. 21 (archbishop elect of York by August 1514); and see p. 29. Common gossips in 1509 were also linking Wolsey's patron Fox with the earl and Buckingham (*Letters of Richard Fox*, p. 44).

237 Pollard, *Wolsey*, pp. 13, 20; *Four Years*, II, 314.

238 The fact that Paulet was at first excluded from Henry VIII's general pardon of 1509 may be significant here (*L.P.* I.11.10, 158.86), since Wolsey may have had a part in drafting it.

239 Some might have seen Riot as Brandon, since the future duke of Suffolk was closer than anyone at this time to being Henry's 'compeer', and Pride as

Compton (see above, pp. 33–34); the two were Henry's special aides in a jousting match in 1510 (Halle, 'Henry VIII', fol. 8v). Among the king's yeoman ushers in 1511 was, oddly enough, one William Riote (*L.P.* I.707).

240 Having been examined in the Star Chamber by Henry on 2 May 1516, apparently on a subject to do with Dacre's administration, Northumberland was committed to the Fleet prison, where he remained in custody until 10 May (*L.P.* II.1836, 1861, 1870, and cf. 2460).

241 *Reliques of Ancient English Poetry* (1765), I, 123. R. L. Ramsay suggests that the characters are psychological aspects of an absent man-type, Pity the virtuous mind and Hick Scorner its vicious aspect, Perseverance the virtuous will and Free Will its vicious aspect, and Contemplation and Imagination the virtuous and vicious understanding respectively; yet Ramsay also observes in the play 'the most complete disappearance of the allegorical element' and the playwright's utter disinterest in the meaning of the characters' names (*Magnyfycence*, pp. clxxxiii–clxxxv, cxcvii). W. Roy MacKenzie, in his *English Moralities from the Point of View of Allegory* (1914), also sees all the play's figures as 'characteristics of men' but evades the point of Ramsay's observations by ignoring 'the realistic embellishments', which MacKenzie says have 'nothing to do with the main plot' (pp. 40, 43). Arnold Wynne's *Growth of English Drama* (1914), on the contrary, thinks the realistic characterisation, particularly of Imagination, has quite overshadowed 'plot-building' (pp. 66–67, 70–71). See also n. 254.

242 Craik, pp. 79–80. Potter agrees that the three sinners are 'a series of Breughel-like genre figures' (p. 41).

243 See p. 32. B. J. Whiting, *Proverbs in the Earlier English Drama*, Harvard Studies in Comparative Literature, 14 (1938), p. 83, points out the title's apparent unsuitability. One would have expected 'The Interlude of Free Will'.

244 For instance, Mankind's coming to Mischief ('despair') after meeting the other vices and Titivillus is allegory (man encounters despair after sinning), not social history (a ploughman who falls in with thieves and convicts will try suicide), but Marlowe's Edward II is visited in prison by one 'Lightborn' because such a man historically murdered him there *and* because, allegorically, the devil 'Lucifer' ('the light-bearer') comes to seize the damned at death.

245 For biographical information, see Appendix I.A. The *Ship of Fools* does not appear to be an influence, except indirectly through *Cocke Lorelles bote* (see above, p. 45), but even its fools, who alone disembark at London, are harmless.

246 The English form of the name was originally 'atte Pole' (*C.P.*, XII, part I, 434, n.d.). Note Hick Scorner's visit to 'Pouille' (312); and see n. 247. None of this innuendo is in the play's known sources.

247 Hick Scorner's jailbird brothers (231, 304) Free 'Will' and (the cleric) Imagination might have recalled, though not in any detail, Richard's two brothers William (imprisoned in the Tower since 1502) and Humphrey (a cleric, died 1513). Ill Will (387), the ship captain and brother to Jack Poller, whose last name also suggests the pretender's, may also allude to this William.

248 For information on his early life, see Appendix I.B.

249 For example, Grimaldi was not, as far as is known, either a cleric or a highway robber, as Imagination is.

250 On a summer 1515 progress Henry evidently also found widespread discontent (Halle, 'Henry VIII', fols. 8r, 57r).

251 Scarisbrick, p. 33.

252 See Appendix I.D., pp. 245–48.

253 See Appendix I.C.

254 Willard Farnham's *Medieval Heritage of Elizabethan Tragedy* (1936) calls the play 'simply a product of disintegration' (p. 215), and Schell says 'the action of the play almost perversely avoids making any particular moral sense' (p. 473).

255 If the play were a psychomachia, presumably Free Will would be the man-type, and the two he summons in, his vices. In that case, why only one of them is converted is obscure (is Free Will, theoretically, not then still partly vicious?); and the status of the opening scene, where virtues (?) congregate without reference to any man-type, is unclear. Farnham also describes the play's rogues as 'like different types of corrupted mankind' (*Medieval Heritage*, p. 214), and later Bevington terms them 'three villains' or 'malefactors' and Pity the 'hero' (pp. 138–39).

256 Ramsay's scheme of the characters and of their relationships (see n. 241) bears some resemblance to that argued here (and below). L. W. Cushman, in *The Devil and the Vice in the English Dramatic Literature before Shakespeare* (1900), first suggested that Free Will and Imagination comprise a single man-type (p. 56). Alois Brandl, ed., *Quellen des Weltlichen Dramas in England Vor Shakespeare*, Quellen und Forschungen, 80 (1898), early argued that Free Will is the central man-type (p. xxviii). Ramsay says *Hick Scorner* has no man-type but instead has two vices converted (*Magnyfycence*, pp. clxviii, clxxi), and MacKenzie agrees 'Man himself is not presented in the action' (*English Moralities*, p. 40).

257 See *H.S.* 177n. 'Imagination' was one of five inward or spiritual 'wits' in medieval psychology (note the five outer 'wits' at *H.S.* 1000), and had an amoral, technical role in abstract perception clearly not referred to by the playwright (cf. Stephen Hawes, *The Pastime of Pleasure*, ed. Wm. E. Mead, E.E.T.S. O.S. 173 [1928], ll. 2845–46). A much broader and also amoral meaning, the faculty similar to memory that forms concepts or images not present to the mind (*O.E.D.*, 3), might sum up both Imagination and (his name after conversion) Good Remembrance (1007). They are here, however, very specific moral concepts.

258 Free Will's oath at this point, 'Cock's passion' (199), may indicate the parody.

259 In *The Castle of Perseverance*, *Caritas* fights against *Invidia*, and cf. *H.S.* 5n. When Hick Scorner's political identity was forgotten after Richard de la Pole's death in 1525, the vice was interpreted as an antichrist, and proverbially applied by both Protestants and Romanists to the heretical Church (see Appendix II).

260 The third of the seven works of mercy, in *Speculum Christiani*, ed. Gustaf Holmstedt, E.E.T.S. E.S. 182 (1933), ordered one to 'Chastise hym that trespasceȝ wyth scharpe reprouynge of wordys, reducynge to god-warde;

or ellys wyth dede, constrenynge ĥym ther-to be scharpe correccyon in due maner' (p. 44).

261 For such resemblances, see n. 210. Here too Pity, like Christ, enters to be accused as a 'thief' (475), ironically saving a thief from a beating (Free Will, like Barabbas), and to be threatened with both hanging and a dagger thrust (499–502).

262 Pity's pursuit of Hick Scorner is analogous to the Towneley 'Harrowing of Hell', where Satan boasts, 'I shall walk eest, I shall walk west', and Christ replies, 'Nay feynde, thou shalbe feste, | that thou shall flyt no far' (*Towneley Plays*, XXV.351, 353–54).

263 Schell says Free Will's rapid shift of allegiance from Perseverance to Contemplation shows that the interlude has a faulty moral sequence (p. 473). Cf. n. 257.

264 Christ also compares his second coming to that of a thief in the night (Matt. xxiv.42–44). Normand Berlin, in *The Base String: The Underworld in Elizabethan Drama* (1968), says that Pity 'is Christ-like in his having to suffer like a thief' (p. 56), and earlier cites (pp. 33–35) the undated Tudor 'sermon of parson Hyberdyne', which draws an elaborate analogy between Christ and condemned English thieves. This sermon is found in *The Fraternitye of Vacabondes*, ed. Edward Viles and F. J. Furnivall, E.E.T.S. E.S. 9 (1869), pp. 92–95.

265 More's Hythlodaeus describes the practice of the Polylerites, who think the 'object of public anger is to destroy the vices but to save the persons and so to treat them that they necessarily become good and that, for the rest of their lives, they repair all the damage done before' (*Utopia*, p. 79).

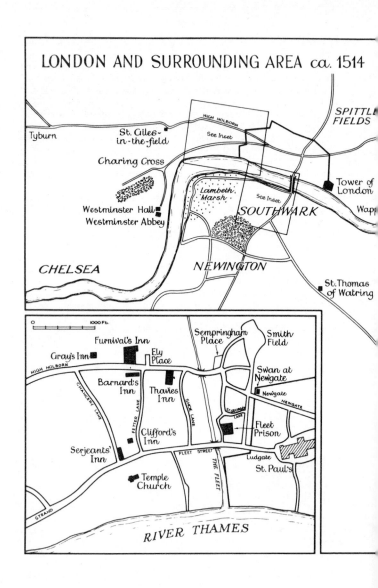

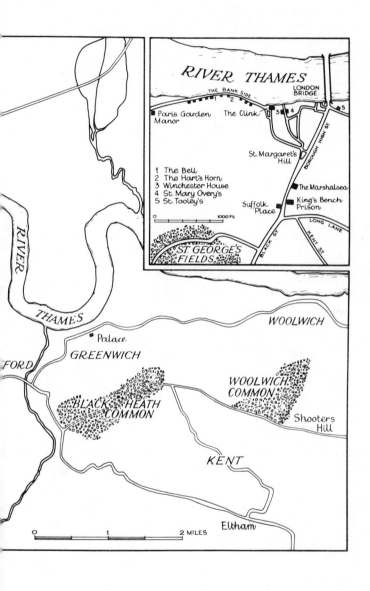

THE INTERLUDE OF YOUTH

The Interlude of Youth

[*Enter* CHARITY.]

Char. Jesu, that his arms did spread
    And on a tree was done to dead,
    From all perils he you defend.
    I desire audience till I have made an end,
    For I am come fro God above   5
    To occupy his laws to your behove
    And am named Charity.
    There may no man saved be
    Without the help of me,
    For he that Charity doth refuse,   10
    Other virtues though he do use—

1. *Char.*] *Q1; not in Q2, Q3.*   5. I] *Q1, Q3; not in Q2.*   fro] *Q1;* from *Q2,*
Q3.   11. though] *Q3;* thought *Q2.*

---

2. *tree*] cross.

dead] 'death', mainly a northern form (Bang, p. 72).

4.] a conventional opening, like 'I pray you all gyue your audyence' (*Everyman*, 1), that yet points to the play's central interest, Charity's argument, which Youth refuses to hear out until 716.

5.] In *Nature* Reason belongs to the 'grace | Of god almyghty / that from aboue ys sent' (I, 227–28), and is 'from heuen in to erth by god . . . sent' out of his 'spyrytuall loue' (I, 305, 297).

6. *occupy*] put into effect, exercise (*O.E.D.*, 6).

laws] the ten commandments (Ex. xx.3–17)? Because Charity is the New Testament's single law (see 30n), the plural is perhaps odd. In *Everyman* Death, sent by God to the world to enforce his 'lawe' (29) and 'commaundement' (65), says: 'Euery man wyll I beset that lyueth beestly | Out of Goddes lawes . . .' (74–75).

behove] behoof, advantage.

8–13.] The primacy of love or good works over, for instance, faith aligns *Y.* firmly with medieval (Romanist) doctrine.

10. *refuse*] (1) eschew the practice of; (2) reject the company of (*O.E.D.*, v., 4).

11. *though*] possibly a northern form in Q2 (Bang, p. 72).

use] (1) practise; (2) associate with (*O.E.D.*, v., 4d).

Without Charity

It will not be;

For it is written in the fay:

Qui manet in charitate, in Deo manet.   15

I am the gate, I tell thee,

Of heaven, that joyful city.

There may no man thither come

But of charity he must have some,

Or he may not come, iwis,   20

Unto heaven, the city of bliss.

Therefore, charity, who will him take,

A pure soul it will him make

12–13.] *This ed.; one line in Q2, Q3.*   12. Charity] *Q3;* charitye *Q2.*   14. fay] *This ed.;* faythe *Q2, Q3 subst.*   15. *manet.*] *Q1;* monet *Q2, Q3.*   16. gate] *Q2, Q3;* yate *Q1.*   17. Of] *Q1, Q2, Q3;* Unto *This ed. conj.*   19. charity] *Q1, Q2, Q3;* Charity *Birmingham.*   20. he] *Q1, Q3;* ye *Q2.*   22. charity] *Q1, Q2, Q3;* Charitie *Halliwell.*   him] *Q1, Q2, Q3;* to him *This ed. conj.*

12–13.] This pair of rhymes occurs four other times (7–8, 35–36, 522–23, 794–95), and four-syllable lines also appear (104, 192, 606, 713, 729).

13. *It*] man's salvation. Such loose construction is regular (23, 184, 290, etc.)

14. *fay*] (1) religious doctrine, the faith (*O.E.D.*, sb.¹, 1); (2) biblical scripture. The term is also a rhyme at 219.

15.] 'Who dwells in love dwells in God' (from 1 John iv.16) belongs to an *A.B.C.* dinner grace (see 25–26n), is the Little Chapter in the ordinary for Terce, and appears in the Epistle for the first Sunday after Pentecost. This passage follows the one quoted at 26.

16. *gate*] (1) gateway (into a walled city; *O.E.D.*, sb.¹, 3b); cf. Christ's parable of the sheepfold: 'I am the door: by me if any man enter in, he shall be saved, and shall go in and out, and find pasture' (John x.9); and also, or perhaps instead, (2) way, road (*O.E.D.*, sb.², 1; mainly northern); cf. Christ's words, 'I am the way, the truth, and the life: no man cometh unto the Father, but by me' (John xiv.6; used at *H.S.* 28), and *Y.* 136, 475, 768. The terms 'thither' (18) and 'Unto heaven' (21) may, like the Q1 form, which is northern (Bang, p. 73), favour the second sense, so that emendation at 17 (cf. *H.S.* 728) may be desirable.

17. *that joyful city*] the New Jerusalem, God's heavenly city (cf. Heb. xi.16), whose twelve gates are never shut, and where there is no more death, sorrow, lamentation or pain (Rev. xxi.4, 21–25).

18–21.] As a quality one must have, loving kindness, rather than as what one must do (in alms-giving), this concept of charity is Pauline (see 1 Cor. xiii.3).

20. *he*] Q2 abruptly breaks Charity's use of the third person (10–11, 19, 23). *iwis*] truly, to be certain.

22.] probably 'Who will to himself take charity' (Ashby suggests '[to] him', fol. 28r); cf. 37.

take] (1) exercise (*O.E.D.*, 51b); (2) befriend (*O.E.D.*, 14).

Before the face of God.
In the A.B.C., of books the least,   25
It is written: *Deus charitas est.*
Lo! charity is a great thing;
Of all virtues it is the king.
When God in earth was here living,
Of charity he found none ending.   30
I was planted in his heart;
We two might not depart.
Out of his heart I did spring

27. charity] *Q1, Q2, Q3;* Charity *Birmingham.*   30. charity] *Q1, Q2, Q3;*
Charity *Birmingham.*

24.] Direct sight of God's face, denied to Moses (Ex. xxxiii.20–23) but granted to John, and to all men at the Last Judgement (Rev. i.7, 14–16), is implicitly prophesied by Paul in his celebration of charity (1 Cor. xiii.12). This line is again unrhymed at 96.

25–26.] Thomas Petyt's 1538 edition of the primer, despite Henry VIII's break with Rome, substantially reproduces a much older text, and the almoner's grace before dinner there (drawn from 1 John iv.8, 16) ends thus: 'The kynge of eternall glory make vs to be pertenars of the celestyall mele. Amen. | God is charite / & he that dwelleth in charite dwelleth in god / and god dwelleth in hym. Let vs pray that god maye dwell in vs / and that we may dwell in hym. Amen' (*The ABC Both in Latyn & Englyshe: Being A facsimile* reprint of the earliest extant English Reading Book, ed. E. S. Shuckburgh [1889], pp. 8–9). See also H. Anders, 'The Elizabethan ABC with the Catechism', *Libr.*, 4th ser., 16 (1935–36), 38–39.

25. *the A.B.C.*] primer, regularly including (besides an alphabet) prayers, creed, the decalogue, the works of mercy, parts of church services, etc.

27–28.] 'And now abideth faith, hope, charity, these three; but the greatest of these is charity' (1 Cor. xiii.13). Among the seven cardinal virtues, however, humility is first (see above, p. 50).

29. *in*] on.

30.] Christ replaced the complex Old Testament Mosaic Law with a single new commandment, brotherly love (John xiii.34–35).

found] provided, gave (*O.E.D.*, 'find', v., 18).

31.] In *Piers the Plowman*, ed. Walter W. Skeat (1886), Love is called 'the plente of pees' (I, B.I.150), and Charity 'a ful trye tree' (I, B.XVI.4). The *Kalender of Shepardes*, printed by Julyan Notary in 1518 (*S.T.C.* 22410), systematically represents the virtues as the branches of a great tree, with charity as the leader (sig. H2r).

32. *might not depart*] could not be separated (*O.E.D.*, 'depart', v., 5). Charity imagines himself, not as Christ's love, which needed no 'might' (34) to release it for mankind, but as his very blood (the communion wine).

33–39.] This passage resembles Knowledge's speech qualifying Five Wits' praise of priests and restating his comment that man's redemption was given by

Through the might of the Heaven-king,
And all priests that be   35
May sing no mass without charity;
And charity to them they do not take,
They may not receive him that did them make,
And all this world, of nought.

[*Enter* YOUTH.]

Youth. [*To the audience*] Aback, fellows, and give me room, 40
Or I shall make you to avoid soon!
I am goodly of person;

36. sing no mass] *Q1, Q2;* not lyue *Q3.*   charity] *Q1, Q2, Q3;* Charity *Birming-ham.*   37. charity] *Q1, Q2, Q3;* Charity *Birmingham.*

God 'out of his herte with grete pyne': 'whan Iesu hanged on the crosse with grete smarte, | There he gaue out of his blessyd herte | The seuen sacramentes in grete tourment; | He solde them not to vs, that Lorde omnypotent' (*Everyman*, 720, 751–54). Priests who do so, Knowledge states, have 'Iesus curse' (756). Cf. *Y.* 167–69. On 6 February 1511/12 John Colet, dean of St Paul's, addressed the Convocation as follows: 'But sens this seculariti was broughte in, after that the secular maner of lyuynge crepte in in the men of the churche, the roote of all spirituall lyfe – that is to say, charite – was extincte. The whiche taken awaye, there can nother wyse nor stronge churche be in God' (Lupton, p. 298). In 1514 Londoners formally complained about their curates' fees, and a petition to parliament in December 1515 charged priests with uncharitability and asked for a bill forbidding them, among other things, to deny to anyone sick the sacraments (*L.P.* I.3602; II.1315).

34. *Heaven-king*] Though a genitive without *s* is northern, this is a common term (*O.E.D.*; *Everyman*, 19).

36. *sing no mass*] Elizabethan Q3 censors a Romanist phrase (which explains 38) kept by Henrician Q1 and Marian Q2.

37. *And*] if.

38. *receive*] to take into the mouth, as the sacrament (*O.E.D.*, 6). Priests were, of course, communicants at their masses; others took communion only on a few main festivals.

39. *of nought*] from nothing.

40–41.] A cry for room generally begins folk drama (Chambers, *E.F.-P.*, pp. 16–17) and interludes. In *Nature* Sensuality, demanding 'a rome' (I, 204) with Reason as Man's counsel, threatens the virtue, 'thou shalt auoyd / myche sonar than thou wenuyst' (I, 267); and cf. Bang, p. 73.

40. *Aback, fellows*] Youth may enter pushing his way through some spectators, or this may be a formulaic demand for more acting space in plays staged extemporaneously under makeshift conditions.

41. *avoid*] leave (*O.E.D.*, 6).

soon] right away.

42. *goodly of person*] physically attractive (cf. 68–69).

I am peerless wherever I come.
My name is Youth, I tell thee.
I flourish as the vine tree. 45
Who may be likened unto me
In my youth and jollity?
My hair is royal and bushed thick,
My body pliant as a hazel stick;
Mine arms be both big and strong; 50
My fingers be both fair and long,
My chest big as a tun;
My legs be full light for to run,
To hop and dance and make merry.
By the mass, I reck not a cherry 55
Whatsoever I do!
I am the heir of all my father's land,

46. likened] *Q3;* likeneth *Q2.*   48. hair] *Q1;* hearte *Q2;* hearre *Q3.*   50. big] *Q1;* fayre *Q2, Q3.*   57. all] *Q1; not in Q2, Q3.*

---

45. *the vine tree*] Youth's claim is also Christ's, 'I am the true vine', where the disciples are his fruitful branches (John xv.1–5). Cf. *Y.* 75–78, where Charity replies to this allusion by further paraphrasing these words of Christ. Henry VIII, who acted as Christ's secular arm, also depicted himself, in his song 'Grene growith the holy, | So doth the ive', as a lover whose faith was as fixed as that vine's hue (Stevens, pp. 398–99); and Henry's coronation tournament gallery used a gilt vine emblematically (Halle, 'Henry VIII', fol. 4v). A Venetian *c.* 1500 tasted grapes from English vines, but wine evidently was not made from them (*Relation*, p. 9; cf. a 1497 remark in *Two Italian Accounts of Tudor England*, trans. C. V. Malfatti [1953], p. 37).

47. *jollity*] (1) light-heartedness; (2) sexual pleasure (*O.E.D.*, 3; cf.*H.S.* 737); (3) splendour (*O.E.D.*, 7). A character of this name is associated with Fellowship in *Everyman* (16), but is not in the play. Cf. *Y.* 172, 211.

48. *royal*] finely arranged, splendid.

bushed] piled out, bushy. A conventional feature of courtiers' hair styles at this time, as with Courtly Abusion in *Magnyfycence* (835–36) and with the gallants in Barclay's *Ship of Fools*: 'To Shyp Galauntes come nere I say agayne. | Wyth your set Busshes Curlynge as men of Inde' (I, 37; cf. I, 63; II, 97, 268). The Song of Solomon beloved, who prefigures Christ, also has abundant hair (v.11; cf. iv.1, vi.5).

50. *big*] McKerrow thinks Q2–Q3 'fayre' an error (p. xxi, n. 1), presumably one attracted by 'fair' in the following line, but 'big' might also have been attracted by its presence at 52.

55. *By the mass*] a commonly inveighed-against oath (e.g., *Songs*, pp. 42–43).
not a cherry] proverbial (*O.E.D.*, 1b).

        And it is come into my hand—
        I care for no mo!
Char. Are you so disposed to do,   60
        To follow vice and let virtue go?
Youth. Yea, sir, even so,
        For nowadays he is not set by
        Without he be unthrifty.
Char. You had need to ask God mercy.   65
        Why did you so praise your body?
Youth. Why, knave, what is that to thee?
        Wilt thou let me to praise my body?
        Why should I not praise it, and it be goodly?
        I will not let for thee.   70
Char. What shall it be when thou shalt flit
        Fro thy wealth into the pit?
        Therefore, of it be not too bold,
        Lest thou forthink it when thou art old.

58. hand —] *Hazlitt;* hande, *Halliwell.*   59. no mo] *McKerrow conj.;* no more
Q1, Q2 subst., *Q3.*   66. did] *Q1;* do *Q2, Q3.*   72. Fro thy] *Q1;* For the
Q2, Q3.

59.] 'I don't care about anything else' (than the land or 'wealth' [72]).

mo] A rhyme on this (with 'do' at 56) is supported by 681–82, though cf. 312.

63. *set by*] regarded, thought much of (*O.E.D.*, 'set', v., 91c).

64. *Without*] unless.

unthrifty] (1) improvident, prodigal (*O.E.D.*, 4); (2) profligate, promiscuous
(*O.E.D.*, 3; cf. *H.S.* 576).

66. *did*] The Q2–Q3 present tense is inconsistent with Charity's past tense at
65, and ignores the two speeches that have occurred since Youth's bragging.

68. *let*] prevent, stop (*O.E.D.*, v.², 1).

70.] a common Tudor defiance. In 1506 a servant of the abbot of Whitby,
intending to exclude the prior of St Andrews forcibly from a property in York,
told the city's mayor bluntly, 'Maister Maier I will not let for you,' and then 'laid
his hand upon his dagger' (*York Civic Records*, ed. Angelo Raine, Yorks. Arch.
Soc. Rec. Ser. 106 [1942], p. 20).

let] desist, leave off (*O.E.D.*, v.², 2).

71. *flit*] (1) fall down (*O.E.D.*, v., 5c); (2) be gone.

72. *Fro thy*] Q2–Q3 attribute Youth's death to his 'wealth', though in this
speech (76–77) Charity emphasises the ephemerality of youth and property, not
their inherent corruptness. Cf. *H.S.* 757.

wealth] (1) prosperity, bodily well-being; (2) possessions.

pit] (1) grave; (2) hell (so called by John in Rev. ix.1–2, xx.1–3; cf. *H.S.* 785).

73. *it*] Youth's body (Bang, p. 74).

74. *forthink*] regret, repent of.

Ye may be likened to a tree: 75
In youth, flourishing with royalty,
And in age it is cut down
And to the fire is thrown.
So shalt thou, but thou amend,
Be burned in hell without end.   80
Youth. Yea, whoreson, trowest thou so?
Beware, lest thou thither go.
Hence, caitiff, go thy way,
Or with my dagger I shall thee slay!
Hence, knave, out of this place,   85
Or I shall lay thee on the face!
Sayest thou that I shall go to hell,
For evermore there to dwell?
I had liever thou had evil fare.
Char. A, yet, sir, do by my rede,   90
And ask mercy for thy misdeed,

---

81. Yea, whoreson,] *Bang;* ye horson *Q2, Q3 subst.;* Ye horson, *Halliwell;* Ye
whoreson! *Farmer;* Yea whoreson! *Schell-Shuchter.*   90. *Char.*] *Q2, Q3;*
youthe. *Q1.*

---

75. *a tree*] Cf. 45 and *Nature*, where Sensuality remarks ironically to Nature
that Man, without his senses, is only 'A lorde made of clow*tes* / or karued out of
tre' (I, 190–94).

76. *royalty*] a king's pomp, splendour.

77–80.] Charity replies from John xv.6, which continues the words of Christ
Youth alludes to at 45: 'If a man abide not in me, he is cast forth as a branch, and
is withered; and men gather them, and cast them into the fire, and they are
burned.' Cf. John the Baptist's warning to the Pharisees and Sadducees: 'And
now also the axe is laid unto the root of the trees: therefore every tree which
bringeth not forth good fruit is hewn down, and cast into the fire' (Matt. iii.10;
cf. vii.19, from Christ's sermon on the mount).

81. *Yea, whoreson,*] Cf. 505 (Bang, p. 74).

trowest thou] do you believe.

85. *place*] (1) manor, residence (*O.E.D.*, sb., 5b); (2) acting locus, theatrical
platea (see Intro., pp. 24–25); (3) public area.

86. *lay thee on the face*] (1) strike you on the face (*O.E.D.*, 'lay', v.¹, 34); (2)
knock you face-down?

89. *liever*] liefer, rather.

evil fare] (1) bad luck; (2) bad journeying.

90. *A*] perhaps a northern invocation (*O.E.D.*, inter., 1).

rede] advice.

And thou shalt be an heritor of bliss
Where all joy and mirth is,
Where thou shalt see a glorious sight
Of angels singing with saints bright   95
Before the face of God.

Youth. What, sirs! above the sky?
I had need of a ladder to climb so high.
But what and the ladder slip?
Then I am deceived yet.   100
And if I fall, I catch a queck;

94. shalt] *Q1;* shal *Q2, Q3.*   97. *Youth.*] *Q2, Q3;* Charite. *Q1.*

92–96.] This passage seems indebted to chapter 15 of Hawes's *Example*, which tells 'How vertu cleymed the enherytaunce longynge to Clennes his wyfe / & how many aungelles & sayntes brought theym to heuen / & how heuen is entayled to Vertu and to Clennes' (p. 2). Virtue's Good Angel showed him heaven, where angels 'dyd proclayme & synge on hye' (2001) and both 'aungels and sayntes for theyr solace | Euermore do loke on goddes face' (2023–24). Cf. *Everyman*: 'I here aungelles synge | And make grete ioy and melody | Where Euerymannes soule receyued shall be' (891–93).

92.] a common Pauline theme: 'we are the children of God: And if children, then heirs; heirs of God, and joint-heirs with Christ; if so be that we suffer with him, that we may be also glorified together' (Rom. viii.16–17; cf. Gal. iii.29, Heb. i.14).

heritor] 'heir', a northern form (Bang, pp. 74–75).

94. *shalt*] The Q2–Q3 reading is not usual (e.g., 71, 79, 92, 136, etc.), but Bang notes 603 and 652 (p. 75).

97. *sirs*] Youth addresses the audience too (Farmer, p. 449).

98. *a ladder to climb so high*] While saying mass for certain souls, St Bernard had a vision of them ascending by a ladder into heaven, and in his honour a *Scala Cœli* mass with a special indulgence attached was provided for chapels so named, as in Westminster Abbey (*O.E.D.*, s.v.), or in parish churches such as those at Lincoln, Boston, Grimsby and Spilsby (*Lincoln Wills*, ed. C. W. Foster, I [1914], Lincoln Rec. Soc., 5, p. 258). In Jacob's dream, the ladder between earth and heaven by which angels ascended to and descended from God (Gen. xxviii.12) was moralised as charity by William of Shoreham (*Poems*, ed. M. Konrath, E.E.T.S. E.S. 86 [1902], p. 2, ll. 36–49); others identify charity as one of the ladder's steps (see below, 101n; and *H.S.* 83n).

99.] Youth is of course thinking of the gallows, where convicts often had to climb a ladder to the rope.

slip] assonance with 100/103, 'yet' (100) then usually being sounded 'yit' (Wyld, p. 133), or with 101–02.

101. *if I fall*] Youth's naive objection to this vision is not uncommon. In *Ane Satyre* the Abbot objects to the two-step ladder to heaven (love of God, and charity; 1554 version, ll. 3492–99), 'Quhat and I fal, than I will break my

I may fortune to break my neck,
And that joint is ill to set.
Nay, nay, not so.

Char. O yet remember and call to thy mind   105
The mercy of God passeth all thing;
For it is written by noble clerks
The mercy of God passeth all works.
That witnesseth Holy Scripture, saying thus:
Miserationes Domini super omnia opera eius.   110
Therefore, doubt not God's grace;
Thereof is plenty in every place.

Youth. What! methink ye be clerkish,
For ye speak good gibb'rish.

105. *Char.*] *Q2, Q3;* youthe. *Q1.* and] *Q1; not in Q2, Q3.* 110. *Miserationes*] *Q1;* Miseratio *Q2, Q3.* 111. God's] *Q1, Q3;* goodes *Q2.* 114. gibb'rish] *Q2, Q3;* garbish *This ed. conj.*

---

bledder' (1554 version, l. 3525; cited by Bang, p. 75); cf. William of Shoreham, 98n above.

    catch a queck] be strangled, be hanged. The term 'queck' is probably a variant of *O.E.D.*, 'quetch', 4, meaning 'twitch' or 'gag' (McKerrow, p. 75), and is onomatopoeic for a choking noise made by a gibbeted person: cf. *The Tale of Beryn*, ed. F. J. Furnivall and W. G. Stone, E.E.T.S. E.S. 105 (1909), ll. 2944–49; *Mankind (Macro Plays)*, l. 808; and *Magnyfycence*, l. 2044 (the last two cited by Bang-McKerrow, p. 75). Cf. Tilley C810, 'He cries CREAK.' The entire phrase may be newly modelled on 'to catch a crike, or muscular neck-spasm, "whiplash"' (*M.E.D.*, 'crike', n. (2); cf. *O.E.D.*, 'catch', v., 30).

    107. *clerks*] (1) members of holy or minor orders; (2) scholars (cf. 113).

    108. *works*] (1) charitable acts, as justifying salvation; (2) conduct in general; perhaps (3) God's creation (cf. 110).

    110.] 'The mercies of God [are] over all his works' (paraphrase of Ps. cxlv.9 [Vulgate 144], 'Suavis Dominus universis; Et miserationes eius super omnia opera eius', which appears in the ordinary of the divine office at Vespers on Saturday after the fourth antiphon). An English translation of this passage, identified as a prophecy by David, is given by Sapience in Hawes's *Example* (806–09).

    111. *God's*] The Q2 form is a variant spelling (cf. 458, *H.S.* 949).

    113. *clerkish*] bookish, like a cleric (in reciting scripture at 110). A Venetian c. 1500 said of the English: 'few, however, excepting the clergy, are addicted to the study of letters; and this is the reason why any one who has learning, though he may be a layman, is called by them *a Clerk*' (*A Relation*, p. 22).

    114. *gibb'rish*] not in the *M.E.D.*, but first recorded after the Q2 instance (c. 1557–59) in 1577 or 1579 by the *O.E.D.* The term is without known etymology ('gibber' is probably a later development) but may come from 'garbage', evidently spelled 'garbish' in the sixteenth century (cf. *O.E.D.*, sb. 3: 'worthless or

> Sir, I pray you, and you have any store,   115
> Soil me a question or ye cast out any more,
> Lest when your conning is all done
> My question have no solution.
> Sir, and it please you this,
> Why do men eat mustard with salt fish?   120

116. any] *Q2, Q3;* ony *Q1.*   117. conning] *Q1, Q2, Q3;* cunning *Haz-litt.*   119. you this,] *Halliwell;* you, this, *Gowans.*   120. salt fish] *Q1, Q3;* salfishe *Q2.*

---

foul literary matter'). This may have been the original *Y.* form, in which case a double rhyme with 'clerkish' exists, and 'cast out' (116) would suggest how Youth regards Charity's words as 'garbage' in its chief sense then, 'offal, (human) entrails' (*O.E.D.*, sb., 1).

115. *any store*] anything in reserve or left over.

116. *Soil*] (1) answer (*O.E.D.*, v.², 3); (2) defile, mess up (*O.E.D.*, v.¹, 1).

Soil me a question] A mock-foolish question is a vice's conventional jest at the expense of a virtue's dignity: cf. Mischief's queries about corn and chaff to Mercy in *Mankind* (*Macro Plays*, ll. 48–52), and Sensual Appetite's spelling problem for Experience in *Four Elements* (sig. C6r). This comic device may develop from plays like the late fifteenth-century *Lucidus and Dubius*, where a doctor of divinity enters 'questiouns to asoyle' (Winchester MS, fol. 54v), theological doubts posed seriously enough by his former clerk. See B. S. Lee, 'Lucidus and Dubius: A Fifteenth-Century Theological Debate and its Sources', *Medium Ævum*, 45 (1976), 79–96.

cast out] (1) utter (*O.E.D.*, v., 26); (2) vomit, throw up (*O.E.D.*, 25, 81e).

117. *conning*] (1) knowledge, expertise; (2) recitation of rote learning (*O.E.D.*, vbl. sb.¹, 2).

119. *this*] 'thus, in this respect' (Bang, pp. 76–77; *O.E.D.*, adv.; cf. *Y.* 632); the demonstrative pronoun is possible (as at 709).

120.] This question must be, unless pointless (and Charity thinks at 124–25 that it can be answered), a trick riddle. Probably the answer depends on a then current total lenten prohibition of flesh, and could be 'Because men can't eat mustard with beef' or a variant of this. The altered *H.S.* version (701) has no seasonal point. Mustard and salt fish, which included the plentiful lenten staples haberdine, or cod, and ling, were regular household provisions, as noted in the fifth earl of Northumberland's household book (Percy 1, pp. 8, 18, 45, 135–36), where 160 gallons of mustard supplied a 166-person court for a year. McKerrow quotes John Russell's advice for salt fish sauce, 'Mustard is / is metest with alle maner salt herynge, | Salt fysche . . .' (*Manners and Meals*, p. 173), and Bang quotes (p. 81) Thomas Nashe's remarks 'that mustard bites a mã so by the nose, & makes him weep & water his plants when he tasteth it; & that . . . the red Herring and Ling, neuer come to the boord without mustard' (*Works*, ed. Ronald B. McKerrow [1905], III, 200). Youth may also be mocking biblical wisdom, since Christ compared heaven to a mustard seed (Matt. xiii.31–32), and Wynkyn de Worde's 1507 edition of *The boke named the royall* (*S.T.C.* 21430) describes that seed's heat allegorically as love (sig. R5v).

Sir, I pray you soil me this question
That I have put to your discretion.
Char. This question is but a vanity.
It longeth not to me
Such questions to assoil. 125
Youth. Sir, by God that me dear bought,
I see your conning is little or nought.
And I should follow your school,
Soon ye would make me a fool.
Therefore, crake no lenger here, 130
Lest I take you on the ear
And make your head ache.

123. This] *Q1, Q2*; Thus *Q3*. a] *Q1; not in Q2, Q3*. 127. conning] *Q1, Q2, Q3*; cunning *Hazlitt*. 129. me] *Q1; not in Q2, Q3*. 130. lenger] *Q1*; longer *Q2, Q3*. 132. ache] *Q1*; to ake *Q2, Q3*.

122. *discretion*] judgement, discernment.
123–25.] Cf. 2 Tim. ii.22–25: 'Flee also youthful lusts: but follow righteousness, faith, charity, peace, with them that call on the Lord out of a pure heart. But foolish and unlearned questions avoid, knowing that they do gender strifes. And the servant of the Lord must not strive; but be gentle unto all men, apt to teach, patient, In meekness instructing those that oppose themselves; if God peradventure will give them repentance to the acknowledging of the truth . . .'
123. *a vanity*] a trifling, idle remark (*O.E.D.*, 4b).
124. *longeth*] (1) is fitting; (2) is (my) business (*O.E.D.*, v.², 1).
125. *assoil*] solve, clear up.
126. *bought*] ransomed, redeemed by barter or sacrifice (*O.E.D.*, 'buy', 4; formulaic in context, as at 665, 711).
128. *school*] (1) doctrine, teaching (*O.E.D.*, sb.¹, 11); (2) disciples, body of pupils and colleagues. Cf. *Four Elements*, where Sensual Appetite says to Ignorance, of Man: 'I shall torne his mynde clene | And make hym folowe my skole' (sig. E2r).
129. *me*] Q2–Q3 is a *non sequitur*, inconsistent with what Youth says elsewhere (127; cf. 151).
130. *crake*] (1) bluster, talk big (*O.E.D.*, 'crack', v., 6; cf. Richard O. Heslop, *Northumberland Words* [1892], I, 192, 194, and *Nature*, where Sensuality says of Pride, 'Another day I am sure he wyll crake | And say suche a gentylman dyd hym make | Very great chere' [I, 908–10]); (2) crow, caw (*O.E.D.*, 'crake', v.¹, 1; perhaps a northern form, as Bang suggests, p. 81).
lenger] longer.
131–32.] In *Nature* Man 'smote Reason so on the hed' at the tavern (I, 1157; also 1167–68).
131. *take*] strike (*O.E.D.*, 5).

Char. Sir, it falleth not me to fight
    Neither by day ne by night.
    Therefore, do by my counsel, I say;   135
    Then to heaven thou shalt have the way.
Youth. No, sir, I think ye will not fight,
    But to take a man's purse in the night
    Ye will not say nay,
    For such holy caitiffs   140
    Were wont to be thieves;
    And such would be hanged as high
    As a man may see with his eye.
    In faith, this same is true.
Char. God save every Christen body   145
    From such evil destiny,
    And send us of his grace
    In heaven to have a place.
Youth. Nay, nay, I warrant thee,
    He hath no place for thee.   150
    Weenest thou he will have such fools
    To sit on his gay stools?

133. me] *Q1;* for me *Q2, Q3.*   134. ne by] *Q1;* ne be *Q2, Q3.*   135. by]
Q1; not in Q2, Q3.   136. the] *Q1, Q3;* thy *Q2.*   149. thee] *Q2, Q3;* ye
Bang conj.

---

133. *falleth*] is fitting (*O.E.D.*, 33b).

134. *ne*] nor.

135. *by*] a Q2–Q3 omission untypical of the play's usage (cf. 607).

136. *have the way*] 'know how to get to' (*O.E.D.*, 'way', sb.[1], 13c).

the] For Q2 'thy', cf. 262.

142–44.] The higher the gallows, the worse the felon. John a Chambre, who
led rebels that murdered the fourth earl of Northumberland at Topcliffe in
1489, was hanged at York, 'vpon a gybbet set vpon a square paire of gallowes,
lyke an archetraytoure, & his complyces & lewde disciples were hāged on the
lower gallowes roūde about theyr mayster' (Halle, 'Henry VII', fol. 16v). For
the execution of Tudor clerics by the secular law, see Intro., pp. 18–19.

147–48.] formulaic; a carol in Richard Hill's commonplace book (early in
Henry VIII's reign) prays that the Son 'will send vs of his grace | In hevyn on
high to haue a place' (*Songs*, I.1.21–22; also I.13.25–27).

151. *Weenest thou*] do you expect.

152. *stools*] (1) chairs of state; (2) low backless seats on legs. Youth imagines,
conventionally (cf. 25–26n), heaven as a court banquet. In Henry VII's household ordinances, a yeoman usher, preparing for the king's well-attended meals,

Nay, I warrant thee, nay.

Char. Well, sir, I put me in God's will
    Whether he will me save or spill.   155
    And, sir, I pray you do so,
    And trust in God whatsoever you do.

Youth. Sir, I pray thee, hold thy peace
    And talk to me of no goodness,
    And soon look thou go thy way,   160
    Lest with my dagger I thee slay!
    In faith, and thou move my heart,
    Thou shalt be weary of thy part
    Or thou and I have done.

Char. Think what God suffered for thee,   165
    His arms to be spread upon a tree;
    A knight with a spear opened his side;
    In his heart appeared a wound wide
    That bought both thee and me.

Youth. God's fast! what is that to me?   170

154. *Char.*] *Bang conj.*; Humi=|litye. *Q2, Q3 subst.*   157. you] *Q1*; ye *Q2, Q3*.   162. and] *Q1*; yf *Q2, Q3 subst.   move*] *Q1, Q3*; mene *Q2*.   163. weary] *Q2, Q3*; wery *Q1*.   169. thee] *Q1*; you *Q2, Q3*.

---

is ordered 'to see & command yeomen to sett vpp y^e king*es* borde & y^t there want noe stooles nor fforemes for ye same' (B.L. Harley MS 2210, fol. 13r).

154. *Char.*] Charity himself implies Humility is not present (185), and so the Q2–Q3 speech heading must be a printer's change (154–57 do show Charity's own humility).

155. *spill*] damn (formulaic in context; see *O.E.D.*, v., 1b).

159. *goodness*] in particular, God's grace (cf. *O.E.D.*, 2a; cf. 106–11, 147).

162. *move*] provoke, anger.

163.] formulaic. On 11 August 1513 before Thérouanne Henry VIII so addressed himself to Scotland's James IV through his herald (*L.P.* I.2157); and cf. the *Vulgaria of Robert Whittinton*, ed. Beatrice White, E.E.T.S. O.S. 187 (1932), p. 72, l. 33.

weary] as at *H.S.* 164, 393; 'wary', meaning 'on guard (against)', develops *c.* 1550 and does not have the Q1 spelling.

part] (1) business, function; (2) part in dialogue (see Intro., p. 26), actor's role.

164. *Or*] before.

167. *knight*] a soldier in John xix.34, in medieval legend usually a knight named Longinus.

170. *God's fast*] his forty days in the wilderness (Matt. iv.1–2), the pattern for Lent; a common oath then (cf. *H.S.* 949).

Thou daw! wilt thou rede me
In my youth to leese my jollity?
Hence, knave, and go thy way,
Or with my dagger I shall thee slay!

Char. O sir! hear what I will you tell,   175
And be ruled after my counsel,
That ye might sit in heaven on high
With God and his company.

Youth. A, yet of God wilt thou not cease
Till I fight in good earnest?   180
On my faith I tell thee true,
If I fight, thou wilt it rue
All the days of thy life.

Char. Sir, I see it will none otherwise be.
I will go to my brother Humility   185
And take counsel of him
How it is best to be do therein.

Youth. Yea, marry, sir, I pray you of that;
Methink it were a good sight of your back.
I would see your heels hither,   190

172. leese] *Q1;* lose *Q2, Q3.*   175. will] *Q1; not in Q2, Q3.*   176. after]
Q1, Q2; of *Q3.*   177. on] *Q1; not in Q2, 13.*   179. A] *Q2, Q3;* And
Schell-Shuchter.   wilt thou] *Q1;* thou wilte *Q2, Q3.*   182. thou wilt it
rue] *Q3;* I tell the true *Q2.*   184. it will] *Q1, Q3; well Q2.*   186. counsel]
Q1; good counsayle *Q2, Q3.*   190. see] *Hazlitt;* se *Q1, Q2, Q3;* set *This
ed. conj.*

---

171. *daw*] fool (literally a jackdaw).

rede] advise.

172. *leese*] lose, give up.

176. *after*] unlike the Q3 reading, typical of the play (728).

177. *on*] an omission in Q2–Q3 again against the play's idiom (455; cf. 98,
792).

177–78.] Cf. Ephes. ii.4–6.

180. *earnest*] An early form (*O.E.D.*, sb.²), stressed on the second syllable,
Bang's conjectured 'earnes' (p. 82) would rhyme with (conjectured) 'cesse' at
179; cf. 496–97.

186. *counsel*] The next line makes the Q2–Q3 addition, though typical of the
play otherwise (774, 779; cf. 355), redundant.

187. *do*] done.

188. *marry*] oath, 'by the Virgin Mary'.

190. *see your heels*] see you in the stocks or in chains (*O.E.D.*, 'heel', sb.¹, 18).
The original reading may well have been 'set your heels' (cf. *H.S.* 479).

And your brother and you together
Fettered fine fast.
Iwis, and I had the kay,
Ye should sing wellaway
Or I let you loose.   195

Char. Farewell, my masters everyone!
I will come again anon
And tell you how I have done.   [*Exit.*]

Youth. And thou come hither again,
I shall send thee hence in the devil's name.   200
What, now I may have my space
To jet here in this place!
Before I might not stir
When that churl Charity was here,
But now among all this cheer   205
I would I had some company here.

---

198. S.D.] *McKerrow; after line 200 in Happé.*   200. shall] *Q1, Q2*; wyll
Q3.   201. What, now] *Halliwell;* What now *Q1;* What nowe, *Q2,*
Q3.   204. that] *Q1;* the *Q2, Q3.*

---

192. *fine fast*] (1) very securely; (2) very quickly. The apparent rhyme is with
195: late sixteenth-century evidence exists for loss of *t* after *s* (Dobson, § 398,
and cf. § 406), and 'fause' is a northern spelling of 'fast' (Brook, p. 89).

194. *sing wellaway*] proverbial (*O.E.D.*, 'wellaway').

195. *loose*] cited in fourteenth- and fifteenth-century spellings 'lause' and
'lawse' by the *O.E.D.*, a.

197. *anon*] in a short while.

200. *shall*] also altered in Q3 at 687.

in the devil's name] i.e., invoking the devil. Youth disposes of Charity, when
he returns, by invoking Riot, who is twice linked with the devil (220, 368).

201. *What*] calling attention to what follows, like modern 'Well!' (*O.E.D.*,
B.I. int., 1).

space] (1) room; (2) opportunity, time.

202. *jet*] (1) strut, move about; (2) riot, live it up (*O.E.D.*, v.^{1}, 5).

204. *Charity*] Youth entered after Charity identified himself, and so could not
have known his name.

205. *cheer*] (1) mirth; (2) hospitable entertainment, as of banquet food and
drink (*O.E.D.*, sb., 6).

206–09.] After complaining, 'Now haue I no maner of company | To helpe me
in my iourney, and me to kepe' (185–86), Everyman turns to Fellowship, and
Kindred and Cousin, roles that Riot, as Youth's 'compeer' (216) and 'brother',
fulfils. Like Fellowship, who offers to avenge wrongs done to Everyman, even
murdering to do so (218, 281–82), Riot later (300) vows to 'beat Charity'.

Iwis, my brother Riot would help me
For to beat Charity
And his brother too.

[Enter RIOT.]

Riot. [*To the audience*] Huffa, huffa! who calleth after
    me?   210
I am Riot, full of jollity,
My heart is light as the wind,
And all of riot is my mind
Wheresoever I go.
But wot ye what I do here?   215
To seek Youth, my compeer.
Fain of him I would have a sight—

207. Iwis] *Q1;* I wis *Q2, Q3;* I wish *Hazlitt.*   211. of] *Q1; not in Q2,*
Q3.   212. is] *Q1;* as *Q2, Q3.*   213. of riot] *Q1;* on Riot *Q2, Q3.*   217.
sight—] *This ed.;* sight, *Halliwell.*

207. *Riot*] (1) prodigal living (see Intro., n. 165). This is, in general, youth's
special vice: 'Ryot is the destruccyon of all yonge men' (*The Vulgaria of John
Stanbridge*, ed. Beatrice White, E.E.T.S. O.S. 187 [1932], p. 22). (2) violent
lawlessness or disorder (cf. 234 and n.). In this sense, 'riot' was the last of six
crimes that Henry VII's parliament of 9 November 1487 declared to be the
special business of the Court of Star Chamber at Westminster, and was defined
as being 'committed when three or more persons assembled to do an unlawful
act and actually did something in pursuance of that intention' (*Select Cases*, pp.
li, cxxix). The only extant case instituted by the Attorney-General concerned the
fifth earl of Northumberland and the archbishop of York (pp. cxxxi, 44).
Henrician efforts to curb and prosecute riot are discussed above, pp. 56–57.
210. *Huffa, huffa*] a gallant's bluster, found in plays at this period, and part of
a refrain from a popular song: '*Huff! a* galawnt, vylabele! | Thus syngyth
galawntys in here revele' (*Historical Poems of the XIVth and XVth Centuries*, ed.
Rossell Hope Robbins [1959], p. 138; my italics). The first *O.E.D.* instance is
from *Four Elements, c.* 1517–18 (sig. B2v), but it occurs earlier among Macro
MS marginalia (*Macro Plays*, p. xxix), in *Magnyfycence* (l. 745), in *Mary Magdalene*, where the gallant enters, saying 'Hof, hof, hof, a frysch new galavnt'
(*Digby Plays*, l. 491), and *Nature*, where Pride says, of Man's effect in his
new-fashioned gown, 'There goth a rutter men wyll say | a rutter huf a galand' (I,
1078–79).
211. *full of jollity*] Cf. *H.S.* 892; and *Johan the Evangelist*, l. 454: 'Lo iouthe is
full of iolyte'.
212. *light*] (1) merry; (2) fickle, changeable.
215. *wot*] know.
216. *compeer*] (1) fellow; (2) equal (in this sense contradicting Youth at 43).

[*Seeing Youth*] But my lips hang in my light!

God speed, Master Youth, by my fay!

Youth. Welcome, Riot, in the devil way!   220

Who brought thee hither today?

Riot. That did my legs, I tell thee.

Methought thou did call me,

And I am come now here

To make royal cheer   225

And tell thee how I have done.

Youth. What! I weened thou haddest be hanged,

But I see thou escaped;

For it was told me here

---

218. lips] *Q1, Q2, Q3;* lids *Ashby conj.*   220. devil] *Q1;* deuels *Q2, Q3.*   221. hither today] *Q1, Q3;* hither to *Q2;* hitherto *Hazlitt.*   223. call me] *Q1;* me call *Q2, Q3.*   225. cheer] *Q1, Q3;* there *Q2.*   227. haddest be hanged] *Q1;* hadst ben henged *Q2, Q3.*   228. escaped] *Q1;* arte escaped *Q2, Q3.*

218.] Tilley L330. Ashby (fol. 29r) seems right about the saying's original form, but no example of it has been found. Skelton's *Magnyfycence*—'thy lyppes hange in thyne eye' (1050)—vies with *Y.* as the place of the proverb's first appearance in this odd form (a foul-case mistake?), as their dates are very close (see, however, Leigh Winser, 'Skelton's *Magnyfycence*', *Renaissance Quarterly*, 23 [1970], 14–25); and much later men like John Heywood and Nashe may have accepted the apparently erroneous form from them.

219. *Master*] a title indicating, not youth, but knightly or spiritual rank (*O.E.D.*, sb.[1], 21a); cf. *Y.* 317, 524, 697.

220. *in the devil way*] (1) exclamation of impatience, with an old genitive plural 'devil' (*O.E.D.*, sb., 19b), the Q2–Q3 form being an unidiomatic modernisation; (2) 'in the devil's business'?

221–22.] Cf. *R3*, I.iv.85–87:

> *Brakenbury.* What wouldst thou, fellow? and how cam'st thou hither?
>
> *1 Murderer.* I would speak with Clarence, and I came hither on my legs.

227–32.] Youth learns about the escape from hanging because someone told him (229) or Riot's *subsequent* mugging enterprise. Later, when Youth asks about 'that jest' (250), he is referring to this apparently accurate story, Riot's three-stage progress 'lately from Newgate' (233–34), outlined here and amplified at 252–68: the rogue's transportation *from* Newgate to Tyburn to be hanged (227, 252–57), his escape (228, 258–61), and his mugging and purse-snatching (229–31, 262–68).

227. *hanged*] a northern form in Q2–Q3 (Bang, p. 83). The rhyme may be with 228 on the unstressed second syllable here, or the passage may be corrupt.

That you took a man on the ear,   230
His purse in your bosom did fly,
And so in new all night he did lie.
Riot. So it was, I beshrew your pate!
I come lately from Newgate,
But I am as ready to make good cheer   235
As he that never came there,
For, and I have spending,
I will make as merry as a king
And care not what I do;
For I will not lie long in prison,   240

230. That] *McKerrow conj. on torn-off Q1 edge; not in Q2, Q3.*   231. His] *This ed. conj. on torn-off Q1 edge;* That his *Q2, Q3.*   232. so] *Q2, Q3;* o   *Q1 torn edge; McKerrow reads Q1 torn edge* d   new all night he] *This ed.;* newe all nyght ye *Q1;* newegate ye *Q2, Q3 subst.;* mew all night ye *This ed. conj.*   233. pate] *Q1, Q3;* parte *Q2.*

---

230. *That*] This word must have dropped one line in Q2–Q3. In Q1 there is clearly room, at the line's beginning, for one more word than appears in Q2–Q3, whereas at 231 Q1 lacks space for the Q2–Q3 reading.

232. *in new all night he did lie*] 'he [the robbery victim] lay all night in pain, a bad way', a perhaps satisfactory reconstruction. Q2–Q3 'Newgate' cannot be correct, because Riot's own account of his Newgate imprisonment (see 227–32n) places it before, not after, the mugging. Q1 'new' seems to be a rare northern form of 'noy', the aphetic form of 'annoy' (*M.E.D.*, 'noi', n.; *O.E.D.*, 'new', sb.[1], meaning 'trouble, sorrow', and elsewhere found only in *York Plays*, ed. Lucy T. Smith [1885], at XLV.144, 'All þat are in newe or in nede and nevenes me be name', and at XXXI.222, XLVII.96, 105; for help with this text I am thankful to Betsy S. Taylor). Because Riot is in delighted high spirits after his crime (211, 224–25, 268), the sufferer must be the robbery victim, felled from his horse by a blow to the head; hence 'ye' (cf. the Q2 misprint at 20) seems either foul-case or a compositor's misreading. Yet there are resemblances between 232, 240 and *H.S.* 422.

233. *pate*] head.

234. *Newgate*] fifth principal (west) gate of the London city wall, and since at least the early thirteenth century a prison, one intended mainly for non-freemen of the city, aliens, felons and those charged with violent crimes (Ludgate, just south of Newgate, was used for freemen charged with less serious crimes such as debt), rebuilt completely by the executors of Sir Richard Whittington in 1423–32, and renowned enough to have had Dublin and Bristol prisons named after it (Pugh, pp. 103–04, 107). Newgate was again rebuilt after 1770, and was at last demolished in 1902.

237. *spending*] ready cash.

238.] Tilley K54.

But I will get forth soon,
For I have learned policy
That will loose me lightly
And soon let me go.

Youth.   I love well thy discretion,   245
For thou art all of one condition:
Thou art stable and steadfast of mind
And not changeable as the wind.
But, sir, I pray you at the least,
Tell me more of that jest   250
That thou told me right now.

Riot.   Moreover, I shall tell thee,
The Mayor of London sent for me
Forth of Newgate for to come
For to preach at Tyburn.   255

241. I] *Q1; not in Q2, Q3.*   242. policy] *Q1; a pollycie Q2, Q3 subst.*   252.
Riot.] *Q2; not in Q3.*

---

242. *learned*] 'scholarly, deeply studied' (the participial adj., though the verb
is possible instead).

policy] cunning (*O.E.D.*, sb.¹, 4); that is, Riot's 'discretion' (245), not 'that
jest' (250). The Q2–Q3 reading (*O.E.D.*, 4b, 'a trick, a device, a plan') is not
supported by the escape's circumstances: Riot plans no jailbreak, but just has
the discreet sense to run once the noose snaps.

243. *lightly*] (1) easily; (2) quickly.

245. *discretion*] In *Nature* Man tells Worldly Affection: 'your counsell ys good
/ do as ye thynk best | I commyt all suche thyng | to your dyscrecyon' (I, 703–04).
Dame Discretion is also one of Youth's counsellors in Hawes's *Example*, and a
character in *Everyman*.

246. *condition*] disposition, frame of mind, character (*O.E.D.*, sb., 11). John
Skelton refers to 'Ryot' among certain 'condycyons' too ('Garlande or Chapelet
of Laurell', *Works*, I, ll. 614–15).

247–48.] Cf. verses on a chamber wall at Wressle, the estate of the fifth earl of
Northumberland: 'If murmur be agaynste trouthe . . . | By vayne wordis
vnstedfast as the wynde | Thy wordis shalbe taken of litill sentens | . . . Not
substanciall nor stabill of lyklyhode shalbe yⁱ warke' (Flügel, p. 497).

248.] Tilley W412: 'As wavering (changeable, fickle, inconstant) as the
WIND'.

250. *jest*] story, exploit.

253–54.] Since 1327 the Mayor of London was one of the justices for jail
delivery of Newgate (R. R. Sharpe, *Memorials of Newgate Gaol* [1907], p. 4; for
his November 1513 warrant, see *L.P.* I.2484.15).

255.] Tilley T646 (first example); cf. G16, 'The GALLOWS is the cutpurse's
pulpit'; *Magnyfycence*, l. 2140, 'And some fall prechynge at the Toure Hyll'; and

Youth. By Our Lady, he did promote thee
      To make thee preach at the gallow-tree.
      But, sir, how diddest thou scape?
Riot. Verily, sir, the rope brake,
      And so I fell to the ground   260
      And ran away safe and sound.
      By the way I met with a courtier's lad,
      And twenty nobles of gold in his purse he had.
      I took the lad on the ear;
      Beside his horse I felled him there.   265
      I took his purse in my hand,
      And twenty nobles therein I fand.

262. By] *Hazlitt;* Be *Q2, Q3.* the] *Q3;* thy *Q2.*

Bang, p. 83. From the late twelfth century, somewhere from Marylebone Road
to the head of the Serpentine, a gallows for Middlesex, including the Westminster and Guildhall courts, was erected at Tyburn or Tye Bourne, a stream then
flowing probably through what is now Regent's Park, Hyde Park and St James's
Park to Westminster (Alfred Marks, *Tyburn Tree* [London, n.d.], pp. 59–61).
The site of the triangular Tyburn gibbet introduced in 1571 and of executions
until the late eighteenth century was Marble Arch, at the junction of Bayswater
and Edgeware Roads, to which the condemned were carted or drawn from
Newgate via Holborn Hill and St Giles-in-the-Fields. Riot also travels this route
in Skelton's 'Bowge of Courte': 'Vnthryftynes in hym [Riot] may well be
shewed, | For whome Tyborne groneth both daye and nyghte' (*Works*, I, ll.
416–17).

   Tyburn] assonance with 'come' (254), *r* being lost before *n* in early speech
(Dobson, I, 112, and II, § 401[c]; cf. *H.S.* 663).

   256. *promote*] (1) prefer, advance in dignity; (2) inform against, prosecute (for
the king). The 1509/10 'Balade of Empson' threatens Empson, Dudley and their
promoters as follows: 'I wyll doo my best, to promoot the on hy | For thy ffals
glose, & dyssymlyd Curtesy | Shewyd to all men, and thy ffals fflateryng | Fyrst
to be drawyn, and than suffyr hangyng' (*Great Chronicle of London*, ed. A. H.
Thomas and I. D. Thornley [1938], p. 347). Bang cites John Taylor's use of the
same witticism a century later (p. 433); cf. *R3* IV.iv.242–43.

   259. *the rope brake*] Collier first noted (II, 314) the similarity of Riot's escape to
New Guise's entry from the gallows in *Mankind* with the rope still partly around
his neck: 'A grace was, þe halter brast asonder: ecce signum' (*Macro Plays*, l.
616).

   262. *lad*] servant.

   263. *nobles*] gold coins first minted by Edward III, also called angels (from
Edward IV) and worth 6s 8d each (Charles Oman, *The Coinage of England*
[1931], pp. 173, 220).

   267. *fand*] found (a northern form; Bang, p. 84).

Lord, how I was merry!

Youth. God's foot! thou diddest enough there

    For to be made knight of the collar. 270

Riot. Yea, sir, I trust to God Almight

    At the next sessions to be dubbed a knight.

Youth. Now, sir, by this light,

    That would I fain see!

    And I plight thee, 275

    So God me save,

    That a surer collar thou shalt have;

    And because gold collars be so good cheap,

    Unto the roper I shall speak

    To make thee one of a good price, 280

    And that shall be of warrantise.

Riot. Youth, I pray thee, have ado,

271. Almight] *Halliwell;* all myght *Q2, Q3.*   275–76.] *This ed.; one line in Q2, Q3.*

---

269. *God's foot*] common oath (*O.E.D.*, 'foot', sb., 1b). See Bang, p. 84, and Intro., n. 211.

270. *knight of the collar*] (1) knight whose order or special favour with the king entitles him to wear an ornamental band or 'chain' (*O.E.D.*, 'collar', sb., 3b); (2) prisoner chained about the neck by an iron collar, customary in medieval English jails (*O.E.D.*, 5); (3) convict hanging on the gallows (cf. 279; for the Tudor use of iron chains as well as hemp nooses, see *Two Italian Accounts of Tudor England*, trans. C. V. Malfatti [1953], p. 69). The *double entendre* also occurs in 'John the Reeve' (Laing, I, ll. 823–30):

    The King tooke a coller bright,

    'Iohn, heere I make thee knight

    With worshippe,' then hee sayd.

    Then was Iohn euill apayd,

    And amongst them all thus hee sayd,

    'Full oft I haue heard tell

    That after a coller comes a rope;

    I shall be hanged by the throate.'

See Intro., pp. 19–20.

272. *sessions*] (quarterly) sitting of the justices of the peace.

273. *by this light*] common oath (*O.E.D.*, 'light', sb., 2b).

277. *surer*] one less liable to snap (cf. 259).

278. *so good cheap*] such a good bargain, so low-priced (*O.E.D.*, 'cheap', sb., 8).

281. *be of warrantise*] (1) be guaranteed or warranted sound; (2) protect you (*O.E.D.*, sb., 3)?

And to the tavern let us go;
And we will drink diverse wine,
And the cost shall be mine.   285
Thou shalt not pay one penny, iwis;
Yet thou shalt have a wench to kiss
Whensoever thou wilt.

Youth. Marry, Riot, I thank thee
That thou wilt bestow it on me,   290
And for thy pleasure so be't.
I would not Charity should us meet
And turn us again,
For right now he was with me
And said he would go to Humility   295
And come to me again.

Riot. Let him come, if he will.
He were better to bide still.
And he give thee crooked language,
I will lay him on the visage;   300
And that thou shalt see soon,
How lightly it shall be done.
And he will not be ruled with knocks,
We shall set him in the stocks

291. be't] *This ed.;* be it *Q2, Q3.*

283–84.] 'Few people keep wine in their own houses, but buy it, for the most part, at a tavern; and when they mean to drink a great deal, they go to the tavern, and this is done not only by the men, but by ladies of distinction' (*Relation*, p. 21).

285. *the cost*] Wine, being entirely imported, was relatively expensive (cf. 445–46): 8d per gallon *v.* 1¼d per gallon of ale in the *Vulgaria of Robert Whittinton*, ed. Beatrice White, E.E.T.S. O.S. 187 (1932), p. 57, ll. 29, 31.

293. *turn us again*] (1) make us go back (from the tavern; *O.E.D.*, 'turn', v., 66g); perhaps quibbling on (2) convert us (to a devout life; *O.E.D.*, 29).

298. *bide still*] stay where he is.

299. *crooked language*] lies, slanders (*M.E.D.*, 'croked', ppl. 4c, and Bang, p. 86; related here to 'crake'? at 130 and 637 it also is followed by the threat to knock Charity down).

304.] George Cavendish's 'Life and Death of Cardinal Wolsey' tells how Wolsey, while a tutor at Limington, Somerset, for the sons of Thomas Grey, marquis of Dorset (died 1501), angered Sir Amias Paulet, a shire justice at nearby Hinton St George, and he 'was so bold to set the schoolmaster by the feet

To heal his sore shins.   305
Youth. I shall help thee, if I can,
    To drive away that hangman.
    Hark, Riot, thou shalt understand
    I am heir of my father's land,
    And now they be come to my hand!   310
    Methink it were best, therefore,
    That I had one man more
    To wait me upon.

        [Enter PRIDE *at a distance.]*

Riot. I can speed thee of a servant of price
    That will do thee good service—   315

309–10. I . . . land, | And . . . hand!] *This ed.;* I . . . lande, | And . . . hand, *Halliwell.*

---

during his pleasure; the which was afterward neither forgotten ne forgiven' (*Two Early Tudor Lives*, ed. Richard S. Sylvester and Davis P. Harding [1962], p. 5; Charles Ferguson, *Naked to Mine Enemies* [1958], pp. 57–58). Among riot cases adjudicated by Henry VII's council was an illegal stocking (*Select Cases*, p. cxxxviii). Paul and Silas in Philippi were also beaten and jailed with their feet in the stocks (Acts xvi.22–23).

the stocks] evidently so named for the two posts holding in place the lower, fixed plank and the upper sliding plank whose edges were provided with the feet-holes (*O.E.D.*, 'stock', sb.[1], 8). Stocks were kept by 1488 for felons in Newgate's lower rooms, and outdoors for vagabonds in 'small howsis' in all London's wards (Pugh, pp. 113, 369, and pl. facing 97).

305.] Actually, the shins, taking the body's weight (the narrow bench for the buttocks was extended far enough away from the stocks so that the legs had to be stretched out straight and taut for support at the ankles), chafed painfully in the wood-holes (cf. *H.S.* 794–98).

307. *hangman*] term of abuse, though ecclesiastical authorities had their own gallows. Bang (p. 86) cites *Magnyfycence*, l. 2190, and *Nature*, where Pride says to Man concerning Reason: 'yt were better ye hangman where in his graue | than euer the lewd fole shold haue | the gouernaunce of you' (I, 980–82).

310. *they*] Such grammatical imprecision (cf. 57–58) is regular, as at 443, 526.

312. *one man more*] As Riot is Youth's equal (207, 216), this remark either indicates he has a (noble) household, or survives from *Nature*, where Man, after receiving lands from the World, tells Worldly Affection, 'I must haue mo seruauntys [than Sensuality and Reason]' (I, 709).

313.1.] Pride must be in sight by the time Riot next speaks.

314. *speed thee of*] provide you with.
of price] of great worth.

I see him go here beside.
Some men call him Master Pride.
I swear by God in Trinity
I will go fetch him unto thee,
And that even anon.   *[Goes.]*   320
Youth. Hie thee apace, and come again,
          And bring with thee that noble swain.

          [RIOT *returns with* PRIDE.]

Riot. Lo! Master Youth, here he is,
         A pretty man and a wise.
         He will be glad to do you good service   325
         In all that ever he may.
Youth. Welcome to me, good fellow!
          I pray thee, whence comest thou?
          And thou wilt my servant be,
          I shall give thee gold and fee.   330

322.1.] *This ed.;* Exit Riot and returns with Pride. *McKerrow; As Riot is going, enter Pride, meeting him. Hampden.*   324. a] *Q3; not in Q2.*   325. you good] *Halliwell;* good you *Q2;* you *Q3.*

316–19.] In *Nature* Sensuality, on the look-out for a servant for Man, tells him, 'Lo wyll ye se lo / here cometh one' (I, 717), but Pride's entering monologue (which then follows) means that there is no awkward pause in the dialogue such as occurs in *Y.* here, where Riot must fetch a Pride who comes in silently (321–22). That an allegorical point is at stake (riot leads one to pride? cf. 319, 361) seems in doubt.

316. *beside*] near by (Pride may be moving in the audience).

317.] In *Nature* Pride calls himself Worship (I, 838), for pride is first among the seven deadly sins, 'the general roote of alle harmes' (Chaucer's *Parson's Tale*, l. 387).

321. *apace*] at once.

322. *swain*] (1) young man; (2) attendant.

325. *you good service*] Q2 is formulaic here (cf. 315), though its errors in this passage make a visual confusion with 327 possible.

328.] unanswered. In *Nature* Man asks Pride at their meeting, 'Whens are ye', to which Pride says, 'I shall tell you or I go' (I, 829); he then tells Sensuality (but not Man) the answer to this question in an aside (I, 836).

330. *fee*] formulaic in context: (1) land 'held on condition of homage and service to a superior lord, by whom it is granted and in whom the ownership remains' (*O.E.D.*, sb.², 1); (2) fixed wage.

Pride. Sir, I am content, iwis,
    To do you any service
    That ever I can do.
Youth. By likelihood thou should do well enow.
    Thou art a likely fellow.   335
Pride. Yes, sir, I warrant you,
    If ye will be ruled by me,
    I shall you bring to high degree.
Youth. What shall I do? tell me,
    And I will be ruled by thee.   340
Pride. Marry, I shall tell you.
    Consider ye have good enow,
    And think ye come of noble kind.
    Above all men exalt thy mind.
    Put down the poor, and set nought by them.   345
    Be in company with gentlemen.
    Jet up and down in the way,

343. think] *Q3;* thing *Q2.*   345. set] *Q3;* se *Q2.*   346. gentlemen] *Q3;* gentel man *Q2.*

331–33.] In *Nature* Pride enters Man's service vowing: 'In good fayth any thyng that I | May do to your pleasure yt ys redy | I am your own' (I, 947–49).

334.] Medwall's Pride says to Man shortly after the service vow: 'And by lykylyhod syr I wys | ye haue wyt accordyng to all thys' (I, 967–68).

By likelihood] probably.

enow] enough.

335. *likely*] (1) apparently suitable; (2) good-looking.

337–38.] Hardiness says to Youth in Hawes's *Example*: 'For I by ryght must nedys enhauncce | A lowe born man to an hyghe degre | Yf that he wyll be ruled by me' (593–95). The formula at lines 337–38 (cf. 452, 619, 621–22, 636, 673, 676, 728) is used elsewhere by Hawes (70, 1221).

338. *degree*] social rank.

342–46.] In *Nature* Pride promises Sensuality to flatter Man to 'thynk how he ys create | To be a worthy potestate | And eke that he ys predestynate | to be a prynces pere' (I, 867–70). Hawes's Youth also meets one called Pride, 'the lady of rychesse | The quene of welth and worldely glory', who asks him 'to company with her noblenesse | And she than wolde promote me shortely | To innumerable ryches and make me worthy | Where I am poore and sette by nought | By her to worshyp I sholde be brought' (1170–76).

342. *good*] possessions (*O.E.D.*, sb., 7b).

343. *kind*] family, ancestors.

346. *gentlemen*] Q2 may have transposed this word and 'gentleman' at 350.

347. *Jet up and down*] formulaic; cf. *Eclogues*, p. 11, l. 363; and Bang, p. 87.

And your clothes—look they be gay.
The pretty wenches will say then,
'Yonder goeth a gentleman,'   350
And every poor fellow that goeth you by
Will do off his cap and make you courtesy.
In faith, this is true.

Youth. Sir, I thank thee, by the rood,
For thy counsel that is so good,   355
And I commit me even now
Under the teaching of Riot and you.

Riot. Lo, Youth, I told you
That he was a lusty fellow.

Youth. Marry, sir, I thank thee   360
That you would bring him unto me.

Pride. Sir, it were expedient that ye had a wife,
To live with her all your life.

Riot. A wife! nay, nay, for God avow,

350. gentleman] *Halliwell;* gentelmen *Q2, Q3.*   359. lusty] *Q2;* lastye
Q3.   364. for God avow,] *Hazlitt;* for, God avow, *Gowans.*

348–53.] In *Nature* Worldly Affection tells Man the merits of Pride's new
fashions: 'Whan ye were on that vestour | Euery man shall do your honour | as
becummeth a man of your hauyour | And so yt shuld be' (I, 1332–35). A
Leconfield maxim also says that clothes 'Causithe men to be honowrede &
muche sett by' (Flügel, p. 473).

350. *gentleman*] a rhyme with 'then' (349), often written 'than' (Q1 136,
Q2–Q3 349), though 'man' in northern and London dialects was sounded like
'men' about this time (Dobson, § 59, n. 2 [a]).

352. *do off*] doff.

make you courtesy] bow down in obeisance, 'curtsy' (*O.E.D.*, sb., 8).

354. *rood*] cross.

362–63.] Hawes's Sapience says, 'youth wyll ye haue a wyfe | And her to loue
durynge her lyfe' (1070–71).

364–73.] Cf. the discussion about the stews' prostitutes in *Nature*: to Man's
question whether they are 'not wedded as other folke be', Sensuality replies,
'Wedded quod a no so mot I the', and explains that men marry them on a simple
kiss, separate as quickly 'yf the woman hap to offend', and 'wed a nother hore on
the morow | Even of the same wyse' (II, 146–57). Marlowe's Mephostophilis also
refuses to get Faustus a wife (marriage being a sacrament) and fetches instead 'a
wife in the devil's name', a 'hot whore' (*Doctor Faustus*, ed. John D. Jump
[1962], v. 148–50).

364. *for God avow*] either (1) '(by) a vow before God' or (2) 'fore God I vow',
where 'a' indicates the northern first person singular (*O.E.D.*, pron., 4; sug-

He shall have flesh enow,   365
For, by God that me dear bought,
Overmuch of one thing is nought.
The devil said he had liever burn all his life
Than once for to take a wife.
Therefore, I say, so God me save,   370
He shall no wife have.
Thou hast a sister fair and free.
I know well his leman she will be;
Therefore, I would she were here,
That we might go and make good cheer   375
At the wine somewhere.
Youth. I pray you, hither thou do her bring,
For she is to my liking.
Pride. Sir, I shall do my diligence
To bring her to your presence.   380

365. enow] *Hazlitt;* inoughe *Q2, Q3.*

---

gested by Collier, II, 314). This oath, otherwise unrecorded by *O.E.D.* or
M.E.D. (cf. *O.E.D.*, 'God', 13), is at 612 and in Medwall's plays: in *Nature*
Pride, eager to hear about Man's fight with Reason, says to Sensuality, 'Tell on
thy tale for god auow' (I, 1122); also see *Fulgens & Lucres*, I.193, and p. 89.
Gowans's punctuation is only impossible in *I Nature*.

365. *flesh*] In a song by William Cornyssh Junior a clerk says, of the girl he has
just seduced: 'The best chepe flessh that evyr I bought' (Stevens, p. 379); and
Nature, where Man wants to visit a stews' 'banket or a rere supper' to get 'some
wanton mete' (II, 200–01).

enow] For rhymes using this form, see 334, 342.

367.] proverbial; cf. 'Over mych is not worth in no thing' ('Stans Puer ad
Mensam', *Remains*, III, l. 79).

368–69.] a reversal of Paul's dictum, 'for it is better to marry than to burn' (1
Cor. vii. 9).

372. *sister*] In *Nature* Man becomes acquainted with one of Pride's 'kynnesmen', Lechery or (Bodily) Lust (I, 1196–98, 1227). The vices are related in
being two of the seven mortal sins.

free] formulaic in context: (1) noble, well-bred (*O.E.D.*, a., 3); possibly also
(2) willing (*O.E.D.*, 20).

373. *leman*] mistress, playmate.

376. *At the wine*] 'at the tavern', modelled on 'at nale' (*H.S.* 419). Cf. *Nature*,
where Reason rebuked Man as he sat 'at the wyne' (I, 1109); *Songs*, V.90; 'New
Notbroune Mayd', *Remains*, III, l. 296.

378. *liking*] (1) taste; (2) sexual pleasure.

Youth. Hie thee apace, and come again.
    To have a sight I would be fain
    Of that lady free.   *[Exit* PRIDE.*]*

Riot. Sir, in faith, I shall tell you true:
    She is a fresh and fair of hue   385
    And very proper of body.
    Men call her Lady Lechery.

Youth. My heart burneth, by God of might,
    Till of that lady I have a sight.
        Intret Superbia cum Luxuria, et dicat Superbia:

Pride. Sir, I have fulfilled your intent   390
    And have brought you in this present
    That you have sent me for.

Youth. Thou art a ready messenger.
    [To Lechery] Come hither to me, my heart so dear.
    Ye be welcome to me   395
    As the heart in my body.

Lech. Sir, I thank you, and at your pleasure I am.

---

383. S.D.] *McKerrow; This ed. conj. after l. 381.*   389.1. *Superbia cum*] *Q2;*
superbis cu *Q3.*   *dicat*] *Q3;* dica *Q2.*   394.] *Q2, Q3;* Come hither to me, |
My heart so dear. *This ed. conj.*   395–96.] *Gowans;* one line in *Q2,*
Q3.   397. I am] *Q2, Q3;* am I *McKerrow conj.*

381–86.] Sapience tells Hawes's Youth: 'Come on your waye walke on a pace |
For ye longe for to haue a syght | Of dame Clennes so clere a face | So goodely of
body in beauty bryght | That there can not be so fayre a wyght' (1233–37; cf.
1072–76).

386. *proper of body*] good-looking.

388. *My heart burneth*] Sapience tells Hawes's Youth that a man in love
complains how a 'sharpe darte' has 'wounded sore his herte | It brenneth hote
lyke fyre certayn' (1331–34; cf. 1560–62).

389.1.] 'Pride enters with Lechery, and says'.

391. *in this present*] just now, this instant (*O.E.D.*, sb.[1], 4a; a northern form?).

392. *That*] what.

393. *ready*] prompt.

messenger] In this sense, 'summoner', the term is used of God's 'myghty
messengere' (63), Death, who summons Everyman to his final reckoning.

395–96.] This conjectural lineation may be preferable to (1) rhyming 'body'
with an emended 'am I' at 397 (and with 398), in that 398 might once have
rhymed 'same' with 'I am'; (2) splitting just 394 after 'me', so that 393–96 is a
quatrain rather than (as now) two couplets; and (3) doing nothing. Cf. 1 Cor.
vi.15–16.

Ye be the same unto me.

Youth. Masters, will ye to tavern walk?

    [*To Lechery*] A word with you there will I talk   400

    And give you the wine.

Lech. Gentleman, I thank you verily,

    And I am all ready

    To wait you upon.

Riot. What, sister Lechery!   405

    Ye be welcome to our company.

Lech. Well, wanton, well! fie, for shame,

    So soon ye do express my name!

    What, if no man should have known?

398.] *Q2, Q3;* Ye be unto me the same *This ed. conj.*   400. there] *Q3;* here *Q2*.
408. my] *Q2;* me *Q3*.   409. What, if . . . known?] *Happé;* What! if . . .
knowne, *Halliwell;* What if . . . wit, *Gowans;* What if . . . known! *Schell-Shuchter.*

398.] 'May you reciprocate.' This, and later lines (466–70), seem to parody Paul's views on marriage (cf. 368–69): 'The wife hath not power of her own body, but the husband: and likewise also the husband hath not power of his own body, but the wife' (1 Cor. vii.4).

400. *there*] Q2 is inconsistent with a future tavern rendezvous (374–76, 462–63).

400–01.] The association of wine and sex is traditional: 'mans flessh may well be likened to a tauerner and þe luste of mans flessh to vyne', and 'mans flesh ʒeues men a tast of þe wyne of lechery by vnclene kyssynges, clippynges, and oþer vnhonest handelynges' (*Sermons*, pp. 234–35).

405–26.] Riot's exclamation suggests that Lechery had left him and Pride (who must have preceded her at 390) behind in going alone to meet Youth at 394, and that only at 399 did Youth invite his fellows to join them towards the exit. The Lechery–Riot skirmish involves threatened fisticuffs (410), and a flirtation (415–17), which Youth, talking with Pride apart and unaware of the ironies of 425, interrupts only at 426–27 with questions that perhaps betray a little jealousy.

407. *Well, wanton, well*] traditional refrain of song mock-chiding one who flirts with eyes (?). Cf. 'Wel wanton ey but must ye nedis pley | Yowre lokis nyse ye let hem renne to wide' (*The English Poems of Charles of Orleans*, ed. Robert Steele, E.E.T.S. O.S. 215 [1941], p. 142, ll. 4235–36; cf. ll. 4241–42, and *Y.* 411–17); and Bang, pp. 87–88. Cf. Tilley W269, 'WELL, WELL is a word of malice.'

408–09.] In *Nature* Sensuality says Lechery, among others, has changed her name (to Lust) 'For to blere hys [Man's] eye' (I, 1204, 1227).

    Iwis, I shall you beat, well, wanton, well!   410

Riot. A little pretty nisot,

    Ye be well nice, God wot!

    Ye be a little pretty pie;

    Iwis, ye go full gingerly.

Lech. Well, I see your false eye   415

    Winketh on me full wantonly.

    Ye be full wanton, iwis.

Youth. [*Aside to Pride*] Pride, I thank you of your labour

    That you had to fetch this fair flower.

Pride. Lo, Youth, I told thee   420

410.]*Q2,Q3;* Iwis . . . beat! | Well . . . well! *Gowans.*   411. A little]*Q2,Q3;* A, lytell *Bang conj.*   nisot] *Bang conj.;* nylet *Q2;* nyset *Q3.*   413–14.] *McKerrow conj.;* one line in *Q2, Q3.*   414. gingerly] *Q3;* gingerie *Q2.*

   411. *A*] Perhaps an interjection is intended, as at 90, but cf. 385, 413.

   nisot] 'wench, coquette', as emended by Bang (p. 88), for rhyme, after Skelton's usage, 'And where I spy a nysot gay | That wyll syt ydyll all the day' (*Magnyfycence*, ll. 1229–30; the only *O.E.D.* example), to which can be added 'Amsot [i.e. 'A nisot'], or folt; Stolidus . . . Baburrus . . . Insons' (*Promptorium Parvulorum*, ed. A. L. Mayhew, E.E.T.S. E.S. 102 [1908], col. 11), and 'Now are þay nysottes of þe new gett, so nysely attyred' (*A Good Short Debate Between Winner and Waster*, ed. Sir I. Gollancz [1920], l. 410; reference courtesy of Professor Sherman M. Kuhn), where 'nysottes' is glossed as 'wanton girls', from OF. *nicette*, fem. of *nicet*. McKerrow (p. 89) thinks Riot means just this, the French diminutive of 'nice' (412), meaning 'innocent, foolish'; cf. also 'nycette', meaning 'breast handkerchief'. Q2 is a foul-case reading of the Q3 term.

   412. *nice*] (1) wanton; (2) coy, affectedly shy (*O.E.D.*, a., 5).

   413–14.] a recollection of a dance refrain. In *Occupation* the gallant Idleness says as he performs his 'trace', 'Queyntly go y, lo, | as prety as a py, lo' (Winchester MS, fol. 66r).

   413. *pie*] (1) wily or cunning one (*O.E.D.*, sb.[1], 2a); Idleness in *Occupation* is also called 'a wyli pye' (Winchester MS, fol. 68r). (2) chatterbox, like a magpie, a bird of black-and-white plumage and a long pointed tail, 'well known for its noisy chatter, and . . . often taught to speak' (*O.E.D.*, 'magpie', 1); cf. Tilley P285, 'To chatter like a PIE'; and *Nature*, where Sensuality says Reason or Innocency 'chatreth lyke a pye' (I, 369).

   414. *gingerly*] (1) warily (regarding her name); or (2) mincingly, daintily? The *O.E.D.* lists the Q2 word, meaning 'ginger-coloured', but foul case here, only in the nineteenth century.

   416.] (1) a conventional expression for flirtation; cf. *Magnyfycence*, where Fortune 'wantonly can wynke' (l. 2023); (2) possibly also 'shuts out, connives at, Lechery's existence' (*O.E.D.*, 'wink', v.[1], 6a).

   418. *labour*] (1) work; (2) lobbying, influence exerted in urging a suit.

   419. *this fair flower*] In the second stanza quoted above at 381–86n Hawes's Youth exclaims, 'Wolde to god I had so fayre a floure' (1078).

That I would bring her with me.
Sir, I pray you, tell me now,
How doth she like you?
Youth. Verily, well she pleased me,
For she is courteous, gentle and free.   425
[*To Lechery*] How do you, fair lady?
How fare you, tell me.
Lech. Sir, if it please you,
I do well enow,
And the better that you will wit.   430
Youth. Riot, I would be at the tavern fain,
Lest Charity us meet and turn us again.
Then would I be sorry
Because of this fair lady.
Riot. Let us go again betime,   435
That we may be at the wine
Or ever that he come.
Pride. Hie thee apace, and go we hence.
We will let for none expense.
Youth. Now we will fill the cup and make good cheer.   440

424. pleased] *Q2, Q3;* pleaseth *Hazlitt.*   428–29.] *This ed.; one line in Q2,*
Q3.   430. wit] *Q2, Q3;* knowe *McKerrow conj.*   433–34.] *McKerrow conj.;*
one line in Q2, Q3.   434. fair] *Halliwell;* farye *Q2, Q3 subst.*   435. again]
Q2, Q3; agayte *McKerrow conj.*

---

423. *like*] please.
424. *pleased*] The tense indicates Youth is speaking to Pride apart from
Lechery.
426.] word-play on 'fair' with 427.
430.] 'And all the better for your wanting to know (how I am).' Cf. Bang, p.
90.
432. *again*] back.
434. *fair lady*] formulaic address (426, 468; Lechery is also termed 'fair' at
372, 385 and 419). The Q2–Q3 form, unattested in the *O.E.D.* as an adjective
until *c.* 1640, must have transposed type.
435.] 'Let us go once more while there is still time.' Riot may imply that
Youth has already been to the tavern: this slip could be an echo of 432, or the
influence of *Nature*, in which Man evidently returns to the tavern (II, 301).
440.] formulaic: a Lord of Misrule, in a Christmas carol *c.* 1500, says, 'Mende
the fyre, & make gud chere! | ffyll þe cuppe, ser botelere!' (*Secular Lyrics of the
XIVth and XVth Centuries*, ed. Rossell Hope Robbins, 2nd ed. [1955], no. 3, ll.
17–18).

I trust I have a noble here.
[*Jingling his coins*] Hark! sirs, for God Almight,
Hearest thou not how they fight?
In faith, we shall them part;
If there be any wine to sell,   445
They shall no longer together dwell.
No, then I beshrew my heart!

Riot. No, sir, so mote I thee,
Let not thy servants fight within thee,
For it is a careful life   450
Evermore to live in strife.
Therefore, if ye will be ruled by my tale,
We will go to the ale
And see how we can do.
I trust to God that sitteth on high   455
To leese that little company
Within an hour or two.

Pride. Now let us go, for God's sake,
And see how merry we can make.

Riot. Now let us go apace.   460

442. S.D.] *Gowans.*   458. God's] *Q3;* goodes *Q2.*

---

443. *they*] not Youth's warring, internal impulses, as Bang and Nugent
Monck (see Appendix IV, pp. 269–70) think, but, as McKerrow queries (p. 90),
Youth's coins, which jingle together in his purse, evidently like clashing dag-
gers, and will be 'parted' (444–45) once they are spent. Ashby is the first to read
this correct sense (fol. 32r).

444. *part*] (1) separate; (2) share (*O.E.D.*, v., 10).

448. *mote I thee*] 'might I thrive' (formulaic).

449.] a standard injunction for servants, as in Henry VII's household ordinances, where every retainer had to swear to avoid 'all mannor of riots, rowts,
vnlawfull assemblies, making of bandes, quarrels, debates, striffs, & controu'-
sies, other w^th^in ye kinges chamber, or w^th^out', and to 'forbid & lett ye same'
(B.L. Harley MS 2210, fol. 9r). Cf. Titus 2.9.

thy servants] Youth's coins, being 'nobles', are properly his servants in that he
is a 'king' (see 592–96).

within thee] in your household (*O.E.D.*, 'within', B.3).

450. *careful*] troubled.

452. *tale*] advice.

453. *to the ale*] to the alehouse.

456. *leese*] lose.

And I be last there, I beshrew my face!

Youth. Now let us go, that we were there
　　　To make this lady some cheer.

Lech. Verily, sir, I thank thee
　　　That ye will bestow it on me,   465
　　　And when it please you on me to call
　　　My heart is yours, body and all.

Youth. Fair lady, I thank thee.
　　　On the same wise ye shall have me
　　　Whensoever ye please.   [*Exit* LECHERY.]   470

Pride. Riot, we tarry long.

Riot. We will go even now with a lusty song.

Pride. In faith, I will be rector chory.

461. be last] *Henderson;* belast *Q2, Q3.*   469.] *Q2, Q3;* On the same wise | Ye
shall have me *This ed. conj.*   470. S.D.] *This ed.; at l. 546.1 in Haz-*
litt.   471. long] *Q3;* very longe *Q2.*

---

467. *My heart is yours*] Hawes's Dame Cleanness also tells Youth, 'ye my hert
haue now in cure' (1567).

470. Exit LECHERY] Lechery's implied invitation at 466 suggests Youth will
meet her at the tavern, not go there with her. Since she speaks no more after 467,
and has nothing to do with Charity's binding (at 574 he only refers to the
'fellows' who chained him), she must exit here, giving her actor ninety-one lines
to change costumes for Humility.

471. *long*] Q3 omits less matter than Q2, this form is found elsewhere (542),
and the delay since Riot first proposed a tavern visit (283) offers plausible
grounds for a Q2 editorial addition.

472. *a lusty song*] Suitable contemporary three-part songs are Dr Cooper's 'In
youth in age both in welth' (Stevens, App. B, no. 152), as well as Henry VIII's
'youth' songs (for their words and music, see *Music at the Court of Henry VIII*,
ed. John Stevens, Musica Britannica, 18 [1962], pp. 22, 52, 70–71; and Intro.,
pp. 25–26.

473. *rector chory*] leader of the choir (*O.E.D.*, 'rector', 2b [from 1546], and cf.
'chore', sb.[1], 4; *M.E.D.*, 'chor(e', a., from 1494; a 1496–97 example appears in
The Medieval Records of a London City Church (St. Mary at Hill) A.D.
1420–1559, ed. Henry Littlehales, E.E.T.S. O.S. 128 [1905], 31). Bang (p. 91)
also notes that Barclay describes in his *Ship of Fools* (1509) this figure's business:
'The rector Chori is made the messanger | He rennyth about lyke to a pur-
suyuant | With his whyte staffe mouynge from syde to syde | Where he is lenynge
talys ar nat skant' (II, 155). The fifth earl of Northumberland provides for the
daily selection of his chapel's two rectors chory (four on principal feasts, and at
the requiem mass celebrated for the deceased knights of the Garter on St
George's night; Percy 1, pp. 198, 370, 374–75; Percy 2, fol. 56v). The choir's
basses, counter-tenors and tenors alternated in this role, for which at the

Youth. Go to it then hardily,
   And let us be agate.   *[They sing.]*   475

         [Enter CHARITY.*]*

Char. *[To Youth]* Abide, fellow! a word with thee.
    Whither go ye, tell me.
    Abide, and hear what I shall you tell,
    And be ruled by my counsel.

Pride. Nay, no fellow, ne yet mate!   480
    I trow thy fellow be in Newgate.
    Shall we tell thee whither we go?
    Nay, iwis, good John a Pepo.
    Who learned thee, thou mistaught man,
    To speak so to a gentleman?   485
    Though his clothes be never so thin,

474–75.] *McKerrow conj.; one line in Q2, Q3.*   474. hardily] *Hazlitt;* hardely
Q2, Q3; hardly *This ed. conj.*   477. Whither] *Hazlitt;* whether *Q2,
Q3.*   479. be] *Q2; not in Q3.*   482. whither] *Hazlitt;* whether *Q2, Q3
subst.*   483. John a Pepo] *Q2, Q3;* John-a-Peepo *Hazlitt.*

Yorkshire matins, mass and evensong they stood at an antiphon-lectern on
either side before the rest of the singers.

474. *hardily*] with gusto.

475. *agate*] on our way (a northern word; Bang, p. 91).

476–77.] Cf. Death's entrance to Everyman: 'Eueryman, stande styll!
Whyder arte thou goynge | Thus gayly?' (85–86).

480. *fellow*] Being so addressed also occasions a dispute between Reason and
Sensuality in *Nature* (I, 311–13).

mate] buddy (*O.E.D.*, sb.^{2}, 1c, used in contempt).

483. *Pepo*] of uncertain meaning, possibly (1) pumpkin, in Latin *pepo* (early
English form 'pepon'), so understood by George Ashby, fol. 32r; (2) sneaky
spying, peeping (*O.E.D.*, sb.^{2}, 1); cf. Tilley B540, 'To play BOPEEP' (first
instance in 1528); (3) shrill, feeble and squeaking in voice (*O.E.D.*, 'peep', sb.^{1},
2)? (4) a place name? there was a Pipe in Herefordshire, Staffordshire and
Warwickshire at least; (5) possibly a minstrel's name? Magdalen College,
Oxford, accounts for 1512 record 'Sol. Petro Pyper pro pypyng in interludio
nocte Sancti Iohannis, vj^d' (Chambers, *M.S.*, II, 249).

486. *thin*] This adjective, oddly chosen to describe a newly well-off heir's
garments (but cf. 348), may echo *Nature*, where the World criticises Man, 'all
naked' with the 'garment of innocencye' (I, 433, 438), as too flimsily clothed for
the climate. Poverty and *thin* clothes are commonly associated: cf. *The Castle of
Perseverance* (*Macro Plays*), ll. 109–10, and de Worde's *lytell geste of Robyn hode*
(*S.T.C.* 13689), sigs. A4v, A6r.

Yet he is come of noble kin.
Though thou give him such a mock,
Yet he is come of a noble stock,
I let thee well to wit. 490
Riot. What! Sir John, what say ye?
Would you be fettered now?
Think nat too long, I pray you.
It may fortune come soon enow;
Ye shall think it a little soon. 495
Char. Yet, sirs, let this cease,
And let us talk of goodness.
Youth. He turned his tale; he is afeard,
But, faith, he shall be scared.
He weeneth by flattering to please us again, 500
But he laboureth all in vain.
Char. Sir, I pray you me not spare,
For nothing I do care
That ye can do to me.
Riot. No, whoreson? sayst thou so? 505

491. ye] *Q2, Q3;* you *McKerrow conj.*   493. you] *Q2, Q3;* ye *Halliwell.*   494. may] *Q3;* mye *Q2.*   496. *Char.*] *Q3;* youthe. *Q2.*   498. *Youth.*] *Q3;* charite. *Q2;* Ryot *Halliwell.*   turned] *Q2, Q3;* turneth *Hazlitt.*   tale] *Q2, Q3;* tail *Hazlitt.*

490.] 'I can set you straight on that' (*O.E.D.*, 'let', v.[1], 13).
491. *Sir John*] a title owing to clergy (Latin *dominus*), and a cleric's name from Chaucer onward (*M.E.D.*, 'Jon', n.), as in *Magnyfycence*, l. 1187, and John Heywood's *Johan Johan the Husband*, ed. G. R. Proudfoot, M.S.R. (1972), and Bang, p. 91.
what say ye?] Besides McKerrow's conjecture, one might have (1) the present form (as at 697), an unrhymed first line to a speech (cf. 716); or (2) 'what sayest thou?' the insulting mode of address (as at 87, 505, 524, 601; cf. *H.S.* 705). The possible double rhyme with 493 tends to support McKerrow.
494. *fortune*] perchance.
496. *Char.*] Q2 gives Charity two successive speeches at 498 and 502, evidently by transposing headings here and at 498.
498. *turned his tale*] (1) changed his mind (cf. 452); perhaps, figuratively, (2) has taken flight, 'turned tail' (*O.E.D.*, 'tail', sb.[1], 11d, a phrase in falconry; cf. Tilley T16, 'To turn TAIL')?
499. *scared*] frightened away, driven off.
501. *laboureth*] pleads.
502-04.] Cf. 1 Cor. xiii.4-7: 'Charity suffereth long, and is kind . . .'

Hold him, Pride, and let me go.   [*Pride seizes Charity.*]
I shall fet a pair of rings
That shall sit to his shins,
And that even anon.

Pride. Hie thee apace, and come again,   510
And bring with thee a good chain
To hold him here still.   [*Exit* RIOT.]

Char. Jesu, that was born of Mary mild,
From all evil he us shield
And send you grace to amend   515
Or our life be at an end,
For I tell you truly
That ye live full wickedly.
I pray God it amend.

[*Enter* RIOT *with fetters.*]

Riot. Lo, sirs, look what I bring.   520
Is not this a jolly ringing?
By my troth, I trow it be.
I will go wit of Charity.

507. fet] *Q3;* set *Q2.* pair] *Halliwell;* prayre *Q2, Q3.*   512. S.D.] *Gowans.*   516. our] *Q2, Q3;* youre *McKerrow conj.*   519.1.] *Hampden.*   523. wit] *Q3;* with *Q2.*

507. *fet*] fetch. In this foul-case variant the term's occurrence elsewhere (319)
and Riot's exit favour Q3.

a pair of rings] Though evidently 'less painful than chains' so called, which
were also reckoned in pairs, 'rings' were still 'a light chain, designed to secure
the prisoner but not to impede his movements' (Pugh, pp. 372–73); cf. 511.

516. *Or*] before.

our] Charity's divine origin does not prevent him using the first person plural
elsewhere (147, 514, 723, 725) for Youth and himself, but here Charity appears
to be influenced by Good Deeds, who accompanies Everyman into the grave.

519.1. fetters] not stocks (as at 304), which are too cumbersome to carry into
the acting area, especially since both Charity's hands and feet (577) are to be
bound.

521. *ringing*] (1) Riot's jingling of the chains, and a pun (507; *H.S.* 690); less
probably (2) according to Bang, a neologism, a collective term for the various
rings in the chains (*O.E.D.*, '-ing'[1], 1f and g).

522–25.] McKerrow thinks these lines possibly belong to Pride, or even
Youth (p. 92), but Riot could answer his own questions and has just addressed
similar taunting queries to Charity (491–95).

523. *wit of*] ask of, find out from.

How sayest thou, Master Charity?

Doth this gear please thee?   525

Char. They please me well indeed.

The more sorrow, the more meed;

For God said, while he was man:

Beati qui persecutionem patiuntur propter justitiam.

Unto his apostles he said so   530

To teach them how they should do.

Pride. We shall see how they can please.

Sit down, sir, and take your ease.

Methink these same were full meet

To go about your fair feet.   535

Youth. By my truth, I you tell

They would become him very well;

Therefore, hie that they were on,

Unto the tavern that we were gone.

Riot. That shall ye see anon,   540

How soon they shall be on; [*Pride and Riot fetter Charity*.]

541. S.D.] *This ed.; They fetter Charity Hampden after l. 544; Youth, Riot and Pride put Charity in the stocks, and go out with Lechery Happé after l. 546.*

527.] a proverb (?), not found elsewhere. The belief is traditional (see *M.E.D.*, 'mede', n. [4] 2[a], the example dated 'a1500[a1415]'); Bang cites Christ's Last Supper counsel to the disciples in John xvi.20: 'ye shall weep and lament, but the world shall rejoice: and ye shall be sorrowful, but your sorrow shall be turned into joy'.

meed] reward.

529.] 'Blessed [are they] who have suffered persecution because of righteousness' (cf. Matt. v.10), preached by Christ to his disciples and the people in his sermon on the mount; and a popular gospel for masses of the saints (such as Abdon and Sennen on 30 July).

532. *they*] the 'pair of rings' (507; cf. 525–26).

533.] on a stool already in the acting area (see Intro., p. 25).

534. *meet*] fit, suitable.

536. *truth*] troth, good faith.

541. Pride and Riot fetter Charity.] Youth evidently takes no active part in the chaining, because he tells the others to do it at 538, and will 'see [it] anon' (540), as if a spectator. The binding may follow Riot's future tense (541), probably occurs as he tells of what they all will do 'after' (542), and may precede 544, because 544–46 echo the words before the first song (473–75), where Youth also voices his agreement after Pride, as the choir leader, brings the other two singers to order. Because Pride has the foot-fetters in his hands by 534–35 (Riot must tie

And after we will not tarry long,

But go hence with a merry song.

Pride. Let us begin all at once.

Youth. Now have at it, by Cock's bones,   545

And soon let us go.

> [YOUTH, PRIDE *and* RIOT *sing, and exeunt.*]

Char. Lo, masters, here you may see beforn

That the weed overgroweth the corn.

Now may ye see all in this tide

How vice is taken, and virtue set aside.   550

Yonder ye may see Youth is not stable,

But evermore changeable;

And the nature of men is frail,

546.1. S.D.] *This ed.; Exeunt Pride, Youth, Riot, and Lechery. Hazlitt.*   551.
Youth] *Birmingham;* youth *Q2, Q3.*   not] *Q3;   not in Q2.*   553.men] *Q2,
Q3;* man *Hampden.*

Charity's hands), however, the binding could be in progress from that moment.

Charity's binding derives from *Everyman*, where Good Deeds, whose meaning is 'charity', complains to Everyman, 'Thy synnes hath me sore bounde, | That I can not stere' (487–88). For a discussion of the fettering-stocking of virtue by vice in *Youth, Hick Scorner, Ane Satyre*, continental woodcuts by Albrecht Dürer (1524) and Peter Flettner (1525), some late moral plays and *King Lear* (II.ii.120–46), see Craik, pp. 93–96, and *H.S.*, 528n.

545. *Cock's*] God's.

547. *beforn*] (1) openly, before you; (2) just previously?

548.] Tilley W242; the first example here is by Malory: 'hit is shame that evir ye were made knyght to se suche a lad to macche you, as the wede growyth over the corne' (ed. Eugène Vinaver, *Works* [1953; rpt. 1966], bk. VII, 8, p. 223); Bang gives others (p. 93). The simile's source is Christ's parable of the sower, some of whose seed 'fell among thorns, and the thorns grew up, and choked it, and it yielded no fruit' (Mark iv.7). Christ interpreted this seed to be 'such as hear the word, And the cares of this world, and the deceitfulness of riches, and the lusts of other things entering in, choke the word, and it becometh unfruitful' (iv.18–19).

corn] seed.

549. *all in this tide*] wholly at this time.

551. *Yonder ye may see*] not to be understood literally; the Youth actor may be changing costumes (see Intro., n. 111).

552. *evermore changeable*] a characterisation suiting more Man in *Nature*, where 'hys dyuers and varyable dealyng' (II, 361) has him twice forsake both virtue and vice, than Youth, who has been hostile to Charity from the start.

553–61.] Meekness tells Man in *Nature* that his 'nature | I[s] frayll / and lyghtly to syn wyll assent | Eyther of purpose / or on wetyng peraduenture' (II,

That he wotteth not what may avail
Virtue for to make. 555
O good Lord! it is a pitiful case,
Sith God hath lent man wit and grace
To choose of good and evil,
That man should voluntarily
To such things himself apply, 560
That his soul should spill.

[*Enter* HUMILITY.]

Hum. Christ, that was crucified and crowned with thorn
And of a virgin for man was born,
Some knowledge send to me
Of my brother Charity. 565
Char. Dear brother Humility,
Ye be welcome unto me.
Where have ye be so long?
Hum. I shall do you to understand
That I have said mine evensong. 570
But, sir, I pray you, tell me now
How this case happened to you.
Char. I shall tell you anon.

557. man] *Q2*; me *Q3;* mē *McKerrow conj.*

1127–29; cf. I, 337, 375). Earlier Man praises God as having given him 'vertue',
an 'vnderstandyng / wherby I may auew | And well dyscerne / what ys tobe done
| yet for all that / haue I fre eleccyon | Do what I wyll / be yt euyll or well' (I,
134–39; cf. 298–302).

556. *case*] turn-of-events (formulaic in context).

557. *man*] McKerrow suggests Q3 intended 'mē' (cf. 553), but Charity mainly
uses the third person singular (554, 559–61).

wit] judgement, understanding.

564–65.] a request that defies allegorical interpretation. In the parallel *Everyman* episode, however, Good Deeds' *sister Knowledge* (519–20) enters to begin a
conversion of the man-type that will raise Good Deeds again to her feet.

568.] a peculiar question: Charity only says he seeks Humility's counsel
(185–87), and Youth assumes the former will return (294–96), but not necessarily the latter.

569. *do you to understand*] make known to you (*O.E.D.*, 'do', v., 22c).

570. *evensong*] vespers, sixth of the seven daily religious hours, performed at
dusk and commemorating the passion's aftermath.

The fellows that I told you on
Have me thus arrayed.   575
Hum. Sir, I shall undo the bands
From your feet and your hands. [*Unfetters him.*]
Sir, I pray you, tell me anon
Whither they be gone
And when they come again.   580
Char. Sir, to the tavern they be gone,
And they will come again anon,
And that shall you see.
Hum. Then will we them exhort
Unto virtue to resort   585
And so forsake sin.
Char. I will help you that I can
To convert that wicked man.

[*Enter* YOUTH, RIOT *and* PRIDE.]

Youth. [*To the audience*] Aback, gallants, and look unto me,
And take me for your special!   590
For I am promoted to high degree.
By right I am king eternal –
Neither duke ne lord, baron ne knight,
That may be likened unto me;

577. S.D.] *Hampden.*   585–86.] *Halliwell; one line in Q2, Q3.*   588.1.]
McKerrow.   593. lord] *Q3;* Lorde *Q2.*

---

574. *fellows*] Charity, when last speaking to Humility, of course had only seen
Youth.

575. *arrayed*] (1) dressed out; (2) afflicted, disfigured (*O.E.D.*, v. 10).

582–83.] the 'anticipated entrance' so common in *H.S.* (see Intro., p. 31).
and perhaps used as a cue: the rogues did not say they would return.

585.] Cf. a proverb written on a wall in the fifth earl of Northumberland's
Wressle castle: 'And in youthe to goode vertues yf thou resorte | In thy age they
shall helpe the . . .' (Flügel, p. 490).

585–86.] For similar lineation, cf. 654–55.

587. *that*] in that, in so far as (Abbott, 284).

589–90.] Pride, describing the effects of Man's new 'gown' in *Nature*, says
'That all the galandys in thys town | Shall on the fassyon wonder' (I, 1060–61).

590. *special*] intimate, particular friend.

592. *king eternal*] epithet for God (*O.E.D.*, 'eternal', a., 1); cf. 34, 783–84.

> They be subdued to me by right,   595
> As servants to their masters should be.
>
> *Hum.* Ye be welcome to this place here.
> We think ye labour all in vain;
> Wherefore your brains we will stir
> And keel you a little again.   600
>
> *Youth.* Sayest thou my brains thou wilt stir?
> I shall lay thee on the ear.
> Were thou born in Trumpington
> And brought up at Hogs Norton?
> By my faith, it seemeth so.   605
> Well, go, knave, go!
>
> *Char.* Do by our counsel and our rede,
> And ask mercy for thy misdeed,
> And endeavour thee, for God's sake,
> For thy sins amends to make   610
> Or ever that thou die.
>
> *Riot.* Hark, Youth, for God avow,
> He would have thee a saint now!
> But Youth, I shall you tell,
> A young saint, an old devil.   615

612. for God avow,] *Halliwell;* for, God avow, *Gowans.*

---

598. *labour*] Youth's urgings at 589–90.

600. *keel*] 'cool (a hot or boiling liquid) by stirring, skimming, or pouring in something cold, in order to prevent it from boiling over', where the early figurative sense, 'to assuage passion or vice', is taken literally (*O.E.D.*, v.¹, 1b, 2). Youth seems to be drunken. Cf. 388, and *Nature*, where Reason advises Man about his conversion: 'Loke what dysease / ys hote and brennyng | take euer suche a medycyn as ys cold in werkyng' (II, 1072–73).

603–04.] Youth's sneer sounds like a university witticism. In *Nature* Pride says Reason's advice is 'the counsell of a karle borne' (I, 1008).

603. *Trumpington*] in Cambridgeshire, just south of Cambridge; the setting in Chaucer's *Reeve's Tale* (Bang, p. 95).

604. *Hogs Norton*] Hook Norton, Oxfordshire. This form, from the fourteenth century, evidently suggested a (possibly later) rhyming jingle, 'Hogs Norton, where pigs play on the organ' (Tilley H505; Margaret Gelling, *The Place-Names of Oxfordshire*, II [1954], 353–54).

606. *knave*] (1) villain; (2) menial, slave.

615.] 'Itt is a comond prouerbe bothe of clerkes and of laye men, "ȝounge seynt, old dewell"' (*Sermons*, p. 159). In a late medieval dialogue, 'Of þe seuen

Therefore, I hold thee a fool,
And thou follow his school.

Youth. I warrant thee, I will not do so.
I will be ruled by you two.

Pride. Then shall ye do well;   620
If ye be ruled by our counsel,
We will bring you to high degree
And promote you to dignity.

Hum. [*To Youth*] Sir, it is a pitiful case
That ye would forsake grace   625
And to vice apply.

Youth. Why, knave, doth it grieve thee?
Thou shalt not answer for me.
When my soul hangeth on the hedge once,
Then take thou and cast stones   630
As fast as thou wilt.

620–21. Then . . . well; | If . . . counsel,] *Schell-Shuchter;* Then . . . well, | Yf
. . . counsell; *Halliwell.*   627. grieve] *Q3;* geue *Q2.*   630. stones] *Q3;*
stones. *Q2.*

Ages', the Angel tells the Child (shortly to be Youth), 'ȝonge saynt alde devell is
ane alde sawe' (R. H. Bowers, 'A Medieval Analogue to *As You Like It* II.vii.
137–66', *Shakespeare Quarterly*, 3 [1952], 110, l. 9). Tilley D311.

623. *dignity*] high rank.

628.] Good Deeds gives 'that ferefull answere' (423; cf. 107) for Everyman.

629–31.] a proverbial passage of considerable antiquity. Cf. the owl's complaint in *The Owl and the Nightingale* (*c.* 1189–1216), ed. Eric Gerald Stanley
(1960), ll. 1607–14:

> Þu seist þat ich am manne loð,
> An euereuch man is wið me wroð,
> An me mid stone & lugge þreteþ,
> An me tobusteþ & tobeteþ;
> An hwanne heo habeþ me ofslahe
> Heo hongeþ me on heore hahe,
> Þar ich aschewele pie an crowe
> From þan þe þar is isowe.

Youth may mean 'When my soul is made a moral example or scarecrow [like the
owl]', or simply 'When my soul is damned [at the Last Judgement]', but in any
case stone-casting is a traditional punishment for sin (John viii.7). For late
examples of the proverbial 'hangeth on the hedge', see Tilley H362, and
O.E.D., 'hang', v., 17b, and 'hedge', sb., 6a (meaning 'to be held in abeyance'
by the seventeenth century).

Char. Sir, if it please you to do thus,
        Forsake them and do after us.
        The better shall you do.
Riot. Sir, he shall do well enow,   635
        Though he be ruled by neither of you.
        Therefore, crake no longer here,
        Lest thou have on the ear,
        And that a good knock.
Pride. Lightly see thou avoid the place,   640
        Or I shall give thee on the face.
        Youth, I trow that he would
        Make you holy or ye be old,
        And I swear by the rood
        It is time enough to be good   645
        When that ye be old.
Youth. Sir, by my truth, I thee say,
        I will make merry whiles I may.
        I cannot tell you how long.
Riot. Yea, sir, so mote I thrive,   650
        Thou art not certain of thy life.
        Therefore, thou were a stark fool
        To leave mirth and follow their school.
Hum. [*To Pride*] Sir, I shall him exhort

638. thou] *Q3;* you *Q2.*

---

638. *thou*] Youth uses this impolite form throughout this attack (601, 603, 628, 630–31); perhaps Q2 wrongly expands 'yᵘ'?

have] 'have (a blow)', an uncommon elliptical construction (*M.E.D.*, 'haven', v. [1]7c[d]; *O.E.D.*, 'have', v., 14d).

641. *give*] strike (*O.E.D.*, 14d). 'If thou make mani wordes I wil geue yᵉ on yᵉ eare' ('A Play of Robin Hood for May-Games', ed. W. W. Greg, *Collections Part II*, Malone Soc. [1908], l. 59).

645–46.] Sensuality in *Nature* tells Reason he can assume control of Man after he has reached forty, in 'Hys croked old age / when lusty youth ys spent' (I, 328). Cf. the proverb on the ceiling of the fifth earl of Northumberland's son's room at Leconfield: 'Youthe in his flowres may lyue at liberte | In age it is conuenient to grow to gravite' (Flügel, p. 483).

648.] proverbial, as in *Castle of Perseverance* (*Macro Plays*), l. 608.

654. To Pride] Humility evidently speaks to his moral opposite, Pride, since he replies. Youth must stand with Riot, to whom he has just spoken, and behind Pride, since Humility has to 'go' to Youth (661, 663).

Unto us to resort   655
And you to forsake.

Pride. Ask him if he will do so,
To forsake us and follow you two.
Nay, I warrant you, nay.

Hum. That shall you see even anon.   660
I will unto him gone
And see what he will say.

Riot. Hardily, go on thy way.
I know well he will say nay.

Youth. [*To Humility*] Yea, sir, by God that me dear bought,   665
Methink ye labour all for nought.
Weenest thou that I will for thee
Or thy brother, Charity,
Forsake this good company?
Nay, I warrant thee.   670

Pride. No, master, I pray you of that,
For anything forsake us nat.
And all our counsel rule you by,
Ye may be Emperor or ye die.

Youth. While I have life in my body   675
Shall I be ruled by Riot and thee.

Riot. Sir, then shall ye do well,
For we be true as steel.

---

663. Hardily] *Hazlitt;* Hardely *Q2, Q3;* hardly *This ed. conj.*   665. by] *Q3;* be *Q2.*   668. thy] *Q2;* they *Q3.*   672. nat.] *Schell-Shuchter;* nat, *Halliwell.*   673. by,] *Schell-Shuchter;* by; *Halliwell.*   676. thee.] *Halliwell;* the? *Happé.*

---

661. *gone*] go.

665. *Yea*] Despite 670, this and the entire line jar with Riot's prediction (664).

669.] Cf. Fellowship in *Everyman:* 'I wyll not forsake the to my lyues ende, | In the waye of good company' (213–14).

674. *Emperor*] Maximilian I, Holy Roman Emperor 1493–1519, offered the title in 1513–14 to Henry VIII (see Intro., pp. 20–21). *Circa* 1515 Pandarus' *Salus Populi* prophesied that the English king who conquered Ireland would win France and the Holy Land and 'dye Emperowre of Rome' (*State Papers*: Henry VIII, II, part III [1834], 31). Cf. *Nature*, where the World agrees that Man be 'ordeyned to reygne / here in thys empiry' (I, 422).

678. *true as steel*] Tilley S840. Riot may show his dagger here (cf. 688n).

Sir, I can teach you to play at the dice,
At the queen's game and at the Irish,   680
The treygobet and the hazard also,
And many other games mo.
Also at the cards I can teach you to play,

---

679. I] *Q3; not in Q2.*   683. play] *Q2, Q3;* ply *This ed. conj.*

---

679. *the dice*] This and cards (683) were in 1495 enacted unlawful games for an apprentice, labourer or servant, except in the Christmas season at his master's house; only play at tables for meat and drink was permitted year-round (*S.R.*, II [1816], 11 Hen. VII. c. 2, p. 569). In Henry VIII's 5 July 1511 proclamation enforcing the Statute of Winchester, servants were again forbidden to play dice and card games, which led to robbery of masters (*T.R.P.*, I, no. 63, pp. 88, 91); and the same prohibitions occur in the 1512 articles for naval war against France (*L.P.* I.1133), and in the 15 May 1513 proclamation of war statutes for Calais (*T.R.P.*, I, no. 73, p. 113). Skelton's Riot in 'The Bowge of Courte' enters as 'on the borde he whyrled a payre of bones, | *Quater treye dews* he clatered as he wente' (*Works*, I, ll. 346–47), and Barclay's *Ship of Fools* makes the same association: 'Some theyr londe and lyuelode in riot out wasteth, | At cardes, and, tenys, and other vnlawful gamys. | And some wyth the Dyce theyr thryft away casteth' (I, 51). For Henry VIII's losses at play, see Intro., p. 56.

680. *the queen's game*] a game at tables, like backgammon, played with dice; also called 'doublets', since 'he that throws Dubblets apace is certain to win, for as many as the Dubblets are, so many he lays down, or bears' (*O.E.D.*, 'queen', sb., 14b; [C. Cotton], *The Compleat Gamester* [1674], p. 162).

the Irish] a more challenging game at tables, termed 'the yresshe game' in Barclay's *Ship of Fools* (I, 21; *O.E.D.*, A.2c, B.3).

681. *The treygobet*] of uncertain meaning, but a dice game: (1) 'trey-gobelet' or 'three dice-boxes' (from French 'gobelet'; cf. *O.E.D.*, 'goblet[1]', 2, 'juggler's cup'); (2) 'three-pieces' (*O.E.D.*, 'gobbet', sb., 2, 'lump or mass'; suggested by Farmer, p. 355); (3) 'three-go-better' (*O.E.D.* conj., 'treygobet').

hazard] (1) a dice game where the caster and onlooker wager on different combinations of two dies; (2) jeopardy, risk or loss. Lilly C. Stone's *English Sports and Recreations* (1960) summarises the game's rules as follows: 'the thrower calls a number between five and nine before throwing. If he throws the number called or a number with a fixed correspondence to it, he "throws a nick" and wins. If he throws two aces or a deuce and ace he "throws out" and loses. If neither, he throws until the first number thrown (the chance) comes up and he wins, or the number first called (the main) comes up, in which case he loses' (p. 24; cf. *Compleat Gamester*, pp. 168–73). Skelton's Riot in 'The Bowge of Courte' invites Dread to play hazard (*Works*, I, l. 393).

683. *play*] an off-rhyme (?) with 684, unless we read 'ply', the aphetic form of 'apply' ('to practise, apply oneself to'; cf. 626 and *O.E.D.*, 'ply', v.[2], 11), though 'play' is formulaic in this context (cf. 679 and *O.E.D.*, 'play', v., 19, where 'ply' is not a variant spelling).

At the triumph and one-and-thirty,
Post, pinion and also ambs-ace,   685
And at another they call deuce-ace.
Yet I can tell you more, and ye shall con me thank,
Pink and drink and also at the blank,
And many sports mo.

684. triumph] *Gowans;* triump *Q2;* triunph *Q3.*   686. another] *Q3;* ad other
Q2.   687.] *Q2, Q3;* Yet I can tell you mo, | And ye shall con me thank, *This
ed. conj.*   shall] *Schell-Shuchter;* shyll *Q2;* wyll *Q3.*

---

684. *the triumph*] card game (from French 'triomphe') where 'trumps' (cards
whose suit temporarily outranks and 'takes' cards of other suits) are played
(*O.E.D.*, 'triumph', sb., 8; 'trump', sb.², 1). Q2 may be dropped type, or a
partial anglicisation towards the technical English term for playing at that game.
Happé suggests Q3 is from Italian 'trionfo' (p. 394).

one-and-thirty] card game like twenty-one; also termed bone-ace, where after
each player gets two cards and a third is turned up, the ace of diamonds or then
the highest card wins the hand, and the game's object is to draw to thirty-one, or
come nearest to it (*O.E.D.*, 'one', *numeral* a., 2b; *Compleat Gamester*, pp.
129–30). In de Worde's *chirche of the euyll men and women*, trans. Henry Watson
(*S.T.C.* 1966), Lucifer claims to have seven special masses, including 'one and
thyrty / and yᵉ tryumphe' (sig. B3v); and cf. Bang, p. 97.

685. *Post*] card game requiring repeated staking; also termed post-and-pair,
where players, after staking at 'post' and 'pair' and getting two cards, stake at
'seat', take a third card, and win the hand with the best three-of-a-kind, and
then either the best pair or cards totalling, or most approaching, twenty-one
(*O.E.D.*, sb.⁴; *Compleat Gamester*, pp. 150–51).

pinion] unknown card game (*O.E.D.*, sb.⁴); perhaps named after *O.E.D.*,
'pennon', 2, meaning 'knight-bachelor', or 1, 'banner' (the *O.E.D.* suggests
'pinion', sb.¹; cf. 6, 'heraldic signs like the saltire and the chevron').

ambs-ace] 'double-ace' (Latin prefix 'amb-'): (1) card game involving drawing
two aces? (2) lowest possible throw with two dice, and a losing combination, as at
hazard (*M.E.D.*, 'ambes-as', a)? (3) bad luck (*M.E.D.*, b)?

686. *deuce-ace*] (1) card game involving drawing an ace and deuce? (2) second
lowest possible throw with two dice, another losing combination, as at hazard
(*O.E.D.*, 'deuce¹', 5)? (3) bad luck?

687. *shall*] a northern form in Q1.

con me thank] show me your thanks (*O.E.D.*, 'con', v.¹, 4).

688. *Pink*] stab, use a dagger or blade (*O.E.D.*, v.¹, 1; so glossed by Farmer,
p. 429). McKerrow (p. 98) and the *O.E.D.* (v.², 1a) interpret as 'blink, as if
nodding from drinking'.

at the blank] (1) at a target's white centre; hence, at archery; (2) a dice game?
Anne of Cleves played at 'blank dice' when in London (Neville Williams, *Henry
VIII and his Court* [1971], p. 178); (3) a card game? in piquet a blank was a hand
without a 'Court-Card', and a winning combination (*Compleat Gamester*, pp. 81,
85–86, 88).

Youth. I thank thee, Riot, so mote I thee,   690
　　　　For the counsel thou hast given me.
　　　　I will follow thy mind in everything
　　　　And guide me after thy learning.
Char. Youth, leave that counsel, for it is nought,
　　　　And amend that thou hast miswrought,   695
　　　　That thou mayst save that God hath bought.
Youth. What say ye, Master Charity?
　　　　What hath God bought for me?
　　　　By my troth, I know nat
　　　　Whether that he goeth in white or black.   700
　　　　He came never at the stews,
　　　　Nor in no place where I do use.
　　　　Iwis, he bought not my cap,
　　　　Nor yet my jolly hat.
　　　　I wot not what he hath bought for me.   705

698. for me] *Q3; not in Q2.*   699. nat] *This ed.;* not *Q2, Q3.*   700.
Whether] *Q2, Q3;* Whither *This ed. conj.*   705. bought for me] *Q2, Q3;*
bought *This ed. conj.*

---

698. *for me*] omitted by Q2 (to rhyme with 699, as at 694/696), leaving 697
rhymeless and Youth's personal emphasis at 703–04 incongruous.

699. *nat*] used in rhyme at 672, and here in assonance with 700 (cf. 188–89).

700. *Whether*] Youth's remarks at 701–02, however, suggest 'Whither'.

white or black] The Carmelites were called White Friars because of the white
cloak covering their brown habit, and the Dominicans or Friars Preachers were
called Black Friars because of the black mantle worn over their white habit.
Christ's raiment was white at the transfiguration (Matt. xvii.2).

701–05.] In *Nature* Pride, who gets a new gallant's outfit for Man, probably
including a scarlet red cap of the kind Pride wears (I, 748–54), says as he goes to
find Man, visiting at the stews: 'Now must I to the stewes as fast as I may | to fech
thys gentylman but syrs I say | Can any man here tell me the way | For I cam
neuer there' (II, 405–08).

701. *the stews*] brothel quarter, specifically the stew-houses available to Londoners in Southwark on Bankside (a street across the Thames from St Paul's and
now running under Southwark Bridge), and then near the bishop of Winchester's palace and under his jurisdiction.

702. *use*] frequent.

703–04.] a gibe at the high price of hats and caps after parliament in 1512
interdicted the sale of cheap foreign-made wear (see Intro., p. 18). Cf. *Nature*,
where Pride complains about his cap's price: 'It cost me a noble at one pyche |
The scald capper sware sythyche | That yt cost hym euen as myche | But there
Pryde had a pull' (I, 752–55).

And he bought anything of mine,
I will give him a quart of wine
The next time I him meet.
Char. Sir, this he did for thee:
    When thou wast bond he made thee free   710
    And bought thee with his blood.
Youth. Sir, I pray you, tell me
    How may this be.
    That I know, I was never bond
    Unto none in England.   715
Char. Sir, I shall tell you.
    When Adam had done great trespass
    And out of paradise exiled was,
    Then all the souls, as I can you tell,
    Were in the bondage of the devil of hell,   720
    Till the Father of heaven, of his great mercy,

708. him meet] *Q2, Q3;* mought *This ed. conj.*

706–08.] a typical blasphemy. In 1485 at Coventry John Falks was charged as 'a very heretic, because he did affirm, That it was a foolish thing to offer to the image of our Lady, saying, Her head shall be hoar ere I offer to her: What is it but a block? If it could speak to me, I would give it an half-penny worth of ale' (John Foxe, *Acts and Monuments*, intro. George Townsend, IV [1846], 134).

707. *a quart of wine*] parodying the communion wine, Christ's blood, given to man.

711.]1 Cor. vi.20: 'For ye are bought with a price . . .'

714. *bond*] bound as a servant, with a (feudal) obligation in villeinage.

716.] This rhymeless formulaic line (cf. 181, 341, 384, 573, 732) is perhaps followed by a lacuna.

717–26.] Cf. *Nature* (II, 1114–23), where Meekness or Humility tells Man that Adam's pride and disobedience caused:

        a great decay and ruyne
In all the progeny / for the same offence
In suche wyse that he / and all that were borne sence
Be vtterly dysheryted / and put fro paradyse
and so we be made / thrall vnto syn and vyce
And lost shuld we be / all of very iustyce
Ne had be that god / of hys mercyfull goodnes
Dyd vs sone after / wyth hys own blode maynpryce
and vs redemed / fro paynes endles

Both passages of course refer to Christ's harrowing of hell, one of the articles of the creed.

717. *trespass*] sin.

Sent the second person in Trinity
Us for to redeem,
And so with his precious blood
He bought us on the rood   725
And our souls did save.

Youth. How should I save it, tell me now,
And I will be ruled after you,
My soul to save.

Riot. What! Youth, will you forsake me?   730
I will not forsake thee.

Hum. [*To Youth*] I shall tell you shortly.
Kneel down and ask God mercy
For that you have offended.   [*Youth kneels.*]

Pride. Youth, wilt thou do so –   735
Follow them and let us go?
Marry, I trow, nay.

Youth. Here all sin I forsake
And to God I me betake.
Good Lord, I pray thee, have no indignation   740
That I, a sinner, should ask salvation.

Char. Now thou must forsake Pride
And all Riot set aside.   [*Youth rises.*]

Pride. I will not him forsake
Neither early ne late.   745
I weened he would not forsake me,
But, if it will none otherwise be,

728–29.] *Hazlitt; one line in Q2, Q3.*

728–29.] Relineation restores a common couplet at 727–28 (e.g., 356–57, 422–23, 571–72).

732.] answering Youth's request (727).

733–34.] Cf. Knowledge's words to a repentant Everyman: 'Lo, this is Confessyon. Knele downe & aske mercy, | For he is in good conceyte with God Almyghty' (543–44).

734. *For that*] because.

739. *to God I me betake*] not literally true, for Youth does not die. Also kneeling before Confession, Everyman says he is bound 'a pylgrymage to take, | And grete accountes before God to make' (550–51).

745.] at any time (*O.E.D.*, 'early', adv., 1c).

I will go my way.
Youth. Sir, I pray God be your speed
    And help you at your need.   [*Exit* PRIDE.]   750
Riot. I am sure thou wilt not forsake me;
    Nor I will not forsake thee.
Youth. I forsake you also
    And will not have with you to do.
Riot. And I forsake thee utterly.   755
    Fie on thee, caitiff, fie!
    Once a promise thou did me make
    That thou would me never forsake,
    But now I see it is hard
    For to trust the wretched world.   760
    Farewell, masters everyone!   [*Exit.*]
Hum. [*To Youth*] For your sin look ye mourn,
    And evil creatures look ye turn.
    For your name who maketh inquisition,
    Say it is Good Contrition,   765
    That for sin doth mourn.

---

750. you] *Q3;* your *Q2.* S.D.] *McKerrow.*   764. inquisition] *Q3;* insicion *Q2.*

749–50.] echoing *Everyman*'s principal formula, as when Cousin says: 'so God me spede, | I wyll deceyue you in your moost nede' (357–58; cf. 229, 254, 285, etc.).

754. *have with you to do*] No direct object for 'have' is needed (*O.E.D.*, 'do', v., 40a).

755.] Cf. *Nature*, where Reason demands Man 'vtterly forsake and dyspyse | All your old seruauntys' (II, 1045–46).

757–58.] This echo of Everyman's complaint, 'For fayre promyses men to me make, | But whan I haue moost nede they me forsake' (370–71; cf. 248, 270, 380–81, etc.), is in keeping with Riot's (comic?) moralisation at 759–60 on Youth's failed vow (at 675–76).

760. *world*] The rhyme or assonance with 759 demands a northern form, 'ward' or 'warld' (Bang, p. 99).

764. *maketh inquisition*] conventional aureate phrase (e.g., *Fulgens & Lucres*, I, 457).

765. *Good Contrition*] defined in the next line. Everyman's new garment is called Contrition (643–45); in *Nature* Man becomes 'contryte' (I, 1414) and visits 'hartys contrycyon' (II, 1407).

Char. [*Giving Youth a garment*] Here is a new array
   For to walk by the way,
   Your prayer for to say.   769
Hum. [*Giving Youth a rosary*] Here be beads for your devotion,
   And keep you from all temptation.
   Let not vice devour.
   When ye see misdoing men,
   Good counsel give them
   And teach them to amend.   775
Youth. For my sin I will mourn,
   All creatures I will turn,
   And when I see misdoing men
   Good counsel I shall give them

770. beads] *Q2;* bokes *Q3.*   772. not] *Q2;* no *Q3.*

---

767. *a new array*] a dominant biblical metaphor for salvation (e.g., Ps. cxxxii.9, 16; Is. lxi.10; 2 Cor. v.1–4). Rev. iii.5 describes the garment as white, and 1 Peter v.5 states: 'ye younger, submit yourselves unto the elder. Yea, all of you be subject one to another, and *be clothed with humility*: for God resisteth the proud, and giveth grace to the humble' (my italics). Youth must receive what covers the habit of one of the virtues. Charity may help Humility off with his priest's (?) over-garment, the chasuble, and then give it to Youth. However, since it 'as touching the mystery signifyeth the purple mantle that Pilate's soldiers put on him [Christ], after that they had scourged him, and as touching the minister . . . signifyeth charity' (C. S. Cobb, *Rationale of Ceremonial, 1540–43*, Alcuin Club, no. 18 [1910], pp. 17–18), Youth may instead receive Charity's (?) chasuble. Earlier plays regularly objectify redemption by costume-changes, sometimes managed while on stage, as in *Everyman* (638–50), and in the older *Occupation*, where Doctrine, putting 'a clothe of clennes' on Idleness, renames him 'Clennes' (Winchester MS, fol. 73r).

768–70.] Charity may have a mendicant order in mind, but Englishmen, a Venetian wrote *c*. 1500, 'all attend Mass every day, and say many Paternosters in public, (the women carrying long rosaries in their hands . . .' (*Relation*, p. 23).

770. *beads*] a rosary or paternoster, stringed beads to keep count of the number of prayers said. Q3's censor, with a book-printer's bias, shows little sense in choosing manageable properties.

772.] Q2 conforms to *Y.* usage (cf. 449), and Q3 may respond to a suspected lacuna in this rhymeless line. It may, however, be non-authorial, since 771–72 together paraphrase the conclusion of the Lord's prayer, 'And lead us not into temptation; but deliver us from evil' (Luke xi.4). Cf. 1 Peter v.8: 'your adversary the devil, as a roaring lion, walketh about, seeking whom he may devour . . .'

777. *creatures*] sinful, wretched people (*O.E.D.*, 3c; the qualifying adj. at *Y.* 763 is not needed).

And exhort them to amend.   780
Char. Then shall ye be an heritor of bliss
    Where all joy and mirth is.
Youth. To the which, eternal
    God bring the persons all
    Here being. Amen.   785
Hum. [*To the audience*] Thus have we brought our matter to an
    end
    Before the persons here present.
    Would every man be content,
    Lest another day we be shent.
Char. We thank all this presence   790
    Of their meek audience.
Hum. Jesu, that sitteth in heaven so high,
    Save all this fair company,
    Men and women that here be.
    Amen, amen, for charity.   795

Finis.

784. God] *Q3;* Go *Q2.*   789. another] *Hazlitt;* onother *Q2, Q3.*   790.
presence] *Hazlitt;* presente *Q2, Q3.*   793.] *Q3; not in Q2.*   795. charity]
Q2, Q3; Charity *Hazlitt.*   795.1.] *Q3; not in Q2.*

783–85.] Cf. the conclusion of *Everyman*: 'Vnto whiche place God brynge vs
all thyder, | That we may lyue body and soule togyder. | Therto helpe the
Trynyte! | Amen, saye ye, for saynt charyte' (918–21).

786–91.] Cf. Reason's closing speech to the audience in *Nature*: 'Here we
make an end | Lest we shuld offend | Thys audyence / as god defend' (I,
1429–31).

786. *matter*] subject, theme.

an end] This loses *d* after *n* and rhymes with 'Amen' at 785 (see Intro., nn. 116,
144; and cf. *Y.* 773–75, 778–80, and *H.S.* 1027–28). A rhyme with 787–89 is
possible in a West Midland pronunciation (Brook, p. 69).

789. *shent*] scolded, blamed (especially servants by their masters).

790–91.] Charity's gratitude for the granting of his opening request (4).

790. *presence*] assembly, company.

795.] 'So be it, for the sake of charity', a formulaic conclusion (*M.E.D.*,
'charite', 4; 'amen', 1c), as in *Everyman* (see *Y.* 783–85n).

HICK SCORNER

The title-page of the quarto published by Wynkyn de Worde *c.* 1515–16;
reproduced by courtesy of the British Library

Hick Scorner

[*Enter*] PITY.

Pity. Now Jesu the gentle, that bought Adam fro hell,
  Save you all, sovereigns, and solace you send!
  And of this matter that I begin to tell
  I pray you of audience till I have made an end.
  For I say to you my name is Pity,   5
  That ever yet hath been man's friend.
  In the bosom of the second person in Trinity

0.1.] *Manly; Pity and Contemplation Farmer.* 1. fro] *Q1;* frō *Q3.* 3. of] *Q1, Q3;* Hawkins reads *Q1* or

---

The title is so split into two words by both Q1 (which prints it as one word elsewhere) and Q3 (generally). Imagination's jest (300) suggests a quibble on 'Hick's Corner', and if the play was written for Brandon's Suffolk Place, such a pun might have been intended, since de la Pole claimed the duke of Suffolk's title (see Intro., p. 34).

  1–9.] adapted from *Y.* 1–9, 31–34 (for *H.S.* 7–8) and 717–26 (for *H.S.* 1, 7) by Charity, and 786 (for *H.S.* 4) by Humility.

  1. *gentle*] noble in birth.

  2. *sovereigns*] masters. Cf. the audience in *Occupation*, 'souereynes semly in se' (Winchester MS, fol. 67r); Mercy's initial appeal to the spectators in *Mankind*, 'O ȝe souerens þat sytt and ȝe brothern þat stonde ryght wppe' (*Macro Plays*, l. 29); and Iris G. Calderhead, 'Morality Fragments from Norfolk', *Modern Philology*, 14 (1916–17), 7.

  solace] good cheer, happiness.

  5. *Pity*] (1) one of the Holy Ghost's seven gifts, which is 'propreliche a dewe and a triacle aȝens al vilenyes, and nameliche aȝens synne of enuye' (*The Book of Vices and Virtues*, ed. W. Nelson Francis, E.E.T.S. O.S. 217 [1942], p. 143; cf. *H.S.* 385), and a Virtue petty captain in *A.G.* (see Appendix III.3, ll. 828, 1080, 1225); (2) Christ, as in the Pietà (*M.E.D.*, 'image', n., 1a). An English woodcut indulgence, known as 'the Image of Pity' and portraying a half-figure of Christ crowned with thorns and surrounded by emblems of the crucifixion, was frequently printed by Caxton, de Worde and others in this period. See Hodnett 350, *459ª, *2016ª; Henry Bradshaw, *Collected Papers* (1889), pp. 84–100; Campbell Dodgson, 'English Devotional Woodcuts of the Late Fifteenth Century', *The Seventeenth Volume of the Walpole Society: 1928—1929* (1929), pp.

I sprang as a plant, man's miss to amend;
You for to help I put to my hand.
Record I take of Mary, that wept tears of blood;   10
I, Pity, within her heart did stand,
When she saw her son on the rood.
The sword of sorrow gave that lady wound,
When a spear clave her son's heart asunder.
She cried out and fell to the ground.   15
Though she was woe, it was little wonder!

9. put] *Q1;* haue put *Q3.*   11. stand,] *Manly;* stonde; *Hawkins.*   12.
rood.] *Manly;* rode, *Hawkins.*   13. wound,] *This ed.;* wounde *Q1;* a wonde
Q3; wounde; *Hawkins;* [a] wounde, *Manly.*   14. asunder.] *Manly;* a sondre
Q1; in sonder *Q3;* a sondre, *Hawkins.*   16. little] *Q1;* no *Q3.*

95–108 and pl. 35; and *H.S.* 11n. For the feast of the 'Iconia Domini Salvatoris'
and a 'Missa Nostrae Dominae Pietatis', see R. W. Pfaff, *New Liturgical Feasts
in Later Medieval England* (1970), pp. 102, 121. The theme also entered late
medieval English drama. In *Christ's Burial and Resurrection* Mary says to John at
the cross: 'Sum dolorose ditee Express now yee, | In þe dew honour of þis ymage
of pitee' (*Digby Plays*, ll. 795–96); cf. the Croxton *Play of the Sacrament*
(*Non-Cycle Plays*, ll. 712.1–2).

8. *miss*] wrongdoing, sin (formulaic with 'amend' in *O.E.D.*, 'miss', sb.[1], 3b).

9. *put to my hand*] make my business (*O.E.D.*, 'put', v.[1], 51b).

10–20.] adapted from 'Testamentum Christi' or an analogue (see Appendix
III.2, especially ll. 268–70, 288, 279, 275, 379), and for *H.S.* 14 see *Y.* 167–69
(Charity).

10. *Record I take of*] I call to witness (*O.E.D.*, 'record', sb., 3c).

tears of blood] a paradox explained in Wynkyn de Worde's 1509 book, *The .vii.
shedynges of the blode of Jhesu cryste* (*S.T.C.* 14572), where Mary 'beholdynge his
body & blody woundes wepeth so pyteously / that ye sanguyn teeres medled w^t
his pcyous blode renne downe on ye deed body' (sig. B2v).

11.] Mary was popularly called the 'moder of pyte', as in de Worde's .vii.
shedynges (sigs. B1v, B2r). His St Paul's Churchyard shop advertised itself at the
sign of 'Our Lady of Pity', a woodcut of whom was sometimes substituted for de
Worde's usual device (E. G. Duff, *A Century of the English Book Trade* [1905], p.
174). The mass of the compassion of the Virgin was alternatively named 'de
Pietate' (R. W. Pfaff, *New Liturgical Feasts*, pp. 97–99). Cf. *H.S.* 17n.

13.] Simeon so prophesies to Mary in the temple (Luke ii.35). This devotional
commonplace occurs, besides in 'Testamentum Christi' and the above noted
mass (*H.S.* 11n), in a song by Gilbert Banastir, Master of the Children of the
Chapel Royal (Stevens, p. 373), and in de Worde's 1519 prose *lamentacyon of our
lady* (*S.T.C.* 17537; cf. sigs. A3r–A4v).

14.] formulaic: in *Johan the Evangelist* John says he 'sawe Longes smyte his
[Christ's] herte a sonder' (l. 246).

16. *woe*] grief-stricken.

This delicate colour, that goodly lady,
Full pale and wan, she saw her son all dead,
Splayed on a cross with the five wells of pity,
Of purple velvet, powdered with roses red. 20
Lo, I, Pity, thus made your errand to be sped,
Or else man forever should have been forlore.

17.] *Q1, Q3; switched with l. 19 Manly (Kittredge) conj.* colour] *Q1, Q3;* colour [had] *Hazlitt.* 19. a] *Q1;* the *Q3.* 22. forlore] *Q3;* forlorne *Q1.*

---

17. *This delicate colour*] this tender culver, soft dove (*O.E.D.*, 'culver¹', of which this is a recorded form; cf. *M.E.D.*, 2b, a term of endearment applied to Christ and the Holy Ghost). A sense, 'lovely complexion', accepted by Hazlitt, Kittredge and others, may be punned on, since Pity's demonstrative adjective suggests that Mary's image is then visible, and his comparison of Christ's wounds to velvet (19–20) that a Pièta is depicted near by, perhaps on Pity's own costume. One Westminster altar was hung with 'cloth [of] golde powderyd with lyonnes and flower de lucys of golde with a riche image of oʳ Lady of Pitye', and a Lincoln cope hood also showed the image (Mackenzie E. C. Walcott, *The Inventories of Westminster Abbey at the Dissolution*, Trans. of the London and Middlesex Archaeological Soc., 4 [1872], p. 2). A Bolton Priory vestment *c.* 1540 was 'of whyt damaske and cremsyn velvett, with half moone and tyretts, and a pycture of Chryst upon the back' (Thomas D. Whitaker, *The History and Antiquities of the Deanery of Craven* [1805], p. 355).

18. *Full pale and wan*] formula describing Christ at death: de Worde's 1514 edition of *The fruyte of redempcyon* (*S.T.C.* 22557) says his body was 'pale and wanne by reason of flowȳges out of blode' (sig. D11r); cf. *The .vii. shedynges*, sig. A4r.

19. *the five wells of pity*] Christ's five wounds, a popular medieval cult and the subject of a Sarum mass (R. W. Pfaff, *New Liturgical Feasts*, pp. 84–91). Pynson's 1520 *lyfe of Joseph of Armathia* (*S.T.C.* 14807) says Christ came on earth the '.v. welles of pyte to open' (sig. A1v).

20. *purple velvet*] Between Pilate's judgement and Christ's journey to Golgotha, he was, as mock king of the Jews, clothed in purple (Mark xv.17, 20) and crowned with thorns (*H.S.* 24). Only Henry VIII and his immediate family could legally wear purple silk or cloth-of-gold at this time (*S.R.*, III [1817], 1 Hen. VIII. c. 14, pp. 8–9; 'Players in enterludes' were among those excepted from this ban).

powdered] strewn, spangled (a heraldic term; *O.E.D.*, 'powder', v.¹, 4, 5).

roses red] 'v roses of rede, þe wiche were þe v princypall woundes in ys [Christ's] bodye' (*Sermons*, p. 38), and which symbolised his charity, as in *The Castle of Perseverance* (*Macro Plays*, ll. 2143–46, 2210–11).

21. *errand*] (1) petition or prayer (submitted through an intercessor); (2) business or purpose (for which one has journeyed). Cf. *H.S.* 146.

sped] successful.

22. *forlore*] lost, ruined.

A maiden so laid his life to wed –
Crowned as a king, the thorns pricked him sore.
Charity and I of true love leads the double reign;   25
Whoso me loveth damned never shall be.
Of some virtuous company I would be fain,
For all that will to heaven needs must come by me;
Chief porter I am in that heavenly city.
And now here will I rest me a little space,   30
Till it please Jesu of his grace
Some virtuous fellowship for to send.

[*Enter* CONTEMPLATION.]

Contem. [*To the audience*] Christ that was christened, crucified
and crowned,

23. maiden] *Q1;* mayde *Q3*.   24. the] *Q1;* and the *Q3*.   25. leads] *Q1;* we
lede *Q3*.   reign] *This ed.;* rayne *Q1, Q3;* rein *Hazlitt*.   26. Whoso] *Q1;* Who
that *Q3*.   27. fain,] *This ed.;* fayne; *Hawkins*.   28. needs must] *Q1;* must
nedes *Q3*.   me;] *This ed.;* me, *Hawkins*.   29. in] *Q1;* of *Q3*.   30. here will
I rest me] *Q1;* wyll I rest me here *Q3*.   31. Jesu] *Q1;* our lorde Jesu
Q3.   32. fellowship] *Hazlitt;* felyshyp *Q1;* company me *Q3*.   send] *Q1, Q3;*
send me *This ed. conj.*   32.1.] *Manly*.   33. christened] *Q1;* chrystene *Q3*.

---

23. *maiden*] virgin man.
  laid his life to wed] (1) vouchsafed his life (*O.E.D.*, 'wed', sb., 2c); and
perhaps (2) pledged himself to marry (with reference to Christ's ultimate
marriage with Holy Church, noted at 43).
  25–29.] adapted from *Y*. 16–21 (Charity).
  25. *leads*] Abbott 336; cf. *H.S.* 70, and also 69, 109, 113, etc.
  28.] 'I am the way, the truth, and the life: no man cometh unto the Father, but
by me' (Christ to Thomas: John xiv.6).
  29. *porter*] gate-keeper, one who keeps the keys (Percy 2, fol. 62v): Pity is the
model for the lowest of the eight holy orders, the doorkeeper or *ostiarius* (Heath,
p. 14), that is, the earthly type of St Peter, to whom Christ gave 'the keys of the
kingdom of heaven' and the power to bind and loose (Matt. xvi.19).
  that heavenly city] New Jerusalem.
  31–32.] conventional entrance cue (Southern, p. 172; cf. *Y*. 582–83n). The
second king in the *York Plays*, ed. Lucy T. Smith (1885; rpt. 1963), prefaces the
third magus's appearance with these words: 'God graunte me happe so þat I
myght | Haue grace to gete goode companye' (XVII.19–20).
  32. *send*] For such irregularities in rhyme, see Intro., n. 116.
  33.] adapted from *Y*. 562 (Humility), but formulaic: 'The awntyrs off
Arthure at the Terne Wathelyn', '[Christ] That was crucyfiede one croyse, and
crownnede with thorne; | Crystynnede and krysemmede with candills and
coude' (Laing, I, ll. 221–22).

In his bosom true love was gaged with a spear.
His veins brast and bruised, and to a pillar bound,   35
With scourges he was lashed – the knots the skin tare.
On his neck to Calvary the great cross he bare;
His blood ran to the ground, as scripture doth tell;
His burden was so heavy that down under it he fell.
Lo, I am kin to the Lord which is God's son.   40
My name is written foremost in the book of life,
For I am Perfect Contemplation,
And brother to Holy Church, that is our Lord's wife.
John Baptist, Antony and Jerome, with many mo,

35. brast and bruised] *Q1;* brused and broken *Q3.*   37. Calvary] *Q1;*
Caluerly *Q3.*   39. down] *Q1; not in Q3.*   40. which] *Q1;* that *Q3.*   42.
am] *Q1;* am called *Q3.*   44. Antony] *This ed.;* Anthony *Q1, Q3.*

34–38.] possibly adapted from 'Testamentum Christi' (see Appendix III.1, ll.
145–54, 221–24) or an analogue like de Worde's 1509 *.vii. shedynges,* which
describes those extra-biblical symbols of the passion also depicted in the 'image
of pity': Christ 'naked boūden to a pyller', his 'flesshe rente fro the bones with
many & fell strokes of the knotted scourges' (sig. A2v), and his clotted wounds
opening with blood that ran to the ground when his clothes were ripped from
him after the scourging (sig. A3r).

34. *gaged*] (1) stabbed, wounded (*O.E.D.,* 'gag', v.², 2a); (2) pledged, offered
as a guarantee (*O.E.D.,* 'gage', v., 2b); (3) measured for depth (as with a spear;
O.E.D., 'gauge, gage', v.¹, 2; see 1523 example).

35. *brast*] burst.

pillar] one of the symbols of the passion, a public whipping post.

36. *tare*] tore.

37.] Only John xix.17 says Christ (elsewhere in the gospels, Simon of Cyrene)
carried the cross.

bare] bore.

41. *book of life*] record of individuals redeemed by God from death and hell, to
be completed on Judgement Day (Phil. iv.3; Rev. xx.12, 15).

42. *Perfect Contemplation*] perfected knowing of God, the end of the second
(contemplative) and higher Christian way of life; and one of Virtue's petty
captains in *A.G.* (see Appendix III.3, l. 849). Cf. M. Patricia Forrest, 'The Role
of the Expositor Contemplacio in the St. Anne's Day Plays of the Hegge Cycle',
Mediaeval Studies, 28 (1966), 60–76.

43.] After Christ's parable of the marriage of the king's son (Matt. xxii.1–14),
Paul interprets the Church as Christ's wife (Eph. v.23).

44. *John Baptist*] Christ's precursor, a desert dweller who heard God's word
there (Luke i.80, iii.2), and preached it by the Jordan river; cf. *A.G.* 1547.

Antony] a desert anchorite and ascetic (died *c.* 350), the founder of Christian
monasticism in Egypt.

Followed me here in holt, heath and in wilderness.   45
I ever with them went where they did go,
Night and day toward the way of rightwiseness.
I am the chief lantern of all holiness,
Of prelates and priests—I am their patron.
No armour so strong in no distress,   50
Habergeon, helm, ne yet no gestron—
To fight with Satan I am the champion
That dare abide and manfully stand.
Fiends flee away where they see me come.

46. them] *Q1;* hym *Q3.*   where] *Q1;* wher so euer *Q3.*   47. rightwiseness]
Q1; ryghtousnes *Q3.*   48. all] *Q1; not in Q3.*   51. Habergeon] *Q1;* Haber-
gon nor *Q3.*   gestron] *This ed. (O.E.D.);* Jeltron *Q1;* geltron *Q3.*   54.
Fiends] *Q1;* Fendes they *Q3.*

Jerome] exegete on whose scriptural translations the Vulgate was based, and
who in 374 became an ascetic and lived in his Bethlehem monastery; cf. *A.G.*
1576.

45. *holt*] a wood.

47. *rightwiseness*] righteousness, 'true wisdom'. Cf. 50–54n; the first of Virtue's four knights in *A.G.* (Appendix III.3, l. 795).

48. *lantern of all holiness*] Cf. Ps. cxix.105: 'Thy word is a lamp unto my feet,
and a light unto my path.' Edmund Dudley's *Tree of Commonwealth* (*c.*
1509–10), ed. D. M. Brodie (1948), says that men in holy orders should be 'the
verie Launternes of Lighte' that 'shew good examples to the temporaltie' (p. 33);
Dudley's phrase recurs later in Skelton's 'Colyn Cloute', *Works*, I, l. 442.

49. *patron*] father superior, protector; as 'One who holds the right of presenta-
tion to an ecclesiastical benefice' (*O.E.D.*, sb., 4).

50–54.] based on Rom. xiii.12, 'let us put on the armour of light', and Eph.
vi.11–18: 'Put on the whole armour of God, that ye may be able to stand against
the wiles of the devil . . . Stand therefore, having your loins girt about with
truth, and having on the breastplate of righteousness. . . . And take the helmet
of salvation, and the sword of the Spirit, which is the word of God: Praying
always with all prayer and supplication in the Spirit, and watching thereunto
with all perseverance . . .' (a passage customarily applied to the active life of
virtue). Contemplation may also allude to the office of the exorcist, one of the
four minor holy orders (Heath, p. 14). Athanasius, in his *Life of Saint Antony*,
trans. Robert T. Meyer (1950), writes that 'meditating on the good things to
come and contemplating the things that are the Lord's' will scatter demons (p.
56), whose temptation of hermits contemporary woodcuts depict (Hodnett 459,
813).

51. *Habergeon*] 'sleeveless coat or jacket of mail or scale armour' (*O.E.D.*)
helm] helmet.

gestron] 'light coat of mail'. Farmer, p. 258, glosses as 'Sheltron = shelter', but
see *O.E.D.*, 'gester(o)n', 'jazerant' and 'sheltron¹' (the last meaning 'troop-
phalanx', etc.).

But I will show you why I came to this land: 55
For to preach and teach of God's sooth saws
Against vice that doth rebel against him and his laws.
Pity. God speed, good brother! Fro whence came you now?
Contem. Sir, I came from Perseverance to seek you.
Pity. Why, sir, know you me?   60
Contem. Yea, sir, and have done long. Your name is Pity.
Pity. Your name fain would I know.
Contem. Indeed, I am called Contemplation,
That useth to live solitarily.
In woods and in wilderness I walk alone   65
Because I would say my prayers devoutly.
I love not with me to have much company,
But Perseverance oft with me doth meet
When I think on thoughts that is full heavenly;
Thus he and I together full sweetly doth sleep.   70

---

55. will] *Q1;* shall *Q3.*   land:] *Manly;* londe *Hawkins.*   56. saws] *Q1;* sawen
Q3.   57. laws] *Q1;* lawen *Q3.*   58. came you] *Q1;* come ye *Q3.*   59.
came] *Q1;* come *Q3.*   60. you] *Q1;* ye *Q3.*   64. solitarily] *Q1;* solytary
Q3.   65. in] *Q1; not in Q3.*   69. is] *Q1;* ben *Q3.*   70. doth] *Q1;* do *Q3.*

---

55. *show*] tell (*O.E.D.*, v., 23).

56. *to preach and teach*] formulaic phrase (e.g., Skelton's 'Colyn Cloute',
Works, I, l. 13).

saws] (1) teachings; and possibly (2) commandments (*O.E.D.*, sb.², 3).

59.] 'noo persone may come to the lyfe contemplatyf / yf he be not fyrst
proued well in the lyf actyf ' (Wynkyn de Worde's 1507 edition of *The boke
named the royall* [*S.T.C.* 21430], sig. Bb1r).

Perseverance] the virtue of the active life: from Christ's promise at Matt.
xxiv. 13, 'But he that shall endure [*perseveraverit*] unto the end, the same shall be
saved', but here adapted from the commander of Virtue's rear-ward in *A.G.*
(Appendix III.3, l. 1094), whose full name appears at *H.S.* 80. The character
occurs also in the *Castle of* [Good] *Perseverance* (*Macro Plays*, ll. 52, 75),
Skelton's *Magnyfycence*, *The World and the Child*, and Stephen Hawes's two
poems, *Example of Vertu* and *Pastime of Pleasure*.

64.] Cf. *A.G.* 922–23 (Appendix III.3).

useth] is accustomed.

70. *full sweetly doth sleep*] the reward of wisdom (Prov. iii.21–24) and of labour
(Eccl. v.12).

Pity. I thank God that we be met together.

Contem. Sir, I trust that Perseverance shortly will come hither.

Pity. Then I think to hear some good tiding.

Contem. I warrant you, brother, that he is coming.

[*Enter* PERSEVERANCE.]

Perse. [*To the audience*] The eternal God, that named was Mes-
      sias,   75

   He give you grace to come to his glory,

   Where ever is joy in the celestial place

   When you of Satan winneth the victory.

   Every man ought to be glad to have me in company,

   For I am named Good Perseverance,   80

   That ever is guided by virtuous governance.

   I am never variable, but doth continue

   Still going upward the ladder of grace;

71. *Pity.*] *Q1; not in Q3.*   72. *Contem.*] *Q1;* Pytye. *Q3.*   73. *Pity.*]
Q1; Contemplacyon. *Q3.*   74. *Contem.*] *Q1;* Pytye. *Q3.*   74.1.]
Manly.   76. his] *Q1;* that *Q3.*   77. celestial] *Q1;* celestycall *Q3.*   78.
winneth] *Q1;* wynne *Q3.*   79. me] *Q3; not in Q1.*   in] *Q1;* in his *Q3.*   82.
doth] *Q1;* alway do *Q3.*

71–74.] Q3 may shift these speech headings forward to give Contemplation
instead of Pity the wish for good tidings, since in Q1 (and presumably in Q3's
copy-text) Pity tells the only news (102).

72.] a standard 'anticipated entrance', according to Southern (pp. 172–73),
but also Contemplation's comment on Perseverance's allegorical nature, 'Still
going upward' (83).

75. *Messias*] 'promised redeemer', 'anointed one', taken from John i.41, iv.25
(Latin form Englished by Wyclif; *O.E.D.*, 'Messiah', a form dating from the
1560 Geneva Bible).

77–78.] Luke xv.10: 'there is joy in the presence of the angels of God over one
sinner that repenteth'.

78. *winneth*] a southern form of the present indicative plural.

81. *is*] The use of the third person form shows that Perseverance elliptically
refers to the abstract virtue he personifies (a switch in inflections that also occurs
at 82).

83. *the ladder of grace*] Cf. *Y.* 98. In various MSS of *Speculum Christiani*, ed.
Gustaf Holmstedt, E.E.T.S. E.S. 182 (1933), two ladders are drawn, one to hell
and one to heaven; in one MS one reads on the ladder's steps, 'Perseuerancia
bona. Paciencia in aduersis. Obediencia in dei preceptis. Iusticia in factis.
Penitencia in vita. Contricio & confessio peccati. Cognicio tui. Caritas. Fides.
Spes' (p. cxci). The topic is also discussed by Samuel C. Chew, *The Pilgrimage of
Life* (1962), pp. 201–02.

And lode in me planted is so true,
And fro that poor man I will never turn my face. 85
When I go by myself, oft I do remember
The great kindness that God showed unto man
For to be born in the month of December,
When the day waxeth short and the night long.
Of his goodness that champion strong 90
Descended down fro the father of rightwiseness
And rested in Mary, the flower of meekness.
Now to this place hither come I am
To seek Contemplation, my kinsman.
Contem. What, brother Perseverance! Ye be welcome! 95
Perse. And so be you also, Contemplation!
Contem. Lo, here is our master, Pity.
Perse. Now truly ye be welcome into this country!
Pity. I thank you heartily, sir Perseverance.
Perse. Master Pity, one thing is come to my remembrance: 100
    What tidings hear you now?

84. lode] *Q1*; loue *Q3*.   85. that] *Q1*; the *Q3*.   93. this] *Q1*; his *Q3*.   101.] *Q1, Q3*; *spoken by Pity? This ed. conj.*

---

84. *lode*] (1) magnetic loadstone (*O.E.D.*, 4; first example in 1509); (2) guidance (Farmer, p. 261; and *M.E.D.*, 2b)? Perseverance compares himself to a ship-compass magnetic needle, turning freely on a pivot but never failing to point (despite the movement of a compass box) to the magnetic pole.

87. *kindness*] (1) tender good will; (2) kinship, likeness in kind?

89.] traditional. In the *Two Coventry Corpus Christi Plays* nativity (ed. Hardin Craig, 2nd. ed., E.E.T.S. E.S. 87 [1957]), the first shepherd says that Isaiah prophesied 'Thatt a chylde schuld be borne of a made soo bryght | In wentur ny the schortist dey | Or elis in the myddis of the nyght' (252–55).

92. *flower*] the most excellent embodiment (*O.E.D.*, sb., 9).

97. *our master*] Perseverance later calls God 'the great master above' (847).

98.] perhaps formulaic: in *Four Elements* Studious Desire says to Experience, 'ye are ryght welcom to this contrey | without any faynyng' (sig. B7v).

101.] Two anomalies suggest that Pity may ask this question, that Perseverance replies at 102, and that the Q1–Q3 speech headings at 121–22 are reversed: (1) Pity's previous remark that he will 'hear some good tiding' from Perseverance (73), who gives no news in either Q1 or Q3; and (2) the oddness of a question about 'tidings' coming to his 'remembrance' (100). The emphasis on poverty (103–08) and the warning about overtrusting mercy (119–20) suit Perseverance (85) more than Pity. However, the term 'piteously' (103; cf. 846) and Pity's subsequent comments about priests' lack of devotion (124–38)—a topic adapted from Charity's opening monologue in *Y.*—support Q1.

Pity. Sir, such as I can I shall show you.
　　　I have heard many men complain piteously;
　　　They say they be smitten with the sword of Poverty
　　　In every place where I do go.   105
　　　Few friends Poverty doth find,
　　　And these rich men been unkind;
　　　For their neighbours they will nought do.
　　　Widows doth curse lords and gentlemen,
　　　For they constrain them to marry with their men,   110
　　　Yea, whether they will or no.

102. *Pity*] *Q1*, *Q3*; *Perse. This ed. conj.*   104. Poverty] *Hawkins;* poverty.
This ed. conj.   105. go.] *Hawkins;* go, *This ed. conj.*   109. doth] *Q1;* do
Q3.

103–08.] Referring to the widespread pulling down of houses and towns, the
loss of jobs and crop-lands, 'Cytees & Market townes brought to grete ruyne &
decaye necessaryes for mannys susten^nce made scarse & dere', and even a
notable depopulation of the realm, the 1515 Parliament strengthened a 1490 act
(*S.R.*, II [1816], 4 Hen. VII. c. 19, p. 542) by legislating against the engrossing
and enclosure of farms for sheep pasture (*S.R.*, III [1817], 6 Hen. VIII. c. 5, p.
127; also 7 Hen. VIII. c. 1, enacted in perpetuity). For a 1514 anti-enclosure
proclamation, see *T.R.P.*, I, no. 75, pp. 122–23. Hythlodaeus in More's *Utopia*
identified the cause of poverty as 'noblemen, gentlemen, and even some abbots'
who, by ordering enclosures, turn sheep to 'devour human beings themselves
and devastate and depopulate fields, houses and towns' (p. 67). Halle notes that
in the summer of 1515 'the kyng toke his progresse Westward, & visited his
tounes & castels there, & hard the complaintes of his pore comminaltie' ('Henry
VIII', fol. 57r). See also Joan Thirsk, *Tudor Enclosures* (1959); and *Tudor
Economic Documents*, ed. R. H. Tawney and Eileen Power (1924), III, 12–81.
　　104. *the sword of Poverty*] Cf. Prov. vi.11: 'So shall thy poverty [*egestas*] come
as one that travelleth, and thy want [*pauperies*] as an armed man'; and Job v.15:
'But he saveth the poor from the sword . . .'
　　106.] Tilley P468, 'The POOR have few friends.'
　　find] (1) discover; (2) provide for, support (as at *Y*. 30).
　　107. *unkind*] (1) unfeeling, cruel; (2) ungenerous, not given to doing charity
(*O.E.D.*, 3e).
　　109–11.] An early Tudor statute prescribes as principal felonies the seizure of
widows (who often had inherited wealth) and their forced marriage to their
captors (*S.R.*, II [1816], 3 Hen. VII. c. 3, p. 512), though such offences had a
long history: cf. C. H. Williams, 'A Fifteenth-Century Lawsuit', *Law Quarterly
Review*, 40 (1924), 354–64. Nevertheless, remarriage of a feudatory's widow
required royal permission and the payment of a large fine to the king (*Relation*,
p. 51).
　　109. *doth*] Abbott 334; cf. *H.S.* 615.

Men marry for good, and that is damnable,
Yea, with old women that is fifty and beyond.
The peril now no man dread will.
All is not God's law that is used in land.   115
Beware will they not till Death in his hand
Taketh his sword and smiteth asunder the life vain,
And with his mortal stroke cleaveth the heart atwain.
They trust so in mercy, the lantern of brightness,
That nothing do they dread God's rightwiseness.   120

Perse. O Jesu, sir, here is a heavy tiding!
Pity. Sir, this is true that I do bring.
Contem. How am I beloved, master Pity, where ye come?

115. law] *Q1;* wyll *Q3.*   117. Taketh] *Q1;* Take *Q3.* smiteth] *Q1;* smyte
Q3. vain] *Q1, Q3;* vein *Hazlitt.*   118. atwain] *Q1;* in twayne *Q3.*   121.
Perse.] *Q1, Q3; Pity This ed. conj.*   122. *Pity*] *Q1, Q3; Perse. This ed. conj.*

112–13.] In 1514 Margaret of Savoy wrote that the previous year Henry VIII,
with her at Tournai during the French campaign, suggested that, 'seeing that it
[widows' remarriage] was the fashion of the ladies of England, and that it was not
there holden for evil' and 'the ladies of his country did re-marry at fifty and
three-score' (that is, past child-bearing), she marry Charles Brandon, then
viscount Lisle (later duke of Suffolk). Margaret refused, saying 'it was not here
the custom, and that I should be dishonoured, and holden for a fool and light'
(*L.P.* I.2941). One notorious case was the marriage of William, a young brother
of Edmund de la Pole, the former (attainted) duke of Suffolk, to Catherine
(formerly married to Lord Grey), 'a widow of fifty, with a fortune . . . of 50,000
crowns . . . patiently to waste the flower of his beauty with her, hoping soon to
enjoy her great wealth with some handsome young lady' (*Relation*, pp. 27–28).

116–18.] In Chaucer's *Pardoner's Tale* a boy servant tells his master how his
old friend just died: 'Ther cam a preuy theef men clepe deth | That in this
countre all the peple sleeth | And wyth his spere he smote his herte in two'
(675–77). Cf. *Everyman*, where Death, referring to his 'darte' (76), warns: 'to
the herte sodeynly I shall smyte | Without ony aduysement' (178–79). Julyan
Notary's 1518 edition of the *Kalender of Shepardes* (*S.T.C.* 22410), which has
several woodcuts of Death with spear (sigs. G5v, G7v), mentions his 'mortall
knyfe' (sig. G8r).

117. *the life vain*] (1) senseless, futile life; (2) the vein of life, the life-
supporting artery (so *O.E.D.*, 'life', sb., 16; cf. 'vein', sb., 2b; and *H.S.* 35)?

119–20.] Bang (pp. ix–x) argues that this couplet is based on lines in Barclay's
Ship of Fools: 'They thynke no thynge on goddes rightwysnes | But grounde
them all, on his mercy and pyte' (I, 85). The proverbial observation, however,
comes finally from Ecclus. v.4–7.

123.] Contemplation must ask for news because he, unlike Perseverance, is a
hermit.

Pity. In good faith, people have now small devotion,
    And as for with you, brother Contemplation,   125
    There meddleth few or none.

Contem. Yet I trust that priests love me well.

Pity. But a few, iwis, and some never adeal.

Contem. Why, sir, without me they may not live clean!

Pity. Nay, that is the least thought that they have of fifteen, 130
    And that maketh me full heavy.

Contem. How, trow you that there be no remedy?

Pity. Full hard, for sin is now so grievous and ill
    That I think that it be grown to an impossible.
    And yet one thing maketh me ever mourning: 135
    That priests lack utterance to show their cunning;

125. with] *Q1; not in Q3.*   127. Yet] *Hazlitt;* Yes *Q1, Q3;* Yes? *This ed. conj.* that] *Q1; not in Q3.*   128. a] *Q1; not in Q3.*   129. live] *Q1;* playe *Q3.*   130. the] *Q3;* y^t *Q1 alternate possible reading.* thought] *Q3;* thoughe *Q1.* that] *Q1; not in Q3.*   132. How] *Q1;* And *Q3.* that] *Q1; not in Q3.*   134. that] *Q1; not in Q3.* impossible] *Q1;* vnpossybyll *Q3.*   135. yet] *Q1; not in Q3.*

---

124. *people have now small devotion*] a frequently made point (344, 583).

125. *as for with you*] as for you, with you (ellipsis: 'with' belongs to the verb at 126).

126. *meddleth*] (1) mingle, associate with; (2) concern themselves with.

128–36.] On 6 February 1511/12 John Colet's sermon to Convocation at St Paul's urged the clergy to reform themselves, since 'all thynge that is in the churche is either concupiscence of flesh, or eies, or pryde of lyfe', or benefice-hunting and 'the continuall secular occupation, wherin prestes and byshops nowe a dayes doth busy them selfe, the seruantes rather of men than of God; the warriours rather of this worlde than of Christe . . . [though] our warrynge is to pray, to rede and study scriptures, to preache the worde of God' (Lupton, pp. 295–97). Colet also attacked indiscriminate admission of men into holy orders, a practice making for 'vnlerned and euyll pristes' (p. 300); and about 1510 Wynkyn de Worde printed *Sermo Exhortatorius* (*S.T.C.* 17806), in which York Minster chancellor William Melton criticised 'the ignorant hordes who in the recent past had entered and then shamed the Church by their inadequate learning' (Heath, pp. 15, 70; cf. pp. 27–38, 70–92). Cf. Skelton's 'Colyn Cloute' (*Works*, I, ll. 85–87, 139–41, 235–39, 278–79); and *H.S.* 599.

adeal] at all.

130.] proverbial: cf. Medwall's *Fulgens & Lucres*, 'Tushe that is the lest care of .xv.' (I.1183).

133. *Full hard*] with great difficulty.

134. *an impossible*] impossibility (to deal with).

136. *lack utterance*] (1) speak out infrequently; (2) are deficient in the art of speech.

And all the while that clerks do use so great sin,
Among the lay people look never for no mending.
Perse. Alas, that is a heavy case,
 That so great sin is used in every place.   140
 I pray God it amend!
Pity. Now God, that ever hath been man's friend,
 Some better tidings soon us send!
 For now I must be gone.
 Farewell, good brethren here!   145
 A great errand I have elsewhere
 That must needs be done.
 I trust I will not long tarry.
 Thither will I hie me shortly
 And come again when I have done.   150

---

139. a] *Q1*; an *Q3*.   142. *Pity.*] *Manly;* Contem. *Q1, Q3 subst.*   145. here]
Q1; dere *Q3*.   146. A great errand] *Q1*; Moche busynes *Q3*.   149. will I]
Q1; I wyll *Q3*.

137–38.] Colet also argued in this way: 'the lay people haue great occasion of euils, and cause to fall, whan those men whose dutie is to drawe men from the affection of this worlde, by their continual conuersation in this worlde teche men to loue this worlde, and of the loue of the worlde cast them downe heedlyng in to hell' (Lupton, p. 297). Cf. *H.S.* 266.

141.] also *Y.* 519.

142. Pity] This exit speech cannot belong to Contemplation (as in Q1), because Perseverance suggests they leave *together* at 155 (Southern, however, manages to accept Q1 by arguing 145 is addressed to the audience [pp. 173–74]). The 142 and 153 speech headings were perhaps confused, as each follows lines by Perseverance. On internal evidence too Pity must have this speech (142 rephrases 5–6, and see 146), unless he either departs without a word before 153 (when Contemplation addresses a single 'Sir', Perseverance) or remains silently until 456 (as Q3 interprets; see 250–51). Manly's emendation, to give Pity the lines at 153, is impossible because both others are present, and the speech is spoken only to one person.

144. *For now*] for the time being (cf. 150).

145–52.] adapted from *Y.* 196–200 (Charity's departure and Youth's response).

146. *A great errand*] evidently Pity's work of mercy for mankind (21). T. W. Craik, in 'The Tudor Interlude and Later Elizabethan Drama', *Elizabethan Theatre*, ed. John R. Brown and Bernard Harris, Stratford-upon-Avon Studies 9 (1966), says Pity's remark has 'no bearing on the future action' and is 'simply a means of his leaving the stage' (p. 41).

Perse.   Hither again I trust you will come.
    Therefore God be with you!   [*Exit* PITY.]
Contem.   Sir, needs I must depart now.
    Jesu me speed this day!
Perse. Now, brother Contemplation, let us go our way.   155
                                     [*Exeunt.*]

[*Enter* FREE WILL.]

Free.   Aware, fellows, and stand a-room!
    How say you, am not I a goodly person?
    I trow you know not such a gest!
    What, sirs! I tell you my name is Free Will;
    I may choose whether I do good or ill,   160
    But for all that I will do as me list.
    My conditions ye know not, perdie;

152. S.D.] *This ed.; at l. 154 in Manly.*   153. *Contem.*] *Q1*, *Q3*; PYTE. *Manly.*
needs I must] *Q1;* I must nedes *Q3.*   155.1 S.D.] *Manly.*   155.2]
Manly.   156. stand a-room] *Q1;* make me roume *Q3.*   158. a gest] *Hawkins;* ageste *Q1;* a ieste *Q3;* a guest *Hazlitt.*   160. do] *Q1;* wyll do *Q3.*   ill]
Q1; euyll *Q3*.

156–59.] adapted from *Y*. 40–44 (Youth's entrance-speech).

156.] Free Will distinguishes between 'fellows', those servants or guests of
low rank near the door who can be brushed aside casually, and seated guests of
higher status, whom he calls 'sirs' (159).
   Aware] beware, watch out.
   a-room] aside.

158. *gest*] (1) guest, one entertained at house or table; (2) stranger; (3) fellow,
guy. The sense 'mien' or 'gesture' (*O.E.D.*, sb.³) is possible, but unlikely.

159. *Free Will*] The name bears three basic meanings: (1) the ability to choose
freely, moral autonomy irrespective of any actual choice (as at 160, 874); (2)
deciding or willing that something be or be done, like Will in *Wisdom*, who 'for
dede oft ys take' (*Macro Plays*, l. 221); and (3) the proper name 'Will', modified
by the adjective 'Free' in senses such as (a) 'one not bound, a freeman', (b) 'one
of gentle birth' (706), (c) 'one not confined in prison' (662, 683) and (d) 'one who
is generous'. The main meaning is the second one, expressed in Free Will's own
use of the term 'will' (e.g., 161, 478, 776, 823, 989), Contemplation's 'thine own
will' (723) and 'wilfully' (754), and references to the man-type's 'ill will' (471)
and 'good will' (890). Q1 writes the name as one word throughout.

161.] adapted from Free Will's remark in *A.G.* (Appendix III.3, l. 1057).
   me list] I want.

162. *conditions*] manners, behaviour, character (*O.E.D.*, sb., 11b).
   perdie] by God.

I can fight, chide and be merry.
Full soon of my company ye would be weary
And you knew all.   165
What, fill the cup and make good cheer!
I trow I have a noble here—
Who lent it me? By Christ, a frere!
And I gave him a fall!
[*Searching for the coin*] Where be ye, sir? Be ye at home? 170
Cock's passion, my noble is turned to a stone!
Where lay I last? Beshrew your heart, Joan!
Now, by these bones, she hath beguiled me!
Let see: a penny my supper, a piece of flesh ten
     pence,
My bed right nought; let all this expense—   175
Now, by these bones, I have lost an halfpenny!

163. fight, chide] *Q1*; chyde/fyght *Q3*.   164. weary] *Hazlitt*; wery *Q1*,
Q3.   165. you] *Q1*; ye *Q3*.   170. S.D.] *Manly*.   172. Beshrew] *Q1*; I
beshrewe *Q3*.   173. these] *Q1*; cockes ten *Q3*.   175. let] *Q1*; let se *Q3*.

163–67.] adapted from *Y*. 54, 163–64, 440–41 (Youth); cf. *H.S.* 401.
    168. *frere*] friar. The mendicant orders were notorious for their begging (e.g.,
Chaucer's *Summoner's Tale*), and so a friar would normally be the last one from
whom a loan would be solicited and expected.
    169. *gave him a fall*] jousting, wrestling or fighting expression (*M.E.D.*, 'fal',
n., 5).
    170.] adapted from *Y*. 443–57 (where Youth also personifies the coins as
'nobles', and Riot makes them servants 'at home' in Youth's household and
vows to lose their company).
    171. *stone*] probably a pun on 'testicle' (*O.E.D.*, sb., 11); cf. Medwall's
Fulgens & Lucres, 'I shall come within two stonys caste: | Of her I aske no more'
(I.854–55). A thief's substitution of stones for coins supposedly victimised a
Robert Coke in 1505 (*Select Cases*, pp. clii, 152).
    172. *Joan*] conventional name for a prostitute (*M.E.D.*, 'Jonete-of-the-
steues', 1).
    173. *by these bones*] Free Will is about to count on his fingers. Cf. 'by these ten
bones' (*O.E.D.*, 'bones', sb., 1c).
    174. *Let see*] Let's see (*O.E.D.*, 'see', v., 15a).
    piece of flesh] 'woman', prostitute (*O.E.D.*, 'piece', sb., 3d); cf. *Y*. 365.
    175. *My bed right nought*] It came with the 'flesh'. One stews regulation stated
that 'No single woman [is] to take money to lie with any man, but shee lie with
him all night till the morrow' (Stow, II, 54).
    let] deduct, subtract (*O.E.D.*, v.[1], 6b).
    176. *I have lost an halfpenny*] not well calculated, a noble being valued at much
more than 11½ pence (see *Y*. 263n).

> Who lay there? My fellow Imagination.
> He and I had good communication
> Of Sir John and Sibley,
> How they were spied in bed together;   180
> And he prayed her oft to come thither
> For to sing 'Lo le, lo lowe.'

179. Sibley] *This ed.;* sybbell *Q1, Q3 subst.*   180. spied] *Hazlitt;* spyed *Q1, Q3;* sped *This ed. conj.*   182. Lo le, lo] *Q1;* lo ly *Q3.*

---

177. *Imagination*] adapted from *A.G.*, where Imagination, as Virtue's messenger sent to warn and rouse his host to gather for battle with Vice (Appendix III.3, p. 263, and ll. 746–60), means 'thinking about, contriving, devising'. Here, however, the term has a pejorative sense: (1) lying, slander, false witness, as of malicious tale-telling (cf. *H.S.* 262, 474–76): e.g., 'by that ymagynacion which is werst of all | They make an hoole tale as thoughe it were true | ffor men be gladde to hire tydynges newe' (*Peter Idley's Instructions to his Son*, ed. Charlotte D'Evelyn [1935], II, ll. 612–14); and one of the heads on a three-headed giant met by La Graunde Amoure in Stephen Hawes's *Pastime of Pleasure*, ed. William E. Mead, E.E.T.S. O.S. 173 (1928), ll. 4333–46; and (2) scheming, plotting means or devices for bad ends (cf. *H.S.* 220n and *M.E.D.*, 'imaginacioun', n. 3). The term's technical meaning in medieval psychology is discussed in the Intro., n. 257.

178. *communication*] (1) news; (2) talk, conversation.

179. *Sir John*] adapted from *Y.* 483, 491.

Sibley] the usual Middle English form: see E. G. Withycombe, *The Oxford Dictionary of English Christian Names*, 2nd ed. (1963), p. 255; cf. the *Ludus Coventriae* Doomsday play, ed. K. S. Block, E.E.T.S. E.S. 120 (1922; rpt. 1960), where 'Sybile sclutte' is a soul damned for lechery (42.118); *Cocke Lorelles bote*'s 'sybly sole mylke wyfe of Islyngton' (sig. B3r); and Skelton's 'Colyn Cloute', *Works*, I, l. 393. The rhymes here (with 173, 176, 182, 185) and later at 391–93 and 737–39 also call for this spelling.

180.] Clerical incontinence is both a standard literary joke (cf. Chaucer's *Canterbury Tales* and *H.S.* 209n) and a historical problem at this time, since for centuries no one in major holy orders, that is, bishops, priests, deacons and subdeacons, had been allowed to marry (Heath, pp. 104–08). Margaret Bowker's *Secular Clergy in the Diocese of Lincoln, 1495–1520* (1968), pp. 115–21, studies some parish case-histories. The first Tudor parliament enacted jail terms for priests and other religious found guilty of 'Avoutrie fornicacion inceste or eny other flesshely incontinency' (*S.R.*, II [1816], 1 Hen. VII. c. 4, pp. 500–01).

How they were spied] Because Free Will tells this anecdote to contrast, as at 183–84, his doubly costly night with Joan (her price and her theft) and Sir John's free enjoyment of Sibley (she comes to *him*), and because one expects '*That* they were spied' but '*How* they were sped [cf. *H.S.* 21]', emendation may be in order, though cf. 210, 465, 656.

182. *sing*] a term parodying religious service (note 'prayed' at 181) and with a

They twain together had good sport,
But at the stews' side I lost a groat.
I trow I shall never i-thee!   185
My fellow promised me here to meet,
But I trow the whoreson be asleep
With a wench somewhere.
How, Imagination, come hither!
And you thrive I lose a feather.   190
Beshrew your heart, appear!

[*Enter* IMAGINATION.]

Imag. What, how, how! Who called after me?
Free. Come near! Ye shall never i-thee!

183. twain] *Q1;* two *Q3.*   187. whoreson] *Q1;* hores sone *Q3.*   190.
thrive] *Q1;* thryue this yere *Q3.*   lose] *Q1;* lese *Q3.*   191. Beshrew] *Q1;* I
beshrewe *Q3.*   192. called] *Q1;* calleth *Q3.*

---

sexual meaning; see Eric Partridge, *Shakespeare's Bawdy,* rev. ed. (1955; rpt.
1961), p. 187 (citing *Troil.* V.ii.9–11).

Lo le, lo lowe] evidently a variant of 'hey trolly lolly' (692); cf. a stage direction
in *The Chester Mystery Cycle,* ed. R. M. Lumiansky and David Mills, E.E.T.S.
S.S. 3 (1974), 'troly loly troly loe' (Play VII, 447n). Possibly we should understand 'Low, lie low, low'.

183.] formulaic: cf. *Cocke Lorelles bote,* 'Therof they had good sporte' (sig.
B2r).

sport] This word is a good rhyme with 184, as *r* here is lost before *t* (Dobson, I,
112; for the vowel, see § 13 [2*b*ii] and 33).

184. *stews' side*] the Southwark Thames bank where the legal stew-houses or
brothels stood (cf. *O.E.D.,* 'stew', sb.², 8). Over half the vagrants discovered in
Southwark during three night raids in 1519 came from the stews, and more were
found in Southwark than in all the other suburbs combined (David J. Johnson,
Southwark and the City [1969], p. 64).

groat] English coin equal to four pence (not Free Will's lost amount at 176).

185. *i-thee*] thrive.

190. *I lose a feather*] proverbial (*O.E.D.,* 'feather', sb., 1b); as in Chaucer's
Troilus, where Fortune 'Gan pulle awey the fetheres brighte of Troie | Fro day to
day, til they ben bare of joie' (V.1546–47); cf. *H.S.* 492. A hat-feather characterised a gallant's pride, as for Troilus in Henry VIII's Epiphany 1516 court revels
(*L.P.* II, p. 1506).

192.] adapted from *Y.* 210 (Riot); cf. *H.S.* 303, 891–93.

how, how] ho, ho (*O.E.D.,* int.¹, 1).

193. *near*] (1) close; (2) nearer (*O.E.D.,* adv.¹, 1)?

Where have ye be so long?

Imag. By God, with me it is all wrong;   195
    I have a pair of sore buttocks.
    All in irons was my song;
    Even now I sat gyved in a pair of stocks.

Free. Cock's passion, and how so?

Imag. Sir, I will tell you what I have do.   200
    I met with a wench, and she was fair,
    And of love heartily I did pray her,
    And so promised her money.
    Sir, she winked on me and said nought,
    But by her look I knew her thought.   205
    Then into love's dance we were brought,
    That we played the pyrdewy.

194. be] *Q1*; ben *Q3*.   198. gyved] *Q1*; gryued *Q3*.   202. pray her] *Q1*;
her praye *Q3*.   203. her money] *Q1*, *Q3*; money her *This ed. conj.*   207.
pyrdewy] *Q1*; pyrdewhy *Q3*.

194.] copied from *Y.* 568 (Charity to Humility).

197.] (1) Imagination's 'song' should be understood sexually, like Sir John's
(182) and the 'pyrdewy' Imagination says he played in 'love's dance' (206–07).
The metaphor probably was suggested by *Y.* 190–95 (and 304–05), where Youth
threatens Charity will 'sing wellaway' in the stocks. (2) Perhaps 'All in irons' was
a popular song.

198. *gyved*] shackled, fettered.

201. *fair*] evidently disyllabic, a double rhyme with 'pray her' (202).

203. *her money*] A double rhyme with 201–02 is possible, but 'money' rhymes
with 207, 210, 213, 216, 219.

204.] Cf. *Y.* 415–16, where Lechery says this of Riot.

206. *love's dance*] traditional phrase (cf. *O.E.D.*, 'dance', sb., 5, 6a; 'love',
sb., 7f; Stevens, pp. 168, 199, 342, 360, 393).

207. *played the pyrdewy*] (1) performed the 'pyrdewy', 'sorte d'air mélancoli-
que', as for dancing (Fréderic Godefroy, *Dictionnaire de l'Ancienne Langue
Française*, VI [1889; rpt. 1969], 174). The term probably comes from 'le doux
père' ('sweet father', an affectionate priest like Sir John?), the name of a French
dance in which dancers kissed (see *Recueil Général des Sotties*, ed. Émile Picot, I
[1902], 100–01; and Howard Mayer Brown, *Music in the French Secular Theater,
1400–1550* [1963], pp. 163–64). (2) fornicated (cf. *H.S.* 180–82). Godefroy's
one example, from *Le Pastoralet* (after 1422), illustrates the entire *H.S.* phrase:

        Car ou hault bois sans descorder
        Les pastouriaulx gais et volages
        En lor flajolz chansons boscages
        Pour resvillier l'esbatement

I wot not what we did together,
But a knave catchpoll nighed us near
And so did us aspy;   210
A stripe he gave me—I fled my touch—
And from my girdle he plucked my pouch.
By your leave, he left me never a penny.
Lo, nought have I but a buckle!
And yet I can imagine things subtle   215
For to get money plenty.
In Westminster Hall every term I am;

210. aspy] *Q1;* espye *Q3.*   213. never] *Q1;* not *Q3.*   215. And] *Q3;* Ane
Q1.

                    Disoient moult sauvagement,
                    Et jouoient le *pirdouy*
                    Tant doulcement que qui l'oy
                    Tout fust lors en merancolie.
The term may have been used in imported French farces, since it also appears in
Recueil de Farces Françaises inédites du XVe siècle, ed. Gustave Cohen (1949): 'Et
nos femmes vont le pirdouy | Dancer par bieu de tous costez' (XVI.663–64).
Two other English examples exist: Skelton's 'Agaynste a Comely Coystrowne'
has 'Hys musyk withoute mesure, to sharp is hys my; | He trymmyth in hys
tenor to counter pyrdewy' (*Works*, I, ll. 25–26); and 'The Tale of Colkelbie Sow'
lists among songs 'Sum *Perdony* sum *Trolly lolly*' (Laing, I, l. 302).

    209. *catchpoll*] sheriff's sergeant, minor officer. Fornicators were liable to
arrest at this period (*L.P.* III.365.5, 10–12). In the early Tudor 'Boke of Mayd
Emlyn' the title heroine was stocked when she was caught with a friar *in flagrante
delictu* by a 'sergeaunt' (*Remains*, IV, ll. 355–76).

    211–12.] In Skelton's 'Bowge of Courte' Dread says, of Deceit's approach,
'For, yf I had not quyckely fledde the touche, | He had plucte oute the nobles of
my pouche' (*Works*, I, ll. 503–04).

    211. *stripe*] (1) blow; (2) lash or weal from a scourge.

    touch] (1) sexual contact; perhaps (2) stroke, hit.

    212. *girdle*] belt.

    214.] Riot in Skelton's 'Bowge of Courte' exclaims, 'Ay, in my pouche a
buckell I haue founde; | The armes of Calyce, I haue no coyne nor crosse'
(*Works*, I, ll. 397–98). Likewise, Fancy in *Magnyfycence* exchanges his purse
with Folly's, and complains, 'Here is nothynge but the bockyll of a sho' (1108).
Cf. Tilley B696.

    215. *imagine*] devise, scheme.

    216. *money plenty*] a normal inversion (*O.E.D.*, 'plenty', adj., 1b).

    217. *Westminster Hall*] The Great Hall, Palace of Westminster, where the
courts of justice kept sessions. At the Hall's entrance were settled the Common
Pleas for civil matters, at the upper end sat the King's Bench for Pleas of the
Crown and the Chancery Court, and adjoining the latter was the Equity Court of

To me is kin many a great gentleman;
I am known in every country.
And I were dead the lawyers' thrift were lost,   220
For this will I do if men would do cost:
Prove right wrong, and all by reason,
And make men leese both house and land;
For all that they can do in a little season.
Peach men of treason privily I can,   225

---

220. the lawyers'] *Hazlitt;* the lawyers *Q1;* lawyers *Q3.*   221. would] *Q1;*
inyll *Q3.*   222. by] *Q1;* by good *Q3.*   223. land;] *Manly;* land *This ed.*
conj.

Requests or Conscience, the 'Poor Man's Court', where after 1493 citizens could
present cases without having money (Mackenzie E. C. Walcott, *Westminster*
[1849], p. 252). Westminster's reputation for corruption was well noticed in
early plays: *Wisdom (Macro Plays),* ll. 789–92; *Johan the Evangelist,* l. 395;
World, sig. C1 (cf. *H.S.* 586n).

every term] time of pleading (Hilary, Easter, Trinity and Michaelmas).

219. *country*] probably 'county', 'shire'.

220. *thrift*] profit.

Imagination is in part modelled on John Baptist de Grimaldi, the most
infamous promoter employed by Henry VII's two lawyer-administrators, William Empson and Edmund Dudley (see intro., pp. 61–62, and Appendix I.B), and
the vice's name was evidently associated with the courts of law: a 1507 response
to a bill before the Star Chamber by members of Furnival's Inn states that it was
'devysed by subtell and Crafty Imachynacionz made to thentent to colour and
kepe from opyn knowlege their manyfold riotes and other gret misdemenours
nightly Committed' (*Select Cases before the King's Council in the Star Chamber,*
ed. I. S. Leadam, Selden Soc., 16 [1903], p. 241). For a study of the validity of
this topical complaint, see E. W. Ives, 'The Reputation of the Common Lawyers
in English Society, 1450–1550', *University of Birmingham Historical Journal,* 7
(1959–60), 130–61.

221. *do cost*] bear the expense, pay the bill (*O.E.D.,* 'cost', sb.[2], 5).

223.] formulaic: cf. *Peter Idley's Instructions to his Son,* ed. Charlotte D'Evelyn
(1935): 'Also flee the Counceill of a man covetous, | ffor he woll for desire of
worldlye goode | Make man to leese bothe lande and house' (I, ll. 288–90).

224.] 'For they [the men who are paying legal fees; or the lawyers] can do all
that [deprive men of their property] in a short time.' Manly's syntax also occurs
at 221, but 'they' refers, strictly, to 'men' at 223: possibly 'Despite all they [the
men who will lose their land] can do [to prevent the loss] in a short time' (cf. 'for'
at 719).

season] period of time.

225. *Peach*] inform against, accuse.

And when me list, to hang a true man.
If they will me money tell,
Thieves I can help out of prison.
And into lords' favours I can get me soon
And be of their privy counsel.   230
But Free Will, my dear brother,
Saw you not of Hick Scorner?
He promised me to come hither.
Free. Why, sir, knowest thou him?
Imag. Yea, yea, man, he is full nigh of my kin,   235
And in Newgate we dwelled together,
For he and I were both shackled in a fetter.

---

229. favours] *Q1;* fauour *Q3.*   230. counsel] *Q1, Q3;* council *Hazlitt.*   236. dwelled] *Q1;* dwell *Q3.*   .237. both] *Q1;* not in *Q3.*

---

226. *to hang a true man*] The infinitive, like 'Peach' (225), follows 'I can' (cf. 461–62 for the same syntax). The phrase is formulaic: in *Magnyfycence* Crafty Conveyance brags he can 'Saue a stronge thefe and hange a trew man' (1360), and 'true man' specifically means 'law-abiding citizen' (*O.E.D.*, 'trueman').

227–28.] as Imagination later does for Free Will (651–84). Since the thirteenth century a jailed offender could pay a fine to the king to obtain release, and pardons were bought (John Bellamy, *Crime and Public Order in England in the Later Middle Ages* [1973], pp. 190–98).

227. *tell*] count out, pay (*O.E.D.*, v., 22).

230. *their privy counsel*] Lawyers wielded great power in both royal and provincial councils: the duke of Buckingham might employ upwards of thirty lawyers, and Henry VII ruled by men like Empson and Dudley (E. W. Ives, 'Reputation of the Common Lawyers', pp. 158–60), who were executed in August 1510 on trumped-up treason charges to placate public outrage at the extortions of the previous reign.

232. *Hick Scorner*] Names formed on the vulgar diminutive of 'Richard', 'Hick' (*M.E.D.*, 'Hikke', n.; 'hykman' in *Four Elements*, sig. B2r; *Cocke Lorelles bote*'s 'hycke crokenec the rope maker', sig. B3v; the meaning 'country bumpkin' is a later development [*O.E.D.*, sb.¹]), and on a type surname. No known dramatic character up to this time has a proper name like 'Hick' unless a historical figure of some sort is being represented. Hick Scorner in part travesties Richard de la Pole, the Yorkist pretender who planned to 'come hither' (233) in spring, 1514 (see Intro., pp. 59–61, and Appendix I.A).

235. *Yea, yea*] Christ, in forbidding swearing and oaths, commands this form of response (Matt. v. 37).

237. *both shackled in a fetter*] All Newgate 'prisoners wore irons unless they could afford to pay for the privilege of going without them' (Margery Bassett, 'Newgate Prison in the Middle Ages', *Speculum*, 18 [1943], 244–45).

Free. Sir, lay you beneath or on high on the sollar?
Imag. Nay, iwis, among the thickest of yeomen of the collar.
Free. By God, then ye were in great fere.   240
Imag. Sir, had not I be, two hundred had be thrast in an halter.
Free. And what life have they there, all that great sort?
Imag. By God, sir, once a year some taw halters of Burport.

---

238. sollar] *This ed.*; seller *Q1*, *Q3*; soller *Manly.*   239. among the] *Q3*;
amŏge yᵗ *Q1*.   240. ye were] *Q1*; were ye *Q3*.   fere] *Q1*; feare *Q3*.   241.
be] *Q1 twice*; ben *Q3 twice*.   an] *Q1*; a *Q3*.   242. have] *Q1*; had *Q3*.   243.
By God] *Q1*; *not in Q3*.   a] *Q1*; in the *Q3*.   some] *Q1*; they *Q3*.

---

238. *beneath*] 1431 Newgate regulations outline three types of accommoda-
tion: the best for honourable persons and freemen of the city, the second best for
aliens and those of low rank, and (for felons) basement cells and 'strongholds',
by 1488 the two lower 'solars' (Pugh, p. 353). These, in the south part of the
prison, 'admitted neither light nor air', being described in 1488 as 'most stronge
and derke' (M. Bassett, 'Newgate Prison', pp. 239, 245). 1874–75 excavations
under Newgate Street found, besides the gate's large stone foundations, a
semi-circular arched passage, about thirty feet long by eight feet high, which
had evidently connected the towers and was both prison and well (Henry B.
Wheatley, *London Past and Present* [1891], II, 590).

  the sollar] upper room open to sunlight (the Q form suggests a typical confusion with 'cellar'; *O.E.D.*, 'sollar', sb.¹, 1). Well-off Newgate prisoners at this
time likely used, besides the chapel and hall, three day-rooms, for a fee walked
about within the jail and on the leads, and slept in tower chambers (Pugh, pp.
356–57, 361). These could be had on payment to the keeper, and 'spacious and
well lighted' recreation rooms stood on either side of the gate's chapel (M.
Bassett, 'Newgate Prison', pp. 239–40).

  239. *thickest*] (1) most crowded; (2) most hefty, thickset.

  yeomen of the collar] 'chained prisoners' (usually found 'beneath' the jail; see
237n, 238n), ironically compared to a servant in a noble household in charge of a
particular function and wearing a collar of livery—such as yeoman of the cellar
(*O.E.D.*, 'yeoman', 2). Cf. *Y.* 270, 278; *H.S.* 588.

  240. *in great fere*] in a great company (*O.E.D.*, 'fere', sb.², 2); as at 950.

  241.] In saying that if the crowd of two hundred had not been put in irons with
him, it would have been condemned to the noose, Imagination implies that
prisoners were either shackled or hanged.

  thrast] thrust.

  242. *all that great sort*] all that large company.

  243. *once a year some taw halters*] 'some tradesmen prepare or heckle (as by
beating, splitting and straightening the fibres) hemp into hanging ropes once a
year', evidently after Michaelmas, when the last crop was harvested (*O.E.D.*,
'hemp', 1).

  Burport] Bridport, Dorset. Cf. Tilley D5: 'Stabbed with a Bridport DAGGER'
(i.e., hanged in a Bridport rope). The town supplied virtually all rope and tackle

Yea, at Tyburn there standeth the great frame,
And some take a fall that maketh their neck lame.   245
Free. Yea, but can they then go no more?
Imag. O no, man, the wrest is twist so sore;
For as soon as they have said 'in manus tuas' once,
By God, their breath is stopped at once.
Free. Why, do they pray in that place there?   250
Imag. Yea, sir, they stand in great fere,
And so fast tangled in that snare
It falleth to their lot to have the same share.

---

244. the] *Q1;* a *Q3.*   245. And] *Q1; not in Q3.*   take] *Q1;* there taketh
Q3.   246. then] *Q1; not in Q3.*   249. By God] *Q1; not in Q3.*   at once]
Q1; by these bones *Q3.*   250. *Free.*] *Q1;* Pytye. *Q3.*   251. *Imag.*] *Q1;*
Contemplacyon. *Q3.*   fere] *Q1 , Q3;* fear *Hazlitt.*

---

for the Tudor navy, and a 1529–30 statute (*S.R.*, III [1817], 21 Hen. VIII. c. 12)
protected the 'Burporte' market from nearby rivals (M. M. Crick, 'The Hemp
Industry', *Victoria History of the County of Dorset*, ed. William Page, II [1908],
345–47, where the *H.S.* reference is given).

244. *the great frame*] gallows (*O.E.D.*, 'frame', sb., 7); not the 1571 triangular
Tyburn gibbet, but 'two uprights and a cross-beam' (as at 254; A. Marks,
Tyburn Tree [n.d.], pp. 63–64).

245.] Cf. *Y.* 101–03.

246. *go*] walk.

247. *wrest*] (1) 'neck', perhaps from *O.E.D.*, sb.[1], 1 ('action of twisting,
wrenching or writhing') or 4 ('peg for tightening a ligature'): in *Magnyfycence*
Cloaked Collusion, termed a hangman (2190), says to another, 'iche shall
wrynge the, horson, on the wryst' (2196); cf. 'Say folysshe fader haddest thou
leuer se | Thy sonnes necke vnwrested wyth a rope' (*Ship of Fools*, I, 48); (2)
'noose', perhaps from *O.E.D.*, 1c ('twist, coil')? (3) 'ankle, instep of foot' (so
defined by *O.E.D.*, 'wrist', 2b) is unlikely, but note 'go' at 246.

248. '*in manus tuas*'] 'into thy hands [I commend my spirit]', the dying words
of Christ (Luke xxiii.46) and of Christians generally (cf. 250): as in *Magnyfycence*, 'by robbynge they rynne to *in manus tuas* quecke' (2044).

251. *fere*] (1) fear (cf. 982); (2) company (cf. 240)? The lawyer in More's
Utopia mentions the practice of multiple hangings for thieves, who 'were
everywhere executed . . . as many as twenty at a time being hanged on one
gallows' (p. 61).

252–53.] 'And, being so tightly caught up in that noose, it falls [quibbling on
the physical drop] to their lot to share one and the same doom.'

252. *snare*] running noose.

Free. That is a knavish sight, to see them totter on a beam.

Imag. Sir, the whoresons could not convey clean,   255
    For and they could have carried by craft, as I can,
    In process of years each of them should be a gentleman.
    Yet, as for me, I was never thief.
    If my hands were smitten off, I can steal with my teeth;
    For ye know well there is craft in daubing.   260
    I can look in a man's face and pick his purse,
    And tell new tidings that was never true, iwis,

---

254. them] *Hawkins;* thē *Q1;* then *Q3.*   255. convey] *Q1;* cary *Q3.*   259.
smitten] *Hawkins;* smytē *Q1;* smyt *Q3.*

---

254. *knavish*] ignominious, evil.

  totter] swing on a gallows rope; cf. *Magnyfycence*, l. 1910, *L.P.* I.1883, and
H.S. 264n and 708n.

  beam] gallows-tree (often used of the cross: *M.E.D.*, 'bem', n., 1b).

  255. *convey clean*] steal without a hitch (*O.E.D.*, 'convey', 6b); a polite
euphemism in idiomatic usage, as in *Fulgens & Lucres*, 'Let them conuay and
cary clene than' (I.138). Death was the penalty for felonies: (1) theft 'yf yᵉ value
passe .xiii. d.'; (2) and theft under that value if not a first offence; but a first theft
of a shilling or under was judged only petty larceny. See *The Justyces of paes*
(Wynkyn de Worde, 1510), *S.T.C.* 14864, sig. A6r.

  256. *carried by craft*] managed skilfully (*O.E.D.*, 'carry', v., 22).

  257.] William Harrison's *Description of England*, ed. Georges Edelen (1968),
describes how whoever 'can live without manual labor, and thereto is able and
will bear the port, charge, and countenance of a gentleman, he shall for money
have a coat and arms bestowed upon him by heralds . . . be called master . . .
and reputed for a gentleman ever after' (p. 114; cf. *H.S.* 681–82).

  In process] in course.

  258. *never thief*] never caught thieving.

  259. *If my hands were smitten off*] an old punishment for thieves (possibly taken
from Matt. xviii.8), for which see John Bellamy, *Crime and Public Order in
England in the Later Middle Ages* (1973), pp. 181–82; and 'who-so settithe eny
trouble in thi reaume or in thi lordschippe, make him to be heded oponly, *id est*
publiquement, to that entente þat other may take example; a theefe, lete his
hande be smeten of . . .' (*The Dicts and Sayings of the Philosophers*, ed. Curt F.
Bühler, E.E.T.S. O.S. 211 [1941], p. 30, and cf. p. 164).

  teeth] probably with *f* for *th*, to rhyme with 258 (as in *Occupation*, fol. 72v): see
Wyld, p. 111.

  260.] Tilley C803.

  daubing] tricking, deceiving.

  261. *purse*] By the loss of *r* before *s*, a common vulgarism (Dobson, § 401[c]),
this rhymes with the next line (as at 660–61 also).

  262. *iwis*] A sixteenth-century spelling, 'iwuss' (see *O.E.D.*), indicates the
pronunciation here.

For my hood is all lined with leasing.

Free. Yea, but went ye never to Tyburn a pilgrimage?

Imag. No, iwis, nor none of my lineages, 265
For we be clerks all and can our neck-verse,
And with an ointment the judge's hand I can grease,
That will heal sores that be uncurable.

Free. Why, were ye never found reprovable?

Imag. Yes, once I stole a horse in the field, 270
And lept on him for to have ridden my way.
At the last a bailie me met and beheld,

264. a] *Q1;* on *Q3.* 265. my lineages] *Q1;* all my lygnage *Q3;* my lineage *Hazlitt.* 266. all] *Q1; not in Q3.* 267. hand] *Q1;* handes *Q3.* 268. that] *Q1;* whiche *Q3.* 272. beheld] *Q1;* beholde *Q3.*

263.] Apparently hoods were used to stow letters and news while they were being delivered (? cf. Chaucer's *Troilus*, II.1109–20).

leasing] deceit, lying.

264. *a pilgrimage*] Cf. *Godly Queene Hester*, ed. W. W. Greg, Materialien zur Kunde des älteren Englischen Dramas, 5 (1904): 'As he that from steylyng, goth to sent thomas watryng | In his yong age. | So they from pytter pattour, may cume to tytter totur | Euen the same pylgrimage' (542–45).

265. *lineages*] family members, kinsfolk (*M.E.D.*, 1a–c, 2). For another off-rhyme between a singular and a plural (264–65), see 573/577.

266. *we be clerks all*] The relative immunity of those in holy orders to punishment by the secular courts encouraged felons to enter a minor order. On 26 June 1514 John Taylor preached before Convocation against 'the brawling and dissolute life of the lower clergy' (*L.P.* I.3033). See Intro., pp. 18–19, and also Heath, pp. 119–33.

can] know.

neck-verse] 'Latin verse [usually the beginning of Ps. li (Vulgate 50): "Miserere mei, Deus, secundum magnam misericordiam tuam; Et secundum multitudinem miserationum tuarum, dele iniquitatem meam"] . . . formerly set before one claiming benefit of clergy . . . by reading which he might save his neck' (*O.E.D.*). Cf. *Y.* 140–43, where Youth says 'holy caitiffs', clerics like Charity (113), are thieves and 'would be hanged'.

Again *r* is lost before *s* (see *H.S.* 261n), and 'verse' rhymes with 267 (for the vowel, see Dobson, § 122, 136).

267.] traditional expression for bribing (*O.E.D.*, 'grease', v., 4b); cf. *Wisdom* (*Macro Plays*), l. 731 and n.; and Tilley M397: 'To grease a MAN in the fist.' Imagination may refer to the practice of buying a pardon (*H.S.* 227–28).

269. *reprovable*] blameworthy, open to punishment.

270. *Yes, once*] This theft of a reddish-brown horse is loosely based on a notorious confession made by John Baptist de Grimaldi (see Appendix I.B).

272. *bailie*] bailiff, sheriff's officer.

And bad me stand—then was I in a fray!
He asked whether with that horse I would gone,
And then I told him it was mine own. 275
He said I had stolen him, and I said nay—
'This is,' said he, 'my brother's hackney'—
For and I had not scused me without fail,
By Our Lady, he would have led me straight to jail.
And then I told him that horse was like mine, 280
A brown bay, a long mane, and did halt behine.
Thus I told him that such another horse I did lack,
And yet I never saw him nor came on his back.
So I delivered him the horse again,
And when he was gone, then was I fain, 285
For and I had not scused me the better
I know well I should have danced in a fetter.
Free. And said he no more to thee but so?
Imag. Yes, he pretended me much harm to do,
But I told him that morning was a great mist, 290

274. whether] *Q1*, *Q3*; whither *Hazlitt*.   278. and] *Q1*; an *Q3*.   scused] *Q1*;
excused *Q3*.   281. behine] *Q1*; behynde *Q3*.   282. that] *Q3*; yᵉ
Q1.   286. and] *Q1*; an *Q3*.   scused] *Q1*; excused *Q3*.   287. I know] *Q1*;
Inowe *Q3*.   290. But] *Q1*; Out *Q3*.

---

273. *fray*] fright.

274–94.] Imagination's contradictory excuses to conceal crimes—he manages
to describe the horse's colour, mane and limp (281) despite the 'great mist' (290)
and megrim headache that so dazzled his eyes that he 'might not well see'
(292–94)—may recall the youngest rogue's collection of ill-disguised pretexts for
buying poison from the apothecary (cf. *H.S.* 669–75) in the *Pardoner's Tale*:

> [He] prayed hym that he wolde hym selle
> Som poyson that he myght his rattis quelle
> And eke therwyth was a polcat in his hawe
> That as he sayd his capons had slawe
> And sayd he wolde wreke hem yf he myght
> Of vermyn that distroyed hem by nyght   (853–58)

278. *scused*] excused.
281. *brown bay*] reddish-brown horse.
did halt behine] limped behind.
287. *danced in a fetter*] hanged (*O.E.D.*, 'dance', v., 3b, only from 1837; for
the use of chains on the gallows, see *Y.* 270n), the punishment for such a theft
being death, not imprisonment (see *H.S.* 255n). Cf. *Mankind* (*Macro Plays*),
'But I thynke he rydyth on þe galouse, to lern for to daunce' (598).

That what horse it was I ne wist.

Also I said that in my head I had the megrin

That made me dazzle so in mine eyen

That I might not well see.

And thus he departed shortly from me.   295

Free. Yea, but where is Hick Scorner now?

Imag. Some of these young men hath hid him in their bosoms,
     I warrant you.

Free. Let us make a cry that he may us hear.

Imag. How, how, Hick Scorner, appear!
     I trow thou be hid in some corner.   300

Hick. [*Without*] Alee the helm, alee! veer! shoot off! veer
     sail! vera!

293. dazzle] *Q1;* to dasell *Q3.*   295. from] *Q1;* fro *Q3.*   297.] *Q3;* Some
. . . in | theyr . . . you *Q1.*   young men hath] *Q1;* felowes haue *Q3.*   298.
Free.] *Q3;* Imagy. *Q1.*   299. *Imag.*] *Q3;* Frewyll *Q1.*   301. S.D.]
Manly.   veer! shoot off!] *Hazlitt;* vere shot of *Q1, Q3;* veer sheet off! *This ed.*
conj.

---

291. *wist*] knew.

292. *megrin*] megrim, piercing headache.

293. *eyen*] eyes.

297.] a compositorial amplification of a shorter line (the rhyme with 296
occurs nine other times)?

298. Free] Though a lacuna of words spoken by Free Will may precede this
line, Q1 seems to have transposed its speech headings here and at 299, since
Imagination has already spoken at 297 and ought to be Hick Scorner's summoner at 299–300: Imagination (not Free Will) appointed to meet with him and
replies to his question, 'Who called after me?' (303).

300. *thou be hid in some corner*] word-play about Hick Scorner being in 'Hick's
corner'? Cf. *Four Elements*, where Ignorance says of Humanity, 'I wot neuer
[where he is] except he be | Hyd here in some corner' (sig. E1v), apparently
within a 'hall' (sig. E3r).

301.] Hick Scorner is a ship's master (despite 389–90) who, possibly blowing a
horn (440), brings his vessel to anchor. Turning the helm or rudder 'alee' (to the
lee side, sheltered from the wind) brings the ship into the wind, and veering ship
(*O.E.D.*, 'veer', v.[2], 2) then turns it down wind, or swings its stern around
towards the wind. Both actions take the way off a ship. Then the anchor is cast
forth or shot (*O.E.D.*, 'shoot', v., 12). Charles N. Robinson, *The British Tar in
Fact and Fiction* (1909), in a similar explanation of this line, suggests one should
read here 'veer the sheet off', meaning 'pay out, or ease off the sheet' (p. 164).
The fourth command, to 'veer sail' (*O.E.D.*, 'veer', v.[1], 1), is to slack off the
sheets (or sail-lines) so that the sails flop without holding the wind. The last
shout, 'vera!', probably means 'veer it!', with 'a' the vestige of the slurred
pronoun.

Free. Cock's body, hark! He is in a ship on the sea!

[*Enter* HICK SCORNER.]

Hick. God speed, God speed! Who called after me?

Imag. What, brother, welcome, by this precious body!

    I am glad that I you see.   305

    It was told me that ye were hanged.

    But out of what country come ye?

Hick. Sir, I have been in many a country,

    As in France, Ireland and in Spain,

302.1.] *Manly.*   303. called] *Q1;* calleth *Q3.*   306.] *Q1, Q3;* That ye were hanged hyt was told me. *Manly conj.*

302.] Hick Scorner's entrance owes much more to Richard de la Pole's anticipated invasion in spring 1514 (see Intro., pp. 59–61, and Appendix I.B) than to Brant's *Narrenschiff.* In Barclay's translation the ship refuses to anchor near London for fear of being overloaded with its gallants (I, 13–14; II, 309). Even in *Cocke Lorelles bote*, where such a ship disembarks at London and gathers more rogues there, having 'banysshed prayer peas and sadnes' as well as 'vertu' and 'deuocyon', the sailors are no threat (unlike Hick Scorner's crew) and only revel at 'colman hedge' between 'tyborne and chelsay' (sigs. C1v–2r) before at last sailing throughout all England (see notes to *H.S.* 389, 622–24, 820–45, however, for the poem's probable influence) with a third of its population on board (sig. C3v). Later figures analogous to Hick Scorner, of course, exist: More's ship-captain in *Utopia*, Hythlodaeus, one 'well-learned in nonsense' (p. 301), and Lindsay's fool Flattery, who enters off a ship out of France (*Ane Satyre*, 1552 version, p. 78 and l. 1730), are two such. Earlier there are dramatic entrances on ship pageant cars in the cycle plays, the Digby *Mary Magdalene* and some Tudor tournaments—in November 1501 the answerers entered the lists before Westminster Hall in one, and on 1 May 1511 the ship Fame met Henry VIII and his court in the fields and led them into the courtyard for jousting (*The Great Tournament Roll of Westminster*, intro., Sydney Anglo [1968], pp. 39, 58–59)—so that, however topical the rogue's appearance may be, it nevertheless belongs to a well-known staging convention.

303–06.] adapted from *Y.* 210, 217 and 219 (Riot), 220, 227 and 229 (Youth).

304. *this precious body*] blasphemous reference to the sacrament, Christ's body (*O.E.D.*, 'precious', 2; *H.S.* 944).

308–24.] Though a literary topic, place-name catalogues appear regularly in early drama too: the Doctor in the mummers' plays (Chambers, *E.F.-P.*, pp. 8, 53), the World in *The Castle of Perseverance (Macro Plays*, ll. 170–78), Aristorius in *The Play of the Sacrament (Non-Cycle Plays*, ll. 95–116), Experience in *Four Elements* (a demonstration rather than a list; sigs. B7v–C1r), Manhood in *World* (sig. A5r), and the Palmer in John Heywood's *Play called The Four PP* (ed. J. S. Farmer, T.F.T. [1908], sigs. A1v–2r).

Portingale, Seville, also in Almain,   310.
Friesland, Flanders and in Bourgogne,
Calabre, Pouille and Arragogne,
Brittany, Biscay and also in Gascogne,
Naples, Greece and in mids of Scotland,
At Cape Saint Vincent and in the new found island.   315

310. Portingale] *Q3;* Port yngale *Q1.*   313. Brittany] *This ed.;* Brytayne *Q1,*
Q3; Britain *Hazlitt.*   314. mids] *This ed.;* myddes *Q1;* the myddest
Q3.   315. Cape] *Q1, Q3; Cape, Hawkins.*

---

310. *Portingale*] Portugal. Cf. *H.S.* 322n below.

Almain] German kingdom of Emperor Maximilian, whose army fought in
Henry's pay in France in 1513.

311.] Lands governed by Margaret, duchess of Savoy, Maximilian's daughter
and Henry's ally in 1513: Friesland is the Netherlands' most northerly province,
on the North Sea; Flanders lies southward, nearer the Strait of Dover; and
Burgundy is a landbound duchy between the upper Loire and Saône rivers.

312. *Calabre*] Calabria, at this time the 'heel' of Italy.

Pouille] Apulia, region on the coast of eastern Italy, adjacent to Calabria; this
spelling was also used for Poland (*L.P.* I.1893).

Arragogne] region in north-east Spain, ruled by Ferdinand II, Henry VIII's
father-in-law.

313. *Brittany*] a province in north-west France against which Henry VIII's
1512–13 naval war was largely waged.

Biscay] region in northern Spain, on the Bay of Biscay, where Henry VIII's
sea-army against Guienne, as commanded by the marquis of Dorset, landed in
1512 and spent a fruitless, mutinous summer.

Gascogne] Gascony, district in south-west France, English from 1152 to 1453;
one of Henry VIII's titles (Halle, 'Henry VIII', fol. 3r).

315. *Cape Saint Vincent*] extreme south-west point of Portugal.

the new found island] coastal America; perhaps Newfoundland. John Cabot
left Bristol in May 1497 to explore the Labrador coast and Newfoundland and
returned early in August, to be rewarded by Henry VII, who also bought hawks,
wild cats and 'popyngays of the new found Island' in 1502–04 (B.L. Add. MS
59899, fols. 38r, 96v). Bristol merchants in 1502 brought back three New World
natives who were 'clothid in Beestes Skynnes', ate raw flesh, and were 'Rude in
their demeanure as Beestes' (*Chronicles*, pp. 258, 328, 337). Barclay's *Ship of
Fools* is the first extant English printed book to mention a 'newe fonde londe' (II,
25): see George B. Parks, *Richard Hakluyt and the English Voyages*, ed. James A.
Williamson (1928), p. 7. Sometime after 1514 Henry VIII was rumoured to be
organising a 'vyage made in to an newfounde land with dyvyrs shypps' (*Original
Letters*, ed. Henry Ellis, 3rd ser. [1846], I, 161–62). Also cf. *Four Elements*, sigs.
A1v, C1r, C3v (John Rastell's thwarted voyage there), and *Old Christmas*, ed.
W. W. Greg in *Collections: Volume IV*, Malone Soc. (1956), p. 37, l. 76 (Riot and
Gluttony are banished there).

I have been in Gene and in Cowe,
Also in the land of rumbelow,
Three mile out of hell,
At Rhodes, Constantine and in Babyland,
In Cornwall and in Northumberland,   320
Where men seethe rushes in gruel.
Yea, sir, in Chaldee, Tartare and Inde,

---

316. Gene] *Q1;* Genes *Q3.*   319. Constantine] *Q1;* Constantynople *Q3.*
Babyland]*Q3;* babylonde *Q1;* Babylon *Hazlitt.*   320. Northumberland]*Q3;*
no northumberlonde *Q1.*   321.]*Q1; precedes l. 319 in Q3.*   322. Tartare]
Q1, Q3; Tartary *Hazlitt.*   and] *Q1;* and in *Q3.*   Inde]*Q3;* Iude *Q1.*

---

316. *Gene*] Genoa. The name was monosyllabic (see *O.E.D.*, 'Geane').

Cowe] Cowes, Isle of Wight, one of Henry VIII's naval harbours for the war in
1512 (*L.P.* I.1133).

317. *rumbelow*] an old, sailors' rowing refrain, perhaps to be read as 'room
below' (cf. 318); as in Skelton's 'Bowge of Courte', 'Heue and how rombelow,
row the bote, Norman, rowe!' (*Works*, I, l. 252); or *Cocke Lorelles bote*, 'some
songe heue and howe rombelowe' (sig. C1v).

318.] possibly formulaic: in 'The Image of Ipocrysy' certain 'sely sowles' are
said to lie in pain 'in the black grange, | Thre myle out of hell' (in Skelton's
Works, II, 444).

319. *Rhodes*] The order of St John of Jerusalem, based here, had holdings in
England, and its Knights Hospitallers included some of Henry VIII's own men
(*L.P.* I.2447).

Constantine] Constantinople (here the name of its first Christian emperor).

Babyland] Babylon (possibly the original *H.S.* form, since the rhymes regularly sound -*and* as [ŏŋ]; see Intro., n. 144), at this time loosely identified with
the 'babbling land' of the Tower of Babel (Gen. xi. 1–9).

320. *Cornwall*] Henry VII suppressed Cornish rebels at Blackheath, Kent, in
June 1497, as well as Perkin Warbeck's invasion of Cornwall that September.

Northumberland] Scotland's James IV, with Perkin Warbeck, twice in 1496
invaded Northumberland, slaughtered its inhabitants, and burned and looted
its towns so that 'all the countrie of Northumberland was by them in maner
wasted, and destroied' (*Holinshed's Chronicles*, III [1808], p. 513). James again
burned towns and crops before his defeat and death at Flodden Field in 1513,
and for decades afterwards the north was barren (see John Hodgson's *History of
Northumberland*, part III, vol. I [1820], 31–40, and vol. II [1828], 32–39,
173–244). Cf. *H.S.* 640n.

321. *rushes in gruel*] Floors were spread with rushes newly every ten days or so
(*Venice*, II, no. 219). Gruel was usually made with ground grain, often oatmeal,
and Sugden describes it as 'the staple of north-country diet' (p. 372).

322. *Chaldee*] Chaldea, country around Babylon (Sugden, p. 108).

Tartare] Tartary: that is, Europe and Asia from the Dnieper river to the Sea of

And in the land of women, that few men doth find,
  In all these countries have I be.
Free. Sir, what tidings hear ye now on the sea?   325
Hick. We met of ships a great navy
  Full of people that would into Ireland,
  And they came out of this country.
  They will nevermore come to England.   329
Imag. Whence were the ships of them? Knowest thou none?
Hick. Harken, and I will show you their names each one.
  First was the *Regent* with the *Michael of Brikilsea*,
  The *George* with the *Gabriel* and the *Anne of Foy*,
  The *Star of Saltash* with the *Jesus of Plymouth*,
  Also the *Hermitage* with the *Barbara of Dartmouth*,   335
  The *Nicholas* and the *Mary Bellouse of Bristow*

323. doth]*Q1*; do*Q3*.   329. They]*Q1*; But they*Q3*. nevermore come to]*Q1*;
neuer returne into*Q3*.   330. ships of them?]*Hawkins*; ships? Of them *This ed.
conj.*   Knowest]*Q1*; knewest*Q3*.   332. with the]*Q1*; with *Q3*.   *Brikilsea*]
Q1; Brystow *Q3*.   333. *Gabriel*]*Q1*; Gabryell₃ *Q3*.   334. *Plymouth*]*Q3*;
plūoth *Q1*.   334. *Dartmouth*]*Q3*; darmouth *Q1*.

Japan, north of the Caucasus and Himalayas (Sugden, p. 501); or perhaps
Tartarus, 'hell' (*O.E.D.*, 'Tartar', sb.[4]).

Inde] In June 1513 Emanuel, King of Portugal, wrote the Pope of the
Portuguese defeat of the Moors at Malacca in India, and of widespread conversions there (*L.P.* I. 1974).

323.] 'Sir Perceval of Galles', ed. Walter H. French and Charles B. Hale in
Middle English Metrical Romances (1930), mentions a man coming from the
'Maydenlande', evidently a faery realm (p. 562, l. 956). The Amazons were
thought to live about the Thermodon river (running into the Black Sea in now
northern Turkey), on the Mediterranean coast of Libya (like the Gorgons) and
elsewhere (*The Bibliotheca Historica of Diodorus Siculus translated by John Skelton*, ed. F. M. Salter and H. L. R. Edwards, E.E.T.S. O.S. 233 [1956], I,
286–88).

326. *navy*] fleet.

327–28.] See Intro., p. 63, and Appendix I.C.

332–37.] See Appendix I.D.

332. Brikilsea] Brightlingsea, East Essex. Q3 did not understand the rhyme
with 333.

333. Gabriel] See R. B. McKerrow, *An Introduction to Bibliography* (1927), p.
322, for the final, questionable type in the Q3 variant.

Foy] Fowey, at the mouth of the Fowey river in Cornwall, here pronounced
'Fee'.

334. Saltash] in Cornwall on the Tamar river, four miles north-west of
Plymouth in Devon, about thirty miles west of Dartmouth.

336. Bristow] Bristol.

With the *Ellen of London* and *James* also.
Great was the people that was in them,
All true religious, and holy women.
There was Troth and his kinsmen,   340
With Patience, Meekness and Humility,
And all true maidens with their virginity,
Rial preachers, Sadness and Charity,
Right Conscience and Faith with Devotion,
And all true monks that kept their religion,   345
True buyers and sellers and alms-deed doers,
Piteous people that be of sin destroyers,
With Just Abstinence and good counsellors,

337. *Ellen*] *Q1;* Heleyn *Q3.*   340. Troth] *Q1;* treuth *Q3;* Truth *Haz-litt.* kinsmen] *Q3;* kynnesman *Q1.*   342. And] *Q1;* An *Q3.*   343. Rial] *Q1;* Good *Q3.*   345.] *Q1;* And the poore in spirite that denyed to haue promocion *Q3.* kept] *Q1;* kepe *Hawkins.* religion] *Hazlitt;* relyon *Q1.*   346. alms-deed] *Q1;* almes deedes *Q3.*

339–52.] The exile or departure of virtues from England is a theme found in traditional complaints (see 546–601n), but these names are largely culled from Virtue's captains (abstractions) and commoners (social types) in *A.G.*, for which see Appendix III.3, ll. 850, 910, 829, 808, 842 (909), 840, 934, 828, 838, 913, 908, 832, 907, 919, 814, 915. *Y.* provides 'Humility' and 'Charity' (also in *A.G.*, 801, 804), 'Mourners for sin' (see *H.S.* 571n), and 352 (cf. *Y.* 767–69). Items at 343 ('Rial preachers'), 348 ('good counsellors') and 349–50 are untraced.

339. *religious*] (1) those bound to a monastic or other formal religious life; (2) the devout, pious?

340. *Troth*] Cf. 520, 579.

kinsmen] Q1 may not be in error (see *Y.* 350n).

343. *Rial preachers*] (1) royal preachers; possibly (2) excellent ones. Yearly in Lent Henry VIII paid various doctors to preach before him, including John Colet, dean of St Paul's (Good Friday, 1512, 1513), and Bryket, the bishop of St Asaph, who with a Dr Egleton preached in March 1514 (*L.P.* II, pp. 1455, 1460, 1463, 1467). Colet, whose 1513 Good Friday sermon controversially objected to war as Henry was about to invade France, apparently preached that day every year from 1510 to 1517 except 1514 (Lupton, pp. 224–25).

Sadness] (1) seriousness; (2) constancy.

344. *Right Conscience*] Cf. *Apius and Virginia*, ed. Ronald B. McKerrow, M.S.R. (1911), where Haphazard says of Conscience: 'sayling by Sandwitche he sunke for his sin' (l. 515).

346. *True buyers and sellers*] Market cheating was a punishable civil offence. In 1500–01 a coal-seller, for instance, was pilloried for not keeping to true measure (*Chronicles*, pp. 233–34).

347. *Piteous*] pious, goodly.

Mourners for sin with Lamentation,
And good rich men that helpeth folk out of prison.   350
True Wedlock was there also,
With young men that ever in prayer did go.
The ships were laden with such unhappy company,
But at the last God shoop a remedy,
For they all in the sea were drowned,   355
And on a quick sand they strake to ground.
The sea swallowed them everyone.
I wot well alive there scaped none.

Imag. Lo, now my heart is glad and merry.
For joy now let us sing 'derry, derry.'   360
Hick. Fellows, they shall nevermore us withstand,

---

356. strake to] *Q1;* stroke on *Q3.*   358. wot] *Q3;* wote wote *Q1.*   alive] *Q1;*
on lyue *Q3.*   none] *Q1;* not one *Q3.*   361. nevermore us] *Q1;* vs neuer *Q3.*

350.] in one of the seven works of bodily mercy (*The ABC Both in Latyn &*
Englyshe, ed. E. S. Shuckburgh [1889], p. 17). Henry VIII, through his
almoner, spent large sums in June 1512 and May 1515 redeeming individuals
from Newgate, Ludgate, the Marshalsea, the King's Bench and the Counters
(*L.P.* II, pp. 1456, 1467), and many others aided prisoners and paid for the
release of debtors (see W. K. Jordan, *The Charities of London: 1480–1660* [1960],
p. 181).

353. *unhappy*] (1) unlucky; (2) trouble-making.

354. *shoop*] contrived (*O.E.D.,* 'shape', v., strong past tense).

356.] Gerard Boate's *Irelands Natvrall History* (1652) describes a great, steep
sands or grounds, some sixty miles long and from two to eight miles from the
shore between Wexford and Dublin in a straight line, and varying between one
and three fathoms deep (pp. 40–41). While the narrow channel between the
shore and the grounds is deep and safely navigable, Boate shows that the Irish
Sea was widely reputed to be stormy and treacherous, and explains its many
shipwrecks as occurring on dark winter nights when, 'some furious storm
arising, the ships are dashed against the Rocks, against the rocky Shoares, or
against those Grounds which extend themselves betwixt the Tuskar [near
Wexford] and the Bay of Dublin, whilst the Steer-men and Pilots by reason of
the darkness not being able to discern the land, or any of their wonted marks, do
not know which way to steer to shun those dangerous places' (pp. 49–50). In
1488 the *Anne of Foy* nearly sank there in such conditions (see Appendix I.D,
pp. 246–47).

strake to ground] run aground, founder (*O.E.D.,* 'strike', v., 60a).

358. *scaped*] escaped.

360. *derry, derry*] refrain of popular song.

For I see them all drowned in the Race of Ireland.

Free. Yea, but yet hark, Hick Scorner:

What company was in your ship that came over?

Hick. Sir, I will say you to understand.   365

There were good fellows, above five thousand,

And all they been kin to us three.

There was Falsehood, Favel and Subtilty,

Yea, thieves and whores, with other good company,

Liars, backbiters and flatterers the while,   370

Brawlers, liars, getters and chiders,

362. see] *Q1;* sawe *Q3.*   364. your ship that] *Q1;* the shyp that ye
Q3.   365. say] *Q3;* sayd *Q1;* aid *Hazlitt.*   367. been] *Q1;* be *Q3.*   368.
Subtilty] *Q1;* sutletye *Q3.*   370. the while] *Q1;* that be whyly *Q3;* the wily *or*
the whilers' *This ed. conj.*   371. liars, getters] *Q1;* great yetters *Q3;* sliers,
getters *This ed. conj.;* liars, jetters *Hazlitt.*

362. *see*] saw (*O.E.D.*, v., A.3a; a vulgar Kentish form).

Race of Ireland] a narrow and strong current in the Irish Sea (*O.E.D.*, 'race',
sb.¹, 6); cf. 827. Hick Scorner's route is through lawless waters, ones infested by
Scottish, Breton and English pirates (E. M. Carus Wilson, 'The Iceland Trade',
Studies in English Trade in the Fifteenth Century, ed. Eileen Power and M. M.
Postan [1933], p. 175; *L.P.* I.2977; *Calendar of the Carew Manuscripts . . .
1515–1574*, ed. J. S. Brewer and William Bullen [1867], no. 15).

364. *came over*] passed over the sea (*O.E.D.*, 'come', v., 66a; cf. *H.S.* 357).

365. *say you*] try to make you (*O.E.D.*, 'say', v.², 5); cf. *Y.* 569.

368–79.] These names are largely taken from Vice's captains (abstractions)
and commoners (social types) in *A.G.*, for which see Appendix III.3, ll. 643, 655
(707), 678, 700, 677, 683, 692, 693, 691, 704, 696 (699), 676, 702, 646, 661, 646
(640), 643, 641. 'Favel' (368) and 'Overthwart Guile' (373) are untraced; the
Pardoner's Tale supplies 377–78.

368. *Favel*] duplicity, false flattery; one of the seven 'subtyll persones' on ship
in Skelton's 'Bowge of Courte' (*Works*, I, ll. 133–34).

370. *the while*] at the time, then. Repetition of 'Liars' later at 371 and the
apparent lack of rhyme suggest textual corruption: (1) 'the wily' (cf. Q3) is
possible, though unattested in this spelling by the *O.E.D.*; and (2) 'chiders' at
371 could rhyme with 'the whilers'' ('a while ago, then', a conjectured form; cf.
O.E.D., 'whilere', adv. [where 'the whilere' is recorded *c.* 1460] and 'erstwhile',
adv.). Q1 'while' was, on the other hand, perhaps disyllabic.

371. *liars*] This is repeated accidentally from the previous line (dittography).
Q3 remodels the line on 'great murderers' (372). Q1 may elide an *s* after
'Brawlers', but more likely a quite different term has been lost and restoration is
impossible. Perhaps it occurs in *A.G.*, 692–93: 'Fyghters Brawlers Brekers of
louedayes | Getters Chyders Causers of frayes'.

getters] (1) braggarts, swaggerers (*O.E.D.*, 'jetter¹'); less likely (2) money-
makers (*O.E.D.*, 'getter', 1).

chiders] quarrellers.

Walkers by night with great murderers,
Overthwart Guile and jolly carders,
Oppressers of people with many swearers.
There was False Law with Horrible Vengeance, 375
Froward Obstination with Mischievous Governance,
Wanton wenches and also michers
With many other of the devil's officers;
And Hatred, that is so mighty and strong,
Hath made avow forever to dwell in England. 380

Imag. But is that true that thou dost show now?

Hick. Sir, every word as I do tell you.

Free. Of whence is your ship? Of London?

Hick. Yea, iwis, from thence did she come,
And she is named the *Envy*, 385

372. great murderers] *Q1;* great murders *Q3*. 373. Overthwart] *Q1;*
Ouerthwart/*Q3 (i.e. virgule)*. 380. avow forever]*Q1;* a vowe*Q3*. 383. Of
whence] *Q1;* Fro whens *Q3*. 384. from] *Q1;* fro *Q3*. 385. named] *Q1;*
called *Q3*.

---

372. *Walkers by night*] night-prowlers, thieves, curfew breakers (*O.E.D.*,
'night-walker', 1). According to *The Justyces of paes, S.T.C.* 14864 (1510),
justices were charged to arrest 'all hasardes that slepe by daye / and wake by
nyght & customably hauntynge the tauernes not haũÿge wheron to lyue and no
man woteth frō whens they come nor whether they wyll' (sig. A7v). Cf. *H.S.*
562, 663–68.

373. *Overthwart*] testy, quick to take offence. The Q3 noun means only
'rebuff' or 'transverse direction'.

carders] card-players.

376. *Froward Obstination*] evil, ungovernable obstinacy.

Mischievous Governance] (1) malevolent government; (2) evil-minded
behaviour.

377. *michers*] (1) pimps; (2) petty thieves.

378. *devil's officers*] devil's agents, sergeants or household servants. This
uncommon phrase (in neither *M.E.D.* nor *O.E.D.*), describing in context
lascivious girls and pimps, occurs both here and in Chaucer's *Pardoner's Tale*, ll.
477–81:

> And ryght anon came in the tomblesteris
> Fetys and smale and yonge frutestris
> Syngars wyth harpys bawdys wafrerys
> Suche as ben very the deuyllis offyceris
> To kyndle and blowe the fyres of lecherye.

380. *made avow*] pledged.

381.] The tale belies itself in the telling: 'Falsehood' (368), 'Liars' (370), etc.

385. *the* Envy] that one of the seven deadly sins directly opposed to charity,
and one of Vice's first captains in *A.G.* (Appendix III.3, l. 622).

I tell you, a great vessel and a mighty.
The owner of her is called Ill Will,
Brother to Jack Poller of Shooters Hill.
Imag. Sir, what office in the ship bare ye?
Hick. Marry, I kept a fair shop of bawdry.   390
I had three wenches that were full pretty,
Jane True, Ann Thriftless and Wanton Sibley—
If ye ride her a journey, she will make you weary,
For she is trusty at need.
If ye will hire her for your pleasure,   395

386. vessel] *Q1;* shyppe *Q3.*   392. Ann] *Manly;* and *Q1, Q3.*   Sibley] *This*
ed.; sybble *Q1;* Sybbyll *Q3.*   394. at] *Q1;* at a *Q3.*

---

387. *Ill Will*] perhaps playing on the proper name, and see Intro., n. 247.

388. *Jack Poller*] Jack 'robber, plunderer' (*O.E.D.*, 'poller', 2; from 'poll', v., 'to give a haircut, to crop the poll or head'); 'Jack' often precedes a type noun to form a quasi-proper name (*O.E.D.*, sb.[1], 35).

Shooters Hill] about 425 feet high, crossed about seven miles south-east of London by the Great Dover Road, on the site of the Roman Watling Street (now Shooters Hill Road), just past Charlton and north of Eltham Palace; there at that time a narrow road overshadowed with trees ('amonge the elmes' according to *Cocke Lorelles bote*, sig. B5v; now Jack Wood and Castle Wood are near by) and a notorious highwayman's ambush (Sugden, p. 464; J. K. Wallenberg, *The Place-Names of Kent* [1934], pp. 3–4).

389. *office*] function, business (at 390–400 associated with pimping, as Hick's 'devil's officers' are at 378; but cf. 461 for an unequivocal usage). On Cocke Lorelle's boat 'There was non that there was | But he had an offyce more or lasse' (sig. C1v).

390. *shop of bawdry*] brothel. One might expect 'shop of fine, rich clothes' (*O.E.D.*, 'bawdry[2]') up to 391–400.

392. *Ann*] Manly's emendation is compelling, as Hick Scorner mentions 'three wenches' (391); for the name, cf. *H.S.* 739n.

393–99.] In Skelton's 'Bowge of Courte' pimping Riot, who lets Malkyn out 'to hyre, that men maye on her ryde' (*Works*, I, l. 402), also brags:

> Had I as good an hors as she is a mare,
> I durst auenture to iourney thorugh Fraunce;
> Who rydeth on her, he nedeth not to care,
> For she is trussed for to breke a launce.   (407–10)

393. *ride*] mount, in copulation (*O.E.D.*, v., 16).

a journey] (1) for a (day's) travel or distance; (2) for a (day's) labour, work (*O.E.D.*, sb., 5).

394. *trusty at need*] proverbial: see *Historical Poems of the XIVth and XVth Centuries*, ed. Rossell H. Robbins (1959), no. 78, l. 36; Bartlett J. Whiting, *Proverbs in the Earlier English Drama* (1938), p. 83.

I warrant, tire her shall ye never,
She is so sure in deed.
Ride, and you will, ten times a day,
I warrant you, she will never say nay,
My life I dare lay to wed.   400
Imag. Now pluck up your hearts and make good cheer,
       These tidings liketh me wonder well!
       Now virtue shall draw arrear, arrear.
       Hark, fellows! A good sport I can you tell:
       At the stews we will lie to-night,   405
       And by my troth, if all go aright,
       I will beguile some pretty wench
       To get me money at a pinch.
       How say you, shall we go thither?
       Let us keep company all together.   410
       And I would that we had God's curse,
       If we somewhere do not get a purse.
       Every man bear his dagger naked in his hand,
       And if we meet a true man, make him stand,

396. warrant] *Q1;* warraunt you *Q3.*   *tire*] *Q3;* tere *Q1.*   shall ye] *Q1;* ye shall
Q3.   397. sure in deed] *Q1;* at nede *Q3.*   398. you] *Q1;* ye *Q3.*   399.
say] *Q1;* saye you *Q3.*   402. liketh] *Q1;* lyke *Q3.*   wonder] *Q1;* wonders
Q3.   405. will] *Q1;* wyll go *Q3.*   413. naked] *Q1;* drawen *Q3.*   414.
stand] *Q1;* to stande *Q3.*

397. *deed*] sexual intercourse (*M.E.D.*, 'dede', n., 1c).

401. *pluck up your hearts*] Tilley H323; cf. Skelton's 'Bowge of Courte', *Works*,
I, l. 386 (Riot).

403.] Cf. Virtue's retreat, and his rearguard under Good Perseverance, in
A.G., Appendix III.3, ll. 962–63, 1063–64.

arrear, arrear] back, to the rear.

405–08.] Though the stew-houses, limited to twelve after 1506, 'were licensed
by official acquiescence and governed by ordinances made in Parliament and
enforced in the Bishop of Winchester's court leet' (David J. Johnson, *Southwark
and the City*, pp. 66–67), no one was allowed to set up a private practice, and
stew-holders only received a set 14*d* rent weekly from a prostitute (Stow, II, 54).

413–18.] Highway robbery, no matter how little the goods or money seized,
was always judged a felony, and thus an act more serious than theft (see 255n),
because of the open threat to the victim's life (*The Justyces of paes*, *S.T.C.*
14864, sig. A5v).

Or else that he bear a stripe.   415
If that he struggle and make any work,
Lightly strike him to the heart
And throw him into Thames quite.
Free. Nay, three knaves in a lease is good at nale!
But thou lubber, Imagination,   420
That cuckold, thy father, where is he become?
At Newgate doth he lie still at jail?
Imag. [*Drawing a dagger on Free Will*] Avaunt, whoreson,
thou shalt bear me a stripe!
Sayst thou that my mother was a whore?
Free. Nay, sir, but the last night   425
I saw Sir John and she tumbled on the floor.
Imag. Now, by Cock's heart, thou shalt lose an arm!
Hick. Nay, sir, I charge you do him no harm.

---

416. and] *Q1;* or *Q3.*   418. Thames] *Q1;* the Tammes *Q3.*   419. lease]
Q1; lese *Q3;* leash *Hazlitt.*   422. at] *Q1;* in *Q3.*   424. was a] *Q1;* is an
Q3.   426. she tumbled] *Q1;* her tomblynge *Q3.*   427. Now] *Q1;* Nay *Q3.*

---

415. *Or else that*] Abbott 382 (ellipsis of an imperative verb complicated by
non-parallel construction).

bear a stripe] See 423n.

416. *If that*] Abbott 287.

make any work] cause trouble (*O.E.D.*, 'work', sb., 31a).

419. *Nay*] emphatic, without negation (*O.E.D.*, adv.[1], 1d).

in a lease] probably (1) in a throng or line, as greyhounds, etc., in coursing
(*O.E.D.*, 'leash', sb., 1; usually tied together in a set of three or 'leash', *O.E.D.*,
2); less likely are (2) in the lurch (*O.E.D.*, 'lash', sb.[1], 4); (3) in a blow or stroke
(*O.E.D.*, 1); cf. *H.S.* 415; and (4) in a lie or trick (*O.E.D.*, 'lease', sb.[2]); cf. Q3
here and *H.S.* 407.

at nale] (1) at ale-drinking, at the alehouse (*O.E.D.*, 'ale', 2a and b; from 'at
þen ale'); (2) at stabbing, dagger-work (*O.E.D.*, 'nall(e', and 'awl', i, 4)? The
context favours the second sense (cf. 413–18, 543), but the probable source here
suggests the first (*Y.* 453).

420. *lubber*] lazy lout.

421. *become*] gone, betaken himself to.

423. *thou shalt bear me a stripe*] I'm going to cut you up. Idleness says to Evil
Counsel in *Johan the Evangelist*: 'In good faythe knaue thou shalte beare me a
strype' (515).

424–26.] Free Will, who has called Imagination a 'whoreson' before (187),
tauntingly identifies his mother with Sibley at 178–83.

Imag. And thou make too much, I will break thy head too.

Hick. By Saint Mary, and I wist that, I would be ago.   430

Imag. Aware, aware, the whoreson shall aby!

    His priest will I be, by Cock's body!

Hick. Keep peace, lest knaves' blood be shed!

Free. By God, if his was nought, mine was as bad.

Imag. By Cock's heart, he shall die on this dagger.   435

Hick. By Our Lady, then will ye be strangled in a halter.

Imag. The whoreson shall eat him as far as he shall wade.

Hick. Beshrew your heart, and put up your blade!

    Sheathe your whittle or, by him that was never born,

    I will rap you on the costard with my horn.   440

    What, will ye play all the knave!

Imag. By Cock's heart, and thou a buffet shalt have!

---

429. make too] *Q1;* prate *Q3.*   433. knaves'] *Hazlitt;* knave's *This ed.*
conj.   435. he] *Q1;* ye *Q3.*   this] *Q1;* my *Q3.*   436. strangled] *Q1;*
stretched *Q3.*   437. shall wade] *Hawkins;* shyll wade *Q1;* wyll wade
Q3.   438. Beshrew] *Q1;* I beshrew *Q3.*   and] *Q1; not in Q3.*   439. him]
Q3; hy3 *Q1;* hyz *Hawkins;* Jis *Hazlitt;* Hyz *Manly.*   441. ye] *Q1;* you
Q3.   all] *Q1; not in Q3.*

---

   429. *make too much*] over-interest yourself here (elliptical; *O.E.D.*, 'make',
v.[1], 21).

   430. *ago*] gone.

   431. *aby*] pay for (that).

   432. *His priest will I be*] 'I will kill him', i.e., give him his last offices, extreme
unction (*O.E.D.*, 'priest', sb., 6). Tilley P587.

   434.] Cf. 707.

   his] Imagination's mother.

   437.] Free Will will get the dagger (down his throat) to the hilt (*O.E.D.*, 'eat',
v., 2d; 'wade', v., 1b). Cf. *Fulgens & Lucres*, 'Nay I had leuer she had etyn my
knyfe' (I.1242); *H.S.* 170 and *O.E.D.*, 'him', 2b.

   shall wade] For the Q1 form, see *Y.* 687.

   439. *whittle*] large knife.

   him that was never born] a snide allusion to Christ's betrayer, Judas Iscariot
(see 546n and Mark xiv.21). Ronald B. McKerrow's *Introduction to Bibliography*
(1927; rpt. 1965) notes that 3 was used commonly for *m* (p. 322).

   440. *costard*] 'large apple', head (earliest instance, but later formulaic in
context: *O.E.D.*, 2).

   my horn] conventional part of a sailor's gear, as in *Cocke Lorelles bote*: 'For Ioye
theyr trūpettes dyde they blowe' (sig. C1v).

   441. *play all the knave*] entirely, or to everyone, act the part of a rogue (cf. 654,
765).

   442. *buffet*] blow.

[*Fights with Hick Scorner.*]

Free. [*To the audience*] Lo, sirs, here is a fair company,
　　God us save!
For if any of us three be mayor of London,
Iwis, iwis, I will ride to Rome on my thumb.　　　445
Alas, a, see! Is not this a great farce?
I would they were in a mill pool above the arse,

442.1.] *Manly.*　　443. a fair] *Q1*; a goodly *Q3*.　　444. any] *Q3*; ony *Q1*.
three] *Q1; not in Q3*.　　445. iwis] *Q1; not in Q3*.　　446. Is not this a] *Q1, Q3*;
are not these *Manly conj.*　farce] *This ed.*; feres *Q1*; feares *Q3*.　　447. mill
pool] *Hazlitt;* myll pole *Q1;* mylpole *Q3*.　　arse] *This ed.*; eres *Q1*; eares *Q3*.

444.] The rise of a low-born man to be Lord Mayor of London was a popular
tale (the post was elective, and no other lordship was), as with the careers of
Richard Whittington (died 1423) and Symon Eyre (died 1459), about both of
whom plays were later written, one being Dekker's *Shoemakers' Holiday.* Cf. *Y.*
253.

445.] Cf. Nicholas Udall's *Roister Doister*, ed. W. W. Greg, M.S.R. (1935), l.
629: 'It were better go to *Rome* on my head than so'; Tilley R164: 'To go (hop) to
ROME with a mortar on one's head' (from 1600).

thumb] possibly 'big toe' (*O.E.D.*, sb., 1b).

446. *farce*] short, broadly comic (French) diversion acted as an interlude in
some larger play or entertainment (the term's first use as such in England? cf.
Chambers, *M.S.*, II, 202; *M.E.D.*, 'farse', n., only defined as 'seasoned
stuffing'): the earl of Kildare (died 1513) owned 'A boke of Farsses in French',
according to a 1525/26 library-catalogue (cited by Donough Bryan, *Gerald
Fitzgerald* [1933], p. 268); and the Scottish court, allied to France, several times
witnessed at a 1508 banquet a 'phairs', James IV (and his queen, Henry VIII's
sister Margaret) saw a 'fars' in 1511/12, and Edinburgh received Albany in 1515
with 'sindre ferses' (Anna Jean Mill, *Mediaeval Plays in Scotland* [1927], pp.
77–78, 330). The word's root is the Latin 'farsa', 'the various phrases interpolated in litanies between the words *kyrie* and *eleison . . .* [and] similar expansions
of other liturgical formulae' (*O.E.D.*, sb.², 1). The first French use of 'farce' in
its secular dramatic sense is in 1398, and among the type's special comic effects
are beatings such as Hick Scorner is getting here (Grace Frank, *The Medieval
French Drama* [1954; rpt. 1967], pp. 245–46).

447.] William Harrison's *Description of England*, ed. Georges Edelen (1968),
says that 'harlots and their mates' (pimps, etc.) were often punished by 'ducking' (p. 189), as on cucking stools. Cf. *Misogonus*, ed. R. W. Bond in *Early Plays
from the Italian* (1911), II.ii.110: 'I woulde they were vp tothe necke ith brooke
all three.'

a mill pool] Southwark's water-mills were near the stews (as in 'Colyn Blow-
bols Testament', *Remains*, I, ll. 166–73), particularly Paris Garden Manor, at
whose east end near the Thames stood a mill and its pond, evidently used for
ducking, since the Manor's court records refer to a cucking-stool: see London
County Council, *Survey of London*, XXII (1950), ed. Ida Darlington, pp. 94, 96;

And then, I durst warrant, they would depart anon.
Hick. Help, help, for the passion of my soul!
    He hath made a great hole in my poll,   450
    That all my wit is set to the ground.
    Alas, a leech for to help my wound!
Imag. [*To Free Will*] Nay, iwis, whoreson, I will beat
        thee or I go.
Free. Alas, good sir, what have I do?
Imag. [*Making to strike at Free Will*] Ware, make room!
    He shall have a stripe, I trow.   455

[*Enter* PITY.]

Pity. Peace, peace, sirs, I command you!
Imag. Avaunt, old churl! Whence comest thou?
    And thou make too much, I shall break thy brow
    And send thee home again.
Pity. A, good sir, the peace I would have kept fain.   460
    Mine office is to see no man slain,
    And where they do amiss, to give them good counsel
    Sin to forsake, and God's law them tell.
Imag. A, sir, I weened thou haddest been drowned and gone;

448. durst warrant] *Q1*; warrant you *Q3*.   450. poll] *Hazlitt*; poule *Q1*,
Q3.   445.1.] *Manly*.   456. sirs] *Q1*; syr *Q3*.   458. make] *Q1*;
prate *Q3*.   shall] *Q1*; wyll *Q3*.   461. Mine] *Q1*; My *Q3*.   462. to] *Q1*;
I *Q3*.

---

there was also one by a stream called 'the sewar' near the Southwark Clink
(Rendle, p. 200). Word-play on Richard de la Pole's family name here and at 450
is discussed in the Intro., p. 60.
    448. *depart*] separate.
    449. *passion*] suffering.
    450. *poll*] top of the head.
    452.] a cry recalling the mummers' 'Call for the Doctor' after their combat
(Chambers, *E.F.-P.*, pp. 38–41).
    leech] physician.
    help] treat, remedy.
    453.] Cf. *Y*. 410 (Lechery's threat to beat Riot for telling her name).
    455. *Ware*] beware.
    457. *old churl*] See Intro., pp. 45–46, and *Y*. 204.
    462–63.] Cf. *Y*. 5–6, 478–79 (Charity), 584–86 (Humility) and *passim*.
    464.] Charity was on Hick Scorner's list of drowned virtues (343; cf. 469).

But I have spied that there scaped one.   465
Hick. Imagination, do by the counsel of me;
    Be agreed with Free Will and let us good fellows be,
    And then as for this churl Pity,
    Shall curse the time that ever he came to land.
Imag. Brother Free Will, give me your hand,   470
    And all mine ill will I forgive thee.
Free. Sir, I thank you heartily.
    But what shall we do with this churl Pity?
Imag. I will go to him and pick a quarrel,
    And make him a thief and say he did steal   475
    Of mine forty pound in a bag.
Free. By God, that tidings will make him sad!
    And I will go fetch a pair of gyves,
    For in good faith he shall be set fast by the heels.
Hick. Have ado lightly, and be gone!   480
    And let us twain with him alone.
Free. Now farewell, I beshrew you, everyone!

---

465. spied that] *Q1;* espyed *Q3.*   scaped] *Q1;* escaped *Q3.*   471. ill] *Q1;*
euyll *Q3.*   475. did] *Q1;* hyd *Q3.*   478. gyves] *Q1;* gyles *Q3.*   479. be
set] *Q3;* besette *Q1.*   heels] *Hazlitt;* heles *Q1, Q3.*   480. ado] *Q1;* ydo
Q3.   be gone] *Q1, Q3;* be go *or* be ago *This ed. conj.*

---

468. *Pity*] Hick Scorner here, Free Will at 473 and Imagination at 484 could
not have known Pity's name, as he never mentioned it. Cf. *Y.* 204n.
    469. *Shall*] Ellipsis of a subject is not uncommon where its meaning is clear
(Abbott 399).
    471.] a witty reminder that Imagination is, allegorically, only an aspect of
Free Will, who can summon (189) and transform him at will (984–85).
    475–76.] adapted from *Y.* 138–41 (Youth), but quite suited to Imagination's
character (225–26, 262–63).
    475. *make*] allege (*O.E.D.*, v.¹, 56).
    477. *sad*] grave.
    478. *gyves*] fetters. This word, sounded with [əz] at 588, may rhyme with an
(unusual) plural form of 'heels' at 479.
    479.] adapted from *Y.* 190–92 (Youth).

Hick. Ho, ho, Free Will, you shrew, and no mo!

[Exit FREE WILL.]

Imag. Thou lewd fellow, sayst thou that thy name is Pity?

Who sent thee hither to control me? 485

Pity. Good sir, it is my property

For to despise sinful living,

And unto virtue men to bring

If that they will do after me.

Imag. What, sir! Art thou so pope-holy? 490

A, see! This caitiff would be praised, I trow.

And you thrive this year, I will lose a penny.

Lo, sirs, outward he beareth a fair face,

But and he met with a wench in a privy place,

I trow he would show her but little grace. 495

By God, ye may trust me!

Hick. Lo, will ye not see this caitiff's meaning?

He would destroy us all and all our kin.

Yet had I liever see him hanged by the chin

---

483. Ho, ho] *Q1;* Howe howe *Q3.*   Free Will] *Q1, Q3;* Farewell *Manly (Kittredge).* shrew] *Manly (Kittredge);* threwe *Q1;* thre *Q3.*   S.D.] *This ed.; at l. 482 in Manly.*   484.] *Q1, Q3;* Thou leude felowe | Sayst thou that thy name is Pite *This ed. conj.*   490. pope-holy] *Q3;* p pe holy *damaged Q1;* pure holy *Hawkins.*   491. would be praised, I trow] *Q1;* I trowe he wolde praysed be *Q3;* wolde be praysed, trowe I. *Manly.*   492. And] *Q1;* An *Q3.*   494. met] *This ed.;* mette *Q1, Q3;* meet *Hazlitt.*   497.ye not] *Q1;* you *Q3.*   498. us all] *Q1;* vs *Q3.*

---

483. *you shrew, and no mo*] Hick Scorner voids Free Will's curse by returning it and then goes one up by cutting him off with the last word (cf. *O.E.D.*, 'fliting', 1, example from 1636).

484. *lewd*] ignorant, base.

486–87. *property | For to despise sinful living*] defining quality, to scorn sin (whereas Hick Scorner despises virtue).

490. *pope-holy*] sanctimonious, hypocritically virtuous.

494.] sexual innuendo (*O.E.D.*, 'meet', v., 11e).

497–502.] adapted from *Y.* 83–86 (*H.S.* 497, 501–02), 142–43 (*H.S.* 499–500), by Youth; and see Intro., p. 46.

498. *all our kin*] Cf. 366–67, and Intro., p. 61.

499.] Cf. *Four Elements*, where Sensual Appetite says of Studious Desire, 'I wolde he were hangyd by the throte' (sig. B3r).

Rather than that should be brought about.　　　　500
And with this dagger thou shalt have a clout,
Without thou wilt be lightly begone.

Imag. Nay, brother, lay hand on him soon,
For he japed my wife and made me cuckold!
And yet the traitor was so bold　　　　505
That he stole forty pound of mine in money.

Hick. By Saint Mary, then he shall not scape!
We will lead him straight to Newgate,
For ever there shall he lie.

[*Enter* FREE WILL *with fetters and rope.*]

Free. A, see! A, see, sirs, what I have brought!　　　　510
A medicine for a pair of sore shins.
At the King's Bench, sirs, I have you sought.

---

502. wilt be] *Q1, Q3;* wylte *Manly.*　begone] *This ed.;* be gone *Q1;* gone
Q3.　503. hand] *Q1;* handes *Q3.*　506. mine] *Q1;* mynd *Q3.*　508. will
lead] *Q1;* wylled *Q3.*　Newgate,] *Hawkins;* Newgate; *Manly.*　509.] *Q1;*
For there he can not ronne awaye. *Q3.*　For ever] *Q1;* For-ever *Manly.*
509.1.] *Manly.*　511. shins] *Hazlitt;* shynnes *Q1, Q3.*

---

502. *Without*] unless.
　be lightly begone] redundancy that takes the imperative 'be gone', two words
often joined, as a past participle of the verb 'go' (instead of 'bego', 'to encom-
pass, surround, beset') on the analogy of 'become' (608).
　504. *japed*] seduced.
　505. *the traitor*] Cf. Imagination's earlier boast (225).
　510–11.] adapted from *Y.* 520, 304–05 (Riot).
　512. *the King's Bench*] one of five prisons in Southwark (Stow, II, 53), shown
in a 1542 map as being on the east side of St Margaret's Hill, Borough High
Street, between St George's Church on the south and the Marshalsea on the
north (Rendle, front. and p. xix). The Court of King's Bench for Pleas of the
Crown, which sat on session days in Westminster Hall's south-east corner and
was named after the king's long marble coronation bench there, did not stock
prison equipment and must be distinguished from the Court's jail, which was
moved from Westminster to Southwark before 1400. See Mackenzie E. C.
Walcott, *Westminster: Memorials of the City* (1849), pp. 251–52; and Pugh, pp.
119–20. The prison's marshal in 1514 was Charles Brandon (see Intro.,
p. 34.
　you sought] searched on your behalf.

But I pray you, who shall wear these?

Hick. By God, this fellow that may not go hence!

I will go give him these hose rings.   515

Now i'faith they be worth forty pence!

But to his hands I lack two bonds.

Imag. Hold, whoreson, here is an halter.

Bind him fast and make him sure.

Pity. O men, let Troth that is the true man   520

Be your guider, or else ye be forlore!

Lay no false witness, as nigh as ye can,

On none, for afterward ye will repent it full sore!

---

513. these] *Q1, Q3;* these [rynges] *Manly;* these gynnes *or* these thynges *This ed. conj.*   515. give] *Hazlitt;* gyue *Q1, Q3.*   516. i'faith] *Q1;* in fayth *Q3.*   517. to] *Q1;* to bynde *Q3.* bonds] *Q1, Q3;* binds *This ed. conj.*   518. an] *Q1;* a *Q3.*   520. Troth] *Q1;* treuth *Q3;* truth *Hazlitt.*   521. guider] *Q1;* guyde *Q3.* forlore] *Manly;* forlorne *Q1, Q3.*

---

513. *these*] The addition of 'gins', a term for 'fetters' (*O.E.D.*, sb.[1], 4, 5b), or of 'rings' or 'things', would make a rhyme with 511 (cf. *Y.* 507–08 and Intro., n. 118), but an off-rhyme on the plural endings is not impossible (as at 586–88).

514. *may not go*] a jest. Pity has 'sore shins'.

515. *give*] punning on 'gyve' (198, 478)?

hose rings] adapted from *Y.* 507–08 (Riot): 'stockings', 'leggings' (only down to the ankle); in the plural 'hose' meant occasionally 'leg-armour, greaves, chain-mail hose' (*M.E.D.*, 2); the quibble in *Ane Satyre*, 'Put in ȝour leggis into the stocks, | For ȝe had never ane meiter hois' (1554 version, ll. 2487–88), was probably old, since men's hose had become known as 'stocks' (*O.E.D.*, sb.[1], 40).

516. *forty pence*] 'customary amount for a wager' (*O.E.D.*, 'forty', A.c; e.g., Stevens, p. 340, and *Johan the Evangelist*, l. 535).

517. *bonds*] probably 'binds', meaning 'ties, bands' (*O.E.D.*, sb., 1; and cf. 'bine'), where the loss of *g* in 'rings' (515) and of *d* here (see Intro., n. 144) gives a rhyme. The couplet could, however, be based on the plural ending (cf. 478–79, 586–88).

518. *halter*] shaped like a hanging noose (243, 499)?

520. *Troth that is the true man*] When God comes to judge at Doomsday he is called Faithful and True, 'Fidelis, et Verax' (Rev. xix.11; cf. *H.S.* 28n, 340, 579).

522. *Lay no false witness*] Moses' ninth commandment (Ex. xx.16). 'It is the easiest thing in the world to get a person thrown into prison in this country; for every officer of justice, both civil and criminal, has the power of arresting any one, at the request of a private individual . . . nor is there any punishment awarded for making a slanderous accusation' (*Relation*, pp. 33–34).

Free. Nay, nay, I care not therefore!

Hick. Yea, when my soul hangeth on the hedge, cast
       stones! 525

    For I tell thee plainly, by Cock's bones,

    Thou shalt be guided and laid in irons.

    They fared even so.   *[They bind Pity.]*

Pity. Away, sir! What have I do?

Imag. Well, well, that thou shalt know or thou go. 530

Pity. O sirs, I see it cannot be amended.

    You do me wrong, for I have not offended.

    Remember God, that is our Heaven-king,

    For he will reward you after your deserving

    When Death with his mace doth you arrest. 535

    We all to him owe fewte and service.

---

527. guided] *Hazlitt;* guyded *Q1;* gyued *Q3.*   528. fared] *Q1;* feared
Q3.   S.D.] *This ed.; at l. 519 in Farmer.*   529. Away] *Q1;* Why *Q3;* Well-a-
way *Hazlitt.*   531. sirs] *Q1;* syr *Q3.*   532. me] *Q1;* to me *Q3.*   534. he]
Q1; hy *Q3.*   deserving] *Manly;* deservygne; *Hawkins.*   535. arrest.] *Manly;*
areest, *Hawkins.*   536. fewte] *Q1;* fayte *Q3.*

---

524. *Nay, nay*] Cf. 235n.

therefore] for that.

525.] adapted from *Y.* 629–31 (*Youth*).

527. *guided*] as at 81 and 521.

528. *They*] Imagination (at 237) and Free Will (at 801–05).

S.D.] George Steevens, in his *Plays of William Shakspeare* (1778), was first to
note the similarity of Pity's treatment to Kent's stocking in *King Lear*, II. ii.
120–46 (IX, 423, n. 1).

530. *Well, well*] See *Y.* 407n.

or] before.

535. *Death . . . arrest*] traditional; cf. de Worde's prose dialogue, *The deyenge
creature* (*S.T.C.* 6035; 1514 ed.): 'Alas that euer I synned in my lyfe to me is come
this daye the dredfull tydynges that euer I herde / here hath ben with me a
sergeaunt of armes whose name is crewelte frome the kynge of all kynges / lorde
of all lordes / and Juge of al Juges lyenge on me his mace of his offyce sayenge
vnto me I arest you' (sig. A2r); and 'The Thrie Tailes of the Thrie Priests of
Peblis', where Death's coming to a man is so described: 'on him laid an officer
his mace, | And summond him, and bad he sould compeir | Befoir the King, and
gif ane count perqueir' (Laing, I, ll. 1176–78); for later usage, see Samuel C.
Chew, *The Pilgrimage of Life* (1962), pp. 245–46.

536. *him*] God the 'Heaven-*king*' (533).

fewte] fealty.

Fro the ladder of life down he will thee threst;
Then mastership may not help, nor great office.
Free. What, Death! And he were here, he should sit by thee.
Trowest thou that he be able to strive with us three? 540
Nay, nay, nay.
Imag. Well, fellows, now let us go our way,
For at Shooters Hill we have a game to play.
Hick. In good faith, I will tarry no lenger space.
Free. Beshrew him for me that is last out of this place! 545
[*Exeunt all but Pity.*]
Pity. Lo, lords, they may curse the time they were born

537. life] *Q1;* lyght *Q3.*   544. lenger] *Q3;* lender *Q1.*   545. Beshrew] *Q1;*
I beshrew *Q3.*   546. born] *Manly;* borne; *Hawkins.*

---

537. *the ladder of life*] Cf. *H.S.* 83 and *Y.* 98–101 (Youth's ladder to heaven, from which he fears to fall).

threst] thrust.

539–41.] Craik compares this situation (p. 93) to Chaucer's *Pardoner's Tale*, where three such rogues vow to slay 'this traytour deth' (699). See Intro., pp. 45–46.

542.] adapted from *Y.* 458, 460, 462, etc.

543. *a game*] after which the hill was named. On May Day 1515 Henry VIII's yeomen of the guard, dressed as Robin Hood's outlaws, entertained him and the court with trick archery on Shooters Hill (Halle, 'Henry VIII', fols. 56v–57r).

544.] adapted from *Y.* 471 (Pride), 542 (Riot).

545.] adapted from *Y.* 461 (Riot). Cf. *Mankind* (*Macro Plays*), where Mischief exits with the other vices in saying: 'I beschrew þe last xall com to hys hom' (724).

546–601.] Pity's complaint is based on at least four sources. (1) It quotes from *Y.* (546–47, 550, 552, 571; cf. 576, 579) and describes its action and themes. Pity echoes Charity in claiming to suffer for God's love (549; *Y.* 528–29), mentions by name Charity (556), Lechery (558), Youth (562) and Pride (577), and comments on Youth's dagger-play (562, 574), Pride's clothes-worship (555, 575) and pimping (566–67), Youth's doctrine of being 'unthrifty' (576; cf. 63–64), and the tavern visit (586–87). (2) Some figures from the opposed armies in *A.G.* appear at 552, 560, 564, 580, 583 and 594 (see Appendix III.3, ll. 637, 678, 649, 838 and 897). (3) Chaucer's *Pardoner's Tale* may influence topics at 554 and 590. (4) A version of *The maner of the world now a dayes*, a title echoed at 551 and 565, is used at 553, 566–67, 574–76, 579, 581 and 584; and an echo of other complaints in this tradition exists at 558. John Peter's *Complaint and Satire in Early English Literature* (1956) discusses this form as the 'England' complaint, and includes Pity's speech among its analogues (pp. 67–68, 190). Personification catalogues, vice's triumph over exiled virtue (cf. *H.S.* 339–52n), and a dependence on proverbs are among the form's conventions, for which see Joseph R. Keller, 'The Triumph of Vice: A Formal Approach to the Medieval Complaint against the Times', *Annuale Mediaevale*, 10 (1969), 120–37.

For the weeds that overgroweth the corn!
They troubled me guiltless and wot not why.
For God's love yet will I suffer patiently.
We all may say 'wellaway!'　　　　　　　　　550
For sin that is now-a-day.
Lo, virtue is vanished forever and aye.
Worse was it never!
We have plenty of great oaths,
And cloth enough in our clothes,　　　　　　555
But charity many men loathes.
Worse was it never!
Alas, now is lechery called love indeed,
And murder named manhood in every need.
Extortion is called law, so God me speed!　　560

547. that] *Q1; not in Q3.* corn!] *Manly;* corne, *Hawkins.*　　548. wot] *Q1;* knewe *Q3.*　why.] *Manly;* why, *Hawkins.*　550–51.] *Manly; one line in Q1,* *Q3.* 552. vanished] *Q1;* banysshed *Q3.* 555. cloth enough] *Q1;* superfluyte of cloth *Q3.* 560. me] *Q1;* be my *Q3.*

546–47.] adapted from *Y.* 547–48 (Charity's complaint).

546.] 'woe unto that man by whom the Son of man is betrayed! it had been good for that man if he had not been born' (Matt. xxvi.24). Cf. *H.S.* 439, 862; *Johan the Evangelist,* l. 212.

548.] 'Then said Jesus, Father, forgive them; for they know not what they do' (Luke xxiii.34).

550.] adapted from *Y.* 194 (Youth to Charity).

552.] adapted from *Y.* 549–50?

553.] the concluding refrain of *The maner of the world now a dayes* (see Appendix III.4, ll. 184, 194).

554. *great oaths*] Chaucer's Pardoner preaches at length against 'othes fals & grete' (629; see 630–59, 472–75), and several that the tale illustrates, 'by goddis precyous herte' (651) and 'goddys armys' (654), recur here (427, 435, 442 and 914), and are not in *Y.*

555.] Henry VIII's first apparel statute attributes much poverty, robbery and extortion to ambition for 'greate and costly array', and varies the maximum quantity of cloth for gowns or coats proportionally to the wearer's social rank (*S.R.,* III [1817], 1 Hen. VIII. c. 14, p. 8).

558. *now is lechery called love*] Cf. *The Pride of Life (Non-Cycle Plays):* 'Lou is nou al lecuri' (337). For the Latin ancestry of this formula, see Carleton Brown, 'The "Pride of life" and the "Twelve abuses"', *Archiv,* 128 (1912), 75–77.

559. *manhood*] manliness.

560. *Extortion*] Cf. *A.G.,* ll. 637, 682 (Appendix III.3). This was a much harped-on early Tudor political issue (e.g., *S.R.,* III [1817], 3 Hen. VIII. c. 12, p. 32).

Worse was it never!
Youth walketh by night with swords and knives,
And, ever among, true men leeseth their lives.
Like heretics we occupy other men's wives
Now-a-days in England.   565
Bawds be the destroyers of many young women,
And full lewd counsel they give unto them.
How you do marry, beware, you young men!
The wise never tarrieth too long.
There be many great scorners,   570
But for sin there be few mourners.
We have but few true lovers
In no place now-a-days.
There be many goodly gilt knives,
And I trow as well apparelled wives;   575
Yet many of them be unthrifty of their lives,
And all set in pride to go gay.

563. leeseth] *Q1*; lese *Q3*.   566. the] *Q1*; *not in Q3*.   568. you] *Q1 twice*;
ye *Q3 twice*.   569. wise] *Hawkins*; wyfe *Q1*, *Q3*. tarrieth] *Q1*; taryed
Q3.   573. now-a-days] *Q1*, *Q3*; now-a-day *This ed. conj.*   577. all] *Q1*; all
is *Q3*.

563.] 'people are taken up every day by dozens, like birds in a covey, and
especially in London; yet, for all this, they never cease to rob and murder in the
streets' (*Relation*, p. 36).

ever among] regularly.

564. *heretics*] In 1499 some English heretics argued that mere copulation
accomplished marriage (*Venice*, I, no. 799). One Agnes Grebill was apparently
burned at the stake after being charged with heresy, in part concerning the
sacrament of marriage (*L.P.* I.752; Charles Sturge, *Cuthbert Tunstal* [1938], p.
19).

occupy] copulate with.

566–67.] Cf. a version of *The maner of the world now a dayes* (Appendix III.4,
ll. 109–12).

568–69.] For this literary convention, see Francis Lee Utley, *The Crooked
Rib: An Analytical Index* (1944).

571.] adapted from *Y.* 762 (Humility).

572. *but few true lovers*] only few who keep to faithful married love (351,
564–69).

574–76.] mainly adapted from a version of *The maner of the world now a dayes*
(Appendix III.4, ll. 45–48); cf. *Y.* 64.

574. *gilt*] gilded, gold-plated.

577.] 'And all [the wives] proudly determined to show off', or 'And all dressed
up showily to flaunt themselves'.

Mayors on sin doth no correction,
With gentlemen beareth troth adown.
Avoutry is suffered in every town.   580
Amendement is there none,
And God's commandements we break them all ten.
Devotion is gone many days sin.
Let us amend us, we true Christen men,
Or Death make you groan!   585
Courtiers go gay and take little wages;
And many with harlots at the tavern haunts—

578. doth] *Q1;* do *Q3.*   579. troth] *Q1, Q3;* truth *Hazlitt.*   580. Avoutry]
Q1; Aduoutry *Q3.*   581. Amendement] *Q3;* Amendyment *Q1.*   583.
many days sin] *Q1;* with many a sen *Q3.*   584. amend us] *Q1;* amende
Q3.   585. groan] *Q1;* to grone *Q3.*   587. haunts] *Hazlitt;* hauntes *Q1, Q3.*

578.] Charles Joseph, summoner and confessed murderer of Richard Hun in
Lollards Tower on 4 December 1514, said to his servant Julian Little (as she
deposed), 'I coulde brynge my Lorde of London [the Bishop] to the dores of
heretyques in London bothe of men and women that ben worthe a thowsand
pound', and also to his daughter, 'lykewyse [as above] & more larger saieng of
the best in London, where to maistres porter [the daughter] answered, the best
in London is my lord Mayer, than Charles sayde, I wil not skuse him quyte for
he taketh this matter whote [Hun's case? 'hot']' (Halle, 'Henry VIII', fol. 52v;
L.P. I.3523).

579. *beareth troth adown*] oppress honest people, insistently oppose the right.

579, 581, 584.] possibly adapted from a version of *The maner of the world now a
dayes* (Appendix III.4, ll. 185–90); but also cf. *Y.* 345–46 for *H.S.* 579.

580. *Avoutry*] (1) adultery, breaking of the (marriage) vow; (2) heresy,
idolatry (*M.E.D.*, 'avoutri(e', 2; and *H.S.* 564–65). Cf. *A.G.*, 649 (Appendix
III.3).

581. *Amendement*] Q spellings of this word (cf. 724) and of its rhyme at 726,
'commandement' (also at 582, 886 and 1026), indicate they were quadrasyllabic
(Dobson, § 306).

583. *sin*] since, ago.

585. *Or*] before.

586. *Courtiers*] residents of the Inns of Court, Lincoln's and Gray's Inns, and
the Middle and Inner Temples; and ten additional Inns of Chancery existed. Cf.
World, where Folly, a Westminster serjeant-at-law living at 'the Innes', says: 'in
holborne I was forthe brought | And with the courtyers I am betaught' (sig. B5).

take little wages] seldom work, earn little in service (*O.E.D.*, 'take', v., 36;
'wage', sb., 2b–c).

587. *harlots*] (1) scoundrels, (male) rogue servants; (2) whores (but cf. 588)?
haunts] rhyming, evidently, on [əz].

They be yemen of the wreath that be shackled in gyves;
On themself they have no pity.
God punisheth full sore with great sickness,   590
As pocks, pestilence, purple and axes.
Some dieth suddenly that death full perilous.
Yet was there never so great poverty.
There be some sermons made by noble doctors,
But truly the fiend doth stop men's ears,   595
For God, nor good man, some people not fears.
Worse was it never!
All truth is not best said,
And our preachers now-a-days be half afraid.
When we do amend, God would be well apaid.   600
Worse was it never!

592. that] *Q1* a *Q3*.   595. men's] *Q1*; theyr. *Q3*.

---

588. *wreath*] 'ornamental band or circlet, generally of gold', here a prisoner's
iron neck-chain or collar; perhaps also a coiled rope or noose.

590. *great sickness*] In Chaucer's *Pardoner's Tale* Death took, among the
'thousande sleyn this pestilence' (679), one of the three rioters' friends (see *H.S.*
116–18n). London experienced serious plague in September–November 1511
(*L.P.* I.865, 933), September 1513–January 1514 (*L.P.* I.2223, 2610), and
April–July 1514 (*L.P.* I.2847, 3050), and regularly before and after. In
1499–1500 some 20,000 Londoners fell before the disease (C. Creighton, *A
History of Epidemics in Britain*, 2nd ed. [1965], I, 243–50).

591. *pocks*] diseases characterised by pustules: small-pox or syphilis, the
'French pox'. The latter reached England in 1503, shortly after which it became
epidemic (C. Creighton, *History of Epidemics*, I, 419).

purple] disease whose chief symptom is purplish pustules, as purpura, where
spots arise from hemorrhage.

axes] ague, a fever marked by paroxysms (pronounced 'áccess').

592. *perilous*] (1) fraught with danger, as for the soul's damnation; (2) terrible,
frightening.

594. *noble doctors*] excellent divines. Cf. *A.G.*, 897 (Appendix III.3).

596. *God, nor good man*] proverbial, as in *The Castle of Perseverance* (*Macro
Plays*), l. 479.

598.] Tilley T594, 'All TRUTHS must not be told.'

599.] In his 1511/12 Convocation sermon Colet said of English priests: 'by
spiritual wekenes and bondage feare, whan they are made weake with the waters
of this worlde, they dare neyther do nor say but suche thynges as they knowe to
be pleasant and thankfull to their princis' (Lupton, p. 298; but see *H.S.* 343n); a
sentiment also appearing in Skelton's 'Colyn Cloute', *Works*, I, ll. 162–65.

600. *apaid*] pleased, contented.

[*Enter* CONTEMPLATION *and* PERSEVERANCE.]

Contem. What, master Pity! How is it with you?

Perse. Sir, we be sorry to see you in this case now.

Pity. Brethren, here were three perilous men,
    Free Will, Hick Scorner and Imagination.   605
    They said I was a thief and laid felony upon me
    And bound me in irons, as ye may see.

Contem. Where be the traitors become now?

Pity. In good faith, I cannot show you.

Perse. Brother, let us unbind him of his bonds.   610

Contem. Unloose the feet and the hands.

                           [*They release Pity.*]

Pity. I thank you for your great kindness
    That you two show in this distress;
    For they were men without any mercy
    That delighteth all in mischief and tyranny.   615

Perse. I think they will come hither again,
    Free Will and Imagination, both twain.

607. me] *Q3;* we *Q1.*   610. bonds] *Q1;* bandes *Q3.*   611.] *Q1;* Vndo you the fete / and I shall lose the handles. *Q3.*   613. show] *Q1;* shew me *Q3.* 615. That delighteth] *Q1;* They delyted *Q3.*   and] *Q1;* and in *Q3.*

602–20.] Here Contemplation and Perseverance largely adapt *Y.* lines: 571–72 (*H.S.* 602–03), 578–80 (*H.S.* 608), 576–77 (*H.S.* 610–11) and 584–86 (*H.S.* 618–20) by Humility, and 582 (*H.S.* 616) by Charity. Perseverance's determination to bring the two rogues to 'virtue' and 'virtuous living' (618–19), however, reflects *A.G.*, where Perseverance 'Betokeneth nomore but the contynuance | Of vertuous lyuyng tyll dethe hath auergone' (1837–38; cf. 1859 and *H.S.* 1025).

606. *felony*] technically, a theft over twelve pence in value (*H.S.* 255n), for which death was normally exacted.

611.] Q3 seems inconsistent with the action. If Contemplation gives Pity the chains at 627 (and *someone* must take them away), he should here unbind Pity's feet (and Perseverance his hands), since the chains are only used for Pity's legs (515–18).

615.] formulaic: cf. 'he delyted all in tyranye' and 'In myscheyff we delyted' ('The Lyfe of Roberte the Deuyll', *Remains*, I, ll. 8, 588).

mischief] evil-doing.

617. *Free Will and Imagination*] As Bevington points out (p. 138), the playwright meant not to bring Hick Scorner back. See Intro., p. 32.

Them will I exhort to virtuous living,
And unto virtue them to bring
By the help of you, Contemplation.   620
Contem. Do my counsel, brother Pity:
Go you and seek them through the country,
In village, town, burgh and city
Throughout all the realm of England.
When you them meet, lightly them arrest   625
And in prison put them fast.
Bind them sure in irons strong,
For they be so false and subtile
That they will you beguile
And do true men wrong.   630
Perse. Brother Pity, do as he hath said.
In every quarter look you aspy
And let good watch for them be laid
In all the haste that thou can, and that privily;

618. to] *Q1; by Q3.*   621. Do] *Q1; Do by Q3.*   623. burgh] *Q1; not in Q3.*   626. put them fast] *Q1; that ye them kest Q3.*   627. sure] *Q1; surely Q3.*   628. false] *Q3; faste Q1.*   632. every] *Q1; euer Q3.* aspy] *Q1; espye Q3.*   634. that thou] *Q1; you Q3.*

618–19.] For the elliptical syntax, see also 414–15.

622–24.] Cf. *Cocke Lorelles bote*, where Cocke and his crew of rogues 'sayled Englande thorowe and thorowe | Vyllage towne cyte and borowe' (sig. C2v); and *Johan the Evangelist*, ll. 384–85.

622. *seek*] (1) search for; (2) pursue in attack, advance against.

625. *lightly*] without delay.

628. *false*] Falseness and subtilty are associated at 368, and a contrast with 'true men' at 630 seems intended. Q1 apparently repeats 'faste' from 626.

632. *aspy*] watch out for.

633. *good watch*] Justices of the peace (see *The Justyces of paes*, S.T.C. 14864, sig. B3r), so as to prevent felons evading capture by going where they were unknown, were charged in 1511 to enforce the neglected Statute of Winchester (1285) by seeing 'from the Day of the Ascension unto the Feast of St. Michael the Archangel, that in every city in the night six men at every gate; in every borough, 12 men; and every uplanded town, six men or four, after the number of people there dwelling. And they shall make watch continually from sunset to sun rising. And if any stranger pass by them, they shall arrest him or them' (*T.R.P.*, I, no. 63, p. 87).

634. *thou*] usually employed for inferiors (as at 705), and not elsewhere spoken by the virtues among themselves; but used between familiars, for which see Abbott 235, and *H.S.* 234. Perhaps Perseverance speaks like a sheriff to his officer.

For and they come hither, they shall not scape   635
For all the craft that they can make.
Pity. Well, then will I hie me as fast as I may
And travail through every country.
Good watch shall be laid in every way
That they steal not into sanctuary.   640
Now farewell, brethren, and pray for me,
For I must go hence indeed.
Perse. Now God be your good speed!
Contem. And ever you defend when you have need!
Pity. Now, brethren both, I thank you.   [*Exit.*] 645

[*Enter* FREE WILL.]

Free. [*To the audience*] Make you room for a gentleman,
        sirs, and peace!
        Dieu garde, seigneurs, tout le presse!

643. speed] *Q3;* spende *Q1;* frende *This ed. conj.*   644.] *Q1, Q3;* And euer
you defende | Whan you haue nede *This ed. conj.*   646. you] *Q1; not in*
Q3.   647. *Dieu garde*] *Hazlitt;* Duegarde *Q1;* Dewegarde *Q3.*

---

636. *craft*] Imagination's special talent (256, 260), used to obtain Free Will's
release from custody (662).

638. *travail*] travel.

country] Cf. 219; but perhaps a legal term for 'neighbourhood' or 'hundred',
the area from which a jury was selected (*O.E.D.*, 7).

640. *sanctuary*] less the ecclesiastical sanctuary in churches (valid only for
forty days, by which time the criminal had to confess his offence publicly and
abjure the realm or be arrested) than the permanent liberties outside the King's
justice (which were destroyed by 1540), such as Westminster (see 842 and n.),
Glastonbury, large parts of Northumberland and Yorkshire, Durham, Chester
and Lancaster, which functioned as safe bases for criminal operations in non-
sanctuary areas. See I. D. Thornley, 'The Destruction of Sanctuary', *Tudor
Studies*, ed. R. W. Seton-Watson (1924), pp. 182–207; *Relation*, pp. 34–35. Great
bands of sanctuary-based robbers attacked Henry VIII's tax-collectors in 1513,
but eighty of the criminals were caught and hanged (*L.P.* I.2072).

647.] 'God save you, sirs, the whole crowd!' Cf. Pilate's greeting to Christ's
torturers in *The Towneley Plays*, 'Dew vows [garde], mon senyours!' (XXIV,
409); and *The Interlude of Wealth and Health*, ed. W. W. Greg, M.S.R. (1907;
rpt. 1963), l. 350.

le presse] One expects *la presse*, but double genders and fluctuation in genders
characterised Middle French (M. K. Pope, *From Latin to Modern French*, 2nd
ed. [1952], § 777).

And of your jangling if ye will cease,
I will tell you where I have been.
Sirs, I was at the tavern and drank wine.   650
Methought I saw a pece that was like mine,
And sir, all my fingers were arrayed with lime,
So I conveyed a cup mannerly.
And yet iwis I played all the fool,
For there was a scholar of mine own school,   655

---

649. been] *Q1, Q3;* be *Manly.*   651. pece] *Q1;* peace *Q3.*   652. arrayed]
Q1; tangled *Q3.*   653. conveyed] *Hawkins;* conuayued *Q1;* connayde *Q3.*

648.] an attention-getting formula, as by Caiaphas in *York Plays*, ed. Lucy T.
Smith (1885; rpt. 1963), 'Pees, bewshers, I bid no jangelyng ȝe make, | And sese
sone of youre sawes, & se what I saye' (XXIX, 1–2).

jangling] chatter.

650.] Cf. Youth's second entrance, from tavern wine-drinking (*Y.* 399–401).

651. *pece*] wine-cup.

652. *sir*] Here and at 656 Free Will confides in an individual spectator (unlike
at 646–47, 650, 663, 688), possibly because he refers to his criminal past, or
because he would demonstrate the theft by snatching an actual banquet cup (cf.
166). At 695 Free Will again singles out an onlooker, but discovers instead
Perseverance. In his translation of Erasmus' *Apophthegmes* (1542), *S.T.C.*
10443, Nicholas Udall comments: 'This custome and vsage, euen yet styl
endureth emong certain of the Germaines . . . (yea and in Englande also) that in
feastes of greate resorte, there is brought in for the nones some iestyng feloe, that
maye scoff and iest vpon the geastes, as they sitten at the table, with the which
iestyng to bee stiered to angre, is accoūpted a thyng much cōtrarie to all courtesie
or good maner' (sig. e2v).

lime] sticky substance prepared from holly bark to catch small birds on twigs,
and found often describing a deft pilferer's fingers (*O.E.D.*, sb.[1], 1), as in
Skelton's 'Bowge of Courte', concerning Deceit the pickpocket: 'Lyghte lyme
fynger, he toke none other wage' (*Works*, I, l. 509); and Tilley F236, 'His
FINGERS are lime twigs.'

653.] The sale of stolen pewter or brass vessels to aliens by thieves was
lucrative and common enough to require a statute prohibiting the practice
(*S.R.*, II [1816], 19 Hen. VII. c. 6, pp. 651–52; III [1817], 4 Hen. VIII. c. 7, p.
51).

mannerly] in a refined, gentlemanlike way.

655. *a scholar of mine own school*] one wise to my game. In 'The Thrie Tailes of
the Thrie Priests of Peblis', the King tells the Fool who tricked him into taking
his own wife as a mistress: 'Thou art ane auld scollar at the scule' (Laing, I, l.
966). Cf. *The Book of Vices and Virtues*, ed. W. Nelson Francis, E.E.T.S. O.S.
217 (1942): 'Þe tauerne is þe deueles scole hous, for þere studieþ his disciples,
and þere lerneþ his scolers' (p. 53).

And sir, the whoreson aspied me.

Then was I rested and brought in prison.

For woe then I wist not what to have done,

And all because I lacked money.

But a friend in court is worth a penny in purse,   660

For Imagination, mine own fellow iwis,

He did help me out full craftily.

Sirs, he walked through Holborn

Three hours after the sun was down,

And walked up toward Saint Giles-in-the-Field.   665

He hoved still and there beheld;

But there he could not speed of his prey,

And straight to Ludgate he took the way.

Ye wot well that pothecaries walk very late.

656. aspied] *Q1;* espyed *Q3.*   657. rested] *Q1;* arested *Q3.*   in] *Q1;* to
Q3.   665. up toward] *Q1;* vpwarde to *Q3.*   669. well] *Q1; not in*
Q3.   walk] *Q1;* waks *Q3;* wake *Manly.*

---

657. *rested*] arrested.

660.] Tilley F687; for early instances, see Chaucer's *Romaunt of the Rose,*
5541–42; and *Songs*, VI.105*a*.64–65.

663. *Holborn*] low street running from Newgate towards Westminster (now
Holborn Viaduct), just north of de Worde's Fleet Street shop; so called from
'Hole Bourne', a valley through which the upper Fleet river flowed down to the
Thames (now at Blackfriars Bridge). Holborn is a legal district, Imagination's
confessed haunt (217–24; cf. 586), and was known for its prostitutes (*Cocke
Lorelles bote*, sig. B4r). The rhyme with 664 is probably improved by the loss of *r*
before *n* here: see *Y.* 255n, *H.S.* 828–29.

665.] that is, from the valley through legal Holborn (and the Inns of Court) up
to High Holborn, a street ending near St Giles-in-the-Field, a parish comprised
of a lepers' hospital, a church and a small village isolated in the fields between
London and Westminster (J. E. B. Gover, *et al, The Place-Names of Middlesex*
[1942], p. 116). Imagination's walk follows the last journey of prisoners drawn
to the Tyburn gallows; they were furnished with a last bowl of ale at St Giles
hospital (Stow, II, 91; and *H.S.* 820–45n).

666.] formulaic: 'He houed styll and behelde vs yerne' (*Kynge Rycharde cuer
du lyon* [de Worde, 1528; *S.T.C.* 21008], sig. B2v, and cf. A6v; Farmer, p. 255).

hoved] waited poised, lurked.

668. *straight to Ludgate*] to London's sixth principal gate (a debtors' prison)
standing on the west side of Ludgate Hill about one-eighth of a mile south of
Newgate, probably via Fleet Street.

669. *pothecaries*] a much-satirised trade, as in the apothecary's sale of poison to
the youngest rogue in Chaucer's *Pardoner's Tale* (851–67), Barclay's comment
that 'the craft of an Apoticary | . . . is all fraude and gilefull pollicy' (*Eclogues*, p.

He came to a door and privily spake   670
To a prentice for a pennyworth of euphorbium,
And also for a halfpennyworth of alum plume.
This good servant served him shortly,
And said, 'Is there ought else that you would buy?'
Then he asked for a mouthful of quick brimstone,   675
And down into the cellar when the servant was gone,
Aside as he cast his eye,
A great bag of money did he spy,
Therein was an hundred pound.
He trussed him to his feet and yede his way round.   680
He was lodged at Newgate at the *Swan*,

672. plume] *Q1; not in Q3.*   674. ought] *Q1;* nought *Q3.*   you] *Q1;* ye
Q3.   675. he asked] *Q1;* asked he *Q3.*   678. spy] *Q1;* espye *Q3.*   679.
hundred] *Q1;* hundreth *Q3.*   680. yede] *Q1;* went *Q3.*

206, ll. 711–12), the Poticary in Heywood's *Four PP* and Romeo's apothecary
(*Rom.* V.i.). Stow locates the apothecaries mainly in Bucklesbury Street within
the City (Stow, I, 260; II, 329–30), but Imagination's purposeful doubling back
and Apothecary Street, which now runs westwards from the City wall one block
south of Ludgate and was so named after the Company of Apothecaries acquired
part of near-by Blackfriars for their hall in 1632 (H. C. Cameron and E. A.
Underwood, *A History of the Worshipful Society of Apothecaries of London*, I
[1963], 58–59), indicate some shops were located about Ludgate much earlier.

walk very late] are stirring, busy themselves (*O.E.D.*, v.¹, 4c), late. The
suburbs were evidently not subject to the City's curfew after dark (e.g., D. W.
Robertson, Jr., *Chaucer's London* [1968], p. 104).

671. *prentice*] apprentice.

euphorbium] highly acrid gum resin used as emetic and purgative, principally
'to purge flewme and melancolyke humours' (Peter Treveris's *The grete herball*,
S.T.C. 13176, sig. I6r).

672. *alum plume*] plume or feather alum, 'a pseudo-alum crystallizing in tufts
of silky fibres' (*O.E.D.*, 'alum', 4; 'plume', sb., 6), another dry substance that,
according to John Arderne's *Treatises of Fistula in Ano*, ed. D'Arcy Power,
E.E.T.S. O.S. 139 (1910), is useful against 'inflacions of þe gomeȝ' (p. 81).

675. *quick brimstone*] fiery sulphur (*O.E.D.*, 'quick', a., 14), 'suche as it
cometh out of the erthe' (*The grete herball*, sig. X2v); for which the servant's
cellar trip is appropriate.

679. *Therein*] in which.

680. *trussed*] betook, bundled.

yede his way round] went round the City wall northwards (to Newgate).

681. *Newgate at the Swan*] an inn-tenement, documented from the fourteenth
to seventeenth centuries, that was located just east of Newgate prison and
London wall, with the king's street on the south, and the city wall again on the

And every man took him for a gentleman.
So on the morrow he delivered me
Out of Newgate by this policy.
And now will I dance an make rial cheer;   685
But I would Imagination were here,
For he is peerless at need.
Labour to him, sirs, if ye will your matters speed!
Now will I sing and lustily spring!
But when my fetters on my legs did ring,   690
I was not glad, perdie;
But now hey trolly lolly!
Let us see who can descant on this same;

683. delivered] *Q1;* delyered *Q3.*   684. this] *Q1;* his *Q3.*   685. an] *Q1;*
and *Q3.*   686. would] *Q1;* wolde that *Q3.*   691–92.] *This ed.; one line in*
Q1, Q3.   693.] *Q1;* Who can synge descant vpon the same *Q3.*

---

north. By 1435 a pipe carrying water from St Bartholomew's Hospital to the
prison ran across the inn's property. See Marjorie B. Honeybourne, 'The
Precinct of the Grey Friars', *London Topographical Record*, 16 (1932), 16–17
(and for a map of 1617 that shows the *Swan*, plate I); Sugden, p. 494; Bryant
Lillywhite, 'London signs' (1973), TS in 19 vols. (in Guildhall Library, London), no. 14282. Imagination's choice of this lodging shows a nice contempt for
the law.

683–84.] Imagination's skill derives from Riot's 'policy', which allows him
also to escape from Newgate (*Y.* 234, 240–44).

684. *policy*] 'stratagem, expedient', here the payment of a fine for a pardon
(227–28n).

685.] adapted from *Y.* 54 (Youth) and 225 (Riot).

an] and.

688. *Labour to*] lobby, solicit earnestly.

matters] 'affairs, business', possibly in a legal sense, 'subjects involving litiga-
tion' (*O.E.D.*, sb.[1], 19c, 20).

692. *hey trolly lolly*] traditional love song refrain expressing carefree mirth. Cf.
Magnyfycence, 'He dawnsys so long, "hey troly loly," | That euery man law-
ghyth at his Foly' (1251–52); *Four Elements*, sig. B2v; Stevens, pp. 401, 413–14,
424. For three musical settings, see *Music at the Court of Henry VIII*, ed. John
Stevens, Musica Britannica XVIII (1962), pp. 32, 57, 95–98.

693. *descant*] extemporise the counterpoint air melody *above* the bass part.
(Free Will must, then, have an adult voice.) Such improvisation on popular
tunes 'formed the staple of chamber-singing by amateurs at court' (Stevens, p.
286). In *Mankind (Macro Plays)* Nought invites the audience's 'yemandry' to
join in the refrains of a 'Crystemes songe' (332–34).

To laugh and get money it were a good game.
[*Sees Perseverance*] What! Whom have we here?   695
A priest, a doctor or else a frere?
What, master doctor dottypoll!
Cannot you preach well in a black boll
Or dispute any divinity?
If ye be cunning, I will put it in a pref: 700
Good sir, why do men eat mustard with beef?
My question can you assoil me?
Perse. Peace, man! Thou talkest lewdly,
And of thy living I rede amend thee.
Free. Avaunt, caitiff! Dost thou 'thou' me?   705
I am come of good kin, I tell thee;
My mother was a lady of the stews' blood born,
And, knight of the halter, my father wore an horn.

696. else] *Q1; not in Q3.*   700. put it in] *Q1;* make *Q3.*   701. beef] *Q1;* salt
befe *Q3.*   703. talkest] *Q1;* spekest *Q3.*   704. amend] *Q1;* to amende
Q3.   705. Dost] *Q1;* Doest *Q3.*   'thou'] *Q1;* mocke *Q3.*   706. of] *Q1;* of
a *Q3.*   708. an] *Q1;* a *Q3.*

695–96.] Free Will's uncertainty can be explained by the fact that Tudor
clerics, though distinguished from some laymen by more sober-looking garb,
had no uniform dress (Heath, p. 108).

695. Sees Perseverance] Until 715 Free Will addresses only one virtue
(696–97, 701, 704), evidently the active one, who should and does reply first
(703).

697. *dottypoll*] (1) blockhead, simpleton, feeble-minded fool (*M.E.D.*, 'doti-
pol'); (2) roundhead, tonsured fool (cf. *O.E.D.*, 'dod', v.¹)?

698. *black boll*] drinking bowl or cup (*O.E.D.*, 'black', a., 19, a 1568 example). Free Will implies that Perseverance, like Chaucer's Pardoner (327–28,
456–61), sermonises well only in an alehouse mood.

700–02.] adapted from *Y*. 116–22 (Youth).

700. *put it in a pref*] bring it to proof, test your claim (*O.E.D.*, 'proof', sb., 4).

701. *mustard with beef*] 'Mustarde is good with brawne, befe . . .' according to
a 1513 de Worde tract, 'The Boke of Keruynge', in *Manners and Meals*, p. 273
(cf. p. 152). Youth's allusion to Lenten fare is lost.

705–10.] suggested in part by *Y*. 484–90 (Pride, of Youth, to Charity); and cf.
Magnyfycence, where Crafty Conveyance says: 'Goddys fote! I warant you I am a
gentylman borne; | And thus to be facyd, I thynke it great skorne' (2216–17).

705. *'thou'*] address as 'thou', as if to a servant, social inferior or one held in
contempt (from 703).

708. *knight of the halter*] Cf. W. Wager's *Enough Is as Good as a Feast*, ed. R.
Mark Benbow (1967): 'Your place is at Saint Thomas-a-Wat'rings, | Or else at

Therefore I take it in full great scorn
That thou shouldest thus check me.   710

Contem. Abide, fellow! Thou canst little courtesy.
Thou shalt be charmed or thou hence pass,
For thou troubled Pity and laid on him felony.
Where is Imagination, thy fellow that was?

Free. I defy you both! Will you arrest me?   715

Perse. Nay, nay, thy great words may not help thee;
Fro us thou shalt not escape.

Free. Make room, sirs, that I may break his pate!
I will not be taken for them both.

Contem. Thou shalt abide whether thou be lief or loath.   720
Therefore, good son, listen unto me,
And mark these words that I do tell thee.
Thou hast followed thine own will many a day
And lived in sin without amendement;
Therefore in thy conceit assay   725

---

711. canst] *Q3;* cast *Q1;* hast *Hazlitt.*   712. pass] *Q1;* paste *Q3.*   717. Fro]
Q1; From *Q3.*   escape] *Q1;* scape *Q3.*   720.] *Followed in Manly by S.D.*
Seizes him.   722. do] *Q1;* shall *Q3.*   723. own] *Q3;* one *Q1.*   724. sin]
Q1; thy synne *Q3.*

Wapping beyond Saint Katherine's. | There will I dub you knights of the halter,
| Among your mates there strongly to tolter' (365–68).

    horn] (1) said to be worn by a cuckold on his brow (*M.E.D.*, 1c[*b*]); (2)
ornamental horn, signifying honour and power; less probably (3) a horn thimble
'used by cutpurses to catch the edge of the knife in cutting the purse-strings'
(*O.E.D.*, sb., 11).

    710. *check*] taunt, insult.

    711. *canst*] Q1 'cast', in the sense 'bestow' (*O.E.D.*, v., 36), is possible, but
'căst' must have been intended: cf. de Worde's *lytell geste of Robyn hode* (*S.T.C.*
13689), 'To suffre a knyght to knele so longe | Thou canst no curteysye' (sig.
B3r).

    712. *charmed*] (1) overcome, subdued (*O.E.D.*, v.¹, 4); (2) protected from evil
by more-than-natural powers?

    714. *that was*] former.

    716. *great*] arrogant.

    719. *for*] despite.

    720. *be lief or loath*] like it or not.

    725. *conceit*] mind.

To ask God mercy and keep his commandement;
Then on thee he will have pity
And bring thee to heaven, that joyful city.
Free. What, whoreson! Will ye have me now a fool?
Nay, yet had I liever be Captain of Calais.   730
For and I should do after your school,
To learn to patter to make me peevish—
Yet had I liever look with a face full thievish!
And therefore prate no lenger here
Lest my knave's fist hit you under the ear.   735
What, ye daws! Would ye rede me
For to leese my pleasure in youth and jollity
To bass and kiss my sweet trully mully,

---

726. commandement] *Q3;* rōmaundement *Q1.*   729. Will ye] *Q1;* wylte thou
Q3.   732. to make] *Q1, Q3;* wolde make *Manly conj.*   733. look] *Q1;* to
loke *Q3.*   734. lenger] *Q1;* longer *Q3.*   736. Would ye] *Q1;* wolde you
Q3.   737. leese] *Q3;* lesese *Q1.*

---

728. *to heaven, that joyful city*] *Y.* 17 (Charity).

729, 731.] adapted from *Y.* 128–29 (Youth).

730. *Captain of Calais*] lieutenant of the castle of Calais; after Henry VIII's coronation this post went to Sir Richard Carewe, Knight for the Body, and then to his son Nicholas (*L.P.* I.104, 414.59, 2484.29), and commanded about fifty soldiers, though *c.* 1500 about 800 guarded the whole town and a contemporary wrote: 'I do not believe that the castle of St. Peter at Rhodes is more strictly guarded against the Turks than Calais is against the French' (*Relation*, p. 45). The title was ancient and prestigious, and the post lucrative (see Robert B. Calton, *Annals and Legends of Calais* [1852], pp. 51–52; K. B. McFarlane, *The Nobility of Later Medieval England* [1973], p. 34). 'Calais' was pronounced like 'challice' (Dobson, § 334) and evidently rhymes with 732–33.

732. *patter*] mumble repeatedly the *pater*noster (or other prayer) in a rapid, automatic way (*O.E.D.*, v.[1], 1); as at *H.S.* 352. During mass literate Tudor women could be found 'taking the office of our Lady with them, and with some companion reciting it in the church verse by verse, in a low voice, after the manner of churchmen' (*Relation*, p. 23).

peevish] foolishly querulous, weak-minded.

734–37.] adapted from *Y.* 130–31, 171–72 and perhaps 47 (Youth).

735. *my knave's fist*] Imagination's (758–59)—an explicit indication of Free Will's superior position.

738. *bass*] buss, kiss.

trully mully] whore (where 'mully' is 'a term of endearment', *O.E.D.*, sb.).

As Jane, Cate, Besse and Sibley?
I would that hell were full of such prims;   740
Then would I run thither on my pins
As fast as I might go!
Perse. Why, sir, wilt thou not love virtue
And forsake thy sin for the love of God almighty?
Free. What! God almighty? By God's fast, at Salisbury— 745

---

739. Sibley] *This ed.;* sybble *Q1;* Sybbe *Q3;* Sybble, [to] *Manly.*   743. virtue]
Q1; of god almyghty *Q3.*   744. God almighty] *Q1;* vertue *Q3.*   745.
What!] *Manly;* What *Hawkins.*   fast, at] *This ed.;* fast at *Hawkins.*

739.] common names for prostitutes (as at 392). 'The Boke of Mayd Emlyn'
says 'these wanton dames | Ofte chaungeth theyr names, | As An, Jane, Besse
and Kate' (*Remains*, IV, ll. 161–63). Cf. also 'The Bowge of Courte', *Works*, I, ll.
369–70; Stevens, pp. 346, 376; *Eclogues*, p. 206, l. 707, and p. 209, l. 799; *Four
Elements*, sig. B7r.

Besse] possibly disyllabic. See Michael J. Preston, *A Complete Concordance to
the Songs of the Early Tudor Court* (1972), p. 374, for a rhyme of 'Besse' with 'me'.

740. *prims*] 'pretty wenches', perhaps a diminutive of 'primeroles' ('early
spring flowers, e.g., cowslip and field daisy', at times applied to girls [*O.E.D.*]).

741. *pins*] legs.

745–53.] Calculated nonsense about times and places, a feature of folk drama
(Chambers, *E.F.-P.*, pp. 48–50), was often spoken by dramatic fools or vices:
e.g., Ignorance's Robin Hood song in *Four Elements* (sig. E8r) and Covetous's
words in W. Wager's *Enough Is as Good as a Feast*, ed. R. Mark Benbow (1967),
ll. 305–10; and cf. Francis H. Mares, 'The Origin of the Figure Called "the
Vice" in Tudor Drama', *Huntington Library Quarterly*, 22 (1958), 18–19. Such
nonsense, however, wittily answers the question Perseverance has just posed
Free Will here. He says he has renounced sin (the Bordeaux wine-drinking) for
God's love (at Canterbury) by doing precisely what the parish church demanded
ordinarily of one during the Easter–Whitsuntide period, that is, by supporting
the church ale (see 748n) in drinking and celebration. A 1544 anti-papal tract
scathingly referred to 'church ales, in the whiche with leappynge, /daunsynge /,
and kyssyng, they maynteyne the profett of their churche (to the honoure of
God, as they both saye and thyncke)' (*A Supplycacion to our moste Soueraigne
Lorde Kynge Henry the Eyght*, ed. J. Meadows Cowper, E.E.T.S. E.S. 13 [1871],
p. 41). In this business the biggest spender was, according to a still later critic,
'counted the godliest man of all the rest' (*Phillip Stubbes's Anatomy of the Abuses
in England in Shakspere's Youth, A.D. 1583*, ed. F. J. Furnivall, Part I, New
Shakspere Soc., ser. VI, nos. 4, 6 [1877–79], p. 150).

745. *By God's fast,*] an oath (as at *Y.* 170n, and *H.S.* 949), but Farmer, with
other editors, reads 'the Lenten fast terminating on Easter-Sunday' (p. 250).

Salisbury] (Wilts.), cathedral city whose order of divine service, the Sarum
use, was adopted in southern England. Sugden says Salisbury Plain was a
well-known robbers' hunting-ground (p. 447).

And I trow Easter-day fell on Whitsunday that year—
There were five score, save an hundred, in my
    company,
And at *Petty Judas* we made rial cheer.
There had we good ale of Michaelmas brewing,
Cheer heaven-high, leaping and springing;   750
And thus did I

---

748. rial] *Q1;* royall *Q3.*   750. Cheer heaven-high,] *Q3;* Chere heuen hye *Q1;*
There heven hye *Hawkins.*

---

746. *Easter-day fell on Whitsunday*] Pentecost or Whitsunday, commemorating the Holy Ghost's descent on the apostles, was the seventh Sunday *after* Easter-day, the end of Lent.

747. *five score, save an hundred*] none. Cf. *Eclogues,* 'Of suche blinde fooles as can not count nor tell | A score saue twentie' (p. 130, ll. 611–12).

748. Petty Judas] 'Little Judas', proverbial name for a dissolute tap-house, and probably not an actual Salisbury tavern. In 1538–39 repairs were made at Boston to some pageant properties, 'de Noe chippe et le pety Judas' (*Records of Plays and Players in Lincolnshire 1300–1585,* ed. Stanley J. Kahrl, Malone Soc. Collections, VIII [1974], pp. xxii, 4), the latter perhaps the alehouse structure where Noah's wife and her gossips drank as the floods rose (cf. *The Chester Mystery Cycle,* ed. R. M. Lumiansky and David Mills, E.E.T.S. S.S. 3 [1974], Play III, 197–244). Cf. *H.S.* 439n.

rial cheer] a reference to the Easter and Whitsun ales. St Edmund's Church in Salisbury at this period bought ale for Maundy Thursday services, and in the three weeks about Whitsunday celebrated the King ale, when a church-operated tap-house sold ale for profit (749), and the clergy sponsored plays, mummers and (morris) dancing (750) inside the church itself as part of the King or Queen of May festival. See Henry J. F. Swayne, ed., *Churchwardens' Accounts of S. Edmund & S. Thomas, Sarum* (1896), pp. xvi–xvii; Sidney O. Addy, *Church and Manor* (1913), pp. 298–302; A. R. Wright, *British Calendar Customs,* ed. T. E. Lones, I (1936), 94–95, 151–57.

749.] Five or six months was the upper storage limit for beer in general (Cruickshank, p. 56), and Michaelmas ale (the feast is 29 September, but the legal term runs from 6 October to late November in general), made from the newly harvested grain, would have soured months before Whitsunday. Hops, which considerably extended the life of ale, were used in beer-brewing before the Reformation but were illegal in brewing ale, and so it was consumed young and made in small quantities (John Bickerdyke, *The Curiosities of Ale and Beer* [n.d.], pp. 67–69, 72, 145).

750. *Cheer heaven-high*] formulaic: cf. *Cocke Lorelles bote,* sig. C2v; and *Fulgens & Lucres,* II.402.

751–53.] Sugden notes (pp. 68–69) a striking parallel in Chaucer's *Pardoner's Tale* (562–71) where a Spanish white wine from Lepe (a small town on the Gulf of Cadiz), surreptitiously mixed with La Rochelle or Bordeaux wines, makes the

Leap out of Bordeaux unto Canterbury,
Almost ten mile between.

Contem.   Free Will, forsake all this world wilfully here,
   And change betime. Thou oughtest to stand in fear,   755
   For Fortune will turn her wheel so swift
   That clean fro thy wealth she will thee lift.

Free.   What, lift me! Ho, and Imagination were here now,
   Iwis, with his fist he would all to-clout you!
   Hence, whoreson! Tarry no lenger here,   760
   For, by Saint Pintle the apostle, I swear

---

755. to] *Q1; not in Q3*.   756. so] *Q3;* to *Q1*.   758. Ho,] *This ed.;* who *Q1, Q3;* who? *Hawkins*.   759. all to-clout] *Q1;* all to cloute *Q3;* all-to clout *Hazlitt*.   760. whoreson] *Q1, Q3;* horesone[s] *Manly*.   761. apostle] *Q1;* postle *Q3*.

---

drinker lose track of where he is. The playwright, probably unfamiliar with Lepe, may have misread 'of lepe' as 'off leap', and associated the passage with the Whitsun morris dances:

   Now kepe you fro the white and fro the rede
   Namely fro the whyte wyne of lepe
   That is to selle in brydge strete or in chepe
   This wyne of spayn crepyth subtylly
   In other wynes growynge fast by
   Of whyche ther ryseth suche fumosyte
   That whan a man hath dronke draught thre
   And wenyth that he be at home in chepe
   He is in spayne ryght at the towne of lepe
   Not at rochell ne at bordeux toun

   752. *Bordeaux*] (1) wine-exporting city in south-west France, an English possession for about three hundred years; (2) Bordeaux wine.

   753.] over 700 miles apart. For a like confusion, see Ill Report in Thomas Garter's *Susanna*, ed. B. I. Evans and W. W. Greg, M.S.R. (1937), ll. 461–70.

   756–57.] Cf. Tilley F617, 'FORTUNE'S wheel is ever turning.' Its lifting elsewhere always indicates a rise, not fall, in fortune (Howard R. Patch, *The Goddess Fortuna in Mediaeval Literature* [1927], pp. 147–77), but Contemplation may be ironically commenting on Free Will's 'leaping and springing' (750). *Y.* 71–72 (Charity to Youth) is probably also an influence here.

   758. *Ho*] as at 192, 299, 483, 928. Q is an obsolete form of *O.E.D.*, int.[1], 1, but the interrogative pronoun is possible.

   759. *all to-clout you*] cover you with blows (*O.E.D.*, 'all', C.14; 'to-', prefix[2], 2).

   761. *Saint Pintle the apostle*] Free Will compares his penis (*O.E.D.*, 'pintle', 1) to the 'twelve apostles', the great cannons that Henry VIII had made for his 1513 invasion of France. Six of these bronze guns, which were each cast in the

That I will drive you both home!
And yet I was never wont to fight alone.
Alas, that I had not one to bold me!
Then you should see me play the man shamefully.   765
Alas, it would do me good to fight!
[*To the audience*]—How say you, lords, shall I
    smite?—
Have among you, by this light!
Hence, whoresons, and home at once,
Or with my weapon I shall break your bones!   770
Avaunt, you knave! Walk, by my counsel!
Perse. Son, remember the great pains of hell.
    They are so horrible that no tongue can tell.
    Beware lest thou thither do go!
Free. Nay, by Saint Mary, I hope not so.   775
    I will not go to the devil while I have my liberty.
    He shall take the labour to fet me, and he will have
      me;
    For he that will go to hell by his will voluntary,

764. bold] *Q1;* bolden *Q3.*   765. you] *Q1;* ye *Q3.*   767. lords] *Q1;* syrs
Q3.   771. you knave] *Q1;* ye knaues *Q3.*   774. do] *Q1; not in
Q3.*   777. fet] *Q1;* fetch *Q3.*

---

likeness of an apostle and in all weighed over 32 tons, were very large siege
weapons that each took thirty horses to pull, fired a 20 lb ball with a charge of 20
lbs of gunpowder, and for Henry symbolised the war's overt purpose, to defend
the Church; the other six were lighter field pieces (Cruickshank, pp. 74–76). See
770n.

763–66.] Possibly Free Will here speaks to the spectators (as at 767).

763. *fight*] with a bawdy sense, like the mock-joust 'at farte pryke in cule' of A
and B in *Fulgens & Lucres* (I.1169). Intercourse is commonly described in terms
of warfare (Eric Partridge, *Shakespeare's Bawdy*, rev. ed. [1955], p. 42), and the
one for whom Free Will looks 'to bold' him to 'play the man shamefully' (i.e., to
obtain an erection; 764–65) is not Imagination.

764. *bold*] embolden, incite (for the bawdy overtones, see *O.E.D.*, a., 4).

768. *by this light*] *Y.* 273 (Riot).

770. *my weapon*] his penis (*O.E.D.*, sb., 3). Apparently like Imagination, who
returns without a dagger (928), Free Will is without a knife, and can only, up to
761, threaten the virtues with his absent fellow's fist (735, 759).

772–88.] amplified from *Y.* 79–82, 87–89 (Youth–Charity).

775. *hope*] think, expect.

The devil and the whirlwind go with him!
I will you never fro thence tidings bring.   780
Go you before and show me the way,
And as to follow you I will not say nay,
For by God's body, and you be in once,
By the mass I will shut the door at once,
And then ye be take in a pitfall!   785

Contem. Now Jesus soon defend us from that hole,
For *qui est in inferno nulla est redemptio*—
Holy Job spake these words full long ago.
Free. Nay, I have done, and you lade out Latin with scoops!

---

782. you] *Q1; not in Q3*.   783. you] *Q1*; ye *Q3*.   784. By the mass] *Q1; not in Q3*.   at once] *Hazlitt*; at ones *Q1*; by cockes bones *Q3*.   785. ye] *Q1*; shall ye *Q3*.   take] *Q1*; taken *Q3*.   786. soon] *Q1*; sone *Q3*.   788. spake] *Q1*; spoke *Q3*.   789. done, and you lade out Latin with scoops!] *Hawkins;* done & you lade out latyu w^t scopes *Q1, Q3 subst.;* done; and you laid out Latin with scope, *Hazlitt*.   you] *Q1*; ye *Q3*.

779.] Tilley D228 (cf. Ps. lviii.9).

784. *at once*] pronounced 'a-tones', a true rhyme with 783 (cf. 248–49).

785. *pitfall*] Free Will refers to a prison's lowest part, the pit, commonly compared to hell (Flint Tower in the Tower of London, for instance, was termed 'Little Hell'), and sometimes accessible both by a door at ground level, and by a ceiling trap-door (see 809) or grated hole, used for observation by those in the overhead jail chamber (Pugh, pp. 354–55, 360). Cf. *Y.* 72; and Rev. xx.1–3, where the devil is shut up in hell-pit by an angel with a key.

786. *hole*] (1) pit, as of hell (*M.E.D.*, 'hol(e', n. [2], 3a); (2) prison dungeon (then possibly a name applied to part of the Counter prison in Wood Street; *O.E.D.*, sb., 2b).

787.] ungrammatical quotation from the Office of the Dead: 'for [?him] who is in hell there is no redemption'. In the third nocturne from Matins, just after the seventh reading (from Job xvii), the full response reads: 'Peccantem me quotidie et non poenitentem timor mortis conturbat me. Quia in inferno nulla est redemptio [Because in hell there is no redemption] miserere mei Deus et salva me' (*Breviarium Ad Usum Insignis Ecclesiae Sarum*, Fasc. II, ed. F. Procter and C. Wordsworth [1879], cols. 277–78). This medieval commonplace, loosely attributed to Job (788; cf. Job vii.9), appears in *Piers the Plowman*, ed. Walter W. Skeat (1886), I, C.XXI.153, *The Parlement of the Thre Ages*, ed. M. Y. Offord, E.E.T.S. O.S. 246 (1959), ll. 642–43, and *Ludus Coventriae*, ed. K. S. Block (1922; rpt. 1960), 26.48, as well as later (Tilley R60).

789. *lade out Latin with scoops*] a nautical metaphor, scoops being used mainly to bail out water (*O.E.D.*, 'scoop', sb.¹, 1). Hazlitt suggests a quibble on 'latten', a yellow copper–tin alloy usually laid out in sheets (for such word-play

But therewith can you clout me a pair of boots?   790
By Our Lady, ye should have some work of me!
I would have them well underlaid and easily,
For I use alway to go on the one side.
And trow ye how? By God, in the stocks I sat tied,
I trow, a three weeks and more, a little stound,   795
And there I laboured sore day by day,
And so I trod my shoon inward, in good fay.
Lo, therefore, methink you must sole them round.
If you have any new boots, a pair I would buy;
But I think your price be too high.   800
Sir, once at Newgate I bought a pair of startups,
A mighty pair and a strong.

792. easily] *Q1;* easlye *Q3.*   794. tied] *This ed.;* tyde *Q1, Q3.*   795. a
three] *Q1;* thre *Q3.* weeks and more,] *This ed.;* weeks, and more *Haz-litt.*   797. trod] *Q3;* tred *Q1.* shoon] *Q1;* sho *Q3.*   798. methink you]
Q1; thynke ye *Q3.*   799. you] *Q1;* ye *Q3.* I would] *Q1;* wolde I
Q3.   801. Sir . . . startups] *Q1, Q3;* Sir . . . bought | A . . . startups *This ed.
conj.* startups] *Q3;* sterlups *Q1 alternate possible reading;* sterrup *Hawkins;*
stirrups *Hazlitt.*

---

later in *Thersites,* see Farmer, p. 260), and though the syntax here demands the
present tense of a different verb, 'lade', a pun probably exists on 'underlaid'
(792), and Hazlitt may be right. In *Mankind (Macro Plays)* New Guise objects to
Mercy's 'Englysch Laten' (124); and Dubius tells Lucidus, 'Thou pratelist
Latyn faste. | Mary, y trow þou be agaste' (Winchester MS, fol. 63v).

790. *clout*] cobble.

792. *underlaid*] with leather or metal plates (as of latten? *O.E.D.*, 'underlay',
v., 1c).

easily] comfortably, not tightly.

793.] Free Will wears down one side of his boots sooner than the other: what
backs his ankles rubs thin under his squirming as they take his body's weight in
the stocks' legholes (cf. *Y.* 304–05), and so the boots need repairs, not only on
the soles, but 'round' (798).

794. *tied*] a reading 'tide' ('a space of time') is possible, but cf. 809.

795. *stound*] time.

797. *trod*] Q1 may be a present tense or a (?northern) past tense (*O.E.D.*,
'tread', v., A.1, 2).

shoon] shoes.

799. *boots*] quibbling on the sense 'remedies' (*O.E.D.*, sb.[1], 7)?

801. *startups*] boots extending high on the leg (see *O.E.D.*, 'stirrup', sb., 2c,
for this correction); here leg-fetters that, though as capable of 'starting up' one's
legs as these boots, are too tight to go past the knee (804). An early form,
'startoppes', assonates with 'bought', though off-rhyme with 806–07 is not
impossible.

A whole year I wore them so long,

But they came not fully to my knee;

And to clout them it cost not me a penny.   805

Even now, and ye go thither, ye shall find a great
    heap;

And you speak in my name, ye shall have good
    cheap.

Perse. Sir, we came never there, ne never shall do.

Free. Marry, I was taken in a trap there and tied by the
    toe,

That I halted a great while and might not go.   810

I would ye both sat as fast there;

Then should ye dance as a bear,

And all by jangling of your chains.

Contem. Why, sir, were ye there?

Free. Yea, and that is seen by my brains;   815

For or I came there I was as wise as a woodcock,

And, I thank God, as witty as a haddock.

Yet I trust to recover as other does,

For and I had once as much wit as a goose,

---

805. not me] *Q1;* me not *Q3.*   808. came never there] *Q1;* neuer came thyther
Q3.   810. while] *Q1;* whyle after *Q3.*   813. all] *Q3;* all all *Q1.*   by
jangling] *Q3;* by gangelynge *Q1;* bejangling *This ed. conj.*

---

803. *so long*] probably 'as long as this [pointing at a place on the leg]', but
perhaps 'that long [a period of time]'.

807. *good cheap*] suggested by Youth's 'gold collars' (278), metaphorically also
chains.

812. *dance as a bear*] A medieval illustration of a dancing bear, bound to the
earth by a neck-collar and a chain of rings, appears in Joseph Strutt's *Sports and
Pastimes of the People of England* (1801), pl. XXII. Sandwich civic accounts for
1516–17 include a payment 'to hym that went wᵗ the dawnsing bere' (*Records of
Plays and Players in Kent 1450–1642*, ed. Giles E. Dawson, Malone Soc.
Collections VII [1965], p. 151). This custom still exists in some parts of Europe.

813. *by*] not unusual (*O.E.D.*, prep., A.35), but possibly an intensifying
prefix (*O.E.D.*, 'be-', 2).

816. *as wise as a woodcock*] a snipe-like bird easily caught in a trap or net for
food; proverbially a type of the gullible (Tilley W746).

817. *as witty as a haddock*] Tilley H3.

818. *other*] any other.

819. *as much wit as a goose*] Tilley G348.

I should be merchant of the bank;   820
Of gold then I should have many a franc
For if I might make three good voyages to Shooters
    Hill,
And have wind and weather at my will,
Then would I never travel the sea more.
But it is hard to keep the ship fro the shore,   825
And if it hap to rise a storm—
Then thrown in a race and so about born

---

820. merchant] *Q1;* a marchaunte *Q3.*   822. to] *Q1;* at *Q3.*   824. travel]
Q1; trauayle *Q3.*   826. hap] *Q1;* happen *Q3.*

820–45.] This extended metaphor of the rogue's ship sailing as a merchant-man 'to Shooters Hill' (822) may develop from *Cocke Lorelles bote*, where Cock's ship, sailing through England, is last seen being 'rowed vp the hyll' (sig. C2v; cf. *H.S.* 834) by a multitude including 'mathew marchaunte of shoters hyll' (sig. B2v) on board. The playwright's storm-and-shipwreck variations, involving word-play (820, 827, 832, 835, 839) and a clever use of London gibbets named for near-by streams (829, 838), may be original. Barclay describes the court as a stormy sea with rocks and sand banks (*Eclogues*, pp. 136–37, ll. 767–70), but this imagery has a long history (see Ernst Robert Curtius, *European Literature and the Latin Middle Ages*, trans. Willard R. Trask [1953; rpt. 1963], pp. 128–30), and Free Will's metaphor is also found much later. Cf. John Lyly's *Gallathea*, ed. Anne Begor Lancashire (1969), I.iv.88–92; and 'A new Ballad against Unthrifts', ed. Joseph Lilly, *A Collection of Seventy-Nine Black-Letter Ballads and Broadsides* (1867): 'some at Newgate doo take ship, | Sailing ful fast vp Holborne Hil; | And at Tiborn their anckers piche' (p. 156).

820. *merchant*] (1) businessman; (2) merchantman, trading vessel (*O.E.D.,* sb., 4).

bank] (1) money-changer's office, 'bank' (*M.E.D.,* n. [3]; *O.E.D.,* sb.³, 2, 7a); cf. Aristorius' lines in *The Play of the Sacrament* (*Non-Cycle Plays*), 'I prey þe rychely araye myn hall | As owyth for a marchant of þe banke' (259–60); (2) the Bank, or Bankside, the Thames Southwark embankment where the stews stood (cf. 184; *O.E.D.,* sb.¹, 11); cf. *Cocke Lorelles bote*, 'By syde London brydge in a holy grounde | Late called the stewes banke' (sig. B4r). Free Will must be thinking of Imagination's earlier proposal (405–18).

821. *many a franc*] French gold coin worth two shillings in 1494 (*O.E.D.*). Cf. *Cocke Lorelles bote*, 'there was | Some relygyous women in that place [the stews] | To whome men offred many a franke' (sig. B4r).

823. *have wind and weather*] formulaic (*O.E.D.,* 'wind', sb.¹, 5).

825. *fro the shore*] from going aground (cf. 834n).

827. *race*] (1) strong current (as at 362); (2) a chase on foot, a race on horseback.

On rocks or breaches for to run,
Else to strike aground at Tyburn,
That were a mischievous case;　　　　　　　　　830
For that rock of Tyburn is so perilous a place
Young gallants dare not venture into Kent.
But when their money is gone and spent
With their long-boats they row on the bay.
And any man-of-war lie by the way,　　　　　　　835
They must tack about and throw the helm alee;
And full hard it is to scape that great jeopardy,

---

828. breaches] *This ed.;* brachis *Q1;* braches *Q2;* broches *Q3;* bracks *Hazlitt.*
for] *Q1, Q2;* sor *Q3.*　　　829. Else] *Q1, Q2;* Or els *Q3.* aground] *Q1, Q2;* on
grounde *Q3.*　　　830. That] *Q1, Q3;* Ther *Q2.*　　　834. long-boats] *This ed.;*
longe botes *Q1, Q2, Q3;* long boots *Hazlitt.* bay] *Q1, Q2;* see *Q3.*　　　835.
And] *Q1, Q2;* And yf *Q3.*　　　836. tack about] *This ed.;* take a bote *Q1, Q2,
Q3.* alee] *This ed.;* a le *Q1;* ale *Q2;* hale *Q3.*

---

828. *breaches*] (1) breakers; surfy, turbulent waters breaking over shallow
rocks (*M.E.D.*, 'brech(e', n., 1b; *O.E.D.*, 'breach', sb., 8, from 1624); Farmer
defines the term as 'an opening in a coast, cliff, or anything similar' (p. 235); (2)
wounds, injuries (*M.E.D.*, 3)? (3) lawbreaking, breaches of the peace (*M.E.D.*,
4)? Q3 intends 'broaches', meaning 'sharp points, spears'. The *O.E.D.* follows
Hazlitt ('brack', sb.[2], from sb.[1], meaning 'breaking, breach').

830. *mischievous*] disastrous.

832. *gallants*] a term often used to describe Tudor ships (*O.E.D.*, a., 4b; cf.
Appendix I.D, p. 247).

Kent] as at Shooters Hill (388, 543). In 1522 the shire was ordered to maintain
watches on its roads to protect travellers from robbers (*T.R.P.*, I, no. 92, pp.
139–40).

834. *long-boats*] large boats, often with mast and sail (*O.E.D.*, the example
from 1769; cf. *M.E.D.*, 'long', adj. [1] 3[a], the example from 1421), used off
ships in landing parties in shallow waters. In *Cocke Lorelles bote* some of Cock's
fools launched the 'lōge bote' (sig. C1r).

835. *man-of-war*] (1) royal navy's armed ship; (2) soldier, law-man.

836. *tack about*] to change a boat's course as it moves upwind by turning the
'helm' to the lee side (see 301n) so as to bring the boat's head into the wind and
about (*O.E.D.*, 'tack', v.[1], 7; the Q forms are typical spellings, and the phrase is
first noted in 1595). To read 'take a-boat' ('board ship, embark'; *O.E.D.*, 'take',
v., 24c; cf. 'a', prep.[1], 2; 'boat', 1d) seems at odds with 834 (unless the gallants
return to their main vessel from smaller landing boats?); and 'tack a boat' is
unidiomatic. The gallants are using evasive tactics, whereas Q3 'hale' is a sailors'
hauling cry (*O.E.D.*, sb.[4], 1).

For at Saint Thomas of Watring and they strike a
    sail,
Then must they ride in the haven of hemp without
    fail.
And were not these two jeopardous places indeed,   840
There is many a merchant that thither would speed.
But yet we have a sure canel at Westminster;
A thousand ships of thieves therein may ride sure,
For if they may have anchor-hold and great spending,
They may live as merry as any king.   845
Perse. God wot, sir, there is a piteous living!

838.a] *Q1; not in Q2, Q3*.   839. hemp] *Q2, Q3;* hepe *Q1*.   840. places] *Q1,*
Q3; pleces *Q2*.   842. canel] *Q1, Q2;* porte *Q3*.   843. ships] *Q1, Q3;*
shappes *Q2*.   844. may] *Q1, Q3; not in Q2*. spending] *Q1, Q3;* spendynke
Q2.   845. merry] *Q1, Q2;* merely *Q3*. any] *Q1, Q3;* one *Q2*.   846. God
wot, sir, there] *Hazlitt;* Good woote syr there *Q1;* God wote there *Q2;* O syr that
Q3.

---

838. *Saint Thomas of Watring*] Surrey gibbet site on the Old Kent Road (which
starts at the end of Southwark's Borough High Street, and leads to Greenwich,
Canterbury and Dover) at the second milestone out of London where a stream
called Earl's Sluice crossed the road, near the boundary between Southwark and
Camberwell, approximately where Shorncliffe Road (near Albany Road) is now
(*Survey of London*, XXV [1955], ed. Ida Darlington, p. 121; Sugden, p. 512).
Cf. Tilley S63: 'SAINT THOMAS A WATERINGS'.
   strike a sail] lower topsail, as to stop the ship or to indicate surrender (*O.E.D.*,
'strike', v., 17).
   839. *ride*] (1) lie at anchor (of a ship); (2) hang (*O.E.D.*, v., 5). Cf. *Johan the*
Evangelist, 'I ryde in a saddyll / but ye shall ryde in a halter' (513).
   haven of hemp] 'gallows'. Hanging ropes and ships' tackle were both made
from hemp (see 243n).
   840. *these two jeopardous places indeed*] Tyburn (831) and St Thomas of
Watring (838) jeopardous indeed.
   842. *canel*] (1) channel, waterway; (2) street water-course, gutter (*O.E.D.*,
'cannel', sb.¹, 2; cf. Thieving Lane below)?
   Westminster] The Abbey precinct served as a sanctuary (cf. the present Broad
Sanctuary; 604n), and persons with rank and money could reside in the Abbey's
northern porch: see Arthur P. Stanley, *Historical Memorials of Westminster*
Abbey, 5th ed. (1882), pp. 346–53. Thieving Lane or Bow Street, destroyed for
Victoria Street, led to the Gate House (J. E. B. Gover *et al.*, *The Place-Names of*
Middlesex [1942], p. 184). The promoter John Baptist de Grimaldi took refuge
here in 1509 (see Appendix I.B).
   844–45.] adapted from *Y*. 237–38 (Riot).
   845.] Westminster Palace was the king's principal London residence.

Then ye dread not the great master above.
Son, forsake thy miss for his love,
And then mayst thou come to the bliss also.
Free. Why, what would you that I should do?   850
Contem. For to go toward heaven.
Free. Marry, and you will me thither bring,
    I would do after you.
Perse. I pray you remember my words now.
    Free Will, bethink thee that thou shalt die,   855
    And of the hour thou art uncertain.
    Yet by thy life thou mayst find a remedy;
    For and thou die in sin, all labour is in vain.
    Then shall thy soul be still in pain,
    Lost and damned for evermore.   860
    Help is past, though thou would fain;
    Then thou wilt curse the time that thou were bore.
Free. Sir, if ye will undertake that I saved shall be,
    I will do all the penance that you will set me.
Contem. If that thou for thy sins be sorry,   865
    Our lord will forgive thee them.
Free. Now of all my sins I ask God mercy.
    Here I forsake sin and trust to amend.

848. forsake] *Q1, Q3;* forseke *Q2.* miss] *Q1, Q2;* myslyuynge *Q3.*   851.]
Q1, Q2, Q3; Towarde heven for to go. *Manly conj.*   852. me thither bring]
Q1, Q2, Q3; me brynge therto *Manly conj.*   853. would] *Q1, Q2;* wyll
Q3.   857. a] *Q1, Q2; not in Q3.*   858. all] *Q1, Q2;* all thy *Q3.*   861.
would] *Q1, Q3;* wolde *Q2.*   862. that] *Q1, Q2; not in Q3.* bore] *Q1, Q3;*
borne *Q2.*   864. you] *Q1, Q2;* ye *Q3.* set] *Q1, Q2;* gyue *Q3.*   866. thee
them] *Q1, Q2, Q3;* them the *Manly.*   868. sin] *Q1, Q3;* synnes *Q2.*

    848–49.] adapted, like 968–70, from *Y.* 91–93 (Charity).
    853. *after you*] as you advise.
    855–56.] adapted from *Y.* 651 (Riot).
    857. *by thy life*] 'because you still live' (not an oath).
    858. *all labour is in vain*] adapted from *Y.* 598.
    859. *still*] continually.
    864.] The two virtues act as priests, who alone can officially impose penance, a
sacrament, on the remorseful confessed sinner.
    867–70.] adapted from *Y.* 733–34, 738, 610 and *passim.*

I beseech Jesu, that is most mighty,
To forgive all that I have offend. 870
Perse. Our lord now will show thee his mercy.
A new name thou need none have,
For all that will to heaven high
By his own free will he must forsake folly;
Then is he sure and save. 875
Contem. [*Giving Free Will a new coat*] Hold here a new
garment.
And hereafter live devoutly,
And for thy sins do ever repent;
Sorrow for thy sins is very remedy.
And Free Will, ever to Virtue apply. 880
Also to Sadness give ye attendance;
Let him never out of remembrance!
Free. I will never from you, sir Perseverance.
With you will I abide both day and night,
Of mind never to be variable, 885

---

869. most] *Q1, Q2;* so *Q3.* 870. forgive] *Q1, Q2;* forgyue me *Q3.* that I
have offend] *Q1;* that I haue offended *Q2;* wherin I dyd offende *Q3.* 871.
now will] *Q1;* wyll now *Q2, Q3.* 872. need none] *Q1;* nedest none to *Q2,
Q3.* 880. to] *Q1, Q2; not in Q3.* 881. Also] *Q1, Q3;* And *Q2.* ye] *Q1,
Q2;* you *Q3.* 882. out of] *Q1;* be out of your *Q2, Q3.* 883. never] *Q1,
Q2;* neuer goo *Q3.*

---

870. *that*] in which (elliptical; *O.E.D.*, relative pron., 8).
offend] an early past participial form.
872–74.] the playwright's self-conscious justification for departing from his
source (*Y.* 764–66), where Youth gets a new name. The easy transition from 'all
that will' to 'he' juxtaposes Free Will's individual and collective roles.
875. *save*] safe.
876.] adapted from *Y.* 767 (Charity). On Pentecost, catechumens wore white
robes for baptism (*O.E.D.*, 'Whit Sunday'). Southern suggests Contemplation
walks out to fetch the clothing from the entry (p. 179).
879. *Sorrow for thy sins*] Cf. *A.G.*, 835 (Appendix III.3).
very] a true, 'indeed'.
880–81.] a recollection of the *A.G.* allegory: Virtue assigned Reaso[n]
supervise Free Will, and Sadness to govern Sensuality (Appendix III.3);
poet concludes, 'But al wey beware be ye yong or olde | That your Fr[e]
Vertue more | Apply than to Vyce' (2075–77).
885–90.] loosely modelled on *Y.* 247–48 (Youth).

At the *Bell*, *Hart's Horn*, ne elsewhere,
Without they have leave of me.
But, sirs, wot ye why I am come hither?
By Our Lady, to gather good company together.
Saw ye not of my fellow, Free Will? 905
I am afeard lest he be searching on a hill.
By God, then one of us is beguiled!
What fellow is this that in this coat is filed?
Cock's death! Whom have we here?
What! Free Will, mine own fere? 910
Art thou out of thy mind?

Free. God grant the way to heaven that I may find,

901. ne] *Q1*, *Q2*; or *Q3*.   903. sirs] *Q1*, *Q2*; syr *Q3*.   904. to gather good]
Q2; togyder good *Q1*; to gather *Q3*.   905. Saw] *Q2*, *Q3*; Saue *Q1*.   912.
that] *Q1*, *Q2*; not in *Q3*.

---

901. *the* Bell] Of eighteen Bankside brothels shut down in 1506, the *Bell* was
among the dozen that later reopened: 'These allowed stewhouses had signes on
their frontes, towardes the Thames, not hanged out, but painted on the walles,
as a Boares heade, the Crosse keyes, the Gunne, the Castle, the Crane, the
Cardinals Hat, the Bel, the Swanne, &c.' (Stow, II, 55). The *Bell*, documented
as early as 1390 (E. J. Burford, *Bawds and Lodgings: A History of the London
Bankside Brothels c. 100–1675* [1976], p. 79), was later owned by the theatre-
owner Philip Henslowe and then by the actor Edward Alleyn (William Rendle
and Philip Norman, *The Inns of Old Southwark* [1888], p. 333). Other *Bell* inns
stood near the Southwark *Tabard* and in Shoreditch and Fleet Street.
  Hart's Horn] probably the Southwark property that belonged to Sir John
Fastolf's estate in 1470, 'le Harte Horne, *alias* le Bucke Head' (Rendle, p. 60),
and the 'Hartshorne' in Southwark mentioned in *The Paston Letters*, ed. James
Gairdner, III (1904), p. 430 (a Paston was one of Fastolf's executors). Several
holders of this stewhouse were fined late in 1505 (Burford, *Bawds and Lodgings*,
pp. 115–16; and for a suggested street-plan of the brothels on Bankside, one
followed by the above map, see pp. 142–43). Perhaps the last reference to this
brothel is in 1519, when authorities made sweeping arrests at the stews, including one called the *Hart* (*L.P.* III.365.5). Several tenements north of the Thames
shared this popular name.
  903–05.] adapted from *Y.* 215–17 (Riot).
  905. *Saw*] The Q1 form, though a recorded variant (*O.E.D.*, 'see', v., A.3c),
may be a quibble.
  906. *a hill*] like Shooters Hill (543); and see Intro., n. 151.
  908–10.] evidently suggested by *Y.* 218–19 (Riot) and by Free Will's repentance disguise in *A.G.* (Appendix III.3, l. 1141).
  908. *filed*] dirtied, 'defiled' (*O.E.D.*, v.², 1, 5).
  910. *fere*] comrade, buddy.
  912.] Cf. *Y.* 136 and *H.S.* 1019.

For I forsake thy company.

Imag. God's arms, my company! And why?

Free. For thou livest too sinfully.   915

Imag. Alas, tell me how it is with thee!

Free. Forsake thy sin for the love of me!

Imag. Cock's heart! Art thou waxed mad?

Free. When I think on my sin it makes me full sad.

Imag. God's wounds! Who gave thee that counsel?   920

Free. Perseverance and Contemplation, I thee tell.

Imag. A vengeance on them, I would they were in hell!

Free. Amend, Imagination, and mercy cry!

Imag. By God's sides, I had liever be hanged on high!

    Nay, that would I not do—I had liever die.   925

    By God's passion, and I had a long knife,

    I would bereave these two whoresons of their life.

    [*To the audience*] How, how, twenty pound for a
        dagger!

Contem. Peace, peace, good son, and speak softer,

    And amend or Death draw his draught,   930

    For on thee he will steal full soft.

    He giveth never no man warning,

    And ever to thee he is coming;

    Therefore, remember thee well!

915. too] *Q1, Q2;* so *Q3.*   916. it is] *Q1, Q2;* is it *Q3.*   918. waxed] *Q1, Q2; not in Q3.*   919. makes] *Q1;* maketh *Q2, Q3.*   full] *Q1, Q2; not in Q3.*   920. wounds] *Q1, Q3;* wounde *Q2.*   922. A vengeance on them] *Q1, Q2; not in Q3.*   in] *Q1, Q2;* bothe at the deuyll of *Q3.*   925. would] *Q1, Q2;* wyll *Q3.*   do] *Q1; not in Q2, Q3.*   926. and] *Q1, Q2;* an *Q3.*   a long] *Q2, Q3;* alonge *Q1.*   927. two] *Q1, Q2; not in Q3.*   928. How, how] *Q1, Q2;* Ho we *Q3.*   929. *Contem.*] *Q1, Q3; not in Q2.*   peace] *Q1, Q2; not in Q3.*   softer] *Q1, Q3;* sefter *Q2.*

913.] adapted from *Y.* 669, *passim.*

925. *Nay, that would I not do*] Imagination appears to realise the ambiguity of his previous oath, being hanged 'By God's sides'.

930. *or*] before.

draw his draught] 'make his move', strike, draw his weapon (*O.E.D.*, 'draught', sb., 11; 'draw', v., 73).

934. *remember thee*] 'Keep your wits about you'.

Imag. A, whoreson! If I were jailer of hell, 935
    Iwis, some sorrow should thou feel,
    For to the devil I would thee sell;
    Then should ye have many a sorry meal.
    I will never give you meat ne drink;
    Ye should fast, whoresons, till ye did stink, 940
    Even as a rotten dog—yea, by Saint Tyburn of Kent!
Perse. Imagination, think what God did for thee!
    On Good Friday he hanged on a tree,
    And all his precious blood spent.
    A spear did rive his heart asunder. 945
    The gates he brake up with a clap of thunder,
    And Adam and Eve there delivered he.
Imag. What, devil! What is that to me?
    By God's fast, I was ten year in Newgate,
    And many more fellows with me sat; 950
    Yet he never came there to help me ne my company.

---

938. meal] *Q3;* mele *Q1;* mely *Q2.*   939. will] *Q1, Q2;* wolde *Q3.* ne] *Q1,*
Q2; nor *Q3.*   941. Tyburn] *Q1;* Thomas *Q2, Q3.*   943. he] *Q1, Q2;* he
was *Q3.*   944.] *Manly;* And spent all his precyous blode *Q1; Q2 and Q3*
subst.   945. asunder] *Q1, Q2;* in sonder *Q3.*   948. What, devil! What]
Q1, Q2; What the deuyll *Q3.*   949. God's] *Q2, Q3;* goodes *Q1.*   950.
many more fellows] *Q1, Q2;* mo felowes I had that *Q3.*   951. Yet] *Q1, Q3;*
Ye *Q2.*

---

935. *jailer of hell*] Christ, traditionally, but he 'bought' (*Y.* 725) man from the
devil's prison, whereas Imagination intends to 'sell' (937) the virtues there.

938–39.] The imprisoned depended on alms for food and drink (Stow, I, 37,
246), and hell's diet here parodies the 'celestyall mele' (*Y.* 25–26n) that heaven
was conventionally thought to provide.

938. *meal*] Q2 intends 'mellay' ('fight').

941. *Saint Tyburn of Kent*] parodying St Thomas à Becket, an object of
pilgrimage, like Tyburn (264)?

942–47.] adapted from *Y.* 709 (*H.S.* 942), 165–68 (*H.S.* 942–45), 717–26
(*H.S.* 947), by Charity.

946. *gates*] of hell (Is. xlv.1–2; Matt. xvi.18).

947. *delivered*] released (as in jail-delivery; cf. 683–84, 967).

948–49.] in part adapted from *Y.* 170 (Youth).

948. *What, devil!*] expression of impatience (*O.E.D.*, 'devil', sb., 20a).

Contem. Yes, he holp thee, or thou haddest not been here
　　　　now.

Imag. By the mass, I cannot show you,
　　　　For he and I never drank together;
　　　　Yet I know many an alestake.   955
　　　　Neither at the stews, I wist him never come thither.
　　　　Goeth he arrayed in white or in black?
　　　　For and he out of prison had holp me,
　　　　I know well once I should him see.
　　　　What gown weareth he, I pray you?   960

Perse. Sir, he halp you out by his might.

Imag. I cannot tell you, by this light,
　　　　But methought that I lay there too long,
　　　　And the whoreson fetters were so strong
　　　　That had almost brought my neck out of joint.   965

Perse. Amend, son, and thou shalt know him

---

953. show] *Q1, Q2, Q3;* sewe *Manly.*   956.] *Q1, Q2;* Nor to the stewes ywys
he came not thyder *Q3.*   957. or in] *Q1, Q2;* or *Q3.*   958. holp] *Q1, Q2;*
holpen *Q3.*   959. see] *Q1, Q2;* haue se *Q3.*   960.] *Q1, Q2, Q3;* I praye
you, what gowne wereth he? *Manly;* What gown weareth he, I pray you? *This
ed. conj.*   961. halp you out] *Q1, Q2;* dyd help you *Q3.*   964. whoreson
fetters] *Q1;* fetters of the horesone *Q3.*   965. That] *Q1;* They *Q3.*   966.]
Q1, Q3; Amende, and thou shalt knowe hym, sone, *Manly.*

952.] God's grace operates in bringing Imagination on stage, allegorically, to
Contemplation and Perseverance. Cf. 958, 967: Christ also descended literally
into hell 'and preached unto the spirits in prison' (1 Peter iii.19), whom he freed
from Satan's power—an event prefigured by Ps. cxlvi.7: 'The Lord looseth the
prisoners.'

　holp] helped.

953–57.] adapted from *Y.* 707–08 (*H.S.* 954), 699–701 (*H.S.* 956–57) by
Youth.

954.] an ironic allusion to the Last Supper, celebrated in the communion, the
'mass' Imagination swears by (953)? Cf. *Tit.* IV.iii.83–85:

　Titus. But what says Jupiter I ask thee?

　Clown. Alas, sir, I know not Jubiter; I never drank with him in all my life.

955. *alestake*] alepole, post erected before a tavern with an identifying sign.

956. *come*] the infinitive (Abbott 349).

959. *see*] also at *H.S.* 362.

961. *halp*] helped.

965.] adapted from *Y.* 102–03.

　That had] Abbott 399; an ellipsis of the subject.

That delivered thee out of prison;
And if thou wilt forsake thy miss,
Surely thou shalt come to the bliss
And be inheritor of heaven.   970
Imag. What, sir, above the moon?
Nay, by the mass, then should I fall soon!
Yet I keep not to climb so high;
But to climb for a bird's nest,
There is none between east and west   975
That dare thereto venter better than I.
But to venter to heaven! What and my feet slip?
I know well then I should break my neck,
And, by God, then had I the worse side!
Yet had I liever be by the nose tied   980
In a wench's arse somewhere,
Rather than I would stand in that great fear.

970. inheritor] *Q1;* one of electe chyldren *Q3.*   974. But] *Q1;* But for
Q3.   976. venter better] *Q1;* better venter *Q3.*   979. And] *Q1;* An
Q3.   worse] *Q1;* worst *Q3.*   982. fear.] *This ed.;* fere, *Hawkins.*

---

971. *above the moon*] The moon's orbit marked, in the medieval world-view,
an end to the spheres' changeless, uncorrupt harmonies and the beginning of the
sublunary, fallen world subject to sin and death. See C. S. Lewis, *The Discarded
Image* (1964), pp. 92–121. Cf. *The Castle of Perseverance (Macro Plays)*, l. 2589,
where *Caritas* says, 'Mary, þi Sone abouyn þe mone'; *Impatient Poverty*, ed. J. S.
Farmer, T.F.T. (1907), sig. C3r; and *Tit.* IV.iii.65–66, where Marcus has just
by arrow shot one of Titus' letters to the gods: 'My lord, I aim a mile beyond the
moon. | Your letter is with Jupiter by this.'
972–73.] adapted from *Y.* 98, 101, 104 (Youth).
973. *keep*] care.
974. *bird's nest*] (1) traditional target for boys' (sexual?) curiosity; cf. Wanton's 'I can spye a sparowes nest' in *World* (sig. A3r), and *Ado* II.i.199–201; (2)
female genitals (*O.E.D.*, 'bird', 1d; and 'nest', sb., in *Slang and its Analogues*,
ed. J. S. Farmer and W. E. Henley [1890–1904; rpt. 1970]); cf. *Ado* II.i.207,
and the Nurse's remark to Juliet: 'I must another way, | To fetch a ladder, by
the which your love | Must climb a bird's nest soon when it is dark' (*Rom.*
II.v.72–74).
976. *venter*] venture, risk going.
977–79.] adapted from *Y.* 99, 102–03 (Youth).
979. *side*] 'deal', outcome.
980–81.] Cf. *Mankind (Macro Plays)*: 'Yt ys grawntyde of Pope Pockett, | Yf ȝe
wyll putt yowr nose in hys wyffys sokett, | ȝe xall haue forty days of pardon'
(144–46); *Fulgens & Lucres*, I.1269–71; *Shr.* II.i.219–20.

For to go up to heaven, nay, I pray you let be!
Free. Imagination, wilt thou do by the counsel of me?
Imag. Yea, sir, by my troth, whatsomever it be!   985
Free. Amend yet for my sake;
 It is better betime than too late.
 How say you, will you God's hests fulfil?
Imag. I will do, sir, even as you will.
 But I pray you, let me have a new coat.   990
 When I have need and in my purse a groat,
 Then will I dwell with you still.
Free. Beware, for when thou art buried in the ground,
 Few friends for thee will be found.
 Remember this still!   995
Imag. No thing dread I so sore as death;
 Therefore, to amend I think it be time.
 Sin have I used all the days of my breath,
 With pleasure, lechery and misusing,
 And spent amiss my five wits; therefore I am sorry. 1000
 Here of all my sins I ask God mercy.
Perse. Hold, here is a better clothing for thee!
 And look that thou forsake thy folly;
 Be steadfast; look that thou fall never!

---

983. heaven,] *This ed.;* heven: *Hawkins.* 985. whatsomever] *Q1;* what that
euer *Q3.* 988. hests] *Q1;* commaundementes *Q3.* 989. sir] *Q1;* syrs
Q3. 990. coat.] *This ed.;* cote, *Hawkins.* 1000. I am] *Q1;* am I
Q3. 1001. all] *Q1; not in Q3.* 1003. thy] *Q1; not in Q3.*

---

 985. *whatsomever*] whatever.
 987.] Tilley L85; cf. *A.G.* 1204.
 988. *hests*] behests, commandments.
 989.] an explicit statement of Imagination's allegorical subordination to Free
Will.
 991.] 'When I am needy, and have [only] a groat in my purse.'
 993–94.] The contemporary works that share this theme are discussed by A.
C. Cawley in his *Everyman* (pp. xiii–xix).
 998. *days of my breath*] formulaic: see *M.E.D.*, 'breth', n. [1], 2a, the example
c. 1475.
 999. *misusing*] (1) adultery, fornication (*O.E.D.*, 'misuse', v., 2b); (2) mis-
conduct, wrongdoing.
 1000. *five wits*] the five senses.
 therefore] for that.

Imag. Now here I forsake my sin forever. 1005
Free. Sir, wait thou now on Perseverance,
    For thy name shall be called Good Remembrance.
    And I will dwell with Contemplation,
    And follow him wherever he be come.
Contem. Well, are ye so both agreed? 1010
Imag. Yea, sir, so God me speed!
Perse. Sir, ye shall wait on me soon,
    And be God's servant day and night.
    And in every place where ye be come,
    Give good counsel to every wight! 1015
    And men ask your name, tell you 'Remembrance',
    That God's law keepeth truly every day.
    And look that ye forget not repentance!
    Then to heaven ye shall go the next way,
    Where ye shall see in the heavenly quere 1020
    The blessed company of saints so holy,
    That lived devoutly while they were here.
    [*To the audience as well*] Unto the which bliss I
        beseech God almighty
    To bring there your souls that here be present,

1006. thou] *Q1;* you *Q3.*   1009. wherever] *Q1;* where *Q3.*   be come] *This ed.;* become *Q1, Q3.*   1012. on] *Q1;* vpon *Q3.*   1014. be come] *This ed.;* become *Q1, Q3.*   1015. to every wight] *Q1;* both day and nyght *Q3.*   1016. you] *Q1;* them *Q3.*

1007. *Good Remembrance*] 'sound memory', a formula used in wills then by those preparing for death; e.g., 'holl of mynde and good remembraunce' (1522; *Wills and Inventories from the Registers of the Commissary of Bury St. Edmund's*, ed. Samuel Tymms, Camden Soc., 49 [1850], p. 115; cf. pp. 131, 133, etc.). The name is from *A.G.*, l. 998 (Appendix III.3); and the device of a name-change is from *Y.* 764–66 (Humility, to Youth).

1015.] adapted from *Y.* 773–74 (Humility), 778–79 (Youth).

wight] person.

1019. *next*] shortest, most direct.

1020–21.] adapted from *Y.* 94–96 (Charity).

1020. *quere*] choir.

1023–24.] adapted from *Y.* 783–87 (Youth, Humility).

And unto Virtuous Living that ye may apply,   1025
Truly for to keep his commandement.
Of all our mirths here we make an end.
Unto the bliss of heaven Jesu your souls bring!
   Amen.

1025. ye] *Q1;* we *Q3.*   1026. for] *Q1; not in Q3.*   1027. our] *Q1; not in Q3.*   an end] *Q1;* endyng *Q3;* an ending *Manly.*   1028.] *This ed.;* Vnto . . . brynge † AMEN. *Q1;* Vnto . . . brynge. † God saue the Kynge. *Q3.*   your] *Q1;* our *Q3.*

   1025.] syntactically parallel to 1023–24: 'And [I beseech God almighty] that you may apply yourselves to virtuous living.' For the *A.G.* influence, see 602–20n, 880–81n.

   1027–28.] adapted from *Y.* 783–86 (Youth, Humility).

   1027. *mirths*] entertainments, merry-making.

APPENDIX I

Hick Scorner: Historical Background

Five sons of John (de la Pole), second duke of Suffolk (died 1492), and Elizabeth (of York), sister of Edward IV and Richard III, were alive when Henry VIII came to the throne in 1509: Edmund, earl of Suffolk (the eldest, executed in 1513); Humphrey, a prebendary in St Paul's Cathedral until 1509, and then rector of Hingham, Norfolk (died 1513); William, knight (died 1539); possibly Geoffrey, a pensioner at Gonville Hall, Cambridge, before 1499; and Richard, the youngest.[1] In August 1501, because of an allegedly planned but thwarted rebellion, Edmund and Richard fled England to the emperor Maximilian in the Tyrol. As a result, Edmund and six others, probably including Richard, were twice publicly excommunicated at Paul's Cross, on 7 November and again on 5 March 1503 solemnly 'w^t book, bell, and Candell'.[2] Henry VII jailed their brother William in the Tower in 1502 (where he remained until his death), outlawed Edmund and Richard at the County Court of Suffolk in Ipswich on 26 December that year,[3] and attainted all three by act of Parliament, January 1503/04. By then, titling himself duke of Suffolk (he legally surrendered the dukedom in 1493) and 'White Rose', Edmund was a very serious Yorkist claimant to the throne. His mother Elizabeth descended from Edmund, duke of York (died 1402), son of Edward III, and Richard III had declared in favour of Edmund's elder brother John, earl of Lincoln (died 1487). In contrast, Henry VII's *de jure* title was questionable.[4] When Edmund left Richard at Aix in 1504 to enlist help from the duke of Saxony in Friesland, Edmund was arrested by the duke of Gueldres and then the archduke Philip, who handed the pretender over to Henry VII to be jailed in the Tower in March 1505/06. Alone then, Richard travelled across the continent to muster support for the de la Pole claim, from Buda in Hungary in 1506–07 to Freiburg in 1510, and then by 1512 into France. Having been (with his jailed brothers) exempted from Henry VIII's 1509 general pardon, Richard assumed Edmund's titles and, with Louis XII's encouragement, claimed the English crown as Richard IV. The French king employed him in the 1512–14 war and in an abortive plan to invade England, but the Anglo-French treaty forestalled this, and Richard retired to Metz in Lorraine from September 1514 to 1519, where Wolsey plotted his abduction or assassination in 1515. Francis I in 1523 supported another of Richard's futile invasion attempts, and his death came gallantly by the French king's side at Pavia 24 February 1524/25. From Edmund's execution in 1513 until then Henry VIII had had no more troublesome rival than Richard, who was termed at his end one 'of the three greatest enemies he [Henry] had in the world'.[5]

Richard de la Pole played three parts in the French response to Henry VIII's attacks in the 1512–14 war. Two were on the battlefield. In Louis XII's service the 'rebel' Richard led a company of German lansquenets in the unsuccessful French invasion of Navarre in October–November 1512, which was seized by Ferdinand of Aragon that summer after Henry VIII's expeditionary force under the marquis of Dorset landed at San Sebastian to join the Spanish in attacking Gascony.[6] Secondly, on 27 July 1513, called 'dry Wednesday' because the armies stood in full battle gear in the hot sun without water for nine hours, the middle-ward of Henry's expeditionary army, commanded by the king in person, met and skirmished with the French army near Tournehem outside the Calais pale.[7] Halle writes that among the leaders of the French army was 'Richard *de la Pole* traytour of England sonne to ye duke Jhon of Suffolke'.[8] Though this engagement was only a minor cavalry exercise, according to a French account Henry 'eut paour d'estre trahy' and surrounded himself with his tough German mercenaries.[9] The presence of a formidable Yorkist pretender commanding enemy forces probably explains Henry's tactics here.

In both 1513 and 1514, finally, Richard stood ready to invade England with a French fleet. On 5 July 1513 Peter Martyr, writing from the Spanish court, indicated that Henry's execution of Edmund de la Pole on Tower Hill on 4 May occurred because he 'held correspondence with Richard De la Pole his brother, an exile in France, and commander of the French fleet, for a rising in England'.[10] This report is unsubstantiated elsewhere, but Louis XII on 8 May did instruct an ambassador to see whether James IV favoured having Richard sent to Scotland with a Franco-Scottish navy of over three hundred ships.[11] No such invasion took place, apparently because Louis had to cope with Henry's own invasion of France that summer, and James himself objected, being married to Henry's sister Margaret.[12] James's death at Flodden Field in September, however, revived the scheme for 1514, as Halle wrote:

> The French king this yere appoincted to Richard de la Pole traitor of England and banished the realme .xii. M. lanceknightes to kepe Normandy, and also to entre into England and to conquere thesame, where they made suche a Riot that many of them were slayn & he was faine to cary them to sainct Malos in

Britaigne [Saint-Malo, Brittany] to take shippe: for the Frenchmen would fayne haue bene rydde of them, they cared not how, their condicions were so vyle and shameful, but by the reason that the French kyng suyd for peace, this iourney toke no effect.[13]

Intelligence of a (spring) expedition to *Scotland* by the French was dispatched to England that year as early as 14 January, when the earl of Surrey reported to Henry's Council that Louis XII would put a fleet and 15,000 men (*L.P.* I.2574; cf. 2578.3) in the command of John Stewart, duke of Albany, whom Scotland by 26 November 1513 had agreed to accept as its regent (*L.P.* I.2461). Richard de la Pole, interestingly, cannot be identified as a participant until May. Five reports for January to March give Albany as the leader, and just one of them notes an English objective for the expedition, the besieging of Berwick, the English border stronghold.[14] Even by 30 April, when Wolsey learned that 20,000 lansquenets (mercenaries such as Richard commanded in 1512) would be sent by the French, no reference to the pretender is made (*L.P.* I.2854), though he was probably involved in some capacity by January.[15] His name at last appears on 22 May (when Louis writes to the captain of Boulogne that he will send there to Richard one Thomas Stanley), a date just three days before Thomas Bohier crossed to England as French ambassador to arrange, not only an Anglo-French peace, but also Louis' marriage to Henry's sister Mary.[16] Then Richard is linked explicitly with Albany, evidently as his (subordinate?) associate in command. On 5 June Sir Thomas Lovell wrote to Richard Fox and Wolsey that 'Ther Rennyth A comyn Brute still here that the duc of Albony maketh preparacōns for goyng in to Scotland and Richard De lapole wᵗ hym', and a Paris report of 15 June says that both, 'with their lanzknechts, have not yet left Normandy for Scotland'.[17] The design of the enterprise may have resembled the obscure invasion of 1523, when Richard, with thirty ships, allegedly split off from Albany's fleet (which kept on to Scotland) to attempt a landing in England, the outcome of which is not known. While Lovell's words suggest Richard's activities were not news on 5 June, they appear to have been an afterthought in Albany's long-planned Scottish adventure. Knowing Henry's fear of the pretender, the French may well have decided to give Bohier, the General of Normandy (from where Richard's force was to set out), a strong hand in the peace negotiations by at the last moment developing Richard's plans. That he posed any serious threat to Henry then is hard to believe, but the English closely watched reports of alien ships in the Irish Sea in June (*L.P.* I.2977), and the treaty was settled quickly. It was thought 'certain' in London by 21 June and signed formally on 7 August.[18] The threat of Richard's invasion, consequently, may only have existed for a month or two. Albany's voyage, which Louis' future sister-in-law Margaret opposed in June (*L.P.* I.3009), was indefinitely postponed. Halle's story of the riot of Richard's lansquenets and of their removal to Saint-Malo is unsubstantiated,[19] but German mercenaries were notoriously ill-disciplined out of battle, and some incident probably occurred. The riot, however, can evidently have been no earlier than mid-June, when Richard was still in Normandy according to the Paris report. Louis resisted English demands for the pretender's arrest and extradition, and his plot ended when he was honourably discharged from French service, rewarded and sent in exile to Metz.[20]

B. JOHN BAPTIST DE GRIMALDI

This naturalised (Genoese) merchant, who by 1495 was already taking part in a crown prosecution (of the London alderman Sir William Capell), soon enriched himself by allegedly unscrupulous business dealings, 'subtyll wordis' and 'ffals promyse', according to the 'legend of Baptyst', a vitriolic verse attack on Grimaldi.[21] He shortly wasted these earnings and faced actions of debt that forced him, thief-like, into hiding in London: there, 'lurkyng, In his denne so vyle', Grimaldi 'Imagynyd' or plotted a legal trick to shake them off. By confessing to theft of a reddish-brown horse, and buying a pardon after the court convicted and sentenced him as a 'ffeloun' to hang, he was apparently able to suppress the other civil suits.[22] In later years, according to the poem, the merchant was accused of many crimes and vices. Rape, incest, open adultery and common bawdry were dominant charges—'this Is he, on whom women may cry | To Tybourn to tybourn, thow worst of all men | For many a vyrgyn, hast thow Ravysshid'—but so were usury, forgery, perjury and even a fraudulent scheme or 'Imagynyng' to collect insurance on non-existent cargo in ships he intended to sink at sea. Once the subject of gossip, this last plot turned Grimaldi, like Imagination, into a night-walker ('as the Bak, worchyth by dyrk evenyng | Soo dyddyst thow walk'), but the merchant was found and jailed in the Counter; and a trial before the London mayor and council earned him a sentence of three days on the pillory, and then banishment. Chancery documents survive for a train of lawsuits that seem to have originated in an action of fraud against Grimaldi about this time.[23] The Exchequer, however, deferred and finally annulled the city's sentences, and probably protected him from other legal actions too. His employment by the crown must have led to this immunity. By 22 June 1507, as a broker, Grimaldi obtained protection to travel to Calais with its lieutenant, Sir Gilbert Talbot,[24] though even this post did not save the merchant from troubles. Having been suspected of treason, Grimaldi had neglected to satisfy Henry VII regarding a 'ransom' for not appearing before his officers to face this accusation, and had consequently been declared an outlaw. After surrendering to the Marshalsea (and presumably paying the usual 16s 4d fine), however, Grimaldi received a pardon on 10 October 1507.[25] With this matter (though perhaps not the 'ransom')[26] behind him, and under Henry VII's chief lawyer-administrators, Edmund Dudley and Richard Empson, Grimaldi became known as the crown's prime 'promoter', one on whose spying, information and accusations the king based the highly lucrative fines he levied on delinquent subjects. Many such prosecutions were unjust, the supporting evidence being flimsy and unverified. Dudley confessed while in prison in 1509–10 to supervising eighty-four cases involving unfair exactions, and because the king himself countenanced obvious extortion the promoters, Grimaldi among them, were not very particular about the truth, source or confidentiality of allegations.[27] The verse satire says that he would regularly 'ffele & tempt men, to knowe theyr counsayll | And afftyr dyscovyr It, to theyr grete dysavayll'. Few details of his promoting activities are known, but he appears to have been involved in a criminal conspiracy on 28 October 1508, and to judge from the apparent reference to him in Skelton's *Magnyfycence*, where Folly describes his pudding-snatching dog as *'Grimbaldus* grēdy' (l. 1156),[28] Grimaldi certainly benefited personally from the job. By 10 February 1509, when he was called the king's servant, Grimaldi's son was granted a customs office for life.[29] Then, after Henry's death on 22 April, disaster struck. The new administration was intent on appeasing the extortion victims, if not on admitting the late king's ultimate responsibility for their plight, and the crown arrested Dudley, Empson and their promoters, except for Grimaldi (then described as 'hym that Is at this daye worst of all men and hath soo contynuyd syne his Infancy'), who fled to Westminster for sanctuary.[30] Henry VIII's general pardon of 30 April, which promised citizens protection from 'forfeiture by reason of any light and untrue informations or wrong surmises of customers, comptrollers, or searchers, or of any persons calling themself promoters', excepted Grimaldi by name; and his son was on 5 June deprived of his office.[31] The verses, which must have been written about this time, end with an allusion to Grimaldi's repentance. Obviously still useful to the crown, he was pardoned 2 February 1510 (*L.P.* I.381 [6]), while Dudley and Empson were executed on 17 August. Grimaldi's political rehabilitation must have been complete by 10 March 1517, when he was again serving as a broker in the retinue of a Deputy of Calais, this time Sir Richard Wingfield (*L.P.* II.3002).

C. IRELAND INVASION DOCUMENTS

1. John Kite, who obtained the archbishopric of Armagh on 24 October 1513 and sailed to Ireland in the spring of 1514, wrote to Wolsey from

Termonfeghin, near Drogheda, on 14 May 1514, to insist on a mooted expedition there by Henry VIII, 'as much bound to reform this land as to maintain order in England, more bound to subdue them than Jews or Saracens'.[32] Kite had told the Irish that Henry would come 'shortly', and wrote again on 7 June (*L.P.* I.2977), but to no avail. The king merely ordered certain reformations to be enacted by an Irish parliament in 1515, about which time Kite went back to London, and after a short return visit to Armagh in 1516 left his see permanently.[33]

2. About 1515 the anonymous tract, 'State of Ireland, and Plan for its Reformation', proposed a 100,000-man immigrant army to occupy Ireland before the king came in force, and quoted extensively from *Salus Populi*, a non-extant fifteenth-century Latin work by an unknown writer, Pandarus.[34] Three extracts follow.

(i) the Pander shewyth . . . that the holly wooman, Brigitta, used to inquyre of her good Anglle . . . 'Of what Crystyn lande was most sowlles damned?' The Angell shewyd her a lande in the weste parte of the worlde . . . for ther the crystyn folke dyeth moste oute of charytie. She inquyrid the cause whye? The Angell sayde, for ther is moste contynuall warre, rote of hate and envye, and of vyceis contrarye to charytie; and withoute charytie the sowlles cannot be saveid. And the Angell dyd shew tyll her the lappes of the sowlles of crystyn folke of that lande, howe they fell downe into Hell, as thyk as any haylle shewrys . . . ther is no lande in this worlde of so long contynuall warre within hymselff, ne of so great shedeing of chrystyn blodde, ne of so great rubbeing, spoyleing, praying, and burneing, ne of so great wrongfull extortion contynually, as Ireland. Wherfor it cannot be denyed . . . that the Angell dyd understande the lande of Ireland. (p. 11)

(ii) that the Kyng ordeyn that ther come dyverse smythes and craftymen oute of Ingland, that canne make and forge gonnes and saletes, bylles and glayves, gonnpowdre and brestes, that shalle dwelle alwaye in every of the sayde cytyes and porttownes. Then, after the Kinges subgettes be put ones in ordre, as aforesayde, Englyshe men, of England, wylbe as desyrous to come and dwelle in to this lande, as ever they were at the fyrste conquest . . . For hyt is necessary that all that partyes be inhabyt with Englyshe men . . . (pp. 23–24).

(iii) yf it please the Kinges Grace to sende one man oute of every paryshe of England, Cornwale, and Wales, into this lande, to inhabyte not only the sayde landes of the countye of Wolster, but also all the Iryshe landes, that lyeth betwyxte the cyttye of Dublyn and the townes of Rosse and Wexford . . . hyt shulde increse to the King, and his heyres for ever, yerely, to more then 30000 markes. (p. 25)

3. Another tract, 'The decay of Ireland' by Patrick Finglas, 'baron',[35] recommends the reformation of Leinster, land-grants to English lords and gentlemen, and the provision of a standing army, but rejects massive re-population from England: 'Touching inhabitants, as it might be dangerous to depeople the realm of England, the lands might be inhabited by some sorts of the Irishry, as at the first Conquest' (p. 6).

D. THE THIRTEEN SHIPS

Records of the Tudor royal or merchant marine 1485–1520 do not prove that any ship Hick Scorner claims to have foundered in the Irish Sea (332–37) did so, but only one (the *Star of Saltash*) is not known to have existed in this period, several (the *Anne* and the *Regent*) actually sank, and three (the *Hermitage*, the *Barbara of Dartmouth* and the *Mary Bellouse of Bristow*) apparently disappeared not long before *Hick Scorner* was written. Proof of actual wreckage is made difficult, not only by the absence or loss of almost all records dealing with privately owned merchant ships, but by problems of vessel identification. Different ships bear the same name simultaneously and must be distinguished by owner or tonnage (as with the *James*); some have multiple names (the *Anne* had four); successive vessels in the same home port have the same saint's name (as with the *Nicholas*); five of the thirteen ships are listed without home port; and the *Anne* sank twice. Even so, we can be fairly sure that the fully identified ships on Hick Scorner's list did sink, somewhere, before 1515, because the only two shipwrecks there that the extant (almost entirely crown) archives should record, those of the two royal ships (the *Anne* and the *Regent*), are in fact recorded. Some of the remaining eleven may, of course, be among the often unidentified vessels that are known to have foundered in four other English naval disasters of the same 1512–13 war that saw those two king's ships go to the bottom. (1) The *Nicholas of Hampton* sank before Brest in April 1513 (see below, p. 247). (2) On 22 April 1513 some French galleys and foists under Prégent de Bidoux ran through the English blockade, and sank at least a ship belonging to William Compton (the *Michael Compton?*), though the French claimed to have destroyed four great ships (including one of 300 tons) and two store vessels.[36] (3) A transport that helped Henry VIII's army cross the Channel to Calais in June 1513 was wrecked in bad weather off the French town of Wissant, and plundered by its citizens, in retaliation for which the English burned the town on 4 July; and (4) that evening a storm sank five English ships in Calais harbour and drowned their crews after, eye-witnesses reported, 'long struggling with the waves'.[37]

The *Regent*

This, Henry VII's prize warship (built 1487–90), served with the *Anne of Foy* against Brittany in 1490 and with her and the *Hermitage* against Scotland in 1497,[38] and was afterwards leased out to merchant adventurers until in 1512 Henry VIII declared war on France. Sir Edward Howard's commission of 8 April 1512 as commander of an eighteen-ship fleet (again including the *Anne*) lists the *Regent* at 1,000 tons with 700 soldiers, mariners and gunners (*L.P.* I.1132). In early August, after some months of Channel plundering, it anchored at Portsmouth with the fleet for Henry's personal inspection, and on 9 August left with the navy (that, besides the *Anne*, included the *James of London*) on its last voyage, captained jointly by Sir John Carew and Sir Thomas Knyvett, who had previously served on the *Anne*.[39] About 11 a.m. the next day, 10 August, St Laurence's day, the fleet met the French navy in Bertheaume Bay outside Brest, where the English (according to their account), after damaging and putting to flight the Vice-Admiral's ship, the *Grand Louise*, turned on two other great ships: the *Nef de Dieppe*, which Howard's *Mary Rose* attacked, and the *Cordelière*, a carrack of about 700 tons captained by Hervé de Porzmoguer that held nearly a thousand persons, among them several hundred knights and gentlemen, many evidently visiting for the day with their wives.[40] This unlucky ship, at first chased and cannonaded by Anthony Ughtred's *Mary James*, and pursued stem-to-stem by the *Sovereign* until by mistake the *Cordelière* was left behind, was then suddenly grappled by the *Regent*, which had left off attacking the *Nef de Dieppe*. The *Regent*'s onslaught of arrows and gunfire, and her 400 boarding soldiers, had almost destroyed the French force when, perhaps by deliberate sabotage of an enemy gunner (*L.P.* I.1403), perhaps by the *Mary James*'s attempt to stave in the *Cordelière*'s stern, its gunpowder store took fire, and consumed and sank both fouled ships before they could be separated.[41] Figures vary, but about 900 French died in the wreck, and only about 200 English survived, excluding Carew and Knyvett.

The *Michael of Brikilsea*

In September 1494 a ship of this name left Exeter–Dartmouth customs (P.R.O., E 122.41/18, fol. 20v).

The *George* with the *Gabriel*

Ships with these saint's names are very common, but we may be intended to identify the *Gabriel* (though less probably the *George*) with Fowey, the home port of the last ship named in l. 333, the *Anne*. Among six Fowey vessels sent to Henry VII's 1489–90 Brittany expeditions are the *George*, the *Gabriel* and the *Anne*.[42] A ship (or ships) called the *Gabriel of Fowey* passed through customs in 1509 and 1517 under the same master, Thomas Walsh (E 122.42/1, fols. 55v, 60v; E 122.116/4, fol. 8v). John Power's *George* or *Little George of Fowey* was, through the good offices of Sir William Trevelyan, who said 'there are few better ships in England of her burden', employed in Henry VIII's fleet to carry 31 men from 15 April to 12 August 1514.[43]

The *Anne of Foy*

This ship's history goes back at least to the reign of Edward IV.[44] After 23 June 1488, the *Anne* sailed from Cornwall across the Irish Sea to

Kinsale under the command of Sir Richard Edgcumbe, comptroller of
Henry VII's household, and with four other ships and 500 men, in
order to pursue English privateers and obtain pledges of loyalty from
the Irish lords.[45] Before reaching Fowey again on 8 August, the *Anne*
(as in Hick Scorner's account) was nearly wrecked several times in the
Irish Sea by foul weather, including a great three-day storm that made
Edgcumbe vow a pilgrimage if ever he got back to England alive. Henry
VII afterwards impressed the privately owned *Anne* into his 1490 and
1497 campaigns, but by 1511 his son had bought her and was leasing
her out to merchants for two voyages, one towards Prussia and back,
the other to Bordeaux and back (*L.P.* I.3608.vi, p. 1503). The first trip
occurred in April–September 1511 (*L.P.* I.3608.ii, pp. 1496–97); the
second, however, was delayed almost three years because of the
Anglo–French war. At this period two other names were given to the
ship because of its new owner and home port: in records from September 1511 to August 1512 she is the *Anne of London*, and from April
1512 to February 1513 the *Anne of Greenwich*.[46] Listed in Sir Edward
Howard's 1512 commission at 160 tons under captain Thomas Lucy
and Sir Thomas Knyvett (who was to die on the *Regent*), the *Anne* was
evidently present at that ship's sinking on 10 August (*L.P.* I.1132,
1453.ii, 3608.iv–v, pp. 1501–02). Then, between 28 October 1512 and
11 February 1513, the *Anne*, having been sailed under master Richard
Fuller to Ratcliff, several miles down-river from London, and placed
inside a special dock, was drastically remodelled.[47] By late February
she was on a list of ships appointed for the fleet from 22 April 1513, with
Anthony Poyntz as captain and Fuller as master, but Henry VIII's own
hand crossed out her name and added instead 'A scyppe off Brystowe'
(*L.P.* I.1661.1). This must be one of three Bristol ships Poyntz was
paid in December and February to acquire and that he provided by 22
March (*L.P.* I.1698, 1728). A construction delay must have caused this
change, for in February and March more materials were taken to
Ratcliff for her, ironwork, a foretop and a maintop were added, and
shipwrights once more employed (these until 5 March); at this point
she was renamed *Anne Gallant*.[48] Lighter at 140 tons and captained by
Walter Loveday, the *Anne* at last is mentioned with the fleet on the
Downs on 22 March 1513 (*L.P.* I.1698). It then left Plymouth with her
on 10 April (*L.P.* I.1771), arrived in Bertheaume Bay the next day to
find the French navy keeping within Brest haven, its entrance guarded
by sunken rocks, and some time before 17 April, when Howard wrote
to Henry, tried to invade the haven, with disastrous results. The
Nicholas of Hampton, in the fleet's vanguard, struck rocks and sank,[49]
and the *Anne* sustained important damages to her hull. After returning
to Plymouth with the navy on 30 April, she sank there before 7 May,
when Thomas Howard, Edward's brother, wrote to Wolsey that 'she

lieth here on dry grownde', would 'not be able to go to the see this yere', and had been replaced.[50] A warrant dated 9 July states that the captain haled her 'on grounde at Plymouth to amend such hurts as the same ship toke upon the rocks in Breten, and when she was in the havyn of Plymouth, the said ship sanke'.[51] This mishap put her out of action for no less than eight months (cf. *L.P.* I.1869, 2217, 2304). The earliest the *Anne* could have been seaworthy was 15 January 1514, but she was still at Plymouth on 26 March, well after late February, when she was appointed for sea-duty the coming year, 6 Henry VIII.[52] She may not have sailed until mid-April, but from 23 or 25 April for six weeks she was with the fleet and after 27 May went northwards to Scotland, where she stayed through July.[53] About her second foundering less is known. In 1516, after the second (Bordeaux) voyage previously contracted to the merchants had taken place in 1514–15, the *Anne* was leased to a Henry Patmer for a voyage into Spain; by October she had returned and was being waterproofed for a second trip there.[54] Her purser was eventually paid for his ship-costs incurred then from 4 November 1516 to 6 January 1517, about which date she presumably sank for good.[55] A later document reports the *Anne* 'was lost at Galisia in the porte of Mongeoy' (*L.P.* II.4606; III.1009), that is, at Mugia, just north of Cape Finisterre on the north-west Spanish coast.

The *Jesus of Plymouth*
In 1525–26 the well-known William Hawkins sailed to Andalusia and back in a ship of this name,[56] but no earlier notice has been found.

The *Hermitage*
This merchantman served in Henry VII's campaign against Scotland in 1497, and sailed from Southampton on trading voyages in 1501 and March 1505, in the latter year for Venice, Florence and Rome.[57] The ship could not have been available by 1512, for it was not then impressed by Henry VIII for war service.

The *Barbara of Dartmouth*
Under various masters this ship passed through Exeter–Dartmouth customs from 1492 to 1503 (P.R.O., E 122.201/1, fols. 16r, 18v, 21v; E 122.41/25, mbs. 10v, 26r). Customs records for these ports in 1507, 1510 and 1516 do not mention the *Barbara*, but a ship with her name is noted under yet another master as leaving Plymouth–Fowey customs in January 1517 (E. 122. 116/4, fol. 5v).

The *Nicholas*
This ship should have the same home port as the *Mary Bellouse* (also at l. 333). Bristol customs record a *Nicholas of Bristol c.* 1486 destined for

Lisbon or the Elbe, and also in 1523 (P.R.O., E 122.20/5, fols. 2v, 9r, 10v; E. 122.21/4, fol. 19v).

The *Mary Bellouse of Bristow*
Her name is from the chapel of the Blessed Mary of Bellhouse, founded before 1491 in Bristol's Church of St Peter and St Paul by the Mary of Bellhouse fraternity.[58] Bristol customs regularly note the movements of this *Mary Bellouse* or *Belhouse* to and from Spain and the Mediterranean in 1492–93 and 1504 (P.R.O., E 122.20/9, fols. 7v, 9r, etc.; E 122.199/1, fols. 29v–30v, 46, etc.) On 12 September 1513 under Robert Waden she left for Ireland (E. 122.21/1, fol. 29r). The next extant customs entries, for 1517, regularly enter an Ireland-destined ship of this name, but one termed a 'Bata' rather than (as before) a 'Nauicula', and under new masters (E. 122.21/2, mbs. 9r, 10v, etc.)

The *Ellen of London*
The *Old Ellen*, a privateer, served the crown c. 1450–58 and 1470–72.[59] Another *Old Ellen* was built by Sir John Fenkyll, citizen and alderman of London in 1496, and in 1499–1500 it left Southampton for Italy.[60] No later record has been found.

The *James*
This is clearly coupled with the *Ellen* as a London vessel, but two so-named ships existed in 1512–13: (1) a 30 ton ship under Peter Aberell or Averell was entered in Kingston-upon-Hull customs in 1512 (P.R.O., E 122.64/3, mbs. 4r, 12r), and helped transport Henry VIII's army for France across the Channel in August–November 1513; and (2) an 80 ton ship owned by Roger Bowterworthe was one of three victuallers to Henry's *Sovereign* in the 1512 naval campaign.[61] In Easter 1516 the *James Trende* or the *James of London* arrived in the Thames from Bordeaux, and in April 1518 Chester customs recorded a *James of London*.[62]

NOTES TO APPENDIX I

1 For information about the de la Pole family generally, see *C.P.*, XII, part I (1953), 451–54, and Appendix I, pp. 21–25.

2 *Chronicles*, pp. 258–59; I. S. Leadam, 'An Unknown Conspiracy against King Henry VII.', *Trans. Royal Hist. Soc.*, new series, 16 (1902), 135; James Gairdner, 'A Supposed Conspiracy against Henry VII.', *Trans. Royal Hist. Soc.*, 18 (1904), 166.

3 Henry A. Napier, *Historical Notices of the Parishes of Swyncombe and Ewelme in the County of Oxford* (1858), pp. 174, 182.

4 S. B. Chrimes, *Lancastrians, Yorkists and Henry VII* (1964), pp. 154–56; Sydney Anglo, 'The *British History* in Early Tudor Propaganda', *Bulletin of*

the John Rylands Library, 44 (1961–62), 17–48; and Scarisbrick, Appendix I, p. 529.

5 *Calendar of . . . State Papers, Relating to the Negotiations Between England and Spain*, III, part I, 1525–26, ed. Pascual de Gayangos (1873), no. 47; the other two were said to be Francis I and the duke of Albany.

6 *L.P.* I.1575; Scarisbrick, pp. 29–31.

7 For a relation of this battle, see Cruickshank, pp. 36–39.

8 Halle, 'Henry VIII', fol. 26v.

9 Cruickshank, p. 38.

10 *L.P.* I.2072; cf. *Venice*, II, no. 248. August–September 1513 records show the French northern fleet commanded by other men (Spont, p. xliv).

11 *Flodden Papers*, ed. Marguerite Wood, Scottish Hist. Soc., 3rd series, 20 (1933), 79, 82; *L.P.* I.2693.

12 *L.P.* I.1297, 1314, 1315, 1340.

13 Halle, 'Henry VIII', fol. 47v.

14 Albany is reported to have been accompanied variously, as by twenty ships and 1,000 men (28 Jan.; *L.P.* I.2605), 10,000 men (15 Feb.; *L.P.* I.2647), Prégent de Bidoux, other sea-captains and German mercenaries (about February; *L.P.* I.2681), the bishop of Murray, 4,000 Germans and 2,000 Normans (19 March; *L.P.* I.2736), and both the French and the Danes (20 March; *L.P.* I.2740). A French costs estimate at Blois on 3 June lists Albany's main forces to be 8,000 soldiers or sailors, 2,500 French infantry and 2,500 lansquenets (*Flodden Papers*, pp. 97–98).

15 German mercenaries had passed through Lorraine (where Richard later went into exile) to France by early January (*L.P.* I.2577), and large forces were assembled about Boulogne against Calais around 4 May (*L.P.* I.2875, 2877–78), where Louis indicated Richard was to be found at that month's end (see below, n. 16).

16 *L.P.* I.2934. For Bohier's departure, see *L.P.* I.2955, 2981.

17 P.R.O., S.P. 1.8, fol. 126r (*L.P.* I.2974); *L.P.* I.3004. There seems to be an obscure reference to the attack of a French fleet against England in a letter of 17 June from London (*L.P.* I.3009).

18 *L.P.* I.3029, 3129. On 11 June Louis was instructing the Scottish ambassador to settle for peace (*Flodden Papers*, pp. 100–07).

19 Part of the Franco–Scottish fleet, however, could be found stalled at Saint-Malo about August 1514 (Spont, pp. 207–08).

20 Richard's dismissal was noted in French letters seen at Rome on 17 August (*L.P.* I.3165, and cf. 3240), and the next day other letters seen there reported that Louis had disbanded a large force including 9,000 lansquenets (*L.P.* I.3173).

21 *The Great Chronicle of London*, ed. A. H. Thomas and I. D. Thornley (1938), pp. 258 and, for the poem (unlineated), 352–65. This piece, by one 'Tom-a-dale of Aylysbury', has been drawn on for otherwise unnoted biographical information: though the verses relate a story that is far from being historically reliable, they do reflect public opinion of Grimaldi *c.* 1510 and present a moralised character that was thought to be true when *Hick Scorner* was written.

22 Paul R. Baumgartner's 'The Date of *Cocke Lorelles Bote*', *Studies in Bibliography*, 19 (1966), identifies this crime with the cause of Grimaldi's outlawry

of 1507 (pp. 180–81), but horse-theft is not likely to be treason, and outlawry was an ordinary court expedient to bring defendants before it (G. R. Elton, 'Henry VII: A Restatement', *Historical Journal*, 4 [1961], 11).

23 A London haberdasher, William Huse (or Husey), brought an action of account against Grimaldi (who was imprisoned about that time) with respect to a balas ruby, but an exchequer writ of privilege evidently got the action discharged. Suits between Huse and Grimaldi's sureties followed (P.R.O., C.1.339/36, 350/42 and 368/31, all dated only 1504–15). The original Huse–Grimaldi case was before parliament itself by 12 February 1515 (*L.P.* II.153).

24 *Calendar of the Patent Rolls . . . Henry VII*, II (1916), 522.

25 *Calendar of the Patent Rolls*, pp. 564–65; Elton, 'Henry VII: A Restatement', p. 11.

26 Grimaldi's forfeiture of a £1,000 obligation to Henry VII was before the exchequer court *c*. 1512, and other late references to the merchant's crown debts occur (*L.P.* I.1493.vi, and p. 1488; *Addenda*, I.49, 816).

27 C. J. Harrison, 'The petition of Edmund Dudley', *English Historical Review*, 87 (1972), 82–99; S. B. Chrimes, *Henry VII* (1972), pp. 309–17.

28 J. P. Cooper, 'Henry VII's Last Years Reconsidered', *Historical Journal*, 2 (1959), 109. The allusion is suggested by Leigh Winser, 'Skelton's *Magnyfycence*', *Renaissance Quarterly*, 23 (1970), 22–23.

29 *Calendar of the Patent Rolls*, p. 625.

30 *The Great Chronicle*, pp. 343–44; Halle, 'Henry VIII', fol. 1r.

31 *T.R.P.*, I.59; *L.P.* I.11 (10), 94 (60). During 1 Henry VIII Parliament also repealed 11 Henry VII. c. 3 (a statute that allowed procedure by information for minor offences) and declared 'it is manifestely known that many Synestr' and craftely feyned and forged informacions have ben pursued' (cited by Elton, 'Henry VII: A Restatement', p. 26). Other actions taken against the promoters are described by Cooper, 'Henry VII's Last Years Reconsidered', pp. 108, 125–26.

32 *L.P.* I.2907. Henry VII's Council in 1506 agreed that the king should invade Ireland, but the plan was not acted on (B.L. Hargrave MS 216, fol. 153r, cited by C. L. Schofield, *A Study of the Court of Star Chamber* [1900], p. 24).

33 *L.P.* II.996; Aubrey Gwynn, *The Medieval Province of Armagh, 1470–1545* (1946), pp. 45–46.

34 *State Papers. King Henry the Eighth*, II, part III (1834), 27 (the whole tract, pp. 1–31, is summarised in *L.P.* II.1366). Among later copies or epitomes of this tract are B. L. Add. MS 4792, fols. 96–110 (Ware MS, *c*. 1600) and Trinity College Dublin MS 581, fols. 31–44v (Ussher MS, *c*. 1600). Pandarus is discussed by Sir James Ware, *The History of the Writers of Ireland*, trans. Walter Harris (in *The Whole Works of Sir James Ware Concerning Ireland* [1764], II), p. 90, and David B. Quinn, 'Tudor Rule in Ireland in the Reigns of Henry VII and Henry VIII', unpublished Ph.D. thesis (University of London, 1933), pp. 156–57, 217, n. 5.

35 Summarised in *Calendar of the Carew Manuscripts, Preserved in the Archiepiscopal Library at Lambeth. 1515–1574*, ed. J. S. Brewer and William Bullen (1867), no. 1, pp. 1–6, and there dated 1515, though Finglas might have been appointed baron of the exchequer in Ireland as late as 1520 (*D.N.B.*, VII, 27), and the tract may thus be later still.

36 Spont, pp. 133, 135–36, 146; G. V. Scammell, 'War at Sea Under the Early Tudors: Some Newcastle Upon Tyne Evidence', *Archaeologia Aeliana*, 4th ser., 38 (1960), 77–78. For Compton's ship, see *L.P.* I.1748, 1882, 1957–58, 2738.

37 *L.P.* I.2391, p. 1058; cf. Cruickshank, pp. 26–27. B.L. Lansdowne MS 818 dates the storm 5 July (fol. 6v), and for subsequent repairs beginning on 6 July see P.R.O., E 36.3, p. 49. Halle does not mention the Wissant wreck (fol. 25v).

38 William Campbell, ed., *Materials for a History of the Reign of Henry VII*, II (1877), 136–37, and cf. 107, 141; and M. Oppenheim, ed., *Naval Accounts and Inventories of the Reign of Henry VII: 1485–8 and 1495–7*, Navy Records Soc., 8 (1896), xxi–xxii, 141–42, 218–23; *Calendar of the Patent Rolls . . . Henry VII*, I (1914), 324.

39 Halle, 'Henry VIII', fol. 21r; *L.P.* I.1371, 1385; Spont, pp. xxi, 36, 50 n. 1; for Knyvett's service on the *Anne*, see P.R.O., E 36.2, p. 6.

40 Spont gives a full account (pp. xxiv–xxvi); and cf. *L.P.* I.1356, 1371, 1385. For the French version (where Porzmoguer takes the initiative in grappling with the *Regent*), see John S. C. Bridge, *A History of France from the Death of Louis XI*, IV (1929), 182–84.

41 An early MS illustration (from Bibliothèque Nationale MS Fr. 1672, fol. 9) is printed by Spont, front. and p. xlvii, and by Bang-McKerrow, p. xi (cf. p. xii, n. 2).

42 M. Oppenheim, 'Maritime History', *The Victoria History of the County of Cornwall*, ed. William Page, I (1906), 484.

43 *L.P.* I.2669, 3137.16 (20); P.R.O., E 36.2, pp. 274, 282, 287, 297 (*L.P.* I.3148.ii–v).

44 J. Payne Collier, ed., *Household Books of John Duke of Norfolk, and Thomas Earl of Surrey* (1844), p. 274; I. S. Leadam, ed., *Select Cases before the King's Council in the Star Chamber*, Selden Soc., 16 (1903), p. 84; *Calendar of the Patent Rolls . . . 1476–1485* (1901), pp. 517–18; Campbell, *Materials*, I (1873), pp. 328–29; P.R.O., C 1.97/32.

45 B.L. Cotton MS Titus B.XI, fols. 282–86; discussed by A. L. Rowse, *Tudor Cornwall* (1941), pp. 114–16.

46 The 'Anne of london [is] other wyse called the Anne of Foye' (*L.P.* I.3608, p. 1497, and cf. pp. 1498–1502); and Richard Fuller is noted as master over the *Anne of Foy* and the *Anne of Greenwich* at different times (*L.P.* I.3318.i [P.R.O., E 36.12, p. 361] and E 36.2, p. 17). Spont also makes these identifications (p. 6, n. 3).

47 P.R.O., E 36.12, pp. 359–77 (*L.P.* I.3318.i).

48 P.R.O., E 36.12, pp. 1–4 (cited by Spont, p. 78, n. 6). For the Fowey–Gallant association, see Harrison's 'Description of the Iland of Britaine' in *Holinshed's Chronicles*, I (1807), 106.

49 Halle, fol. 22v; *L.P.* I.1786 (dated 17 April), 2305.iii (150).

50 Spont, p. 160.

51 Spont, p. 160, n. 1 (*L.P.* I.2305.266); cf. P.R.O., S.P. 1.4, fol. 114r (*L.P.* I.2305.147).

52 P.R.O., E 36.12, pp. 534 (cf. *L.P.* I.3318.iv), 639; *L.P.* I.2574, 2680, and I.2055.12, 2686–87.

53 *L.P.* I.2842, 2851, 2946, 2959, 3148; P.R.O., E 36.12, p. 655.

54 For the Bordeaux voyage, see P.R.O., C 1.504/18, 19, and *L.P.* II.304 and p. 1488; the Patmer records are in P.R.O., E 36.10, fols. 5Ar, 6r, 17, 19, 23r, 25r; cf. *L.P.* III.54, 2074.7; *Addenda*, I.299.

55 Cf. *L.P.* II.3585, 4606. The usually quoted date, 1518, refers to documents that record the ship's loss; see, for instance, M. Oppenheim, *A History of the Administration of the Royal Navy*, I (1896), pp. 66, 68.

56 Gordon Connell-Smith, *Forerunners of Drake* (1954), pp. 10, 62.

57 *Cal. Pat. Rolls . . . Henry VII*, II (1916), 87–88, 91; Oppenheim, *Naval Accounts*, pp. xlv–xlvi, 281. Alwyn A. Ruddock, *Italian Merchants and Shipping in Southampton: 1270–1600* (1951), pp. 236–37; and Ruddock, 'London Capitalists and the Decline of Southampton in the Early Tudor Period', *Economic History Review*, 2nd ser., 2 (1949–50), 141, 143; P.R.O., C 1.283/30 (*c.* 1504–15).

58 George Pryce, *Notes on the Ecclesiastical and Monumental Architecture and Sculpture of the Middle Ages in Bristol* (1850), pp. 204–05; T. P. Wadley, *Notes or Abstracts of the Wills . . . In the Council House at Bristol* (1886), p. 177.

59 *Calendar of the Patent Rolls . . . Henry VI*, V (1909), 383, 442, 447; VI (1910), 175, 405, 411; *Calendar of the Patent Rolls . . . 1467–1477* (1900), pp. 201, 250, 355; *Acts of Court of the Mercers' Company, 1453–1527*, ed. Laetitia Lyell and F. D. Watney [1936], p. 63.

60 W. E. C. Harrison, 'Maritime Activity Under Henry VII', unpublished M.A. thesis (University of London, 1931), p. 80; Ruddock, *Italian Merchants*, p. 221.

61 P.R.O., E 101.56/16, fol. 8r (cf. *L.P.* I.2326); and Spont, p. 41, n. 2.

62 P.R.O., C 1.547/32, 42; K. P. Wilson, ed., *Chester Customs Accounts: 1301–1566*, Record Soc. of Lancashire and Cheshire, III (1969), 42.

APPENDIX II

Selected Tudor *Hick Scorner* Allusions

1. Nicholas Udall, trans., Erasmus' *Apophthegmes* (London, 1542), *S.T.C.* 10443 (no example found in Udall's earlier works):

(a) zeno beeyng outright alltogether a Stoique vsed to call Socrates the scoffer, or the Hicke scorner of the citee of Athenes: because of his merie conceiptes and tauntyng, that he neuer ceassed to vse . . . (sig. ***2r; noted in *O.E.D.*).

(b) Signifiyng that Sophistrie dooeth no helpe, vse ne seruice to dooynges in publique affaires or bearyng offices in a commen weale. Whiche publique offices whoso is a suiter to haue, it behoueth the same not to playe hicke skorner with insolubles, & with idle knackes of sophisticacions, but rather to frame and facion hymself to the maners and condicions of menne, and to bee of suche sorte as other menne bee (sig. B6v; noted by J. O. Halliwell, in *Shakespeare Society's Papers*, 4 [1849], 34).

2. John Bale (pseud. H. Stalbrydge), *The Epistel Exhortatorye of an Inglyshe Chrystian* (1544), *S.T.C.* 1291:

Ye playe altogether hicke scorner vndre the fygure of Ironia. That ye saye ye hate, ye loue, and that ye saye ye loue / ye hate. Lett all faythfull menne beware of suche double daydreamers ād holow harted traytours, and thinke where as they beare the Rule / nothing shall com ryghtly foreward neyther in fayth nor commen welth (fols. 27v–28r; noted by Thora Balslev Blatt, *The Plays of John Bale* [1968], p. 132).

3. *Prayers and Other Pieces of Thomas Becon*, ed. John Ayre, IV, Parker Society (1844), from *The worckes of T. Becon* (entered in Stationers' Register in 1560), *S.T.C.* 1710:

(a) Thy Son ministered the sacraments without putting on of any disguised apparel: the papists deck themselves like hickscorner in game-players' garments (p. 232; noted in *O.E.D.*; cf. p. 260).

(b) This your fool's coat, gaily gauded, signifieth your pleasant fineness and womanly niceness, and your delectation in the verity or change of Venus' pastimes, because ye will not be cumbered with one lawful wife. Thus, as men well harnessed for an interlude, ye come forth to play hickscorner's part with your shameless, smooth, smirking faces, and with your lusty, broad, bald shaven crowns, antichrist's brood of Rome (p. 259).

(c) Shortly after the *Agnus* ye kiss the *pax*, which was the ordinance of pope Innocentius, in the year of our Lord four hundred and ten. And while the boy or parish-clerk carrieth the *pax* about, ye yourselves alone eat up all and drink up all. Ah, what riding fools and very dolts make ye the people! Ye send them a piece of wood or of glass or of some metal to kiss, and in the mean season ye eat and drink up altogether. Is not this a pageant of hickscorner? Is not this a toy to mock an ape withal? (p. 279).

(d) Mass ended, he looked always when the people should have been called to eat and drink with hickscorner that heaved the bread and cup over his head; but no man had part with him: he devoured all alone, like Sim Slap-sauce (p. 281).

(e) The massmonger, like hickscorner, being dressed with scenical and game-player's garments, as with an humeral or ephod, with an alb, with a girdle, with a stole, with a maniple, with an amice, with a chesible, with a fannon, &c., cometh unto the altar with great pomp, and with a solemn pace (p. 361).

4. Thomas Harding, *A Reioindre To M. Jewels Replie* (Antverpiae, 1566), *S.T.C.* 12760 (cf. *The Works of John Jewel*, ed. John Ayre, Parker Society [1848], pp. 139–40, 529, 626):

(a) There was neuer any Hickescorner, that ieasted more pleasantly at any toye in an Enterlude, then M. Jewel scoffeth blasphemously at the most holy and dredful Mysteries. And may no man be so hardy as to name him a Lucian, or a Scoffer? (sig. CC2r).

(b) I perceiue our M. John of Sarisburie would faine play Hicke Scorner, if he had a mery parte, for it semeth he hath on him a fooles cote already. But Syr I pray you, keepe your sporte in store vntil an other time, and perhaps if you play the Vise wel and varletlike, you may chaunce to make a good company laugh their bellies ful (fol. 251v).

5. *The Works of James Pilkington*, ed. James Scholefield, Parker Society (1842), from *A godlie exposition vpon certeine chapters of Nehemiah*, *S.T.C.* 19929 (1585; written *c*. 1575):

. . . we, for our bitter taunting, scoffing, reviling, disdaining, and despising of God's true ministers at these days, shall be given into our mortal enemies' hands. What is more common in these days than, when such hickscorners will be merry at their drunken banquets, to fall in talk of some one minister or other? Nay, they spare none, but go from one to another, and can spy a mote in other men, but cannot spy their own abominations. Christ was never more spitefully and disdainfully scoffed at, than these lusty ruffians open their mouths against his preachers: but the same Lord Christ saith of his disciples, that 'he which despiseth them despiseth him' (p. 357).

6. James Bell, trans., *Aganst Ierome Osorivs*, Walter Haddon, continued by John Foxe (1581), *S.T.C.* 12594:

Here you play hickscorner concernyng the reformation of our maners after the rules of the Gospell: *Where you sportyngly promise, that you will sayle ouer vnto vs, to learne this notable discipline of life*. Come not at vs I pray you, except you throw away your hypocritical visour, and cal to your memory the saying of the Propheticall kyng. *Thy worde O Lord is a lanterne to me feete*: which sentence lyeth drowned amongest you in so deepe a dongeon of bald ceremonies and mens traditions, that like night owles you are starke blynd in the midday: and are not able to endure the bright beames of the cleare shynyng Gospell (fol. 12v; noted in *O.E.D.*).

7. George Puttenham, *The Arte of English Poesie 1589* (Scolar Press, 1968):

Or when we giue a mocke with a scornefull countenance as in some smiling sort looking aside or by drawing the lippe awry, or shrinking vp the nose; the Greeks called it *Micterismus*, we may terme it a fleering frumpe, as he that said to one whose wordes he beleued not, no doubt Sir of that. This fleering frumpe is one of the Courtly graces of *hicke the scorner* (p. 159).

8. Marphoreus, pseud., *Martins Months Minde* (1589), *S.T.C.* 17452:

Naie he goeth farther, and setting his face against the heauens, he makes a mock of the *Saints* of God; yea the mother of *Christ*, (with his single sold *Sirs*) & the Scriptures themselues he beastlie abuseth to his hick scorners iestes (sig. B3r; noted in *O.E.D.*).

9. Gabriel Harvey, *Pierce's Supererogation 1593* (Scolar Press, 1970):

. . . had I bene Martin [Marprelate] . . . I would haue beene so farre from being mooued by such a fantasticall Confuter, that it should haue beene one of my May-games, or August-triumphes, to haue driuen Officials, Commissaries, Archdeacons, Deanes, Chauncellors, Suffraganes, Bishops, and Archbishops . . . to entertaine such an odd

light-headded fellow for their defence; a professed iester, a Hick-
scorner, a scoff-maister, a playmunger, an Interluder; once the foile of
Oxford, now the stale of London, and euer the Apesclogg of the presse,
Cum Priuilegio perennitatis (pp. 74–75; Harvey seems to speak of John
Lyly).

Source and Analogue Materials

Italicised words or phrases in texts 2, 3 and 4 are found also in the plays.

1. The *Revesby Play*, now B.L. Add. MS 44, 870,[1] is entitled 'Oct. 20. 1779—Morrice Dancers at Revesby' (the Lincolnshire abbey estate then the seat of Sir Joseph Banks, the naturalist and President of the Royal Society). Banks made an annual visit to Revesby from September to early November, during which stay he attended the yearly village fair, 'when Mummers and Morris dancers vied with up-to-date entertainers in making the most of a joyous day'.[2] The Revesby entertainment was undoubtedly performed then with Banks as its *'master of the house'* (421.2–3).[3] In a witty and often ironic way, the play mixes the traditional 'Hero Combat' (of which it is the first extant text) and other folk dramatic types with local Lincolnshire references, contemporary eighteenth-century banter, and a Song of the Landlord and the Tenant that culminates in a money-collection that probably served to gather the semi-annual rentals from Banks' tenants.[4]

Three of the playwright's dramatic models were from the north: the sword dance, the Plough Monday Fool's Wooing, and *Youth*.[5] Since its influence appears only in the last Revesby episode, the wooing of Cicely, he could have adapted *Youth* indirectly from a lost partial recension in an early Plough Monday play, and in fact three other Lincolnshire mummers' plays, the 1823 Bassingham and Broughton texts, reproduce *Revesby* material that is partly taken from the interlude.[6] If these late texts derive simply from Revesby (as seems likely), however, its playwright might have used *Youth* in original quarto form.[7] His main debt is to Youth's first monologue, which is split between Blue Britches and Pepper Britches, who enter with their brothers to court Cicely with set speeches after their father (and her favourite), the Fool, has displeased her by first chasing them away.

> *Blue Britches.*　I am a youth of jollitree;
> 　　　　　　　　Where is there one like unto me?
> 　　　　　　　　My hair is bush'd very thick;
> 　　　　　　　　My body is like an hasel stick;

My legs they quaver like an eel;
My arms become my body weel;
My fingers they are long and small:
Am not I a jolly youth, proper and tall?

(308–15; cf. *Y*. 44–54)

Pepper Britches.   I am my father's eldest son,
And heir of all his land,
And in a short time, I hope,
It will fall into my hands.

(330–33; cf. *Y*. 57–58)

Two recollections of Youth's meeting with Lechery may also survive later when the Fool successfully woos Cicely away from his sons. She greets him with Lechery's words to Youth, 'You are kindly wellcome, sir, to me' (360; cf. *Y*. 395–97, 406), and the Fool soon notes in an aside: 'For a thousand pounds she loves me best! | I can see by the twinkling of her ee' (374–75; cf. *Y*. 415–16).

NOTES

1 R. Flower, 'The Revesby Play', *The British Museum Quarterly*, 11 (1936), 23–24. The MS was presented to the Museum by Lady Gomme, and previously W. S. Thoms had been given it by Sir Henry Ellis. Sometime before John Brand (who was a northerner) died in 1806, he described the MS, which he evidently possessed, in an unfinished revision of his 1777 *Observations on Popular Antiquities* that was later edited, with Brand's notes, by Ellis in 1813 (I, 401). W. Carew Hazlitt's *Faiths and Folklore* (1905) states Brand's MSS went to Ellis (I, vi).

2 *The Banks Letters*, ed. Warren R. Dawson (1958), p. xxv; and Edward Smith, *The Life of Sir Joseph Banks* (1911), p. 306.

3 'The Revesby Sword Play', *Specimens of the Pre-Shaksperean Drama*, ed. John Matthews Manly, I (1897), 296–311. All quotations are from this edition.

4 Chambers, *E.F.-P.*, pp. 120–23; Alan Brody, *The English Mummers and their Plays* (1970), pp. 148–55. Violet Alford, in her *Sword Dance and Drama* (1962), suggests the play honoured Rent Day (p. 56).

5 The sword dance appears mainly in Yorkshire, Durham and Northumberland (Brody, *English Mummers*, p. 72), and the Fool's Wooing in Lincolnshire and Nottinghamshire (though some instances occur in Leicestershire, Rutland, Yorkshire and East Anglia): see M. W. Barley, 'Plough Plays in the East Midlands', *Journal of the English Folk Dance & Song Society*, 7 (1953–54), 68, 72–73.

6 Charles R. Baskervill, 'Mummers' Wooing Plays in England', *Modern Philology*, 21 (1923–24), p. 242, ll. 17–20, p. 246, ll. 18–21, and p. 254, ll. 96–99.

7 If *Youth*'s rhymes at 45/47, 'vine tree' / 'jollity', explain the odd *Revesby* reading 'jollitree' (308; possibly 'Iollitrie' in the MS), the *Revesby* playwright should have had a quarto copy before him.

2. 'Testamentum Christi' (from B.L. MS Harl. 2382, fols.
111v–18r), ed. F. J. Furnivall, *The Minor Poems of the Vernon MS.*,
Part II, E.E.T.S. O.S. 117 (1901), 637–57; see Carleton Brown and
Rossell Hope Robbins, *The Index of Middle English Verse* (1943), no.
4154, 'The Long Charter of Christ' (B-text):

They made scourges hard & grete,	145
ther-with my body shuld be bete;	
and thogh y wold haue pleyned me,	
ther shuld to me no socour haue be.	
ful sore a-ferd, for-sothe y was,	
when they led me so gret a pas!	150
To a piler y was bound al þe nyght,	
togged & betyn til day-light,	
and wasshen with myn owne blode,	
that al the erthe aboute cold stode.	154

with a spere of Stile myn hert was stonge	221
thurf my syde & thurf my lunge;	
apon my side they made a wonde,	
myn herte-blode ran doune to grounde . . .	224

for loue of the y hong on a tre,	260
But [seid] 'my fader, y pray now the,	
apon myn enmyes thu haue pite;'	
And as y do, do thu to thyne,	
and saued shalt þᵘ be fro helle-pyne.	
Here [of] be wittenesse mo then on:	265
Mark, Mathew, Luke and Iohñ,	
and namely my moder swete,	
that for me *blody terys gan lete.*	
for, there she stode *vnder the rode,*	
she sawe my body al on blode	270
that fro my fete vnto my hede	
y was not els but al blode-rede;	
No word to me þer myght she speke,	
it semed ny here herte wold breke;	
no wonder was thogh she were woo	275
when she sawe me on þe crosse y-do.	
ffor sorwe of here y made a cry	
and seid ful lowde 'heli lamaʒabathany.'	
anone *she fell doune* in sownyng,	
right be-fore me at myn endyng.	280
the peynes that y suffred were ful sore,	
but for my moder they were the more.	

when y layd my hed here & there,
my moder chaunged al here chere;
ful fayn she wold haue holpe me,   285
but for the Iewys it myght not be.
my peynes were tho fulle smerte,
the swerd of sorwe perced here herte . . .   288

A cote-armuur I bere here with me,   373
the which y toke of thy lyuere;
this cote is riche & wel fyne,   375
the champe is now of red satyne;
a wel faire mayde me it be-tought
and out of here boure I it broght;
poudred it is with v. roses red,
wondes y suffred with peynes of ded.   380

3. *The assemble of goddes* (Westminster? Wynkyn de Worde, *c.* 1500),
S.T.C. 17006. (Some typical variant readings are noted for three other
texts: *S.T.C.* 17005, by de Worde in 1498; *S.T.C.* 17007, by de Worde
in 1500? and Trinity College Cambridge MS 599.)

Summary. The poet, wondering how to reconcile Reason and Sensuality, falls asleep and has the following dream. After debating the
complaint of Diana and Neptune against Eolus at Pluto's parliament
and then at Apollo's banquet, the pagan gods hear Atropos' charge that
Virtue alone withstands death, and Pluto offers his bastard son, Vice,
to war on the upstart (1–610). Vice enters with his seven principal
captains, Pride, *Envy*, Wrath, Covetise, Gluttony, Lechery and Slouth
(610–34). A list of the lesser captains (635) who attend them then
follows:

sacrylege symony & dyssymulacyon
Manslaughter mordre theft & *extorcyon*

Arrogaūce Presūpcyon wyth contumaci
Contēpcyon Cōtempt & Inobedyence
Malyle *Frowardnes* grete Jelasy   640
wodnes *Hate* Stryf and Impacyence
Vnkyndnes Opp̄ssyon wᵗ wofull neglygēce.
Murmur *Myschef Falshod* & detraccyon
Vsury Periury Ly and adulacyon

Wrong Rauyne Sturdy vyolence   645
Fals Jugement wᵗ *Obstynacyon*
Dysceyt Dronknes & Improuydence.

646. *Obstynacyon*] S.T.C. *17006*; obstynacy S.T.C. *17005, 17007*; *TCC.*

Boldnes in yll wᵗ foule and Rybaudy.
Fornycacyon Incest and *Auoutry*
Vnshamfastnes wᵗ Prodygalyte   650
Blasfeme vaynglory & worldly vanyte

Ignoraũce Dyffydence wᵗ Ipocrysy
Scysme Rancour Debate and Offence
Heresy Errour wᵗ Idolatry.
New fangylnes and *sotyll* false Pretence   655
Iordynat desyre of worldly excellence
Fayned pouerte wyth apostasy
Dysclaunder scorn & vnkynd Jelousy

Hoordom baudry false mayntenaunce
Treyson abusyon and pety brybry   660
Vsurpacyon wᵗ *horryble vengaunce*
Came alder last of that company

Then Idleness sets in battle order the commons (666–72), which is
accordingly catalogued:

There were bosters crakers & brybours
Praters sasers strechers and wrythers
Shamefull shakelers soleyn slauedours   675
Oppressours of people and myghty crakers
Mayntenours of quarels horryble *lyers*
Theues traytours wᵗ false *heretykes*
Charmars sorcerers & many scysmatykes.

Preuy symonyakes wyth false vsurers   680
Multyplyers coyn wasshers & clyppers
Wrong vsurpers wyth grete extorcyoners
Bacbyters Glosers and fayre *flaterers*.
Malycyous murmurers with grete claterers
Tregetours Tryfelers Feyners of tales   685
Lastyuous lurdeyns and Pykers of malys.

Rouners Vagabundes Forgers & lesingis.
Robbers Reuers Rauenous Ryfelers.
Choppers of Chyrches Fynders of tydynges
Merrers of maters and mony makers.   690
Stalkers by nyght wyth Euysdroppers.
Fyghters *Brawlers* Brekers of louedayes
Getters Chyders Causers of frayes.

Tytyuyllis Tyraũtis wᵗ Tourmentours.
Corsyd apostatis Relygyous dyssymulers.   695

Closshers *Carders* wyth comon hasardours.
Tyburne colops and Purskytters.
Pylary knyghtys double tollyng Myllers.
Gay Joly tapters w^t hostelers of the stewes.
Hores and Bawdes that many bale brewes   700

Bold blasfemers wyth false Ipocrytes.
Brothellers Brokers abhomynable *swerers*.
Dryuylls Dastardes dyspysers of ryghtis
Homycydes Poyseners & comon *morderers*
Scoldis Caytyues Comberous clappers.   705
Idolatrēs Enchauntors w^t false regenates.
Sotyl ambydextrys and sekeers of debatis.

Pseudo Prophetes false Sodemytes.
Quesmers of chyldren wyth fornycatours.
wetewoldes that suffre syn in their syghtis.   710
Auoutrers and abhomynable auauntours.
Of syn grete clappers & makers of clamours
Vnthryftes & vnlustes came al to that game
w^t lusk*es* & loselis y^t might not thryue for shaͫ

Morpheus secretly leaves Apollo's court to warn Virtue, who then sends his messenger *Imagination* to summon to the field Virtue's friends, and they gather in a host (715–70). Baptism secures the battleground from Crime Original, Vice's messenger, who had occupied it but runs off at the sacrament's approach (771–82). Virtue then enters the field with his four knights, *Rightwiseness*, Prudence, Strength and Temperance (783–98), and his seven captains, *Humility, Charity, Patience*, Liberality, *Abstinence*, Chastity and Good Business (799–826). The petty captains (827) follow them and include

     trew *feyth* & hope mercy pease & *pyte*.
Ryght *trouth mekenesse* w^t rood enteut.
Goodnes concorde & parfyte vnyte.   830
Hoeest trewe loue with symplycyte.
Prayer fastȳg preuy *almysdede*.
Joyned with ye artycles of the crede.

Confessyon contrycyon & satyffaccyon.
With *sorow for synne* & grete repentaunce.   835
Foryeuenesse of trespas w^t good dysposycyon.
Resystence of wrong performȳg of penance.
Holy *deuocyon* wyth good contynaunce
Presthode hem folowed with the sacramētis

696. *Carders*] S.T.C. *17006*, *17007*; *TCC*; cardes S.T.C. *17005*.

And *sadnesse* alse wyth the commaūdementes   840

Suffraunce in trouble wyth Innocensy
Clennes contynence and *virgynyte*
Kyndnes reuerence wᵗ curteysy
Content & pleased wyth pyteous pouerte
Entendyng wel mynystryng equyte   845
Twene ryght & wrong hole indyfferently
And labouryng the seruyse of god to multyply

Refuse of ryches & worldly vaynglory
Perfeccyon wyth *perfyghtcontemplacyon*
Relygyon professyon wel kept in memory   850
Verry drede of god wyth holy predycacyon
Celestyall sapyence wyth gostly inspyracyon
Grace was the guyde of al this meyne

Besides these, the arts and practical virtues like Moderate Diet appear, though others (like Negromancy) are rejected and desert to Vice (854–89). Then the commoners (890–96) come forth, as follows:

There were *noble* and famous *doctours*.
Example yeuers of lyuyng gracyous.
Perpetuel prestes and dyscrete confessours.
Of holy scrypture declarers fructuous.   900
Rebukers of syn & myscheues odyous.
Fysshers of soules & louers of clennes.
Dyspysers of veyn and worldly rychesse.

Peasyble prelatys Justycyal gouernours.
Founders of chyrches wyth mercyfull peres.   905
Reformers of wrong of her progenytours
On peynfull pore *pyteous compassyoners*
well menyng marchaūtes wᵗ *trew artefecers*
Vyrgyns pure and also Innocentes
Hooly matrones wᵗ chast contynence   910

Pylgrymes & palmers wᵗ trew laborers
Holy heremytes goddys solycytours
Monesteryal monkes & well dysposed freres
Chanonsand nonnes feyth *p*rofessoures
Of worldly people trew coniugatours.   915
Louers of Cryst Confounders of yll.
And all that to godward yeue her good wyll

Mayntenours of ryghte verey penytentes.

897. *noble*] S.T.C. *17006*; notable S.T.C. *17005*, *17007*; *TCC*.

Dystroyers of errour causers of vnyte.
Trew actyf lyuers that set her ententis   920
The dedis to performe of mercy and pyte
Contemplatyf people that desyre to be.
Salytary seruauntis vnto god alone.
Rather thē to haboūd in rychesses echone.

Both armies advance to the battlefield, Macrocosm, where *Free Will* is lord and *Conscience* stands as judge (925–96). Pluto charges Vice, 'draw not arere | But put yᵉ forth boldly to ouerthrowe Vertu' (962–63). To Free Will Virtue sends three ambassadors, Reason, Discretion and Good Remembrance, and Vice a like number, Temptation, Folly and Sensuality, but Free Will gives 'Answere . . . none to neyther party' (1009). He says he will await the battle's outcome, and 'not restrayne his lyberte. | Whan he come where sorow shold awake. | Than it shold be know what part he wyl take' (1013–15). At this point Vice has 'wanton' Sensuality (1238; cf. 1230, 1362) enter Macrocosm as a spy and seed it with slippery, rank weeds, so that, when Free Will, Vice and Virtue meet 'as tripartite' (1031) there, Virtue's host is encumbered by the weeds and must turn to the defensive at two assaults by Vice's army, and Free Will is convinced by Sensuality to forsake Virtue for Vice (1016–55). When Reason objects, Free Will replies, 'Noforse . . . I wyll do as my lyst' (1057). Consequently, he joins Vice in constraining Virtue 'clerely by duresse. | A lytyll tyne abacke to make abew retret' (1063–64), and he is driven 'out of the feld it was the more pyte' (1080). *Good Perseverance*, however, rallies the rear ward to attack, urges Virtue to re-enter the field, and personally defeats Vice in single combat (1093–134). After coming forward to repent before Conscience, Free Will, 'Dysguysed yᵗ he were not knowen as he wente' (1141), is directed to Humility, and in turn to Confession, Contrition, Satisfaction and Penance (1135–48). God then sends Prescience to punish Vice, and Predestination to reward Virtue with a heavenly crown, and some of Vice's host are redeemed through Baptism (1149–217). When Virtue summons Free Will to answer who advised him 'Vyces party to take' (1220), the kneeling penitent prays Virtue, 'let pyte your eres to me enclyne' (1225), and confesses Sensuality was responsible (1218–28). Virtue then demotes Free Will to bailiff of Macrocosm under Reason and places Sensuality, who has been tamed and converted by a fear of death (2003–16), under the control of his captor, Sadness (1229–81). The allegory ends after Atropos, having entered God's service as Death, lays waste to Macrocosm and himself vanishes, leaving Virtue to ascend to heaven (1282–467). The dreamer then visits Doctrine for an explanation of world history, the allegory's meaning, and the dreamer's own initial problem, the reconciliation of Reason and Sensuality (through the fear of Death).

4. Cf. *The maner of the world now a dayes* (single folio; *S.T.C.* 17255), published by G. Simson? *c.* 1590; but see *The Britwell Handlist* (1933), II, 630 (now Huntington 18348). The line-numbering is from the text published in Skelton's *Works* (I, 148–54).

> So *many* proper *knyues*
> So *well apparrelled wyues*   45
> And so yll *of theyr lyues*
> > Saw I neuer.
> > > > 48

> So many alle sellers.
> In baudy holes and sellers   109
> Of yonge folkes yll counsellers
> > sawe I neuer.
> > > > 112

> To the lord I make my mone   181
> For y^u maist healpe vs euerichone
> Alas the people is so wo begone
> > *worse was it neuer*
> > Amendment   185
> Were conuenient
> But it may not be
> > We haue exiled veritie
> God is neither dead nor sicke
> > He may amend al yet   190
> And trowe ye so in dede
> > As ye beleue ye shal haue mede
> After better I hope euer
> > For worse was it neuer.   Finis.   194

A shorter version of this poem, with ll. 45–48 above, exists in the late fifteenth-century Missenden Abbey Register (B.L. MS Sloane 747, fols. 88v–89r), and is edited in *Works* also (II, 199–203).

5. What follows is an index to those parallels between *Youth* and *Hick Scorner*, and their sources or analogues (including scripture), that may be found in the annotations to this edition.

Assemble of goddes: HS 5, 42, 44, 47, 59, 64, 161, 177, 339–52, 368–79, 371, 385, 403, 546–601, 560, 580, 594, 602–20, 879, 880–81, 908–10, 987, 1007, 1025.
'Bowge of Courte': Y 255, 679, 681; HS 211–12, 214, 317, 368, 393–99, 401, 652, 739.
Cocke Lorelles bote: HS 179, 183, 232, 302, 317, 388, 389, 440, 622–24, 663, 750, 820–45, 820, 821, 834.

The Nugent Monck and Barry Jackson *Youth* Revivals

Youth was a founding production of two major acting companies, Nugent Monck's Norwich Players, later at the Maddermarket Theatre, and Sir Barry Jackson's Pilgrim Players, who became the Birmingham Repertory. What sent them independently to *Youth* was William Poel's widely successful *Everyman* revival, acted by the Elizabethan Stage Society in July 1901 in the Master's Court, the Charterhouse, London.[1]

Once a member of Poel's *Everyman* production, Nugent Monck formed the English Drama Society in May 1905 to 'protest against modern over-staging, under-acting, and to reanimate the national drama' (as he wrote).[2] The Society's second production was *Youth*. It was performed six times at Bloomsbury Hall in London, on 12–14 December 1905, the opening night being delayed until Poel's patrons, the duke and duchess of Argyll, arrived.[3] This not-well-received revival had an afternoon performance on 8 January 1906 at the Great Queen Street Theatre, and still later was in a Lenten week's programme, alternating with Robert Arthur's *Everyman* revival and another play on 25 and 28 March 1907 at the Coronet Theatre, Notting Hill Gate.[4] During this period Monck also probably produced *Youth* at Oxford and privately before the Queen, but after the Society collapsed in 1909 following the police suppression of his *Ludus Coventriae* passion plays at the Fortune Playhouse, scheduled for 7–10 April,[5] Monck turned with *Youth* to the provinces. Emily Horniman, the owner of the Manchester Gaiety Theatre, invited him to perform it with *The Second Shepherds' Play* there on 28 February and 1–2 March 1510.[6] By then he had moved to Norwich, where in the autumn he formed the Norwich Players, one of whose first productions, acted in the upstairs sitting-room of Monck's medieval house, the 'Crypt', was *Youth*.[7] This and *The World and the Child* were in their repertoire, and in 1911, after a dress performance of *Youth* in the Norwich Grammar School crypt, the troupe put on both interludes before the bishop of London and the archbishop of Canterbury in Lambeth Palace Crypt.[8] Late in this year Monck moved to Dublin. W. B. Yeats had decided to found a second Abbey group, a Theatre School of Acting, to occupy the stage when the main company was on tour and to be a permanent dramatic academy, and he asked Monck to be director.[9] On 16 November 1911, before a privately invited audience that included Maude Gonne, Jack Yeats and his wife, Maire O'Neill, Padraic Colum and W. B. Yeats himself, this second company premiered with *Youth* (Monck taking the title role).[10] According to Yeats, the play was chosen because 'None of their players had ever seen Sir H. Tree play "The Interlude of Youth," and that fact helped them to do something very charming and fresh'.[11] Joseph Holloway, who grew to like the play, at first only said it 'was mildly effective & impressive without being unduly so', and public performances of it and *The Second Shepherds' Play* followed on 23–25 November, and of *Youth* on 7–9 December, but the School was no great success, and Monck returned to Norwich after spending a period with the Abbey Players in America.[12] On 10 July 1913, however, Monck and the renewed Norwich Players, this time with the choristers of the Temple, again acted *Youth* at Lambeth Palace; and the troupe got a permanent Norwich theatre when Monck converted Sir John Paston's fifteenth-century inn loft into the 'Old Musick Room', and on opening nights, 7–8 January 1914, he gave a programme of eight items, including *Youth*.[13] After the war Monck established the Maddermarket Theatre in an eighteenth-century Catholic church, where the interlude was revived in 1924.[14]

Monck's *Youth* inherited, not only Poel's *Everyman* costumes, still in use in 1910 by the Norwich Players,[15] but his *fin-de-siècle* medievalism. The 1905 Bloomsbury Hall programme promised 'medieval methods of staging', by which Monck meant Poel's 1901 techniques: no front curtain, actors who in entering 'seemed to be of the audience', a cathedral-like setting with a 'high altar under a canopy' at the hall's eastern end, and acting characterised by 'slowness and solemnity', 'posturing and declamation', and 'a sort of chant' (in the Abbey performances).[16] The 1905 production was a decorous psychomachia framed by extraneous church ritual. After a twenty-minute organ overture (and incense-burning at the Queen Street Theatre), a procession of one priest, two monks and a three-boy choir, bearing a crucifix and chanting *Adeste Fideles*, marched up the hall.[17] Charity appeared with the wings of a 'pre-Raphaelite angel', Lechery became Luxury, a regal lady wearing crown, furpiece and flowing gown, and Pride's song was *Roister Doister*'s 'I mon be married on Sunday' (despite Riot's lines at 364–67).[18] When Youth reached into his pouch for a 'noble' (441) to pay for their tavern visit, he produced, not a coin, but 'a small crucifix and rosary', at which he gazed 'awe-stricken' (in 1907 Monck interpolated a hymn during a critical pause here) and spoke the ensuing lines (442–47) in 'terror'—a rendering that William Archer properly said depended on mistaking '"Hearest thou how they fight?" as referring to the contest of the powers of good and evil for his soul'.[19] After Youth's conversion, which involved his reception of a cloth of rue, a rosary and a Bible, he went up the altar steps 'into the arms of the Church as represented by an angel', who held up the sacramental chalice to give him what Everyman obtained off-stage.[20]

Youth was also the first and staple production of Sir Barry Jackson's Pilgrim Players. Arnold Pinchard, vicar of Birmingham's St Jude's Church, who had helped to bring Poel's Everyman to Birmingham in late 1901, was present, early in the autumn of 1907, when Jackson and other amateurs acted Youth in the Jackson family's dining-room at 'The Grange'.[21] Pinchard then persuaded the 'Grange' company to act publicly at the St Jude's Mission Hall in Inge Street on 2 October, and himself prefaced Youth by a short talk in which he called medieval drama 'the Daughter of the Church'.[22] Despite poor attendance, press notices were good, and another performance was given a fortnight later.[23] Six weeks after, Jackson formed the Pilgrim Players; they were to present Youth some twenty-eight times by 1914. Audiences saw it at Queen's College, Birmingham (spring 1909), the Corn Exchange, Stratford-upon-Avon (April 1909), St Jude's again (24–25 March 1911), the Liverpool Repertory Theatre (April 1912), the Stratford-upon-Avon Festival at the Shakespeare Memorial Theatre (August 1912), eventually the Birmingham Repertory itself (14 June 1913, its first year), and in various Warwickshire towns during the Players' tours there in the summer of 1911 (as at Stratford's Memorial Theatre Gardens) and in the early 'twenties.[24] In the summer of 1933 some students at the Central (London) School of Speech and Acting assumed the Pilgrim Players' name and made a similar country tour with the interlude. Sir Barry Jackson, finally, revived it again (coupled with Marlowe's Doctor Faustus on the same night) for the 1934 Malvern Festival programme in a completely new production by Godfrey Baxter, designed by Paul Shelving, and acted by both seasoned professionals and at least one of these students, Mavis Walker.[25]

Jackson's production in 1907, like Monck's, opened with ritual: the chanting of an Ave Maria by an unseen choir, and a procession (accompanied by a hymn) up the St Jude's hall aisle by 'acolytes swinging censers and carrying tapers', followed by the actors, one of whom, Bache Matthews, later admitted their Youth had 'the solemnity of a religious ceremonial'.[26] Jackson's heavily bowdlerised and emended text bears out this remark. Lechery again becomes Luxury, oaths sworn with God's name disappear, some fifty lines are cut (most serious and comic references to the Trinity, and Lechery's bawdry), textual revision gives Youth symptoms of a psychomachic internal conflict, and Humility's speeches are generally reassigned to Charity, perhaps to stress the Catholic doctrine of good works (though John Drinkwater's acting strength may have been responsible).[27] Staging, costumes and acting were, however, unaffected and balanced. The set used 'bright green curtains hung in a semi-circle' with three entrances, over each of which was 'a panel of brown board which bore, in clear shapely letters, the name of the place to which it was supposed to lead: "The World," "The Citie of Blyss," "The Tavern"', while the virtues dressed simply as monk and nun, and the vices each had a spirited song or dance to Pinchard's small orchestra.[28] Years later Drinkwater could say that the production was at ease with both fashionable and slum audiences.[29]

Jackson's imaginative Malvern Festival production in 1934, though adapting features of the 1907 staging, took its central impulse from gothic art and perhaps the *commedia dell' arte*. Malvern used the three-door setting of 1907, much elaborated: between a towered castle World and a Tavern building stood the City of Bliss, a church behind whose steeples shone a great sun.[30] These 'gates' (cf. *Y.* 16, 136, 220, etc.) objectified Youth's abstract choices. Riot, Pride and Lechery emerged from the World (cf. *Y.* 760), whereas Charity and presumably Humility came from the City (*Y.* 17, 21, 570), which Youth passed by on the way to the Tavern. This objectification was also true of Paul Shelving's costuming. Youth was in green (with a lacquered wig)[31] and resembled the pagan, vegetative figure of his opening monologue (*Y.* 45). Half-masks for the virtues and vices stressed both their abstractness and, by contrast, Youth's (unmasked) humanity.[32] Charity was a monk, and Humility a nun (as in 1907), but a nimbus depersonalised both. Riot wore brilliant scarlet,[33] and had a grotesque animal face staring from his belly (as in medieval demon-illustrations), apparently to suggest his role as a devil (cf. *Y.* 220). Pride and Lechery, herself at last, were spectacularly overdressed, evidently in velvet damasks and cloth-of-gold, a fine brother–sister pair; and Pride, as 'rector chory' (*Y.* 473), carried a staff of office. Youth did not change costume while at the tavern, but seems to have been crowned by Riot with a belled cap of folly[34] that would have given point to Youth's later jest (*Y.* 703–04). Jackson's Birmingham edition was abandoned for an unbowdlerised text with the original assignment of speeches, and though the musical setting included 'arrangements of Gregorian Plainsong',[35] there were no liturgical processions, and *Youth* at last emerged out from under the pall of Poel's *Everyman*.

NOTES TO APPENDIX IV

1 Robert Speaight, *William Poel and the Elizabethan Revival* (1954), pp. 161, 282; for this and later productions, see Winifred F. E. C. Isaac, *Ben Greet and The Old Vic* [1964–65], pp. 75–85; and Potter, pp. 1–5, 222–25.

2 Biographical information on Monck appears in June Ottaway's 'Nugent Monck of Norwich', *Christian Drama*, 2, no. 6 (1953), 21; *The Times* (23 October 1958), p. 17; *Who Was Who: 1951–1960* (1961), p. 776; and Martin Kinder, 'Early Days With the Norwich Players', *Eastern Daily Press* (Norwich: 9 December 1960), p. 8. For Monck's words about the Society, see *The Athenaeum* (20 May 1905), p. 636.

3 *The Times* (5 December 1905), p. 6; *Holborn and Finsbury Guardian* (16 December 1905), p. 3; Harold Child partially lists these productions in 'Revivals of English Dramatic Works, 1901–1918, 1926', *R.E.S.*, 3 (1927), 171. The cast included Ina Royle (Charity), Catherine Stuart (Humility), Arthur Goodsall (Youth), Arthur Curtis (Riot), Bertram Forsyth (Pride) and Mina Legh (Luxury). Costumes were designed by Jennie Moore.

4 Joseph W. Barley, *The Morality Motive In Contemporary English Drama* (1912), p. 116; *The Morning Post* (1 January 1906), p. 8; *The Stage* (28 March 1907), p. 15; *The Referee* (31 March 1907), p. 3. Papers noting 26 March Coronet performances seem in error.

5 Barley, *Morality Motive*, p. 116; *The Athenaeum* (27 March 1909), p. 388 and (17 April 1909), p. 476; *The Times* (8 April 1909), p. 11; Ottaway, 'Nugent Monck', p. 22.

6 Rex Pogson, *Miss Horniman and The Gaiety Theatre, Manchester* (1952), p. 201 (the entry for those dates in 1911 on p. 202 is incorrect); *Manchester Guardian* (1 March 1910), p. 7.

7 Kinder, 'Early Days', p. 8; M.S. and F.W.W., *The Norwich Players* (1920), pp. 9–10, 27–28.

8 Kinder, 'Early Days', p. 8; Ottaway, 'Nugent Monck', p. 22. Archbishop Davidson has, in his large 1911 diary (now deposited in Lambeth Palace Library), noted a 'Play' on 17 February. The occasion was in part memorable because the bishop of London took Lady Lechery to dinner between a rehearsal and the performance.

9 Yeats's *Countess Cathleen* had just been acted in Norwich (*The Norfolk Chronicle* [25 February 1911], p. 10).

10 'MS. [Joseph] Holloway. Impressions of a Dublin Playgoer. July–December 1911', National Library of Ireland MS 1812, pp. 783–85; Lennox Robinson, *Ireland's Abbey Theatre* (1951), p. 106.

11 *The Freeman's Journal* (Dublin: 17 November 1911), p. 9.

12 Nat. Lib. of Ire. MS 1812, pp. 785, 907, 912; *The Irish Times* (21 November 1911), p. 4; *The Saturday Herald* (2 December 1911), p. 4; *Who Was Who: 1951–1960* (1961), p. 776.

13 A programme of the Lambeth performance exists in the Maddermarket Theatre archives (as of 24 August 1971, according to its Secretary, James Livock). E. G. W. Bill, Librarian of Lambeth Palace Library, found two entries for 10 July in the diaries of archbishop and Mrs Davidson: his reference to an 'Evening Party & Morality Play', and her item, '*Evening Party 9.30–*' (letter of 6 November 1974). H.R., 'The Norwich Players' Venture: New Lamps for Old', *Norwich Mercury* (10 January 1914), p. 4; *Eastern Evening News* (6 January 1914), p. 4; T. L. G. Burley, *Playhouses and Players of East Anglia* (1928), p. 94.

14 Harold Child, 'Revivals of English Dramatic Works, 1919–1925', *R.E.S.*, 2 (1926), 180; Burley, *Playhouses*, p. 97.

15 Kinder, 'Early Days', p. 8.

16 For a copy of the programme, see British Library Playbills 341, no. 61; *The Daily News* (13 December 1905), p. 8; William Archer, 'The Theatre. "The Interlude of Youth." ', *The World* (19 December 1905), p. 1074; *The Globe* (9 January 1906), p. 4; Nat. Lib. of Ire. MS 1812, p. 784.

17 *The Daily Chronicle* (13 December 1905), p. 5; *The Era* (13 January 1906), p. 17; *Holborn and Finsbury Guardian* (16 December 1905), p. 3; Archer, 'The Theatre', p. 1074.

18 Archer, 'The Theatre', p. 1074; the photographs in *The Sketch* (13 December 1905), pp. 6–7; *The Referee* (17 December 1905), p. 2.

19 Archer, 'The Theatre', p. 1074; *The Times* (27 March 1907), p. 3.

20 J. T. Grein, 'The English Drama Society', *Sunday Times* (17 December 1905), p. 4; *The Tatler* (24 January 1906), pp. 138–39, with pictures of Riot, Humility and the Angel (giving the sign of benediction); *The Sketch* (13 December 1905), pp. 6–7, with pictures of these (the Angel holding up a chalice), Charity, Luxury and Youth.

21 Bache Matthews, *A History of the Birmingham Repertory Theatre* (1914), pp. 2–3; and Isaac, *Ben Greet*, p. 75. The cast included Herbert S. Milligan (Youth), John Drinkwater (Charity), Barry V. Jackson (Riot), Thomas J. Kennedy (Pride), Cathleen Orford (Humility), Louise de Lacy (Luxury).

22 *Birmingham Daily Mail* (10 October 1907), p. 4.

23 John Drinkwater, *Discovery* (1932), p. 142.

24 Matthews, *History*, pp. 16, 19–20, 28–29, 32–33, 38, 94–95, 199, 212 and *passim*; *The Scallop-Shell*, ed. J. Drinkwater, no. 1 (February 1911), 29–30; T. C. Kemp and J. C. Trewin, *The Stratford Festival* (1953), p. 98; *The Gong*, ed. Alan Bland, 1 (1922), 287, 323 and 436.

25 The cast (a programme, *Sixth Malvern Festival 1934*, is in Malvern Public Library) included Geoffrey Toone (as Youth; understudied by Errol Flynn), W. E. Holloway (Charity), William Heilbronn (Riot), Vernon Harris (Pride), Margaret Hood (Lechery) and Mavis Walker (Humility). The musical setting was by Ernest Irving. Among Malvern Festival morning lectures was F. S. Boas's topic, '*Youth* and the English Morality Plays'.

26 Birmingham, pp. 22–24; Matthews, *History*, pp. 3, 6–7; cf. *The Birmingham Daily Post* (3 October 1907), p. 6.

27 Lines 166–69, 344, 348, 351, 365–66, 386, 407–17, 466–70, 528–31 and 699–708 are among those omitted. Emendation at ll. 496–99 alters Youth's character, Charity speaks Humility's part at ll. 597 and 792, and speech headings at ll. 607, 624 and 632 are interchanged.

28 Matthews, *History*, pp. 3, 6. Photographs of many in the cast are in the Pilgrim Players' album, *The Interlude of Youth* (British Library shelfmark 11797.ff.5). Three are reproduced in Drinkwater's *Discovery* (facing pp. 140, 142 and 148; and cf. p. 141). Charity's hazel staff (cf. *Y.* 49) shows how Jackson's designs enhanced the text.

29 Gowans, p. v.

30 See Allardyce Nicoll, *The Development of the Theatre*, 2nd ed. (1937), fig. 249 (reproduction of a photograph of the cast and Paul Shelving's setting).

31 These details I discovered from Geoffrey Toone.

32 *The Stage* (2 August 1934), p. 11.

33 *The Malvern Gazette* (28 July 1934), p. 6.

34 Riot seems to hold such a cap in Nicoll's reproduction. This suggestion I owe to Mavis Walker.

35 *Malvern Festival MCMXXXIV*, the complete festival brochure (copy courtesy of Geoffrey Toone), p. 27. Among other medieval and modern tunes was Riot's song, 'Mr. Lane's Maggot'.

Glossarial Index to the Annotations

This index does not include annotations on grammatical constructions, points of dialect, or general literary, thematic or historical information. Character names and place names are indexed, but not historical figures. Words and phrases appear in the form in which they occur in the texts, and phrases are also normally lemmatised under their key words. When a gloss is (basically) repeated in the annotations, only the first occurrence is listed. An asterisk indicates that an annotation gives significant information on sense or usage not found in the *O.E.D.* Annotations concerning proverbial phrases and stage business are also collected below under those headings. A separate list of parallels between *Youth* and *Hick Scorner*, and their sources or analogues (including scripture), may be found in Appendix III.5.

Race, *HS* 827
Race of Ireland, *HS* 362
ready, *Y* 393
receive, *Y* 38
record I take of, *HS* 10
rector chory, *Y* 473
rede (sb.), *Y* 90
rede (vb.), *Y* 171
refuse, *Y* 10
religious, *HS* 339
remember, *HS* 934
Remembrance, Good, *HS* 1007
reprovable, *HS* 269
rested, *HS* 657
rial cheer, *HS* 748
Rial preachers, *HS* 343
ride, *HS* 393, 839
rightwiseness, *HS* 47
*ringing, *Y* 521
rings, hose, *HS* 515
rings, a pair of, *Y* 507
Riot, *Y* 207
rood, *Y* 354
royal, *Y* 48
royalty, *Y* 76
rumbelow, *HS* 317

Sad, *HS* 477
Sadness, *HS* 343
sail, strike a, *HS* 838
sail, veer, *HS* 301
Saint Pintle the Apostle, *HS* 761
Saint Thomas of Wat'ring, *HS* 838
Saint Tyburn of Kent, *HS* 941
salt fish, mustard with, *Y* 120
sanctuary, *HS* 640
save, *HS* 875
saws, *HS* 56
say you, *HS* 365
scaped, *HS* 358
scared, *Y* 499
scholar of mine own school, *HS* 655
school, *Y* 128
scoops, *HS* 789
scused, *HS* 278
season, *HS* 224
see, *HS* 362
see your heels, *Y* 190
seek, *HS* 622

sessions, *Y* 272
set by, *Y* 63
share, *HS* 253
shent, *Y* 789
shoon, *HS* 797
shoop, *HS* 354
shoot, *HS* 301
Shooters Hill, *HS* 388
shop of bawdry, *HS* 390
show, *HS* 55
Sibley, *HS* 179
side, *HS* 979
side, stews', *HS* 184
sin, *HS* 583
*sing, *HS* 182
Sir John, *Y* 491
snare, *HS* 252
soil, *Y* 116
solace, *HS* 2
sollar, *HS* 238
so long, *HS* 803
soon, *Y* 41
sort, all that great, *HS* 242
sought, you, *HS* 512
sovereigns, *HS* 2
space, *Y* 201
special, *Y* 590
sped, *HS* 21
speed thee of, *Y* 314
spending, *Y* 237
spill, *Y* 155
sport, *HS* 183
stable, full, *HS* 887
(Stage business), *Y* 40, 97, 313.1, 316,
     405–26, 424, 443, 470, 519.1, 533,
     541, 551, 582–83, 654, 678, 767;
     HS 20, 31–32, 72, 146, 156, 302,
     611, 617, 628, 652, 695, 763–66,
     803
startups, *HS* 801
stews, *Y* 701
stews' side, *HS* 184
still, *HS* 859
still, bide, *Y* 298
stocks, the, *Y* 304
stone, *HS* 171
stools, *Y* 152
store, any, *Y* 115
stound, *HS* 795